PROPOSAL PREPARATION AND MANAGEMENT HANDBOOK

PROPOSAL PREPARATION AND MANAGEMENT HANDBOOK

ROY LORING, MS., MBA
Davy McKee Corp.
Cleveland, Ohio

HAROLD KERZNER, Ph. D.
Baldwin Wallace College
Berea, Ohio

VNR VAN NOSTRAND REINHOLD COMPANY
NEW YORK   CINCINNATI   TORONTO   LONDON   MELBOURNE

Library of Congress Catalog Card Number: 81-16145
ISBN: 0-442-25437-7

Manufactured in the United States of America

Published by Van Nostrand Reinhold Company Inc.
135 West 50th Street, New York, N.Y. 10020

Van Nostrand Reinhold Publishing
1410 Birchmount Road
Scarborough, Ontario MIP 2E7, Canada

Van Nostrand Reinhold Australia Pty. Ltd.
17 Queen Street
Mitcham, Victoria 3132, Australia

Van Nostrand Reinhold Company Limited
Molly Millars Lane
Wokingham, Berkshire, England

15 14 13 12 11 10 9 8 7 6 5 4 3 2 1

Library of Congress Cataloging in Publication Data
Loring, Roy J.
    Proposal preparation and management handbook.
    Bibliography: p.
    Includes index.
    1. Proposal writing in business. I. Kerzner,
Harold. II. Title.
HF5718.5.L67   658.4′04   81-16145
ISBN 0-442-25437-7   AACR2

To Carol and Gail

Preface

This book is about proposal preparation and management in our time. In this age of high technology and sophisticated information processes, many of the older methods of occasional adjustments of organizations or ad hoc approaches to organizing and managing a proposal effort are no longer satisfactory. What was once only mandatory to handling aerospace or Department of Defense proposals is now required for almost any type of project. During the 1980s, more and more industries are adopting a professional approach toward their proposal efforts. These industries are using project and systems management concepts in order to control their resources more efficiently and effectively.

This book has been prepared with the intention of providing an up-to-date view of the proposal management function. Our focus is on the management of the effort. Under current conditions, the old methods are no longer satisfactory. We require now a more disciplined, precise approach to handling the management of proposals. The manager is expected to understand in clear terms what tools are available and how they can be related to the performance of the system at hand. The goal of this book is to provide a modern approach to organizing for the preparation and management of successful proposals.

To understand the approach taken by this book, it is essential that the manager recognize the relationship of the various elements that contribute to the proposal effort and their interaction. The proposal manager must recognize that the proposal activity is a system composed of many different activities being done by many different operations. The manager must appreciate the interacting roles of such groups as marketing, finance, engineering, purchasing, and so forth, and the psychological, physiological, and sociological factors that govern their behavior. The manager must also recognize the interactions of the internal system with the external world. These include the effects or competition as well as the legal and governmental restraints, economic factors, community attitudes, and the social system factors in general. It is widely agreed that many external and internal factors contribute to the success or failure of a business. Yet time after time, while firms in a particular industry may be facing tough economic conditions, one company will be achieving great success. This fact leads to our contention, which is expressed in this book, that the individual is the key factor in the success or failure of a business.

This book therefore deals with total proposal preparation and management. It strives to show how to blend into one framework the organization structure, the people, and the environment in which people must function in order that a company can achieve maximum efficiency in obtaining new business. It does not attempt to separate structure, people, environment, or the intangible aspects of organization. Instead, it tries to provide a fundamental and systematic basis for blending these aspects into an effective organization that produces optimum results.

This book was developed to provide a hands-on approach toward learning the necessary tools and techniques by which proposal activities can be integrated throughout an organization, regardless of the organizational size or project complexity. The book is addressed not only to those individuals who wish to understand the contributions to successful proposals resulting from proven management applications, but also to those functional managers and upper-level executives who must, either directly or indirectly, provide their continuous support to all proposals. This book is also written with the recognition that the average manager is a "doer."

This book has combined research and academic knowledge of the subject with practical day-to-day operating experience gained from a wide range of companies and organizations. There are very few books and articles that cover this subject, particularly in the manner covered here. We therefore felt a strong need for a practical book such as this. The book suggests methods and techniques that will minimize a company's chance of failure and optimize its chances of success. While the emphasis is on corporations, most of the book is also applicable to other types of enterprises as well as nonprofit institutions and government departments. To satisfy its role as a handbook, the subject matter and scope of areas covered are broad.

We acknowledge with appreciation the many sources over the years which supplied material and ideas for figures, tables and in some cases, text. Most of the information in this book has been either tested in actual work environments or present in the form of seminars over many years. In both situations, the reaction, comments and lengthy discussions with clients, colleagues and participants at seminars, gave us the encouragement to write this book.

Our gratitude to others is vast, and the list which follow is incomplete. Grateful acknowledgment is given to Art Serrin, Manager of Contracts, Davy McKee corporation for use of material regarding contracts and his overall comments and suggestions. Valuable criticisms and contributions were made by many colleagues. In particular, Irwin Hess, Vice-President of Operations, H. O. Materials, provided considerable comments on how to present the information to individuals not already engaged in the world of proposals. We are also indebted to Warren Willits for his invaluable contributions of time and effort for the artwork presented herein. Finally, to Mark Collier, Vice-President for Academic Affairs, we offer our sincere gratitude for the time, opportunity, and support necessary to conduct meaningful research.

Roy J. Loring
Harold Kerzner

Contents

Chapter 1
Preproposal Work

1.0 INTRODUCTION

In industrial, governmental, and academic circles, the word *proposal* is well understood. It is the device used to bring income or revenue to the requesting organization. The proposal could be requesting a grant to fund a new research and development effort or to sell an item of equipment. It could be an offer to perform services on a project or to build a complete facility. While the end item may be different and relevant specifically to the requesting organization, the means of getting it are basically the same. Because the proposal is the major tool by which many companies secure new business, the importance of proposals to the success of a firm cannot be overemphasized.

From a client's standpoint, a proposal is the primary, if not the only, source of information from which decisions are made to select a contractor. The proposal must stand alone in conveying to the client the ideas, concepts, and capabilities of the firm. The proposal must tell the client what the offeror wants to do, the services involved, what the offeror charges for doing it, the facilities and manpower available to do the job, and the overall experience of the offeror. No matter how good a company may be, if the proposal does not explain the key information properly, it can easily lose the job. The company's reputation and future growth rest on the success of its proposals. One poorly written proposal can cause a company to lose a major account. The proposal is the primary document used by the sales department in meeting the goals and objectives of the company.

Because the proposal is the prime document of a sales effort for many companies, it should be made an integral part of the company's marketing or sales activity. All too often a proposal is prepared on a job-by-job basis, with no prior planning or format. These types of proposals have very little chance of success. The reason for their limited success is the lack of preparing a proposal in a professional manner, and as a part of the company's long-range plan.

To help create the proper proposal setting, there must be a certain amount of preproposal work. This allows you to do a more effective job during the time you are actually preparing a proposal. It is work that keeps you from getting bogged down in non-proposal-related aspects. It is the preproposal work that helps you avoid being caught by surprise. It also allows you to make the right decisions with greater ease.

Typical of the preproposal activities, covered in Chapter 1 in detail, are the following:

- Setting marketing/sales objectives and goals
- Developing a proposal preparation guide
- Formalizing the inquiry screening and proposal authorization procedure
- Developing standard qualifications and boilerplate
- Developing a boilerplate and talent/skills inventory retrieval system
- Establishing arrangements with outside service and supply companies
- Advertising and promotional activities.

1.1 PROPOSALS AND THE MARKETING FUNCTION

Time in any organization is a scarce resource and time spent on proposal preparation is limited to selecting the best projects to bid on; projects which most satisfy the goals and objectives of the organization. There are many different kinds of objectives that are important to an organization at one time or another, such as:

- Performance objectives
- Marketing objectives
- Operational objectives
- Technical objectives
- Financial objectives
- Personal objectives
- Scheduling or end-item objectives
- Organizational objectives.

Although these objectives are different, the approach taken to achieve each of them follows a similar procedure. This procedure is to *plan in advance for their accomplishment.* A plan is a scheme of action, procedure, or operation established for a definite purpose to accomplish a project, objective, or work effort. The primary purpose of planning in pursuit of an objective is to know to some extent in advance what is to be done, when it is to be done, who will do it, and how it will be done. Considering the complex and dynamic nature of our environment, some degree of planning, both for the short and long term is necessary for all organizations, regardless of their size. Because planning is done on the basis of future happenings, which cannot be predicted with total certainty, alternate courses of action must be incorporated into the overall plan. Figure 1-1 shows the systems approach to planning, illustrating the incorporation of alternates into the planning effort.

The systems analysis process begins with systematic examination and comparison of those alternative actions that are related to the accomplishment of the desired objective. The alternatives are then compared on the basis of the resource cost and the associated benefits. The inputs from the constraints and limitations identify the explicit consideration of the uncertainty variables. The loop is then completed by using feedback in order to determine how compatible each alternative is with the objectives of the organization.

The above analysis can be arranged in steps:

- Input data to mental process
- Analyze data
- Predict outcomes
- Evaluate outcomes and compare alternatives

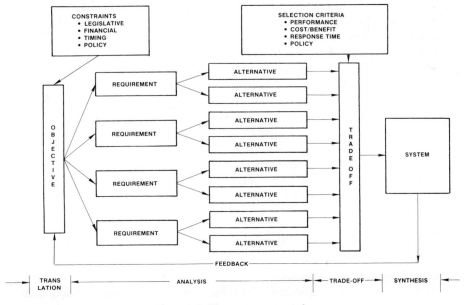

Figure 1-1. The systems approach.

- Choose best alternative
- Take action
- Measure results and compare with predictions.

All successful companies have a well-organized marketing function, which in turn has developed a meaningful market plan that is updated on an annual basis. The marketing plan guides the activities of the company and tells the staff what they should be doing today to achieve the goals of tomorrow. It is a dynamic plan that continually points the company in the direction it wants to go. As marketing involves the entire sales activity of an organization, proposals must be looked upon as part of the marketing function. In a great many organizations, the proposal function is centralized under a marketing or sales group. There is an equally large number of companies, especially those of smaller size, that have no special group to handle proposals. These companies use whatever sources of manpower are available at the time. The success of their proposal reflects the professionalism and planning that is used in preparing them.

Proposals are used to sell the products and services of a company, and they should be developed to satisfy the markets aimed for by the company. In other words, the overall proposal effort must be in tune with the thinking of the marketing plan. The capabilities discussed in the proposal must be developed long before the actual preparation. Everything that is required to satisfy and convince the client of a company's ability to do a job must be in hand before attempting to write a proposal to the client. For example, if certain specialized manpower or equipment is needed to perform a task, then the company must obtain this manpower or equipment prior to the submittal of a proposal. The further in advance the company can secure the necessary items, the better it can project their availability in the proposal as a company resource or capability. The complexity of determining where the company fits in on the total scheme of things and what services it will provide can be seen from Figure 1–2, the development of an industrial plant project. Because of size constraints, the company could be interested in only doing the market or economic feasibility study, or acting as consultants to the development of the concept. It may be appropriate for your organization to do the engineering, or construction, or both. Your company may be capable of assuming the overall project management for the whole effort.

1.2 ESTABLISHING OBJECTIVES, GOALS, AND ACTION PROGRAMS

Most business firm systems include such functions as resource control, decision making, and production. The relationships among these functions is

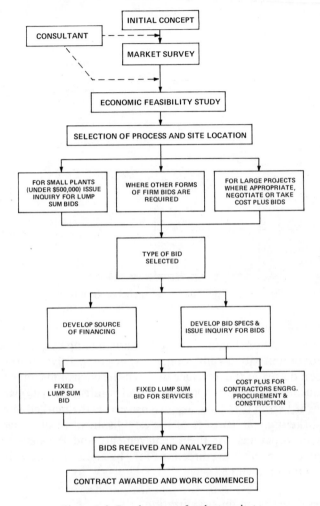

Figure 1-2. Development of a plant project.

shown in Figure 1-3 in which the business firm is represented as a dynamic systems model. For every decision that management makes, actions and strategies are developed in order to achieve the most effective utilization of the resources of money, equipment, facilities, technology, manpower, and materials. The output from resource control, together with the management policies developed during decision making, provide input to the production function. The output from the production function can be a product, services, or some other form of end-item.

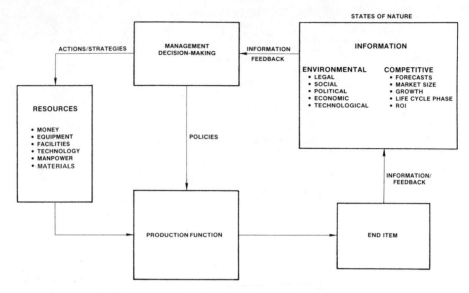

Figure 1-3. A dynamic system model of the business firm.

The rate of output of the end-item provides information that is used as feedback for additional management decision making by comparing the end item rate of output with the environmental and competitive information. This comparison occurs at the interface between the environmental systems level and the business firm level. One key action/strategy activity performed by management, which uses feedback extensively, is the marketing plan.

The marketing plan consists of the establishment of objectives, the formulation of programs for their achievement, and the determination of policies governing the future direction of the business. The marketing plan accomplishes the following:

- Gives direction to the organization
- Provides realistic and measurable sales objectives
- Determines the resources needed to meet the objectives
- Provides the lead time to develop the capability of resources needed
- Forms the basis for scheduling and budgeting the efforts of the organization.

In setting up the marketing plan, to be most effective in meeting organizational needs, objectives must be:

- Specific
- Not overly complex

- Measureable, tangible, verifiable
- Appropriate level-challenging
- Realistic and attainable
- Within the bounds of the organization
- Consistent with resources available or anticipated
- Consistent with organizational plans, policies, and procedures.

The basic operating objective of any organization is to make the most efficient and effective use of its total resources. These resources usually consist of:

- Manpower
- Equipment
- Facilities
- Money
- Information/technology
- Materials.

The use of these resources is achieved within set budgets, schedules, and performance levels. The use of these resources must also adhere to the ever-changing environmental input factors around us, such as:

- Legal
- Social
- Economical
- Political
- Technological.

The marketing plan optimizes the technical, managerial, and economic capabilities of the organization. It allows the organization to utilize its total services fully, specialized technology, and resources as a whole. At the same time, the marketing plan is used to coordinate and monitor all activities of the organization. Table 1-1 shows the content of a typical marketing plan for a medium size organization.

1.3 SELECTING MEANINGFUL PROJECTS

The marketing plan describes the company mix of products and services to be offered in meeting the goals of the company. It identifies the areas of business that the company is interested in developing. For example, if the firm is interested in entering the energy area, the marketing plan spells out the specific ways the company sees as a method to enter the area. The marketing plan not only identifies the projects to go after, it establishes a baseline to measure against. It tells what size a company should be to meet its goals, what

Table 1-1. Representative Marketing Manual Content

SECTION	DESCRIPTION	PAGE
1	General notes to the Manual	-
2	Executive Summary	1
3	Organization and Marketing Philosophy	9
4	Marketing Coordination/Responsibility plan	13
5	Sales Projection for the Year	16
6	Details of Specific Sales Activities	20
7	Principal Industry Markets	25
8	Identification of New Markets and Territories	72
9	Domestic Accounts	76
10	Foreign Accounts	86
11	Advertising and Promotion Plan	95
12	Licensing and Royalty Policy	100
13	Contract Agreement Policy	104

manpower it needs, how much R&D to do, etc. It is also a continuous measure of how well a company is moving toward its objectives. The sales staff seek new business in relation to the marketing plan and proposals are prepared for projects identified in the plan. The success of the proposals means the success of the marketing plan and eventually the success of the firm. Once the projects are identified, the services are developed and priced, resources are organized, and sales promotion and advertising can begin.

To be prepared properly to have a winning proposal, certain advance preparation of the proposal activity must be accomplished along with securing the necessary resources or specialized conditions required by the upcoming projects. The marketing plan allows you to do this by giving a measure to:

- Set up the necessary sales organization
- Establish the marketing, action, and R&D programs
- Determine the operating organizational structure
- Develop the personnel and equipment requirements
- Develop facilities requirements
- Develop the management and financial organization
- Prepare a timetable to work from and measure against

The revenue of an organization is made up of the continual flow of overlapping projects. Figure 1-4 shows the nature of these projects and their contribution to the total revenue of an organization. Managers and planners of the organization secure new work so that the resources of the organization are being utilized completely with scheduled availability for new work. It is the

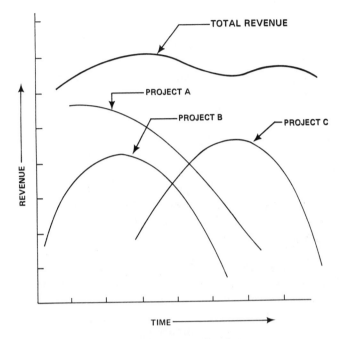

Figure 1-4. A stream of projects.

proper balance of obtaining new work that most effectively uses the resources of the organization.

1.4 ANALYZING THE MARKETPLACE

Each organization, depending on the particular industry, has different factors or variables that govern its operation. These variables indicate what is important to that organization and how to deal with them.

In order to get people to accept and participate in a structured plan which can stand up under pressure, visible, targeted objectives must be established as standards for measurable marketing and project objectives. Identification of these variables is a necessary step prior to the development of a program and/or marketing plan. The variables must be identified and described such that an explicit definition of future posture can be assessed with regard to constraints on existing or projected resources. Top management support must be available for strategic planning variable identification such that effective decision making can occur at the operating level. Final decision making always rests at the upper levels of management, regardless of the organizational structure.

The identification and classification of these "strategic" variables are necessary to establish relative emphasis, priorities, and selectivity among alternatives, to anticipate the unexpected, and to determine the constraints of the program. Universal systems for the classification process are nonexistent because of the varied nature of organizations and programs. General guidelines, however, can be developed for the variable classification process.

Katz has developed a set of seven variables for strategic planning:[1]

1. The market segments to be pursued
2. Products and services to be developed, offered, or discontinued
3. Channels of distribution and promotion to be utilized
4. Pricing policies and quality/price trade-offs followed
5. Investment policy and capital expenditures
6. Means of financing and spending constraints
7. The key people required by the strategy.

Each of the variables represents a broad spectrum of possible cases. In order to simplify the process somewhat, we can further classify variables as *intra-company* and *extra-company*. Intra-company variables would include such topics as management skills, resources, overhead, wages and salaries, government freezes on hiring, hiring of minority groups, and lay-offs.

Extra-company variables normally fall into three categories. The first extra-company variable is technology. Technological changes in such areas as data processing and electronics require systematic analysis during a program. Keeping up with the technology of the competition is a costly process, especially if competitive bidding is included. The second variable is the social or political nature of the environment. Changes in government, both national and international, can produce major system changes because of imports of raw materials or exports of finished goods. Labor unions and availability of the work force must also be included. The third variable is the economic characteristics of the environment. This includes per capita income and output as measured by national indicators such as Gross National Product (GNP), Consumer Price Index (CPI), and prime interest rate.

The following examples illustrate the variables that are critical to two different industries.

Example 1-1: Chemical Engineering Industry

Company Z is a manufacturer of chemical cooling towers for industrial applications. The company considers itself a member of the chemical industry and deals primarily with cooling water efficiency applications. Company Z

[1]Katz, Robert L., *Cases and Concepts in Corporate Strategy,* Prentice Hall, 1970.

maintains less than 5 percent of the market share. The industry leader maintains a 30 percent market share.

1. *External factors*
   A. GNP Growth
      This variable provides a measurement of what the real growth is, and an idea of how inflation is behaving. A look at customer industries for this year compared to last year gives a rough indication of how much sales should increase.
   B. Industry Trends
      What type of cooling equipment is required? For instance; would a chemical treatment be preferred over a hardware device?
   C. Legislative Trends
      This includes EPA actions. For instance, Company Z uses chromate in 8 percent of its products. Chromate has been used in cooling systems for the last 30 years, but recently it is considered a dirty word for the environmentalists. As a result, Company Z is changing its chemical formulas to contain low amounts of chromate.
   D. Political Situation
      The political relationship between the U.S. and Rhodesia must be evaluated. (Rhodesia is a raw material supplier of chromate.) This relationship is important for any foreign supplier.
2. *Internal Factors*
   A. Growth by Product
      It is important to know what product is growing in order to anticipate future resource needs. Product growth is important for financial forecasting.
   B. Expansion Rate
      Industrial bankruptcy is caused primarily by overexpansion. Company Z has been growing at 30 to 40 percent annually for the last three years. Maintaining a stable rate of growth is important for capital expenditures, financing, and acquisitions.
   C. Sales Effectiveness
      Company Z looks at competitors only from the viewpoint of maintaining market shares. The sales force is the major aim of the company, so training salespersons is important. A lead time of 1-½ years is typical until a salesperson becomes profitable, because competence in the sales and technical areas must be learned. This time also allows for a build-up of customer confidence.

Example 1–2: International Engineering/Construction Industry

The international engineering/construction industry is characterized by a large corporate headquarters with multiple divisions, most often with worldwide locations. Normally, all divisions operate on the systems approach to management. Strategic variables are established at the corporate level. Divisions then set their own strategic variables and objectives in relation to corporate plans. The variables are essentially the same among contractors with only the magnitude of the dollar volume varying.

The basic product policy variable is to provide engineering, procurement, and/or construction services. The customer policy variable defines to whom these services are offered. For instance, one large corporation offers the above services to owner/operators in the heavy industries such as refineries chemicals, steel, nonferrous metals, and foods. Within each area, specific fields are defined such as chlorine/caustic plants, silicone plants, catcrackers, and reformers.

The marketing areas are worldwide. The engineer/contractor has very little, if any, input as to plant location. So construction site and project value are uncontrolled variables. However, the location of the plant can determine where engineering and procurement are performed. An example would be a project plant site in Latin America. The engineering could be done in the U.S., Mexico, or Argentina, depending on the expertise required, customer preference, and major supplier locations.

Most members of this industry depend upon reputation and sales force effort as their promotion policy. Regardless of justifications from the marketing personnel, reputation is the key. Of course, reputation includes technical and financial qualifications.

Expertise in a given field is the competitive emphasis. Each engineer/contractor has expertise in several key areas like polymer processing, blast furnace design, and reformers. This then establishes what specific customer policies apply to the promotion policy.

Efforts are made continually to increase the technical base to meet market demands and penetrate new markets. One large contractor is presently expanding its technical base in polymer science and coal gasification. This results from answering the customer policy question, "Where are our major market opportunities?"

The major variable with regard to pricing is the type of contract, including *cost-plus, fixed fee,* and/or *lump sum* contracts. (See Chapter 9 for a comparison of these contracts.) The type of contract is dependent upon the market. Cost-plus contracts are preferred because they reduce risk. The actual fee is determined relative to the size of the project.

All strategic variables within this industry are interrelated. One variable cannot be established without looking at the others. The location of a plant determines where work is performed; the type of plant and size determines the level of competitive advantage; the market, customer, and work level with respect to capacity determines the type of contract. A brief summary of the strategic variables for the industry follows:

1. *Capital expenditures on new plant by the major petroleum and chemical companies.* This industry acts as a service firm. It provides engineering construction services to firms contemplating new plants or additions to existing ones. The magnitude of such plants reflects in their capital expenditure allocations and, in turn, the volume of business is dependent upon it.

2. *Customer or client requirements.* Clients, in sending out job inquiries for an overseas project, often require that the successful contractor have previous experience at completing a job in that specific country. Similarly, the client may require that a certain process be incorporated in his plant's design. A contractor's success in securing work also depends on the ability to satisfy these types of customer requirements.

3. *Availability of both quantity and quality of labor.* Many projects today are quite complex and massive in scale. The ability to handle a job of such magnitude, while allowing for the manning of other jobs concurrently, demands sufficient numbers of people. Likewise, the technical expertise must be present to handle different types of plants or those employing special processes. Obviously, this availability of manpower widens the number of jobs the firm can bid on and possibly obtain. (Note also the relationship to customer or client requirements.)

4. *Location of offices in relation to those of the client.* In situations where the contractor has an office near a client's existing or proposed plant site, a distinct advantage over the competition exists. The reasons are obvious: travel costs are minimized, communications maximized, and problems solved in a shorter time span by the necessary decision makers. Similarly, having an office located near the headquarters of major oil and chemical firms allows numerous and quick contact with minimal expense. Such considerations play a major role in decisions to relocate European headquarters to London, for example. Nearly all the Arabian oil companies, as well as many U.S. firms, have major offices in London.

5. *Types of jobs available.* The reference here is to whether lump sum or cost-plus contracts are available. The firm seeks to minimize the amount of work it bids on a lump sum basis, but, of course, the market ultimately governs such decisions. A glut of available lump sum work, for example, would force the contractor to re-evaluate some of its internal procedures as well as sharpen its pricing arrangements to meet competition. The risks involved with lump sum work are greater than those associated with the cost-plus variety and so the risks in profit making are increased as well. Very definitely, the type of jobs available on the market could influence the company's financial performance greatly.

1.5 DEVELOPING A MARKETING STRATEGY

As a beginning step, the person responsible for the proposal function should attend the market planning meeting. It is at this meeting that the market planning objectives (Company objectives) are passed on to the sales force and operations people. This meeting directs the sales force what areas to concentrate their efforts on. It also tells the operating people how they should prepare themselves for future work.

A typical overview of what may be covered at the market planning meeting is the following:

- Diversification of activities
- Penetration of international markets
- Changing from small to large project emphasis
- Developing a preferred position
- Entering the alternate fuels market
- Organizing for greater flexibility.

Diversification of activities relates to the broadening of the industries that the organization serves. For example, if your primary business is in the chemical plant construction area, you may want to move into other related areas, such as environmental facilities, pipelines or waste recycling. Another form of diversification is to go from a pure service or product organization to one with an equity participation in the project.

As your organization grows or market demands dictate, moving into the international market place may be a new objective. It may mean extending your sales activities into a new country or a region such as South America, or may be expanding your sales activities on a worldwide basis. Making the move from a company that handles mostly small projects to one that is interested in large projects depends on the size of your organization, the industry you serve, and the growth projected for the marketplace. Figure 1–5 illustrates the progress of an organization that has grown from one handling projects with an average value of $20 million for many years to one handling projects with an average value of over $80 million. Table 1–2 shows the same kind of trend by summarizing the organization's proposal activities over the same time span.

One objective of an organization may be to establish itself in a preferred (number one) position, one that is recognized throughout the industry, both by competitors and clients alike. It means being known as the best in the business. An organization that has performed 70 out of 85 projects of a certain type is recognized as the leader in that type of work. Having specialized technology or notable personnel on your staff can provide you with a preferred position. A preferred position can also be geographic, by having your

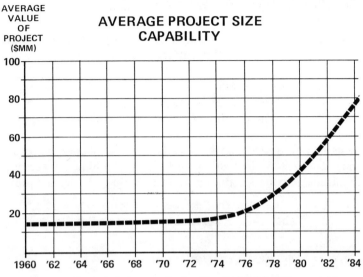

Figure 1-5. Average Project Size CAPABILITY.

organization known as the major element in doing business in a particular part of the world.

As new products, processes, or industries develop, your organization may choose to enter into one or more of these new areas. For example, considering the current energy crisis we face and the enormous amount of interest and

Table 1-2. Summary of Proposal Activity

PROJECT VALUE ($MM)	1974	1975	1976	1977	1978	1979	1980	1981
0–10	21	11	11	5	4	6	13	11
11–20	4	5	7	6	1	10	2	7
21–30	1		1	1			2	4
31–40	2	1	1	1		1	3	2
41–50								2
51–60		1		1				1
61–70			1					2
71–80		1						
81–90						1		
91–100						1	3	
101–200								2
200+							2	4
Totals	28	19	21	14	5	19	25	35

resources being committed to offset it, an organization may find it advantageous to enter into the area of alternate fuels development.

The transition from corporate goals to action objectives could be as shown in the example below. Corporate goals may be:

- Goal No. 1—increase profits
- Goal No. 2—increase stock value
- Goal No. 3—insure continuing company success

Objectives are now developed to satisfy these goals. Increasing profits means more new business or instituting cost-saving techniques. Increased profitability, leadership in the industry, and developing stability and predictabil-

Table 1-3. Goal No. 1—Increase Profits

OBJECTIVE 1—PREFERRED POSITION

    A. Conduct a market review of four new processes
    B. Develop two new markets: one technical, one geographic
    C. Establish a new technical area:
- Develop one from the market review
- Acquire technical rights in two new areas
- Make two improvements on existing processes

    D. Develop early position by performing:
- Technology review and interchange
- Three feasibility studies in new technology
- One design contract in new technology

    E. Professional participation:
- Attend technical meetings
- Present seven technical papers
- Foster continuous educational development

    F. Improve client satisfaction:
- Perform continuous client project review

OBJECTIVE 2—FULL-RANGE PROJECT CAPABILITY

    A. Handle five projects simultaneously
    B. Increase staff by 10 percent
    C. Develop ability to handle super-size project
    D. Widen scope of services offered
    E. Hire selected key position personnel

OBJECTIVE 3—BEST VALUE

    A. Improve existing operations
    B. Control overhead
    C. Develop cost-saving techniques

ity will satisfy Goal No. 2. Developing a professional organization, providing career development, establishing an *esprit de corps* in the organization, keeping current with new technology can contribute to accomplishment or Goal No. 3.

For example: Goal No. 1, increase profits can be subdivided into several objectives and subobjectives (action programs) as shown in Table 1–3.

The corporate goals, once put into general objectives, can then be translated into marketing objectives, such as:

Three-Year Marketing Objectives

- Financial
- Large projects
- Best in the business (technical and geographic)
- Best value (execution and economic)
- Diversification

These marketing objectives can then be developed into a marketing plan (action programs) and presented in a more quantitative manner as shown below:

THREE-YEAR MARKETING PLAN

Financial

	1978	1979	1980
• New business (minimum)			
• Plant value ($MM)	350	400	450
• Home office mhrs (MM)	1.5	1.7	2.0
• As sold profit ($MM)	7.5/6.0	9.0/6.0	10.5/6.8
• Risk on project (% min risk)	95	90	85
• Self-financing work (%)	75	75	75
• New operating income ($MM)	4.0	4.5	5.0

Large Projects
- Secure seven new projects in the $100–200 MM range
- Secure three new projects in the over $200 MM range
- Increase permanent staff by 50 percent

Best in the Business (Technical and Geographic)
(Secure 25 percent of the business available)
- Develop professional management
  - Training
  - Position descriptions
  - Annual objectives
  - Performance standards
  - Succession charts
- Technical marketing position (preferred position)
  (Develop action programs for new markets)
  - Environmental
    - Bioengineering

- Alternate fuels
1. Shale oil
2. Coal conversion
3. Tar sands
- Pharmaceuticals

Best Value (Execution and Economics)

- Overhead cost—reduce by 10 percent as measured by: $\dfrac{\text{overhead charges}^*}{\text{contract charges}}$
- Contract cost—develop three new systems to reduce job cost

Diversification

- Technical—establish position in *new* industries to expand market by 20 percent
  - Cement
  - Pulp and paper
  - Power plants
  - Textiles
  - Offshore terminals
  - Stack clean-up
- Geographic—establish position in two new parts of the world
- Middle East
- Venezuela

Individual Objectives

- Profit related to new business will be as a minimum $4/H.O. man-hour or 3 percent of plant value
- Risk not greater than objectives, self-funding per objectives
- Contract/study in technical area not principally served by company
- Contract/study in technical area not previously served by company
- Assist management by identifying process development or process licensing opportunities that will promote three-year plan
- Operate within budget

*Excluding money set aside for action programs and special opportunities.

1.6 DEVELOPING A PROPOSAL PREPARATION GUIDE

Now that we have fully informed the responsible proposal-producing staff of the needs and objectives of the marketing plan, we must turn to other preproposal procedures and activities to aid in proposal preparation. One of these activities, relegated not to a specific proposal but the entire proposal effort, is the creation of a proposal preparation guide or manual. Having a proposal guide to aid you in preparing proposals is of great value and by far worth the time and money it takes to prepare it. Its help is invaluable during times of heavy proposal workload and in training new individuals. The guide's true value cannot be fully appreciated until an organization has spent the time and effort developing and using it. Table 1–4 shows the contents of a typical proposal preparation guide.

The purpose of the proposal preparation guide is to clarify the responsibilities and procedures involved in proposal preparation and management. The guide conveys the current philosophy and practices of the company. The guide is intended for use by full-time members of the proposal group sales, personnel, and anyone assigned temporarily to work on a proposal. The value to the latter is particularly important because these personnel are most likely not familiar with the procedures used in preparing proposals.

Table 1-4. Proposal Preparation Guide: Typical Contents

SUBJECT	SECTION
Introduction	1.0
Purpose of guide	
How to use guide	
Duties of the Proposal Manager	2.0
Role and primary function	
Specific responsibilities	
Other related duties	
Coordination with other groups	
Proposal Types and Forms	3.0
Qualification proposals	
Commercial proposals	
Letter proposals	
Preliminary proposals	
Detailed proposals	
Presentations	
Authorization of Proposal Work	4.0
Inquiry screening procedures	
Management review and approval	
Proposal approval and assignment of number	
Proposal numbering system	
Initiating the Proposal Effort	5.0
Defining proposal scope and objectives	
Organizing the proposal effort	
Kick-off/coordination memo	
Kick-off meeting	
Preparing the proposal outline	
Proposal Scheduling	6.0
Preparing and verifying the schedule	
Proposal schedule format	
Factors affecting proposal schedule	
Proposal Budgets and Cost Control	7.0
Obtaining proposal man-hours	
Preparing the proposal budget	
Controlling proposal costs	
Carrying out the Proposal Work	8.0
Proposal Manager's Functions	
On large proposal efforts	
On small proposal efforts	
On sales support efforts	
On special assignments	
Proposal Team Functions	
Engineering	
Estimating	
Scheduling	

(*continued*)

Table 1-4 (*Cont.*)

SUBJECT	SECTION
Procurement	
Construction	
Personnel and employee relations	
Legal	
Other support Departments	
Special Considerations	9.0
Client's confidential information	
Secrecy agreements	
Licensing agreements	
Dealing with Communist-bloc countries	
Restrictive trade agreements and boycotts	
Publishing the Proposal	10.0
Writing, editing, and organizing the proposal	
Final review and approval	
Preparing and assembling proposal documents	
Reproduction and binding techniques	
Delivery to the client	
Follow-on Procedures	11.0
Additional information/presentations	
Contract negotiations	
Support work for project initiation	
Standard Distribution and Filing	12.0
Standard distribution list	
Standard proposal filing system	
Standard (Boilerplate) Proposal Write-ups	13.0

In general, the guide describes the following:

1. Procedures for initiating, preparing, and publishing proposals, paid studies, and presentations.
2. A list of responsibilities of the Proposal Manager and the proposal team.
3. The techniques for managing the effort with special emphasis on scheduling and cost control.
4. Organizational structure of the proposal department or function and its relationships with other departments in the company.
5. The format used for proposals, including typical examples of written sections, organization charts, schedules, and other material.
6. The writing and publishing routine, including where and how to obtain information, materials, and services.

The proposal guide enables the Proposal Manager to control and monitor the development of the proposal with successful and familiar procedures. Without the use of a guide, the effort becomes random and disorganized, allowing the opportunity for relevant information to be omitted. A good proposal preparation guide provides the proposal function with three worthwhile features:

1. Regardless of change in personnel, proposal activity carries on with consistency and continuity.
2. It insures that all individuals working on a proposal follow the same general philosophy of proposal preparation and management.
3. It helps the proposal team in doing their work with maximum efficiency and minimum assistance.

It is good practice before starting a proposal to have all participants not familiar with the guide read it and then use it during actual proposal preparation.

1.7 INQUIRY SCREENING AND PROPOSAL AUTHORIZATION

Inquiries normally come to an organization through pre-established channels, such as the Sales Department. In the majority of cases, they are sent directly to the organization by the customer. In some cases, the organization may have to request the inquiry from the customer. Inquiries may also be received through other individuals or groups in the organization, such as the Project Staff, Engineering Department, or Executive Management. There will also be situations, based upon some specially developed in-house expertise, where the organization may submit an unsolicited proposal to a customer. In all of these cases, the information received from or developed for a potential customer should be handled in a logical and orderly manner.

Some organizations and individuals believe incorrectly that the number of contracts awarded to an organization is directly proportional to the amount of proposals they send out. In other words, send out more proposals and your chances of getting work increases. The true relationship between proposals and awards is in how much care and professionalism goes into planning, organizing, and preparing. The more advanced and scrutinized planning that goes into gearing up to turn out a meaningful product, the more success an organization will have in winning a job. A badly prepared proposal not only loses a job but may also create a bad image of your organization in the eyes of the customer. In addition, the preparation of a proposal is time-consuming and costly. It ties up key personnel in your organization that could be assigned to other more rewarding work.

Therefore, an organization must select projects to bid on carefully, so that the organization can maximize its chance for success. It is also a selection based upon the objectives of the marketing plan of the organization. To allocate its resources properly, the decision makers must, in addition, have enough knowledge about the industry to anticipate upcoming inquiries so that it does not commit all its people too quickly. All too often, an organization faces a situation where they have committed all their professional people to some proposals leaving only untrained personnel to prepare a proposal for a "must-win" project. The allocation of all resources, including people, must be done carefully with advanced planning.

As shown in Figure 1-6, the flow of work from inquiry stage to the proposal product, the first activity that is required is to receive and log all inquiries from the customer. The log can be as simple as a chronological tabulation on a sheet of paper to a formal recordkeeping document, as shown in Figure 1-7.

Some organizations assign a number (inquiry) to all inquiries that they receive from a customer whether they bid the work or not. Some only assign a number (proposal) after a decision to bid has been made, while still others assign numbers based on the type or size of their response to an inquiry. For example, a response of a qualifications brochure or standard and preprinted material has one type of number while a normal commercial proposal follows a different series of numbers. They can be called inquiry numbers, proposal numbers, estimate numbers, job numbers, or a whole host of other things. Whatever method or title is selected is not important so long as some record of inquiries and proposals is maintained. This log or list is very valuable for the future when trying to back check a project or client activity. This list also aids in formulating future market strategy by providing a source of data on:

- Types of inquiries received
- List of clients and frequency of inquiry
- Percent of proposal responses
- Percent of proposal wins and to what clients

The logging in of inquiries or proposal efforts can be done by someone such as the secretary to the proposal manager. In some organizations, the handling of inquiries and bid decisions are kept within the sales group and it is only after a decision to submit a proposal is made that a proposal department becomes involved. In large organizations, the recording of inquiries and proposals is put on computer cards to aid in retrieval of information. One such system could retrieve data based upon anyone of the following descriptions:

- Client
- Type of project

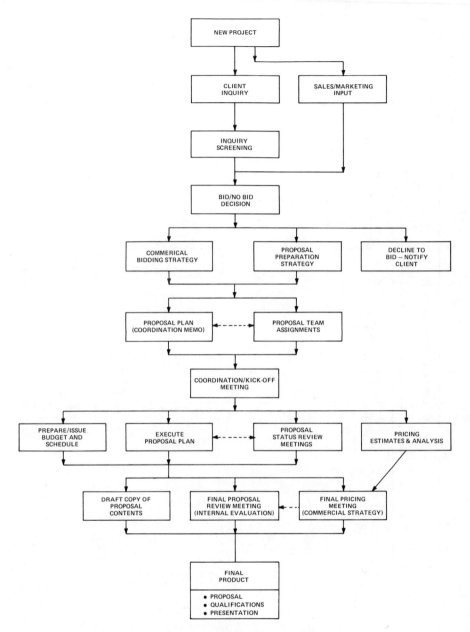

Figure 1-6. Flow of work from inquiry to proposal.

LOG OF INQUIRIES RECEIVED

FROM _____ TO _____

CLIENT	PROJECT DESCRIPTION	PROJECT LOCATION	DATE REC'D	DATE DUE	SERVICES REQUIRED	APPROX. VALUE	INQUIRY REVIEW MEETING (DATE)	PROPOSAL NUMBER – IF ASSIGNED	PROPOSAL MANAGER ASSIGNED	REMARKS

Figure 1-7. Recordkeeping documentation.

- Location
- Type of bid
- Date of bid
- Sales representative

1.8 THE BID-NO BID DECISION

After the inquiry is received and logged in, it should be screened as soon as possible to facilitate the *bid–no bid decision*. Because most inquiries have a short response time, the sooner a decision can be made, the longer you have to prepare your proposal. As part of the screening process, it is important that the sales representative or proposal manager review the document thoroughly to determine its total value to the organization. It also allows the decision-makers to determine if they have the capabilities required to bid on the job. The technical nature of the current marketplace is such that organizations must compete in specialized areas of an industry. While you may find anywhere from 10 to over 50 organizations bidding on a project, only a handful are serious competitors capable of performing the work. The rest are just wasting time and money. Therefore, an organization must concentrate its proposal efforts in areas that assist in their success by satisfying the objectives of the organization. Careful screening of the inquiry may also reveal that more information is needed to prepare a responsive proposal properly. A bid–no bid decision is usually made based upon a set of criteria judged to be important in selecting projects that contribute to an organization's continued growth and success. A typical set of criteria to be answered is shown in Table 1–5. In any event, the decision to bid or not to bid is very important to the resource allocation and should be made by senior management. In making the decision to bid, management must be convinced that the project is good for the company, they have the necessary resources and capabilities, and they have a good chance of winning. An organization must be realistic; if they cannot be competitive or responsive in meeting the requirements of the project, then they should not waste their time preparing a proposal. In some instances, an organization may feel obligated to submit a proposal to the customer to show interest and to develop a rapport for future work. If a decision to bid is made, a commitment to provide full resources toward preparation of the proposal must follow.

All proposal efforts must have the endorsement of the commercial or sales department, and, where needed, legal and operations departments. It is the sales representative or proposal manager's responsibility to obtain this clearance. For proposal efforts budgeted under a certain amount, say, less than $500 or $1000, no further management authorization is needed. The proposal manager must, however, have the agreement of either the General Sales

Table 1-5. Request for Approval of Bid Preparation Strategy/Approach Critique

1. Does company have capabilities and resources to perform the work?
2. Can company phase in the work to meet client schedule?
3. What is company's technical position?
4. What is company's approach to project execution?
5. Is project of special importance to client?
6. Would doing project enhance our reputation?
7. What has been our past experience and contractual relationship with client?
8. What is company's commercial approach and price strategy?
9. What are client's future capital expenditures?
10. Who is the competition and do they have any special advantages?
11. Does client have preferred contractor and if so, why?
12. What is the probability of project going ahead?
13. Does project meet the immediate or long-range objectives of the company?
14. Other work prospects for company in next six months? one year?
15. Other special factors and considerations?

Manager or the operation's general manager to proceed with each such proposal to assure compliance with the group's profit plan and staffing.

Proposal efforts identified as costing in excess of this breakpoint must have the approval of an *inquiry review committee* (IRC). It is the sales representative's responsibility to complete a *request for approval of bid preparation form,* as shown in Table 1-6. The proposal manager obtains inputs on costs and staffing from the selected group and provides this to the sales representative for inclusion in the request for approval of bid preparation.

The IRC usually meets once a week. All inputs must be in the marketing departments on the day prior to the meeting. The IRC is usually chaired by the senior vice President of marketing. The members of the Committee may include the vice presidents of operations, engineering, research and development, legal, financial, and the manager proposal. The proposal manager discusses the workload of his department so members of the IRC can make the proper decision on resource allocation. In addition to providing proposal budget authorization, the agreement to spend money on preparing a proposal, the IRC essentially provides a review

- To provide management guidance and support for the sales efforts
- To insure that day-to-day activities are consistent with long-term objectives
- To reduce the risks of making premature, conflicting, or nonproductive commitments.

As can be seen previously from Figure 1-6, input from the sales group is required during the inquiry screening and bid–no bid decision stage. The sales representative has certain information or ideas that cannot be picked up from the inquiry. In many cases, the inquiry is the end point of a long series of thinking and planning regarding a project. This planning may or may not involve outside help. The sales representative, through his normal contact with a client, has a feel for the customer's thinking on such areas as:

- Technical approach
- Management organization
- Operational systems
- Plans and schedules
- Related and future work
- Dollars budgeted for project

The sales representative may also find out such information as strengths and weaknesses of the competition, and if the customer is biased toward a particular competitor. The sales representative knows the customer's organization, their key players, their evaluators, and the decision makers involved

Table 1-6. Request for Approval of Bid Preparation

Date: _____

No.: _____

1. Client_____
2. Project_____
3. Units and Capacities _____
4. Location_____
5. Scope of Work_____
6. Value of Project _____
7. Type of Contract _____
8. Type of Proposal _____
9. Proposal Cost _____
10. Due Date of Proposal_____
11. % Probability to go ahead _____
12. % Probability for Award to company _____
13. Other Factors
    a. Timing of Award (if long range) _____
    b. Financing (if financing involved _____
    c. Source of Know-How (if other than company) _____
    d. Special Contract Conditions (if not company standard) _____
    e. Manpower Availability (if not readily available) _____
    f. Secrecy Conditions (if any) _____
    g. Competition (if known)_____
    h. Unusual Factors (if any)_____

Management Review Committee

Approved By: _____   Date: _____

in awarding a contract. In general, you want to know as much as possible about the customer's total requirements so you can present the best possible proposal to him. This contact with the customer works both ways, and after completion of the proposal, the sales representative conveys as much information as possible to the customer regarding the proposal. The sales representative, if possible, explains key portions of the proposal, especially new concepts, points of strength, and the specific approach. In some instances, a visit by the customer to your facilities and a discussion with the project team becomes part of the proposal effort.

Once a decision is made not to bid on a project, the customer should be notified in writing. Some organizations respond with a form letter, but this could cause the customer to interpret this as lack of interest and loss of future work. A specific letter for that inquiry should be prepared, explaining to the customer why your organization could not respond. It is good policy to explain honestly to the client that although you were interested in bidding you felt for one reason or another you were not qualified. You may also indicate your intention to rectify the situation in the future by hiring additional personnel, expanding facilities, or developing new techniques.

1.9 PROPOSAL APPROVAL AND NUMBER ASSIGNMENT

Each proposal effort is budgeted against the annual group allocation of proposal funds. Upon approval by the IRC, the marketing department issues authorization to the general manager of the nominated group with copies to other required departments. The sales representatives requests a proposal number using the request for proposal form. After having it confirmed at the required level, marketing endorses for issuance of a proposal number. The system of numbering proposals assigned should be part of a company-wide system of numbering all jobs, estimates, sales development efforts, and projects. This system should be in effect in all parts of the company and become part of the corporate general ledger.

1.10 STANDARD QUALIFICATIONS AND BOILERPLATE

In order to enhance the effectiveness of a proposal, it is recognized that a highly professional look and detailed responsiveness is required. A significant amount of the information used in a proposal falls into the category of *qualifications* or *boilerplate*. This information includes descriptions of how you work, project experience, personnel policies, and manpower data. To provide the information and do it with a professional look, a significant amount of time and effort is required in assembling the necessary material for the proposal. Because it is not unusual that proposals are assembled on a tight schedule, any help in reducing the effort employed during preparation of a proposal is rewarding. One such helpful activity is to prepare, independent of any specific proposal effort, as much standard qualifications or boilerplate as possible.

While this standard information or boilerplate is prepared independent of any specific proposal, its use is usually common to all proposals. In many cases, the use of this information is necessary for the submittal of a successful proposal. The type of material that is considered to be standard qualifications or boilerplate usually falls into the following categories:

- Description of services offered by organization
- Project qualifications and experience summaries
  - Areas of technology or industries
  - Geographical areas or unusual conditions
  - Use of engineering tools and procedures
  - Different size project
  - Capabilities in procurement, financing, training, etc.
- Standard operating procedures for organization disciplines
- Management monitoring, control, and reporting system, including MIS
- Organization charts for corporate, division, office, etc.
- Resumés of personnel who would be assigned to a project
- Standard description such as, personnel practices, EEO, minority hiring and subcontracting plans
- Contractual and cost information
- Other material, such as diagrams and photographs

Generally, standard qualifications and boilerplate information originates from other groups or departments in the organization, such as marketing, engineering, procurement, construction, personnel, etc. These initial writeups on standard qualifications, which include policies and procedures, usually are written by a specialist from the group or department and usually are written in language too specialized for a proposal. In most instances, to enhance the effectiveness of these writeups, it is necessary to rewrite them. To be used properly, these writeups must be tailored to the required format and proposal style language before being given to a customer. In obtaining these writeups and rewriting them, it is necessary to spend a sizable amount of time. As mentioned earlier, proposals usually are prepared under a short time limit and anything done prior to and independent of the proposal can only be an advantage.

The specialist assigned to rewrite these write-ups should be most familiar with proposal formats but know enough about the organization to understand the specific write-up. This specialist must know enough about these areas to understand their relative importance to the client and their contribution to the project.

We mentioned previously that boilerplate material is information and data which, in general, are common to most every proposal. In other words, the message it conveys to a customer is broad enough in scope to be used satisfactorily each time without needing to be changed. While the proposal may be different each time, the type of information required to explain your capabilities to a customer is the same.

For example, technical and operational write-ups contain descriptions of project management, engineering disciplines, and internal flow of work responsibilities, including client interface. These write-ups tell the client how you function as an organization. They include project organizations, design aids, and control techniques. Procedures can be established and used in preparing proposals for large projects, or projects requiring small staffing such as studies, or projects which involve multioffice/contractor arrangements. Other information of interest to a customer could be your model making capability, computer hardware and software usage, pollution control expertise, or your construction and startup techniques.

One widely used type of boilerplate information is the *experience summary*. Experience summaries (and lists) tell a customer in the shortest way possible the amount and scope of your background and project capabilities. These summaries can demonstrate experience that is exactly like the proposal's objective or experience that is related, showing a wide breadth of expertise. It outlines for a customer through actual projects why you think you are qualified for the job and gives the customer a feeling of how successful you will be in performing the work. A list of repeat business for the same customer shows to the current customer a series of successful projects with satisfied customers.

For customers who like more detailed information, specific sheets identifying the important technical, commercial, and other specialized factors of the work can be prepared.

Another important section for standardization is in the area of contracts. Contract terms and conditions, including limits of liability, insurance, payment terms, etc., can be written in standard language and put into the form of a model contract agreement. Typical of the contractual documents that can be prepared independent of a specific proposal are:

- Cost-plus fixed fee agreement
- Cost-plus percentage fee agreement
- Lump sum service agreement
- Engineering service agreement
- Definition of mechanical completion.

Equally important, but often overlooked, is the documentation used to describe the cost basis of an organization. While the organization may feel its costing system is perfectly clear and logical, to a customer it may be a maze of confusion. Worse yet, it may even anger the customer by giving him the feeling that you are trying to put something over on him. To relieve the fears of the customer and give him a feeling of confidence in your costing methods, a certain amount of effort is required to develop a clear and meaningful document. By standardizing the cost information, you provide to the customer the best organized and clearest information for his review. As with contracts, standardizing the information also provides continuity from job to job. One method used for cost-plus work is to put the costing information into a summary that describes the charges a customer must pay. These charges can be broken down: charges at a specified rate, charges passed along at cost, and the fee basis under which the organization is paid.

This summary cost document can also contain other cost-clarifying sections of interest to the customer, such as:

- Rates charged for office personnel
- Rates charged for field personnel
- Categories of billable and nonbillable personnel
- Printing and reproduction services
- Computer and data processing services
- Relocation and living expenses, both domestic and foreign
- Tool and equipment rental.

The charging summary, which reflects the basis used to develop the estimate of the work, allows the customer to understand how the estimate was established for the project.

Boilerplate information should not be used in each proposal simply because it is available. Each proposal is different and the use of boilerplate material depends on the specific requirements of the request for proposal. Proposals are made up of different parts and these parts are selected and organized to satisfy the needs of the proposal request. You will find that in each proposal request, the emphasis placed upon each specific area is different. Therefore, when responding, there is no need to include a 10-page boilerplate section when several paragraphs will do. Use the unabridged boilerplate *only* when required. Loading up a proposal with information, no matter how good, usually is counterproductive to your purpose.

1.11 BOILERPLATE RETRIEVAL SYSTEM

While the ideal use of boilerplate materials is in its complete and untouched form, occasionally it is necessary to rewrite the information before it can be used. To avoid recreating the boilerplate material for each proposal and to serve as an aid during situations in which editing is required, a retrieval system is mandatory. Once a proposal boilerplate section is prepared, it should be maintained in a file of standard writeups. Putting this boilerplate information in a retrieval system, possibly, but not necessarily computerized, allows a rapid recovery of the information. It also allows the inexperienced person to have a starting place in preparing the proposal sections. Equally important, if not more so, using the same information as a basis each time provides a continuity and consistency of response in each proposal submitted. Experience has shown that without a retrieval system, much good information is lost and eventually forgotten about once a proposal is submitted.

A simple retrieval system is to file one copy of each proposal under some numbering, chronological, or customer name order. This allows anyone to be able to refer to past proposals to review what has already been done and to determine what can be revised for the current proposal. Another method could be to take apart one copy of a proposal and file each part or section under its subject heading. Still another simple method is to fill out a card for each proposal, listing all important sections contained in it. All three methods allow the inexperienced person to have a start in preparing their proposal. These methods can be combined with a computerized system enabling the user to obtain the necessary information as quickly as possible.

Whatever system is employed, the material should be dated so that users know how current the information is. Boilerplate, like all information retained in a retrieval system, must be updated on a periodic basis to make sure it reflects the current status of the organization. In any event, the material should be reviewed at least annually to see if it needs updating. Experience summaries and lists usually are updated on at least a yearly basis to incorporate the experience gained during that year.

Because time is a critical resource during the preparation of a proposal, anything that can save time is a welcomed help. A boilerplate retrieval system, if set up properly, can be a great time-saving aid and prove invaluable during the proposal preparation stage.

1.12 TALENT INVENTORY

Another worthwhile preproposal activity is the development of a personnel *talent* or *skills inventory,* and many organizations have set up such a system or program for their professional staff. Whether manual or through the use of a computer program, the background, experience, and skills of the organization's staff are recorded in detail for future retrieval. Key words are established for specific areas of information and provided as a checklist in the retrieval process. Anyone needing to know certain information, such as experience with specific product, can, using the proper keyword, retrieve a list of people with that experience. Typical information that can be keyworded for retrieval is:

- Project experience broken down by types
- Specific client experience
- Geographic or climatic experience
- Job classification
- Education and experience level
- Professional membership and licenses
- Language skills.

Information for the inventory can be obtained from initial employment data gathered by the personnel department or through a formal skills inventory survey form that is given to each employee to fill out. Some department or group must also be given the responsibility for updating this information on an annual basis. To be most effective, the inventory information must be as up-to-date as possible. Whatever method may be used, information for each individual should be placed in the inventory soon after joining the organization so that the full capability can be available to the proposal.

An offshoot of the talent inventory and an item that is used quite frequently in proposals is the *skills matrix*. This matrix or grid relates an individual to a whole series of skills or experience. It shows in one composite form the skills and background that a team of people can bring to a project. An example of the skills matrix is shown in Figure 1-8.

1.13 USE OF OUTSIDE SERVICES

While not as important to the client as the content of a proposal, the overall look and format of a proposal is important in providing an attractive and easy-to-read document. It shows the customer that you are thorough and organized in what you do. It shows the customer that you have reviewed the inquiry and have planned your response carefully. Anything that gives the customer a good feeling and a clearer understanding of the content can only be considered a plus toward a winning proposal. The materials and format used for a proposal can be established as a preproposal activity. To aid in setting up the material and services used on proposals, a list of outside companies that supply these materials and services can be established. To save time during the proposal effort, prearrangements on providing these materials and services can be made. Typical of these services or supply companies are:

- Printers: for covers, special documents and paper, decals, logos
- Tabs and other types of dividers

FUNCTIONAL AREAS OF EXPERTISE	PRATT, L.	OLIVER, G.	NEWTON, A.	MAYER, O.	LEDGER, D.	KLEIN, W.	JULES, C.	IMHOFF, R.	HENRY, L.	GREEN, C.	FRANKLIN, W.	EASLEY, P.	DIRK, L.	COOK, D.	BAKER, P.	ABLE, J.
ADMINISTRATIVE MANAGEMENT		a			a	a			a		a				a	
COST CONTROL		b	b		b	b				b	b	b		b	b	
ECONOMIC ANALYSIS	c			c				c	c				c			c
ENERGY SYSTEMS	d	d		d			d			d		d		d	d	
ENVIRONMENTAL IMPACT ASSESSMENT				e		e		e						e	e	e
INDUSTRIAL ENGINEERING							f					f				f
INSTRUMENTATION		g				g					g		g			g
PIPING AND DESIGN LAYOUT				h			h				h	h		h		h
PLANNING AND SCHEDULING	i		i		i				i			i	i		i	
PROJECT MANAGEMENT		j				j					j		j			j
PROJECT REPORTING	k		k		k			k	k			k		k	k	
QUALITY CONTROL								l	l	l	l			l	l	
SITE EVALUATION			m				m	m			m				m	
SPECIFICATION PREPARATION	n			n		n				n			n, n	n		
SYSTEMS DESIGN		o			o		o		o	o		o		o	o	

Figure 1-8. Personnel skills matrix.

- Artwork and keylines
- Photostats of artwork, photoprocess lettering
- Photography
- Slides, flip charts, and other presentation material.

Arrangements that can be worked out in advance with the individual service companies would include such items as quantities required, timing, type of print, color, format style, and so on. It is good practice to line up more than one company for each service or supply required. Chapter 10 discusses in greater detail the design and publication techniques that are used in proposal preparation.

1.14 ADVERTISING AND PROMOTION

A great deal of the material and documents prepared during the preproposal effort can also be used in the organization's advertising and promotional activities. Project description, qualifications writeups, photography, and overall experience all lend themselves to use in advertising the organization's capabilities and expertise. There is no reason to "invent the wheel" when so much effort has already been expended in creating the existing documents.

Typical of the advertising and promotion objectives that are usually of importance to an organization and that relate directly to information developed for proposals are the following:

- Create a desirable overall image of the firm
- Develop an awareness of and demand for the firm's services
- Introduce a new capability to established specifying influences
- Increase awareness of an existing capability
- Maintain market awareness of extensive experience of the firm
- Expand into new geographic markets.

Each one of the objectives can be broken down further to allow more specific types of information to be selected for use. For example, creating an image of the firm can be broken down into the following subcategories:

- Broad capability and experience
- Quality services and dependable modern techniques and innovation
- Satisfied customers
- Professional staff
- Technologically oriented.

Chapter 2
The Proposal Manager

2.0 INTRODUCTION

Successful proposal management, regardless of the organizational structure, is only as good as those individuals and leaders that are managing the key functions. Proposal management is not a one-person operation; it requires a group of individuals dedicated to the achievement of a specific goal. Proposal personnel could include:

- A manager of proposals
- A proposal manager
- An assistant proposal manager or coordinator (if necessary)
- A proposal team
- A home office support group
- Outside participating personnel.

Generally speaking, proposal team personnel are assigned full-time to the project and work out of the home office, whereas the support group members work out of the functional units and may spend only a small percentage of their time on this proposal. Normally, the proposal team reports directly to the proposal manager.

Before the staffing function begins, four basic questions are usually considered:

- What are the requirements necessary to become a successful proposal manager?
- Who should be a member of the proposal team?

- Who should be a member of the supporting group?
- What problems can occur during the proposal activity?

On the surface, these questions may not seem overly complex. But when we apply them to a proposal environment, which is defined as a "temporary" situation, and with the requirement of a constant stream of proposals necessary for corporate growth, staffing problems become overly complex. Conflicts and priority setting become a way of life during the staffing function.

2.1 THE PROPOSAL MANAGEMENT FUNCTION

The proposal manager's major activity is that of a manager, and like every manager, in order to complete his task he must do the following:

- Sets objectives
- Establishes plans
- Organizes
- Staffs
- Sets up controls
- Issues directives
- Motivates
- Applies innovation for alternative actions
- Remains flexible and can handle change.

Common to contractors is the concept of executing proposals under a *proposal management system,* in which one person represents the contractor to the client and the client to the contractor, and is responsible for all management aspects of the proposal to the satisfaction of both parties. For the sake of simplicity, we call this person the proposal manager. He has various responsibilities, depending on the particular company, but in most cases he is directly responsible for the development of the proposal from the initial inquiry, through the planning and actual preparation, to the submission of the finished document to the client.

The proposal manager is much like that of a project manager, only instead of managing a project, he manages a proposal. In doing so, he has an organization or team to direct, and a budget to follow. Different from a project manager, however, the proposal manager is faced with the following conditions:

- Finite and short-term objectives
- Hastily assembled team

- Short life for the organization
- Critical decisions made quickly
- Frantic pace
- Lack of interest in the functional department.

Contractors use many different approaches or organizational set-ups in preparing a proposal. Some assign a project manager to supervise development of one or more proposals. At award of a contract, he would follow through in his normal position as project manager. Other companies have a proposal department with several proposal managers who have complete supervision over the development of one or more proposals. Still other companies separate the technical and commercial volumes of the proposal; responsibility for each lies with a separate department or individual.

If the scope of the project is large, one or more project engineers will be assigned to the proposal manager, with responsibility for directing and approving the technical portion of the proposal. The proposal manager also directs the efforts of design engineering, estimating purchasing, construction, scheduling, and legal departments toward the common goal of preparing the proposal, and maintains a balance among scope, budget, and time variables. All information from the owner is screened and passed on to the proper recipients, through the proposal manager, who likewise passes all questions from the proposal team to the owner.

During the proposal preparation effort, the proposal manager's prime responsibilities are to:

- Plan and manage the proposal effort
- Define the scope of work to be done
- Establish the proposal budget and schedule
- Obtain adequate staffing
- Coordinate the efforts of the proposal team
- Exercise adequate control in maintaining budget and schedule
- Edit (or write) and publish the proposal.

The specific duties of the proposal manager in meeting these responsibilities include the following:

- Develop and guide the proposal effort from its inception to the presentation of the proposal to the client
- Develop the format of each assigned proposal and to specify the contents of each section. This may be done with the guidance of management and the corresponding sales representative

- Prepare man-hour and financial budgets based on the proposal requirements and review with management
- Develop organization requirements and recommend candidates to fill positions on proposal team so that proper level of staffing is maintained to all work assignments at all times
- Prepare a detailed schedule, setting dates for completion of all key inputs and deadlines for work assignments based on schedule requirements
- Monitor the costs and progress of work continuously to insure completion of the effort on time and within budget
- Review and edit all technical and other written material prepared outside the proposal group for its ultimate suitability, accuracy, applicability, and completeness by understanding the content of this material fully and ascertaining that it has been reviewed properly by the responsible department
- Develop all man-hour estimates and review critically any estimates prepared by other departments, by making judicious use of man-hour statistics and factors which may be available to justify
- Review methods used in preparing material take-offs and pricing to ascertain that the effort required and the results obtained conform to the accepted proposal strategy
- Review, in depth, the quote calculations prepared for the work and resolve any questions prior to passing these on for final approval
- Keep management and the sales department apprised at all times of problems or potential problems relating to staffing, scheduling, budget, or content
- After completion of each major proposal and in accordance with instructions of management, prepare a close-out report summarizing the significant aspects of the effort.

The proposal manager may perform nearly all of the work on some proposals. However, on major proposals, he directs and coordinates the work of others strictly. Where responsibility for preparation of a write-up is assigned to another individual or department, this responsibility encompasses delivery to the proposal manager of a completed piece of work requiring only minimal editing for final incorporation into the proposal.

Figure 2-1 shows the graphical representation of the proposal management function and its interrelationship between the various activities and groups which contribute to the proposal effort. Note that the proposal manager is the center or focal point of all interchange of information and activity between the various groups.

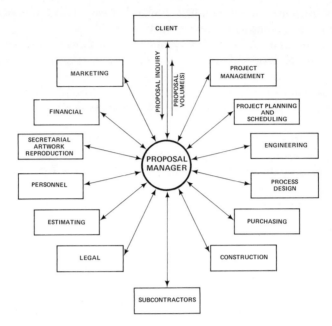

Figure 2–1. Graphic representation of proposal management.

2.2 CHARACTERISTICS OF THE PROPOSAL MANAGER

In order to understand fully the proposal management function, we must first investigate the characteristics of proposal management. The characteristics to be discussed include the proposal environment, the proposal management process, and the proposal manager.

There are two major problem areas under the proposal environment characteristics: personnel performance problems and personnel policy problems. Personnel performance poses difficulties for many individuals because the proposal environment is a change in the way of doing business. Most individuals prefer a stable situation. Regardless of how competent they are, they find it difficult to adapt continually to a changing situation. As a result, some people have come to resent change. Unfortunately, proposals, by definition, are temporary assignments. On the other hand, there are many individuals who thrive on temporary assignments because it gives them a "chance for glory." These individuals are usually highly creative and enjoy challenging work. The challenge has a greater importance than the cost of failure.

The second major performance problem lies in the proposal/functional interface where an individual suddenly must report to two bosses, the functional manager and the proposal manager. If the functional manager and the proposal manager are in total agreement as to the work to be accomplished, then performance at the interface will not be hampered. But if conflicting directions are received, then the individual at the interface, regardless of capabilities and experience, may suffer a decline in performance because of this compromising position.

Personnel policy problems can create havoc in an organization, especially if the "grass is greener" in a proposal environment than in the functional environment. Functional organizations are governed normally by unit-manning documents that specify rank for the employees. Proposal offices, on the other hand, have no such regulations because by definition, each proposal is different and therefore necessitates different structures.

The proposal management process is organized:

- To achieve a single set of objectives
- Through a single proposal of a finite lifetime
- Which operates as a separate company entity (except for administrative purposes).

Because each proposal is different, the proposal management process dictates that each project can establish its own procedures, rules, and standards, provided they fall within the broad company guidelines. Each proposal must be considered as a project by top management so that the proposal manager has the delegated authority necessary to enforce the procedures, rules, and standards.

Proposal management is successful only if the proposal manager and the team are dedicated totally to the successful completion of the proposal. This requires that each member of the team and supporting office has a good understanding of the fundamental requirements. These include:

- Directing
- Planning
- Controlling
- Evaluating
- Reporting
- Customer liaison.

Each member of the proposal team must become an authority in the ability to satisfy these requirements. Because these requirements generally cannot be fulfilled by single individuals, members of the supporting office as well as functional representatives, must work together as a team. This teamwork concept is vital to the success of a proposal.

Ultimately, the person with the greatest influence is the proposal manager. Because the proposal manager is dependent upon the input of individuals from various disciplines in the organization, he must be an effective leader and organizer. Proposal managers, by virtue of their characteristics, have the ability to either attract or deter highly desirable individuals. They must exhibit a great amount of enthusiasm and must motivate the team to have enthusiasm for their part of the work. Recognizing the short duration of a proposal, the proposal manager must have a considerable amount of drive and perseverance to keeping the team moving toward completion of the proposal effort. A proposal manager must like trouble and be adept in evaluating risk and uncertainty. Other basic characteristics include:

- Honesty and integrity
- Understanding personnel problems
- Tact and diplomacy
- Understanding project technology
- Business management competence
  - Management principles
  - Communications
- Alertness and quickness
- Versatility and inventiveness
- Energy and toughness
- Decision-making ability.

The proposal manager must exhibit honesty and integrity to the staff, thus fostering an atmosphere of trust. The proposal manager should not make unfulfilled or often impossible promises. Honesty, integrity, and an understanding of personnel problems can often eliminate any problems or conflicts that detract from the creation of a truly dedicated environment. Most proposal managers have "open-door" policies for personnel problems. On temporarily assigned activities, such as a proposal, managers cannot wait for personnel to iron out their own problems for fear that time, cost, and performance requirements will not be satisfied.

Proposal managers should have both business management and technical understanding competency. The proposal manager must also have a broad knowledge of his company's operation, its services, products, personnel, and manpower so that these elements can be presented properly in the proposal. It is necessary to know the techniques and policies followed in developing the various sections of the proposal, including engineering, estimating, and contractual. The proposal manager must understand the fundamental principles of management, especially those involving the rapid development of temporary communication channels. The proposal manager must understand the technical implications since he is ultimately responsible for all decision making. He may have a staff of professionals to assist him. Many good proposal managers have failed because they get too involved with the technical side of the project rather than the management side. Finally, the proposal manager must be conscientious and thorough in following through with a well-organized and professional-looking document. The individual write-ups must be edited, proofread, and corrected, so that the proposal reads like one person wrote it. As a selling document, the proposal must be packaged aesthetically with eye appeal.

In the proposal environment, because of its relatively short duration, decision making must be rapid and effective. The manager must be alert and quick in his ability to perceive "red flags" that can eventually lead to serious problems. He must demonstrate his versatility and toughness in order to keep his subordinates dedicated to goal accomplishment.

Another area of concern in the proposal environment, is motivating the temporarily assigned members of the proposal team. Basically, proposal managers must appeal to the individual's needs of esteem and self-actualization. Motivating employees so that they have a feeling of security and well-being on the job is not easy, especially because proposals have a finite lifetime. Specific methods for producing security in a proposal environment include:

- Letting your people know why they are where they are
- Making the individuals feel that they belong where they are
- Placing individuals in the positions for which they are properly trained
- Letting your team members know how their efforts fit into the big picture.

2.3 SELECTING THE PROPOSAL MANAGER

To both the client and contractor, the proposal is vitally important; its quality affects the execution of the project directly. The proposal document, upon award of a contract, entails the scope of work or guiding instructions for the project-execution phase. A badly prepared proposal can hurt the owner or contractor seriously, and destroy any chances of future agreements between them. This is one reason a capable individual must manage the preparation of a proposal.

Probably the most difficult decision facing upper-level management is the selection of the proposal managers. Some managers work best on long-term projects where decision making can be slow, whereas others may thrive on short-term projects that results in a constant pressure environment. Upper-level management must know the capabilities and short-comings of their managers. A director was once asked who he would choose for a key manager position: an individual who had been a manager on previous programs but did a relatively poor job, or a new aggressive individual who may have the capability but has never had the opportunity. The director responded by choosing the seasoned veteran assuming that the previous mistakes would not be made again. Stewart has commented on this type of situation:[1]

Though the manager's previous experience is apt to have been confined to a single functional area of business, he must be able to function on the project as a kind of general manager in miniature. He must not only keep track of what is happening but also play the crucial role of advocate for the project. Even for a seasoned manager, this task is not likely to be easy. Hence, it is important to assign an individual whose administrative abilities and skill in personal relations have been convincingly demonstrated under fire.

The selection process for proposal managers is not an easy one. Five basic questions must be considered:

1. What are the internal and external sources?
2. How do we select?
3. How do we provide career development in proposal management?
4. How can we develop proposal management skills?
5. How do we evaluate proposal management performance?

Proposal management cannot succeed unless a good proposal manager is at the controls. Upper-level managers should therefore see fit to select a qualified person. The selection process is an upper-level management responsibility because the proposal manager is delegated the authority of the general manager to cut across organizational lines in order to accomplish the desired objectives successfully. It is far more likely that a proposal manager will succeed if it is obvious to the subordinates that the general manager has made the appointment. The major responsibilities of the proposal manager include:

- Producing the end item with the available resources and within the constraints of time, cost, and performance/technology

---

[1] John M. Stewart, "Making Project Management Work," *Business Horizons,* fall 1965, p. 63.

- Meeting organizational profit objectives
- Making all required decisions
- Acting as the customer (external) and upper-level and functional management (internal) communications focal point
- "Negotiating" with all functional disciplines for accomplishment of the necessary work packages within time, cost, and performance/technology
- Resolving all conflicts, if possible.

A proposal manager, in order to fulfill his responsibilities successfully, must demonstrate the various skills of interface, resource, and planning and control management. These implicit responsibilities are shown below:

- Interface Management
  - Product interfaces
    - Performance of parts or subsections
    - Physical connection of parts or subsections
  - Project interfaces
    - Customer
    - Management (functional and upper-level)
    - Change of responsibilities
    - Information flow
    - Material interfaces (inventory control)
- Resource Management
  - Time (schedule)
  - Personnel
  - Money
  - Facilities
  - Equipment
  - Material
  - Information/technology
- Planning and Control Management
  - Increase equipment utilization
  - Increase performance efficiency
  - Reduce risks
  - Identify alternatives to problems
  - Identify alternative resolutions to conflicts.

Yet even with these personal characteristics and desired traits that proposal managers should possess, and even though the job descriptions are often clearly defined, management still persists in selecting the wrong person. The following are common justifications given by upper-level managers and the corresponding results of the assignment:

- *"Anne is available. Let's use her as project manager."* Using Anne just because she is available may fulfill a present requirement but may ultimately lead to disaster if she is not qualified. Although it is often not a good policy to reassign project managers in midstream, there might be no choice if a minimum risk position is to be maintained.
- *"Project Z is a high-technology project. Let's promote Jim, one of our best engineers, to project manager."* This philosophy will work if and only if Jim can divorce himself from the engineering side of the firm and fulfill his responsibilities as project manager. Although Jim is obviously highly capable, he might find it more difficult to become a manager than a doer.
- *"John belongs to the same outside clubs and organizations as our client. He'll have an inside track."* Being able to communicate with the customer does not guarantee that the project will be a success or managed correctly.
- *"Richard has performed well as assistant project manager for production and technology. Let's give him a new exposure and make him project manager for cost. He should know how to handle money."* This philosophy can lead to disaster if Richard does not understand cost control. Critical project decisions are almost always based upon cost, schedule, or technology. Good program/project managers for cost cannot be trained overnight. There should be an apprenticeship period.
- *"Sandra is a hard-nosed individual who drives her people into the ground. The work always gets accomplished on time and within cost. She will make sure that all objectives are met."* Applying hard-nosed tactics to one's subordinates, especially professionals, can create a very demoralizing atmosphere. It is true that pressure must be applied in time of crises. However, it should not be considered a way of life, or else eventually Sandra will not find qualified people who wish to work with or for her.
- *"Dennis has worked in almost every division of our organization. This knowledge should make him an excellent project manager."* This is faulty rationale. Although it is true that a good knowledge of total company operations is a valuable asset to a manager, there is no guarantee that he can perform effectively as a manager.
- *"Tom was hired from the outside to become a manager. He brought with him two of his assistants to help him direct project activities. His assistants work well with him. They always do what he wants. They make up a strong team."* There is no guarantee that Tom and his two pals are making decisions in the best interest of the company. His assistants are probably "yes" men. A strong team is dedicated to completion of the project objectives as long as it is in the best interest of the

company. Unfortunately, conflicts can arise as to the best interest of the company versus the best interest of the project.

Finding the man or woman with the right qualifications is not an easy task because proposal managers are selected more according to their personal characteristics than to the job description. In Section 2.2, a brief outline of desired characteristics are presented. Archibald defines a broader range of desired personal characteristics:[2]

- Flexibility and adaptability
- Preference for significant initiative and leadership
- Aggressiveness, confidence, persuasiveness, verbal fluency
- Ambition, activity, forcefulness
- Effectiveness as a communicator and integrator
- Broad scope of personal interests
- Poise, enthusiasm, imagination, spontaneity
- Able to balance technical solutions with time, cost, and human factors
- Well-organized and disciplined
- A generalist rather than a specialist
- Able and willing to devote most of the time to planning and controlling
- Able to identify problems
- Willing to make decisions
- Able to maintain a proper balance in the use of time.

Most companies would prefer to find, and possibly train, proposal managers from within. On-the-job training is probably one of the most important aspects in the development of a proposal manager. The individual selected from within knows the structure of the organization, its policies and procedures, and the key people to work with. This allows the proposal manager to do a quality job in a quicker time. In addition, these individuals have already proven themselves on other assignments, which gives upper-level management a better insight into their ability to do the job.

One of the most important, and often least understood, characteristics of a good proposal manager is the ability to understand both his (or her) own strengths and weaknesses and those of the employees by understanding human behavior. In order for an employee to perform efficiently, the manager has the responsibility to:

- Know what is supposed to be done, preferably in terms of an end product
- Have a clear understanding of authority and its limits

---

[2] Russell D. Archibald, *Managing High-Technology Programs and Projects,* New York: John Wiley & Sons, 1976, p. 55.

- Know what the relationship with other people is
- Know what constitutes a job well done in terms of specific results
- Know when and what is being done exceptionally well
- Show concrete evidence that there are just rewards for work well done and for work exceptionally well done
- Know where and when efforts are falling short
- Be aware of what can and should be done to correct unsatisfactory results
- Feel that the superior has an interest as an individual
- Feel that his superior is anxious for success and progress.

Thus far, we have assumed that the project is large enough for a full-time proposal manager to be appointed. This is not always the case. There are four major problem areas for proposal management responsibilities:

1. Part-time versus full-time assignment
2. Several proposals assigned to one proposal manager
3. Proposals assigned to functional managers
4. The proposal management role retained by the general manager.

The first two problem areas are related to the size of the proposal. If the proposal is small (short duration and low cost), then a part-time proposal manager may be selected. However, it is a common practice for one proposal manager to control several proposals, especially if they are either similar or related.

If the project is a high-technology effort that can be performed by one department, then it is not unusual for the functional manager to take on a dual role and act as proposal manager also. This can prove difficult to do, especially if the functional manager is required to give priority to the work under his supervision.

Probably the worst possible situation is when the general manager retains the role of proposal manager for a particular effort. The difficulty lies in the fact that the general manager may not have the time necessary to dedicate himself totally to the achievement of the proposal. The general manager cannot make decisions as a proposal manager while still discharging his normal duties.

2.4 THE PROPOSAL STAFFING PROCESS

Staffing the proposal organization can become a complicated and tedious effort, especially on large and complex engineering projects. Three major questions must be answered:

- Which people will be required?
- Where will the people come from?
- How will the team be organized?

Determining people resources must include a description of types of individuals (possibly by job descriptions), how many individuals from each job category are needed, and when these individuals will be required.

Key considerations to make when selecting members for the proposal team are that:

- People should be assigned to tasks commensurate with their skills
- Whenever possible, the same person should be assigned to related tasks
- The most critical tasks should be assigned to the more responsible people.

The proposal manager must realize that not all the personnel assigned to the proposal are part of the full-time proposal team. The factors that control whether or not individuals are part-time or full-time team members and the amount of members required in general are as follows:

- Project size
- Project complexity
- Type of project (R&D, qualification, production)
- Level of technical competency required
- Importance to the organization (Is it a strategic project?)
- Customer requirements
- Interfacing requirement with organization.

Once the resources are defined, the next question to consider is whether staffing will be from within the existing organization or from outside sources such as other offices or consultants. Outside consultants are advisable if and only if internal manpower resources are being fully utilized on other programs or if the company does not possess the required project skills. The answer to the last question should describe the organizational form that is best for achievement of the objectives. The form might be a matrix, product, or staff project management structure.

As with any organization, the subordinates can make the superior look good in the performance of his duties. Unfortunately, the proposal environment is symbolized by temporary assignments in which the main effort put forth by the proposal manager is to motivate his (temporary) subordinates toward proposal dedication and to make them understand fully that:

- Teamwork is vital for success
- *Esprit de corps* can perpetuate success
- Conflicts can occur between proposal and functional ties
- Communication is vital for success
- Conflicting orders may be given:
  - Proposal manager
  - Functional manager
  - Upper-level manager
- Unsuccessful performance may result in transfer or dismissal from the proposal as well as disciplinary action.

Except in the case of a major proposal, in which a full-time group of specialists is assembled, the usual approach is to place the proposal effort on top of the individual's existing workload. The individual involved exerts a certain amount of resistance to having this "extra" work imposed upon what is considered to be the normal duties. The proposal manager must also realize that the most qualified personnel may not always be available to work on the proposal.

The following are key factors to keep in mind when selecting the proposal team members:

- Upper-level management must have an input into the selection process
- Establishing proposal requirements should be a joint effort between the proposal manager and functional management
  - Functional managers may have more expertise and can identify problem areas
  - Functional managers develop a positive attitude toward the proposal through early participation in the planning phase
- Are there any special requirements in the way of:
  - Technical specifications?
  - Customer requests?
  - Organizational structuring that deviates from existing policies?

The worst position for a proposal manager is to attempt to get top-quality personnel to volunteer for the proposal after unfulfilled promises have been made on previous proposals. Under this condition, even if top management assigns key individuals to the proposal, they will always be skeptical about any promises.

Selecting the proposal manager is only one part of the staffing problem. Selecting the proposal team and support personnel often can be a time-consuming chore. The proposal team consists of personnel that are usually assigned as full-time members of the proposal. The first step in selecting the proposal staff requires that the proposal manager evaluate all potential candidates, regardless of whether or not they are now assigned to another project. This evaluation process should include active proposal team members, functional team members available for promotion or transfer, and outside applicants.

Upon completion of the evaluation process, the proposal manager meets with upper-level management. This coordination is required to assure that:

- All assignments fall within current policies on rank, salary, and promotion.
- The individuals selected can work well with both the proposal manager (formal reporting) and upper-level management (informal reporting).
- The individuals selected have good working relationships with the functional personnel.

Good proposal team personnel cannot be trained overnight. Good training is usually identified as exposure on several types of projects. Proposal managers do not "train" proposal team members primarily because time might not permit this luxury. Proposal team personnel must be self-disciplined, especially during the first few assignments.

The third and final step in the staffing of the proposal is a meeting of the proposal manager, upper-level management, and the manager from whose department the requested individuals are currently assigned. Department managers are very reluctant to give up qualified personnel to the staff of other offices. Unfortunately, this procedure is a way of life in a proposal environment. Upper-level management attends these meetings to represent to all negotiating parties the fact that top management is concerned with maintaining the best possible mix of individuals from available resources and to help resolve staffing conflicts. Staffing from within is a negotiation process in which upper-level management establishes ground rules and priorities.

2.5 LEADERSHIP IN A PROPOSAL ENVIRONMENT

Leadership can be defined as a style of behavior designed to integrate the organizational requirements and one's personal interest into the pursuit of some objective. All managers have some sort of leadership responsibility. If time permits, successful leadership techniques and practices can be developed.

Leadership is the composition of several complex elements, the three most common being:

- The person leading
- The people being led
- The situation (i.e., the proposal environment).

Project and proposal managers are often selected or not selected because of their leadership styles. The most common reason for not selecting an individual as a project or proposal manager is his inability to balance the technical and managerial functions. Wilemon and Cicero have defined four characteristics of this type of situation:[3]

- The greater the Project Manager's technical expertise, the higher the propensity that he will overly involve himself in the technical details of the project.
- The greater the project manager's difficulty in delegating technical task responsibilities, the more likely it is that he will over involve himself in the technical details of the project (depending upon his expertise to do so).
- The greater the project manager's interest in the technical details of the project, the more likely it is that he will defend the project manager's role as one of a technical specialist.
- The lower the project manager's technical expertise, the more likely it is that he will overstress the non-technical project functions (administrative functions).

These four points are important particularly in selecting the appropriate person to head the proposal function. Some organizations have the tendency of promoting technical specialists who have demonstrated writing skills into proposal management. If the employee is not willing to surrender that technical ability in order to develop a good balance, then the proposal may suffer. This same result can occur if we promote an individual who overemphasizes the managerial duties.

There have been several surveys to determine what leadership techniques are best. The following are the results of a survey by Richard Hodgetts:[4]

- Human Relations-Oriented Leadership Techniques
  - *"The Project Manager must make all the team members feel that their efforts are important and have a direct effect on the outcome of the program."*
  - *"The project manager must educate the team concerning what is to be done and how important its role is."*
  - *Provide credit to project participants."*

[3] David L. Wilemon and John P. Cicero, "The Project Manager: Anomalies and Ambiguities," *Academy of Management Journal,* Vol. 13, 1970, pp. 269–282.
[4] Richard M. Hodgetts, "Leadership Techniques in Project Organizations," *Academy of Management Journal,* Vol. 11, 1968, pp. 211–219.

- *"Project members must be given recognition and prestige of appointment."*
- *"Make the team members feel and believe that they play a vital part in the success (or failure) of the team."*
- *"By working extremely close with my team I believe that one can win a project loyalty while to a large extent minimizing the frequency of authority gap problems."*
- *"I believe that a great motivation can be created just by knowing the people in a personal sense. I know many of the line people better than their own supervisor does. In addition, I try to make them understand that they are an indispensable part of the team."*
- *"I would consider the most important technique in overcoming the authority gap to be understanding as much as possible in the needs of the individuals with whom you are dealing and over whom you have no direct authority."*
- Formal Authority-Oriented Leadership Techniques
  - *"Point out how great the loss will be if cooperation is not forthcoming."*
  - *"Put all authority in functional statements."*
  - *"Apply pressure beginning with a tactful approach and minimum application warranted by the situation and then increasing it."*
  - *"Threaten to precipitate high-level intervention and do it if necessary."*
  - *"Convince the members that what is good for the company is good for them."*
  - *"Place authority on full-time assigned people in the operating division to get the necessary work done."*
  - *"Maintain control over expenditure."*
  - *"Utilize implicit threat of going to general management for resolution."*
  - *"It is most important that the team members recognize that the project manager has the charter to direct the project."*

These remarks apply not only to project managers but to proposal managers as well.

2.6 ORGANIZATIONAL IMPACT

In most companies, whether or not project-oriented, the impact of management emphasis upon the organization is well known. In the proposal environment, there also exists a definite impact because of leadership emphasis. The leadership emphasis is best seen by employee contributions, organizational order, employee performance, and by the proposal manager's performance.

- Employee Contributions
  - A good proposal manager encourages active cooperation and responsible participation. The result is that both good and bad information is contributed freely. This is particularly important during proposals where good preliminary planning is a necessity.
  - A poor proposal manager maintains an atmosphere of passive resistance with only responsive participation. This results in information being withheld.
- Organizational Order
  - A good proposal manager develops policy and encourages acceptance. A low price is paid for contributions.
  - A poor proposal manager goes beyond policies and attempts to develop procedures and measurements. A high price is normally paid for contributions.
- Employee Performance
  - A good proposal manager keeps people informed and satisfied (if possible) by aligning motives with objectives. Positive thinking and cooperation are encouraged. A good proposal manager is willing to give more responsibility to those willing to accept it.
  - A poor proposal manager keeps people uninformed, frustrated, defensive, and negative. Motives are aligned with incentives rather than objectives. The poor proposal manager develops a "stay out of trouble" atmosphere.
- Performance of the Proposal Manager
  - A good proposal manager assumes that employee misunderstandings can and will occur, and therefore does not blame. A good proposal manager attempts to improve constantly and to be more communicative by relying heavily on moral persuasion.
  - A poor proposal manager assumes that employees are unwilling to cooperate and therefore blames subordinates. The poor proposal manager demands more through authoritarian attitudes and relies heavily on material incentives.

Management emphasis also impacts the organization. The following four categories show this management emphasis resulting for both good and poor proposal management:

- Management Problem Solving
  - A good proposal manager performs problem solving at the level for which he (or she) is responsible through delegation of problem-solving responsibilities.
  - A poor proposal manager performs subordinate problem solving in

known areas. For areas that are unfamiliar, the poor proposal manager requires that approval be given prior to idea implementation.

- Organizational Order
  - A good proposal manager develops, maintains, and uses a single integrated management system in which authority and responsibility are delegated to the subordinates. In addition, occasional slippages and overruns that do occur are acted upon to minimize their effect.
  - A poor proposal manager delegates as little authority and responsibility as possible, and runs the risk of continual slippages and overruns. A poor proposal manager maintains two management information systems: one informal system for personal guidance and one formal ("eyewash") system simply to impress superiors.
- Performance of People
  - A good proposal manager finds that subordinates accept responsibility willingly, are decisive in attitude toward the project, and are satisfied.
  - A poor proposal manager finds that subordinates are reluctant to accept responsibility, are indecisive in their actions, and seem frustrated.
- Performance of the Proposal Manager
  - A good proposal manager assumes that his key people can "run the show." By exhibiting confidence toward individuals working in unfamiliar areas and exhibiting patience with people working in familiar areas, the proposal manager builds mutual trust. A good proposal manager is never too busy to help people solve personal or professional problems.
  - A poor proposal manager has visions of being indispensable, is overcautious with work performed in unfamiliar areas, and becomes overinterested in work that is familiar. A poor proposal manager is always tied up in meetings.

Two other major problem areas in the proposal environment are the determination of the "who has what authority and responsibility" question, and the resulting conflicts associated with the individual at the project/functional interface. Almost all proposal problems in some way or another involve these two major areas.

Authority is the key to the management process and is usually defined as a legal or rightful power to command, act, or direct the activities of others. To be effective, the proposal manager must have broad authority over all elements of the proposal, sufficient enough to draw upon all necessary managerial and technical actions required to complete the proposal successfully. The proposal manager manages across functional and organizational lines to bring together diverse activities. In addition, the proposal manager accomplishes these objectives through personnel who are primarily professional. For professional people, proposal leadership includes the rationale of the effort as well as the more obvious function of planning, organizing, directing, and controlling.

Project authority is covered in greater detail in Chapter 3. Managing conflict is discussed in a later section of this chapter.

2.7 MANAGER PROBLEMS

On the manager level, the two most common problems involve personal values and conflicts. Personal values are often attributed to the "changing of the guard". New managers have a sense of values different from those of the older, more experienced managers. Miner identifies some of these personal values attributed to new managers:[5]

- Less trusting, especially of people in positions of authority
- Increased feelings of being controlled by external forces and events, and thus believing that they cannot control their own destinies. This is a kind of change that makes for less initiation of one's own activities and a greater likelihood of responding in terms of external pressures. There is a sense of powerlessness, although not necessarily a decreased desire for power.
- Less authoritarian and more negative attitudes toward persons holding positions of power
- More independent, often to the point of rebelliousness and defiance
- More free and uncontrolled in expressing feelings, impulses, and emotions
- More inclined to live in the present and to let the future take care of itself
- More self-indulgent
- Moral values that are more relative to the situation, less absolute, and less tied to formal religion
- A strong and increasing identification with peer and age groups and with the youth culture
- Greater social concern and greater desire to help the less fortunate
- More negative toward business, the management role in particular. Clearly, a professional position is preferred to managing.

---

[5] John B. Miner, "The OD-Management Development Conflict," *Business Horizons,* December 1973, p. 32.

- A desire to contribute less to an employing organization and to receive more from the organization

Previously, we defined one of the attributes of a manager as liking risks. Unfortunately, the amount of risk which today's managers are willing to accept varies not only with their personal values but also with the impact of current economic conditions and top management philosophies. If top management views a specific project as vital for the growth of the company, then the proposal manager may be so directed to assume virtually no risks during the execution of the proposal. In this case, the proposal manager may attempt to pass all responsibility to higher or lower management by claiming: "My hands are tied!" The amount of risk that a manager will accept also varies with age and experience. Older, more experienced managers tend to take little risks whereas the younger, more aggressive managers may adopt a "risk-lover" policy in hopes of achieving a name for themselves.

Conflicts exist at the proposal/functional interface regardless of how conscientiously an attempt is made to structure the work. Authority and responsibility relationships can vary from proposal to proposal. In general, however, there does exist a relatively definable boundary between the proposal and functional manager. According to Cleland and King, this interface can be defined by the following relationships:[6]

- Proposal (Project) Manager
  - What is to be done?
  - When will the task be done?
  - Why will the task be done?
  - How much money is available to do the task?
  - How well has the total project been done?
- Functional Manager
  - Who will do the task?
  - Where will the task be done?
  - How will the task be done?
  - How well has the functional input been integrated into the project?

Another difficulty arises from the way the functional manager views the proposal. Many functional managers consider the proposal as simply a means toward an end and therefore identify problems and seek solutions in terms of their immediate duties and responsibilities rather than looking beyond them.

---

[6] David I. Cleland and William Richard King, *Systems Analysis and Project Managment,* 1968, 1975 by McGraw-Hill, p. 237.

This problem also exists at the horizontal hierarchy level. The problem comes about as a result of authority and responsibility relationships, and may not have anything at all to do with the competence of the individuals concerned. This situation breeds conflicts that also have an impact on the amount of risk that a manager wishes to accept. Killian defines this inevitable conflict between the functional and project manager:[7]

> The conflicts revolve around items such as project priority, manpower costs, and the assignment of functional personnel to the project [proposal] manager. Each project [proposal] manager will, of course, want the best functional operators assigned to his project. In addition to these problems, the accountability for profit and loss is much more difficult in a matrix organization than in a project organization. Project managers have a tendency to blame overruns on functional managers, stating that the cost of the function was excessive. Whereas functional managers have a tendency to blame excessive costs on project [proposal] managers with the argument that there were too many changes, more work required than defined initially, and other such arguments.

Another major trouble area is in problem reporting and resolution. Major conflicts can arise during problem resolution sessions, not only because of the reasons mentioned above, but also because the time constraints imposed on the proposal often prevent both parties from taking a logical approach. Proposal managers have the tendency of wanting to make immediate decisions, after which the functional manager asserts that his way is "the only way" the problem can be resolved. One of the major causes for prolonged problem solving is the lack of pertinent information. In order to ease potential conflicts, all pertinent information should be made available to all parties concerned as early as possible.

2.8 THE CONFLICT ENVIRONMENT

Previously, we stated that proposal objectives can exist anywhere in the organization—company, division, department, project, individual—and can be interpreted differently at each level if not defined properly. Therefore, to assist in resolving conflicts, objectives should be given priority.

The most common factors influencing the establishment of proposal priorities include:

- The risks that the company incurs, financially or competitively
- The penalties that can accompany late delivery dates

---

[7] William P. Killian, "Project Management-Future Organizational Concepts," *Marquette Business Review,* No. 2, 1971, pp. 90–107.

- The amount of influence that the customer possesses, possibly because of the size of the project
- The impact on other projects
- The impact on affiliated organizations
- The impact on a particular product line

The ultimate responsibility for establishing priorities rests with top-level management. Yet even with priority establishment, conflicts still develop. Wilemon has identified several reasons why conflicts still occur:[8]

- The greater the diversity of disciplinary expertise among the participants of a project team, the greater the potential for conflicts to develop among the members of the team.
- The lower the project manager's degree of authority, reward and punishment power over those individuals and organizational units supporting his project the greater the potential for conflicts to develop.
- The less the specific objectives of a project (cost, schedule, and technical performance) are understood by the project team members the more likely that conflict will develop.
- The greater the role played by ambiguity among the participants of a project team the more likely that conflict will develop.
- The greater the agreement on superordinate goals by project team participants, the lower the potential for detrimental conflict.
- The more the members of a functional area perceive that the implementation of a project management system will adversely usurp their traditional roles, the greater the potential for conflict.
- The lower the percent need for interdependence among organizational units supporting a project, the greater the potential for dysfunctional conflict.
- The higher the managerial level within a project or functional area, the more likely that conflicts will be based upon deep-seated, parochial resentments. By contrast, at the project or task level, the more likely cooperation will be facilitated by task orientation and professionalism that a project requires for completion.

2.9 MANAGING CONFLICT

Temporary management situations produce conflicts. This is a natural occurrence resulting from the differences in the organizational behavior of in-

---

[8] David L. Wilemon, "Managing Conflicts in Temporary Management Situations," *Journal of Management Studies,* Vol. 10, 1973, pp. 282–296.

dividuals, the differences in the way that functional and proposal managers view the work required, and the lack of time necessary for proposal managers and functional personnel to establish ideal working relationships.

Regardless of how well planning is developed, proposal managers must be willing to operate in an environment that is characterized by constant and rapid change. This turbulent environment can be the result of changes in the scope of work, a shifting of key personnel because of new priorities and other unforeseen developments. The success or failure of a proposal manager is quite often measured by the ability to deal with change.

In contrast to the functional manager who works in a more standardized and predictable environment, the project (proposal) manager must live with constant change. In order to integrate various disciplines across functional lines, the proposal manager must learn to foster a climate that promotes the ability of his personnel to adapt to the pressures of this continuously changing work environment. Demanding compliance to rigid rules, principles, and techniques is often counterproductive. In such situations, an environment conducive to effective management is missing and the leader too often suffers the same fate as heart-transplant patients' rejection![9]

There is no one single method that suffices for managing all conflicts in temporary management situations because:

- There exist several types of conflicts.
- Each conflict can assume a different relative intensity over the life cycle of the proposal.
- For each proposal, different conflicts will be more critical.

The detrimental aspects of these conflicts can be minimized if the proposal manager can anticipate their occurrence and understand their composition. The prepared manager can then resort to one of several conflict resolution modes in order to manage the disagreements that can occur more effectively.[10]

Conflict is defined as the behavior of an individual, a group, or an organization which impedes or restricts (at least temporarily) another party from attaining its desired goals. Although conflict may impede the attainment of one's goals, the consequences may be beneficial if they produce new information which, in turn, enhances the decision-making process. By contrast,

---

[9] H. S. Dugan, H. J. Thamhain, and D. W. Wilemon, "Managing Change in Project Management," *Proceeding of The Ninth Annual International Seminar/Symposium on Project Management,* Chicago, October 22–26, 1977, pp. 178–188.

[10] The remainder of Section 2.9 is devoted to Hans J. Thamhain and David L. Wilemon, "Conflict Management in Project Life Cycles," *Sloan Management Review,* Summer 1975, pp. 31–50. Reprinted by permission.

conflict becomes dysfunctional if it results in poor project decision making, lengthy delays over issues that do not affect the outcome of the project significantly, or a disintegration of the team's efforts.

Project (proposal) managers indicate frequently that one of the requirements for effective performance is the ability to manage various conflicts and disagreements that invariably arise in task accomplishment. While several research studies have reported on the general nature of conflict in project management, few studies have been devoted to the cause and management of conflict in specific project life-cycle stages. If project (proposal) managers are aware of some of the major causes of disagreements in the various project life-cycle phases, there is a greater likelihood that the detrimental aspects of these potential conflict situations can be avoided or minimized.

The following are the seven major potential sources of conflict that may be faced by the manager:

- *Conflict over project priorities.* The views of project participants often differ over the sequence of activities and tasks that should be undertaken to achieve successful project completion. Conflict over priorities may occur not only between the project team and other support groups but also within the project team.
- *Conflict over administrative procedures.* A number of managerial and administrative-oriented conflicts may develop over how the project will be managed, i.e., the definition of the project manager's reporting relationships, definition of responsibilities, interface relationships, project scope, operational requirements, plan and execution, negotiated work agreements with other groups, and procedures for administrative support.
- *Conflict over technical opinions and performance trade-offs.* In technology-oriented projects, disagreements may arise over technical issues, performance specifications, technical trade-offs, and the means to achieve performance.
- *Conflict over manpower resources.* Conflicts may arise around the staffing of the project team with personnel from other technical and staff support areas or from the desire to use another department's personnel for project support even though the personnel remain under the authority of their functional or staff superiors.
- *Conflict over cost.* Frequently, conflict may develop over cost estimates from support areas regarding various project work breakdown packages. For example, the funds allocated by a project manager to a functional support group might be perceived as insufficient for the support requested.

- *Conflict over schedules.* Disagreements may develop around the timing, sequencing, and scheduling of project-related tasks.
- *Personality conflict.* Disagreements may tend to center on interpersonal differences rather than on "technical" issues. Conflicts often are "ego-centered."

A number of research studies indicate that managers approach and resolve conflicts by utilizing various conflict resolution modes. Blake and Mouton, for example, have delineated five modes for handling conflicts:[11]

- *Withdrawal.* Retreating or withdrawing from an actual or potential disagreement.
- *Smoothing.* Deemphasizing or avoiding areas of difference and emphasizing areas of agreement.
- *Compromising.* Bargaining and searching for solutions which bring some degree of satisfaction to the parties in a dispute. Characterized by a "give-and-take" attitude.
- *Forcing.* Exerting one's viewpoint at the potential expense of another. Often characterized by competitiveness and a win/lose situation.
- *Confrontation.* Facing the conflict directly which involves a problem-solving approach whereby affected parties work through their disagreements.[12]

2.10 TYPICAL POSITION DESCRIPTIONS

In establishing a permanent proposal department, it is necessary for successful operation that the department and the individuals who are assigned to it have their roles defined clearly. While the proposal group is responsible for the planning, organizing, monitoring, controlling, and assembly of the proposal, the functional departments (i.e., engineering, cost, scheduling, etc.) are still responsible for preparing the individual sections of the proposal. To provide a smooth flow of interaction and information between the proposal group and the functional group, the positions of the proposal staff should be defined clearly in writing. The following are typical position descriptions for three levels of proposal staffing. They are:

- Manager of Proposals (Department Head Position)
- Proposal Manager
- Proposal Coordinator

---

[11] R. R. Blake and J. S. Mouton, *The Managerial Grid,* Houston: Gulf Publishing, 1964.

[12] For a fuller description of these definitions, see R. J. Burke, "Methods of Resolving Interpersonal Conflict." *Personnel Administration,* July 1969, pp. 48–55.

Specific functions of the proposal department staff include, but are not necessarily limited to:

- Prepare proposals for new work
- Prepare qualifications, technical capability, or other brochures as may be needed for the development of new business
- Process inquiry screening requests to obtain management quoting decisions
- Establish budgets, monitor and control costs for preparation of proposals, and other sales support efforts
- Provide support services to the sales staff as needed for the development of new business
- Arrange for and coordinate assistance from operations when needed for the development of new business
- Assist in new business contract negotiations and see to the issuance and distribution of contractual documents
- Help train and develop new project and sales staff personnel
- Perform other assignments or duties as may be assigned.

As part of the overall function, the proposal department develops and maintains the following documents that are useful to the new business development effort:

- Standard basic descriptions of various aspects of operations and services
- Experience summaries and other data in a format useful for sales promotion
- Procedures or manuals for proposal preparation and sales coordination
- Organization charts
- Manpower breakdown and availability curves
- Standard commercial and contractual terms
- Visual aides for sales presentations.

Position Description: Manager of Proposals

General Function: The manager of proposals has responsibility for organizing and managing the preparation of proposals and maintaining and developing the proposal staff to perform and increase the efficiency of the work. The manager of proposals reports to the vice president of sales.

Specific Responsibilities: The manager of proposals is responsible for the following specific tasks:

1. After management authorization of a bidding effort, arrange for the preparation of proposals based on information generated by sales,

engineering, operations, and estimating. Guide and expedite the work of all groups concerned with the development of proposal information, insure that the ultimate product of this effort meets the requirements of the inquiry and that it is completed on time.

2. Assign and direct proposal managers and proposal coordinators to staff the proposal so that each proposal effort is implemented properly.
3. Keep in close contact with sales, and participate in meetings with clients, to insure that sales' thinking permeates the proposals.
4. Furnish to sales preliminary pricing information based on data compiled in consultation with estimating.
5. Supply copies of key proposals to branch operations and subsidiaries, and maintain vigilance over their use and whereabouts.
6. Aid sales in the evaluation of competitive offerings and customer feedback information as a guide to future selling.
7. Review all proposals, estimates, and letters to assure the inclusion of necessary commercial terms, time limitations, technical limitations, etc.
8. Supplement the sales staff in direct client relationships, when requested.
9. Provide assistance and direction for development projects, inquiries, and consulting projects as requested.
10. Review cost of operation of the proposal component regularly and exert continual effort to reduce this overhead item.
11. Appraise performance of personnel and provide for continual improvement by instruction, training, and recruiting.
12. Review salary structure periodically within proposal department.
13. Review, interpret, and secure understanding and acceptance of company objectives, policies, and procedures with all members of the department.
14. Submit recommendations and justifications for personnel addition and reduction to management.

Position Description: Proposal Manager

General Function: The proposal manager has the authority and overall responsibility to initiate work, assemble and manage assigned personnel, and complete bid proposals on time, within budget, and in conformity with company's bidding objectives, based on the suggested sales strategy established by the sales department. The proposal manager reports to the manager of proposals.

Specific Responsibilities: The proposal manager is responsible for the following specific tasks:

1. Review staffing and supervise the activities of assigned personnel to develop all technical and commercial information required for the proposal.

2. Direct development of clear and persuasively written proposals having adequate detail, following established proposal preparation procedures.
3. Direct preparation of technical proposal, specifications, and commercial proposals for approval by the manager of proposals.
4. Establish the form and extent of detail, schedule the proposal effort, and establish progress controls to complete proposal on time, within budget, and in conformity with company's bidding objectives. These items are to be detailed in the form of a kick-off or coordination memo.
5. Provide liaison with clients and sales department on matters relating to assigned proposals.
6. Plan, arrange, and/or participate in visits to plant sites as required to survey local conditions and secure data as required for preparation of proposals.
7. Review proposal, including estimate, to determine compliance of the estimate with the proposal and with client's requirements, and to ascertain that reasonable technical assumptions are used as a basis of establishing minimum cost design.
8. Participate in technical sales effort for assigned proposals specifically and also generally where technical sales assistance is required.
9. Direct the work of the proposal coordinator (when assigned) so that he acts in conjunction with all departments to follow the technical aspects of a proposal.
10. Assist in contract negotiations, document all changes to the original scope, and prepare additional contract data as may be required.
11. After contract award, coordinate with project manager to provide orderly transfer of all documents defining the plant as it was sold.
12. Provide proposal management assistance and direction for development projects, inquiries, and consulting services as requested.
13. Perform the functions of the proposal coordinator as required or when a proposal coordinator is not assigned.

Position Description: Proposal Coordinator

General Function: The proposal coordinator is responsible for the technical and cost execution of his assigned proposal, acting under the direction of the assigned proposal manager. The proposal coordinator reports to either the proposal manager or the manager of proposals.

Specific responsibilities: The proposal coordinator is responsible for the following specific tasks:

1. Read and understand the client's specification and proposal scope letter. Analyze the provisions of these documents for their effect on the technical execution of the project.

2. Establish with the proposal manager the technical scope of work required to fulfill the client's requirements and company's objectives.
3. Distribute all inquiry documents as required to prepare the proposal properly.
4. Assist the proposal manager in all phases of the proposal effort with particular emphasis on the technical aspects.
5. Participate in the development of the plot plan, engineering flow sheets and, where applicable, the process flow sheets.
6. Insure that all data sheets, specifications, equipment sizes, equipment quantities, and equipment numbers are compatible with the flow sheets and plot plan.
7. Assist the scheduling department in the development of a project schedule for the proposal.
8. Provide assistance to the purchasing department in soliciting bids requested by the estimating department.
9. Provide the proposal manager with assistance as required to meet schedules and get the proposal and estimate completed on schedule.
10. Coordinate the preparation, collection, editing, and assembly of all proposal documents.
11. Act as the proposal manager on small inquiries as required and perform the task normally assigned to the proposal manager.
12. Participate in training programs as required to develop further skills and competence in the present position, and in the possible future position of proposal manager.

Chapter 3

Improving Managerial Effectiveness

3.0 INTRODUCTION

Quite often, the effectiveness and success of project managers are measured by how well they can negotiate with both upper-level and functional management for the resources necessary to achieve the project objective. The two most important characteristics of a project manager are his interpersonal and communicative skills. Unfortunately, many organizations have not realized as yet the necessity to develop these characteristics within the proposal manager.

If the proposal is considered to be a project, as it is in most companies, then the proposal manager must have the same characteristics as the project manager. In many organizations, both the project manager and future project team report to the proposal manager during the proposal period. In addition, it is also possible for project vice presidents to report informally to the proposal manager during the proposal stage, regardless of the grade level of the proposal manager. This is quite common in the construction industry.

Proposal managers must understand the importance of managerial effectiveness. The proposal manager must plan, organize, schedule, control, and direct functional resources (all of which report formally to a line manager) in order to accomplish the time, cost, and performance requirements of the proposal. Generally speaking, the proposal manager has more delegated authority to go with the same amount of responsibility as would the project or program manager. In large organizations, the proposal manager can draw upon vast organizational resources and can communicate directly with top corporate executives. Management skills for the proposal managers are equally as important in the small company because the proposal manager not only works closely with top management but may have to wear "two hats," performing functional responsibilities as well as proposal responsibilities. In small companies, it is not uncommon for engineering functional managers and functional personnel to act, at one time or another, as proposal managers and to be solely responsible for the entire proposal, from beginning to end.

The intent of this chapter is to identify for the proposal manager methods to improve managerial effectiveness of projects. Given the fact that each proposal is a project, proposal managers must understand the basic management functions and principles, as well as other related topics on interpersonal skills such as time management, communications, and how to run better meetings. For the remainder of this chapter, the words "proposal manager" and "project manager" are used synonymously.

3.1 PROPOSAL PLANNING

The most important responsibilities of a proposal manager are planning and integrating functional plans into a unified document for the customer. Almost all proposals, because of their relatively short duration and often prioritized control of resources, require formal, detailed planning. The integration of the planning activities is necessary because each functional unit may develop its own planning documentation with little regard for other functional units.

Planning, in general, can best be described as the function of selecting the enterprise objectives (which may have been set forth by the customer) and establishing the policies, procedures, and programs necessary for achieving them. Planning in a proposal environment may be described as establishing a predetermined course of action within a forecasted environment. The customer sets the major milestones and the contractor's line managers hope that they can meet them. If the line manager cannot commit because the milestones are perceived as unrealistic, the proposal manager may have to develop alternatives, one of which may be to request the customer to move the milestones. Upper-level management must become involved in the selection of alternatives during any part of the proposal stage. Planning is, of course, decision making because it involves choosing among alternatives. Planning is a required proposal management function to facilitate the comprehension of complex problems involving interacting factors.

One of the objectives of project planning is to define completely all work required (possibly through the development of a documented project plan) so that it is readily identifiable to each project participant. This is a necessity in a proposal environment because:

- If the task is well understood prior to being performed, much of the work can be preplanned with a reasonable degree of accuracy and assurance.
- If the task is not understood, then during the actual task execution more knowledge is learned which in turn, leads to changes in resource allocations, schedules, and priorities, as well as surprises for the customer.
- The more uncertain the task, the greater the amount of information that must be processed in order to insure effectiveness performance. (This could easily result in a drain of the corporate bid and proposal budget.)

These three facets are important in a project environment because each project can be different, requiring a variety of resources that has to be performed under time, cost, and performance constraints with little margin for error. Figure 3-1 identifies the type of project planning required during the proposal to establish an effective monitoring and control system and to convince the customer that the proposal was well planned. The boxes in the upper portion of the curve represent the planning activities, and the lower portion identifies the proposed "tracking" or monitoring system to be employed. The customer is interested in both the upper as well as lower boxes.

Without proper planning, programs and projects can start off "behind the eight ball" because of poorly defined requirements during the initial proposal planning phase. Below is a list of the typical consequences of poor planning:

- Project initiation
- Wild enthusiasm
- Disillusionment
- Chaos
- Search for the guilty
- Punishment of the innocent
- Promotion of the nonparticipants
- Definition of the requirements.

Obviously, the complete definition of the requirements should have been the first step. This is discussed in greater detail in Chapter 6.

There are four basic reasons for well-defined project planning:

- Eliminate or reduce uncertainty
- Improve efficiency of the operation
- Obtain a better understanding of the objectives
- Provide a basis for monitoring and controlling work

There are involuntary and voluntary reasons for planning. Involuntary reasons can be internally mandatory functions of the organizational complex-

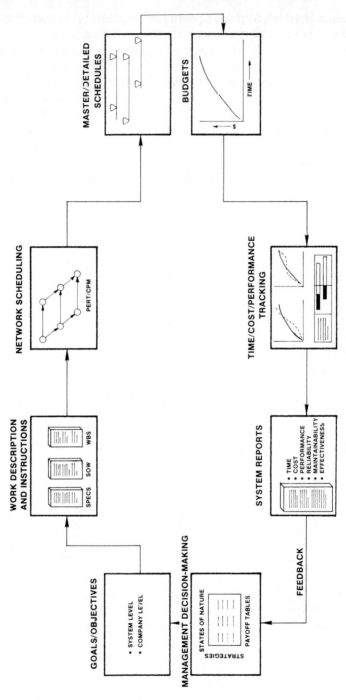

Figure 3–1. The project planning and control system.

ity and organizational lag in response time, or externally correlated to environmental fluctuations, uncertainty, and discontinuity. The voluntary reasons for planning are attempts to secure efficient and effective use of operations should the contract be won.

Planning is decision making based upon futurity. It is a continuous process of making entrepreneurial decisions with an eye to the future and methodically organizing the effort needed to carry out these decisions. Futhermore, systematic planning allows an organization to set internal goals in concert with external customer requirements. The alternative to systematic planning is decision making based upon history. This generally results in reactive management leading to crisis management, conflict management, and "fire fighting."

Planning is determining what needs to be done, by whom, and by when, in order to fulfill one's assigned responsibility. There are nine major steps which must be developed during the proposal planning phase:

- *Objective:* a goal, target, or quota to be achieved by a certain time, probably customer-specified
- *Program Plan:* the strategy to be followed and major actions to be taken in order to achieve or exceed the objectives of the customer
- *Schedule:* a plan showing when individual or group activities or accomplishments will be started and/or completed
- *Budget:* planned expenditures required to achieve or exceed objectives
- *Forecast:* a projection of what will happen by a certain time
- *Organization:* design of the number and kinds of positions, along with corresponding duties and responsibilities, required to achieve or exceed objectives
- *Policy:* a general guide for decision making and individual actions, including customer participation
- *Procedure:* a detailed method for carrying out a policy
- *Standard:* a level of individual or group performance defined as adequate or acceptable i.e., manufacturing learning curves

Several of these steps require additional comments. Forecasting may not be easy, especially if predictions of environmental reactions are required. For example, planning is customarily defined as either *strategic, tactical,* or *operational.* Strategic planning is generally five years or more, tactical can be one to five years, and operational is the here and now of six months to one year. Although most proposal projects are operational, they can be considered strategic especially if spin-offs or follow-up work is promising. Forecasting also requires an understanding of strengths and weaknesses, such as:

- Competitive situation
- Marketing
- Research and development
- Production
- Finance
- Personnel
- Management structure

If project planning is strictly operational, then these factors may be clearly definable. However, if strategic or long-range planning is necessary, then the future economic outlook can vary, say year to year, and replanning must be accomplished at regular intervals because the goals and objectives can change. This procedure can be seen in Figure 3-1.

The last three factors, policies, procedures, and standards, can vary from project to project because of their uniqueness. Each project and proposal manager can establish project policies provided that they fall within the broad limits set forth by top management. Policies are predetermined general courses or guides based upon the following principles:[1]

- Subordinate policies are supplementary to superior policies
- Policies are based upon known principles in the operative areas
- Policies should be complementary for coordination
- Policies should be definable, understandable, and preferably in writing
- Policies should be both flexible and stable
- Policies should be reasonably comprehensive in scope

Project policies must often conform closely to company policies, and are usually similar in nature from proposal to proposal. Procedures, on the other hand, can be drastically different from proposal to proposal, even if the same proposal activity is performed. For example, signing off manufacturing plans may require different signatures on two selected projects even though the same end item is being produced. Customer requirements may also cause modifications to internal policies and procedures.

Planning varies at each level of the organization. At the "individual" level planning is required so that cognitive simulation can be established before taking irrevocable actions. At the "working group" or "functional" level, planning must include:

- Agreement on purpose
- Assignment and acceptance of individual responsibilities

---

[1] Edwin Flippo and Gary Munsinger, *Management,* 3rd edition. Boston: Allyn and Bacon, 1975, p. 83.

- Coordination of work activities
- Increased commitment to group goals
- Lateral communications.

At the "organizational" or "project" level, planning must include:

- Recognition and resolution of group conflict of goals
- Assignment and acceptance of group responsibilities
- Increased motivation and commitment to organizational goals
- Vertical and lateral communications
- Coordination of activities between groups.

The important point is that each level can have its own goals and objectives. It is vitally important during proposal activities that all organizational levels align themselves to the goals and objectives of the proposal.

As part of proposal planning, the proposal manager must supply answers to several planning questions in order for alternatives and constraints to be fully understood. A partial list of these questions would include:

- Analyzing the Environment
  - Where do we stand within the environment?
  - How did we get here?
- Setting Objectives
  - Are proposal objectives compatible with company objectives?
  - Is this where we want to be?
  - Where would we like to be in one year? In five years?
- Listing Alternative Strategies
  - Will this proposal help us to continue as before?
  - Is this where we want to go?
  - If not, how can we get there, and what major changes are necessary?
- Listing Threats and Opportunities
  - What might prevent us from getting there?
  - What might help us get there?
- Preparing Forecasts
  - What are we capable of doing?
  - What do we need to take us where we want to go?
- Selecting Strategy Portfolio
  - What is the best course for us to take?
  - What are the potential benefits?
  - What are the risks?
- Preparing Action Programs
  - What do we need to do?

- When do we need to do it?
- Who will do it?
- Monitoring and Controlling
  - Are we on course? If not, why?
  - What do we need to do to be on course?
  - Can we do it?

One of the most difficult activities in the proposal environment is to keep the planning on course. Below are typical procedures that can assist managers during planning activities:

- Let functional managers do their own planning. Too often operators are operators, planners are planners, and never the twain shall meet.
- Establish customer and contractor goals before you plan. Otherwise, short-term thinking takes over, resulting in suboptimization.
- Set these goals for the planners. This guards against the nonessentials and places your effort where there is a pay-off.
- Stay flexible. Use person-to-person contact and stress fast response.
- Keep a balanced outlook. Don't overreact and position yourself for an upturn.
- Welcome top management participation. Top management has the capability to make or break a plan, and may just well be the single most important variable.
- Beware future spending plans. These may eliminate the tendency of underestimating.
- Test the assumptions behind the forecasts. This is necessary because professionals are generally too optimistic. Do not depend solely upon one set of data.
- Don't focus on today's problems. Try to get away from crisis management and "fire fighting."
- Reward those who dispell illusions. Avoid the Persian messenger syndrome i.e., behead the bearer of bad tidings. Reward the first person to come forth with bad news.

3.2 IDENTIFYING STRATEGIC PROJECT VARIABLES

For long-range or strategic projects, the project manager must continuously monitor the external environment in order to develop a well-structured program that can stand up under pressure. These environmental factors play an integral part in planning. The proposal manager must be able to identify and evaluate these strategic variables in terms of the future posture of the organization with regard to constraints on existing resources.

In the project environment, strategic project planning is performed at the horizontal project proposal hierarchy level, with final approval by upper-level management. There are three basic guidelines for strategic project planning:

- Strategic project planning is a job that should be performed by project managers, not for them.
- It is extremely important that upper-level management maintains a close involvement with project teams, especially during the planning phase of the proposal.
- Successful strategic proposal planning must define the authority, responsibility, and roles of the strategic planning personnel.

For the proposal to be successful, all members of the horizontal team must be aware of those strategic variables that can influence the success or failure of the project plan. The analysis begins with the environment, subdivided as internal, external, and competitive, as shown below:

- Internal Environment
  - Management skills
  - Resources
  - Wage and salary levels
  - Government freeze on jobs
  - Minority groups
  - Lay-offs
  - Sales forecasts

- External Environment
  - Legal
  - Political
  - Social
  - Economical
  - Technological

- Competitive Environment
  - Industry characteristics
  - Company requirements and goals
  - Competitive history
  - Present competitive activity

- Competitive Planning
  - Return on investment
  - Market share
  - Size and variety of product lines
  - Competitive resources

Once the environmental variables are defined, the planning process continues with the following:

- Identification of company strengths and weaknesses
- Understanding personal values of top management
- Identification of opportunities
- Definition of product market
- Identification of competitive edge
- Establishment of goals, objectives, and standards
- Identification of resource deployment.

Complete identification of all strategic variables is not easily obtainable during proposal preparation. Internal or operating variables are readily available to proposal personnel by virtue of the structure of the organization. Normally, the external variables are tracked under the perceptive eyes of top management. This presents a challenge for the organization of a system. In most cases, personnel in the horizontal hierarchy of the proposal are more interested in the current operational plan and tend to become isolated from the environment, losing insight into the factors influencing the rapidly changing external variables in the process. Proper identification of these strategic variables requires that communication channels be established between top management and the proposal manager.

Top management support must be available for strategic variable identification so that effective decision making can occur at the proposal level. The participation of top management in this regard has not been easy to implement. Many top-level officers consider this process a relinquishment of some of their powers and choose to retain strategic variable identification for top-level management.

The systems approach to management does not attempt to decrease top management's role in strategic decision making. The maturity, intellect, and wisdom of top management cannot be replaced. Ultimately, decision making rests with upper-level management, regardless of the organizational structure.

The identification and classification of the strategic variables are necessary to establish relative emphasis, priorities, and selectivity among the alternatives, to anticipate the unexpected, and to determine the restraints and limitations of the proposal. Universal classification systems are nonexistent because of the varied nature of organizations and projects. However, variables can be categorized roughly as internal and external, as shown in Table 3–1.

A survey of 50 companies was conducted by the authors to determine if

Table 3-1. Strategic Planning Variables in the Tire Industry

INTERNAL	EXTERNAL

• Operating
  • Product changes
  • Volume (economies of scale)
  • Wages vs. automation
  • R&D
	• Operating
	  • Customer Requirements
	  • Capacity of plants
	  • Borrowing expenses
	  • Technological advances

• Legal
  • Product quality
  • Union and safety considerations
	• Legal
	  • OSHA noise levels
	  • Product liabilities
	  • DOT requirements

• Economic
  • Market indicators
  • Division of market
  • Production runs (timing)
  • Pricing/promotion policy
	• Economic
	  • Forecast of industry
	  • Inventory (on hand/dealers)
	  • Steel and chemical output
	  • Competition

• Sociopolitical
  • Allocation of resources
  • Raw material price/availability
  • Feasibility of exporting
  • Productivity levels
	• Sociopolitical
	  • Produce what is profitable
	  • Primarily third world
	  • Threat of imports
	  • Stability of free market

lower-level and middle management, as well as project managers, knew what variables in their own industry were considered by top management as important planning variables. The following results were obtained:

- Top management considered fewer variables as being strategic than did middle managers.
- Middle management and top management in systems-oriented companies had better agreement on strategic variable identification than did managers in non-systems-oriented companies.
- Top executives within the same industry differed as to the identification of strategic variables, even within companies having almost identical business bases.
- Very little attempt was made by top management to quantify the risks involved with each strategic variable.

As an example of the differences between the project manager and upper-level management, consider the six strategic variables that are characteristic of the machine tool industry:

- Business markets and business cycles
- Product characteristics
- Pricing and promotion policies
- Technology changes
- Labor force and available skills
- Customer organization restructuring.

Both project managers and upper-level management agreed on the first four variables. The last two were identified by upper-level management. Because many products are now made from material other than steel, the question arises as to the availability of qualified workers. This poses a problem in that many customers perform a *make-or-buy analysis* before contracting with machine tool companies. The machine tool companies surveyed felt that it was the responsibility of upper-level management to communicate continuously with all customers to ascertain if they are contemplating developing or enlarging their machine tool capabilities. Obviously, the decision of a prime customer to develop its own machine shop capabilities could have a severe impact on the contractor's growth potential, business base, and strategic planning philosophy.

3.3 PROJECT AND PROPOSAL PLANNING

Successful proposals, whether they are in response to an in-house project or a customer request, must utilize effective planning techniques. From a systems point of view, management must make effective utilization of resources. This effective utilization over several different types of projects requires a systematic plan in which the entire company is treated as one large network subdivided into smaller ones.

The first step in total program scheduling is understanding the project objectives. These goals may be to develop expertise in a given area, become competitive, modify an existing facility for later use, or simply to keep key personnel employed.

The objectives are generally not independent; they are all interrelated, both implicitly and explicitly. Many times it is not possible to satisfy all objectives. At this point, management must prioritize the objectives as to which are strategic and which are not.

Once the objectives are clearly defined, four questions must be considered:

- What are the major elements of the work required to satisfy the objectives and how are those elements interrelated?

- Which functional divisions will assume responsibility for accomplishment of these objectives and the major element work requirements?
- Are the required corporate and organizational resources available?
- What are the information flow requirements for the project?

At what point does upper-level management become involved? If the project is large and complex, then careful planning and analysis must be accomplished by both the direct and indirect labor-changing organizational units. The project organizational structure must be designed to fit the project; work plans and schedules must be established such that maximum allocation of resources can be made; resource costing and accounting systems must be developed; and a management information and reporting system must be established.

Effective total program planning cannot be accomplished unless all of the necessary information becomes available at project initiation. These information requirements are:[2]

- Statement of Work (SOW)
- Project Specifications
- Milestone Schedule
- Work Breakdown Structure (WBS).

The *statement of work* (SOW) is a narrative description of the work to be accomplished. It includes the objectives of the project, a brief description of the work, the funding constraint if one exists, and the specifications and schedule. The schedule is a "gross" schedule and includes such items as the

- Start date
- End date
- Major milestones
- Written reports (data items)

Written reports should always be identified so that if functional input is required, the functional manager will know to assign an individual who has writing skills. After all, it is no secret who would write the report if the line people do not.

The last major item is the *work breakdown structure*. The WBS is the breaking down of the statement of work into smaller elements so that better visibility and control can be obtained.

---

[2] A more detailed analysis is given in Chapter 6.

3.4 ROLE OF THE EXECUTIVE IN PLANNING

Many proposal managers view the first critical step in planning as obtaining the support of top management, because once it becomes obvious to the functional managers that top management expresses an interest in the project, they (the functional managers) are more likely to respond favorably to the project team's request for support, partly as a self-protection measure.

Executives are also responsible for selecting the project and proposal managers. The people chosen should have adequate planning expertise. Not all technical specialists are good planners. As Rogers points out:[3]

> The technical planners, whether they are engineers or systems analysts must be experts at designing the system, but seldom do they recognize the need to "put on another hat" when system design specifications are completed and design the project control or implementation plan. If this is not done, setting a project completion target date of a set of management checkpoint milestones is done by guesswork at best. Management will set the checkpoint milestones, and the technical planners will hope they can meet the schedule.

Executives must not arbitrarily set unrealistic milestones and then force line managers to fulfill them. Both proposal and line managers should try to adhere to unrealistic milestones, but if a line manager says it cannot be done, executives should comply with this judgment. The line manager is supposedly the expert at this level. Sometimes executives can lose sight of the long-range objectives. As an example, a bank executive took the six-month completion date milestone and made it three months. The project and line managers rescheduled all of the other projects to reach this milestone. The executive then did the same thing on three other projects and again the project and line managers came to the rescue. The executive began to believe that the line people did not know how to estimate and that they probably loaded up every schedule with "fat." So the executive, acting on a "gut feeling," changed the milestones on *all* of the other projects to make them more "realistic." You can imagine the chaos that followed.

Executives should interface with project, proposal, and line personnel during the planning stage in order to define the requirements and establish reasonable deadlines. Executives must realize that creating an unreasonable deadline may require the reestablishment of priorities and, of course, changing priorities can push milestones forward.

---

[3] Lloyd A. Rogers, "Guidelines for Project Management Teams," *Industrial Engineering,* December 1974, p. 12. Published and copyright 1974 by the American Institute of Industrial Engineers, Inc., Norcross, Ga. 30092.

3.5 WHY DO PLANS FAIL?

No matter how hard we try, planning is not perfect and sometimes plans fail. Typical reasons why plans fail include:

- Corporate goals not understood at the lower organizational levels
- Plans encompass too much in too little time
- Poor financial estimates
- Plans based upon insufficient data
- No attempt to systematize the planning process
- Planning performed by a planning group
- No one knows the ultimate objective
- No one knows the staffing requirements
- No one knows the major milestone dates, including written reports
- Project estimating by best guesses, not based upon standards or history
- Not enough time given for proper estimating
- No one bothered to see if there would be personnel available with the necessary skills
- People not working toward the same specifications
- People consistently shuffled in and out of the project with little regard for schedule.

Why do these situations occur, and who should be blamed? If corporate goals are not understood at the lower planning levels, it is because corporate executives were negligent in providing the necessary strategic information and feedback. If a plan fails because of severe optimism, then the responsibility lies with both the project and line managers for not assessing risk accurately. Project and proposal managers should ask the line managers if the estimates are optimistic or pessimistic, and expect an honest answer. Erroneous financial estimates are the responsibility of the line manager. If the project fails because of a poor definition of the requirements, then the proposal manager is totally at fault.

Project and proposal managers must be willing to accept failure. Sometimes, a situation leads to failure, and the problem rests with either upper-level management or some other group. As an example, consider the major utility company with a planning group that budgets (with help of functional groups) and selects those projects to be completed within a given time period. A project manager discovered that one of the projects should have started a month earlier in order to meet the completion date. It is in cases like this that project managers will not become dedicated to projects unless they are active during the planning and know what assumptions and constraints were considered in development of the plan.

Sometimes, when the project manager is part of the planning group, and part of a feasibility study is asked to prepare, with the assistance of functional managers, a schedule and cost summary for a project that will occur three years downstream (if the project is approved at all). Suppose that three years downstream, the project is approved. How does the project manager get functional managers to accept the schedule and cost summary that they themselves prepared three years before? It cannot be done because technology may have changed, people may be working at a higher or lower level on the learning curve, and salary and raw material escalation factors are inaccurate.

Sometimes project plans fail because simple details are forgotten or overlooked. Examples of this might be:

- Neglecting to tell a line manager early enough that the prototype is not ready and that rescheduling is necessary
- Neglecting to see if the line manager can provide additional employees for the next two weeks because it was possible six months ago.

Sometimes plans fail because the project manager and his team "bite off more than they can chew," and then something happens. Even if the project manager were effective at doing a lot of work, overburdening is unnecessary. Many projects have failed because the project manager was the only one who knew what was going on and then got sick, leaving the project at a standstill.

3.6 STOPPING PROJECTS

There are always situations in which projects have to be stopped after the proposal has been accepted and the project is underway. Below are several reasons:

- Final achievements of the objectives
- Poor initial planning and market prognosis
- Better alternative has been found
- Change in company interest and strategy
- Allocated time has been exceeded
- Budgeted costs have been exceeded
- Key people have left the organization
- Personal whims of management
- Problem too complex for the resources available.

Once the reasons for cancellation are defined, the next problem is how to go about stopping the projects.

- Orderly planned termination
- The "hatchet" (withdrawal of funds and removal of personnel)
- Reassignment of people to higher priority
- Redirection of efforts toward different objectives
- Burying it or letting it "die on the vine," i.e., not taking any official action.

There are three major problem areas to be considered in stopping projects:

- Worker morale
- Reassignment of personnel
- Adequate documentation and wrap-up.

Sometimes, executives do not realize the relationship between projects, and what happens if one is cancelled prematurely. As an example, the following remarks were made by an executive concerning data processing operations:

When 75–80% of the resource commitment is obtained, there is the point of no return and the benefits to be obtained from the project are anticipated. However, project costs, once forecast, are seldom adjusted during the project life cycle. Adjustments, when made, are normally to increase costs prior to or during conversion. Increases in cost are always in small increments and usually occur when the corporation is "committed," i.e., 75–80% of the actual costs are expended, however, total actual costs are not known until the project is over.

Projects can and sometimes should be cancelled at any point in the project life cycle. Projects are seldom cancelled because costs exceed forecasts. More often, resources are drained from successful projects. The result of the action is the corporation as a whole becomes marginally successful in bringing all identified projects on line. One might assume individual projects can be analyzed to determine which projects are successful and which are unsuccessful. However, the corporate movement of resources makes the determination difficult without elaborate computer systems. For example, as Project A appears to be successful, resources are diverted to less successful Project B. The costs associated with Project A increase dramatically as all remaining activities become critical to Project A completion. Increasing costs for Project A are associated with overtime, traveling, etc. Costs for Project B are increasing at a straight time rate and more activities are being accomplished because more manpower can be expended. Often resources, particularly manpower working on Project B, are charged to Project A because the money is in the budget for Project A. The net result is Project A and B overrun authorized budgets by about the same percentage. In the eyes of top corporate management, neither project team has done well nor have the teams performed poorly. This mediocrity in performance is often the goal of corporate project management techniques.

These statements have severe implications for proposal managers. As part of proposal manpower planning, the proposal managers should work closely with functional managers to ascertain whether or not functional resources will be drained if this new proposal is accepted. If sufficient time is not available to train new employees, then the company may wish to choose a no-bid strategy rather than run the risk of having to cancel ongoing successful projects.

3.7 CONTROLLING

Controlling is a three-step process of measuring progress toward an objective, evaluating what remains to be done, and taking the necessary corrective action to achieve or exceed the objectives. These three steps are defined below:

- *Measuring:* determining through formal and informal reports the degree to which progress toward objectives is being made
- *Evaluating:* determining cause of and possible ways to act on significant deviations from planned performace
- *Correcting:* taking control action to correct an unfavorable trend or to take advantage of an unusually favorable trend.

After proposal acceptance and contract signing, the project manager is responsible for insuring the accomplishment of group and organizational goals and objectives in accordance with the program plan. This requires a thorough knowledge of standards, cost control policies, and procedures enabling a comparison between operating results and pre-established standards. This may or may not be included as part of the proposal or program plan. The project manager must then take the necessary corrective actions. Both proposal and project managers must understand organizational behavior in order to be effective, and must have strong interpersonal skills. This is especially important during the controlling function. As stated by Doering:[4]

---

[4] Robert D. Doering, "An Approach Toward Improving the Creative Output of Scientific Task Teams," *IEEE Transactions on Engineering Management,* February, 1973, pp. 29–31.

The team leader's role is crucial. He is directly involved and must know the individual team member well, not only in terms of their technical capabilities but also in terms of how they function when addressing a problem as part of a group. The technical competence of a potential team member can usually be determined from information about previous assignments, but it is not so easy to predict and control the individual's interaction within and with a new group, since it is related to the psychological and social behavior of each of the other members of the group as a whole. What the leader needs is a tool to measure and characterize the individual members so that he can predict their interactions and structure his task team accordingly.

The proposal manager must exercise the same type of control during proposal preparation as would the project manager during project execution. Furthermore, the proposal manager must make sure that the management and possibly the cost volumes of the proposal delineate clearly the methods and mechanisms of control that will be utilized during the execution of the project.

3.8 DIRECTING

Directing is the implementing and carrying out (through others) of those approved plans that are necessary to achieve or exceed objectives. Directing involves the following steps:

- *Staffing:* seeing that a qualified person is selected for each position
- *Training:* teaching individuals and groups how to fulfill their duties and responsibilities
- *Supervising:* giving others day-to-day instruction, guidance, and discipline as required so that they can fulfill their duties and responsibilities
- *Delegating:* assigning work, responsibility, and authority so others can make maximum utilization of their abilities
- *Motivating:* encouraging others to perform by fulfilling or appealing to their needs
- *Counseling:* holding private discussions with others about how he might do better work, solve a personal problem, or realize ambitions
- *Coordinating:* seeing that activities are carried out in relation to their importance and with a minimum of conflict.

Directing subordinates is not an easy task because of both the short duration of the proposal and the fact that the employees might still be assigned to a functional manager while temporarily assigned to your effort. The luxury of getting to "know" one's subordinates may not be possible in a proposal environment.

Proposal managers must be decisive and move forward rapidly whenever directives are necessary. It is better to decide an issue and be 10 percent wrong than it is to wait for the last 10 percent of a problem's input and cause a schedule delay and improper use of resources. Directives are most effective when the KISS (keep it simple, stupid) rule is applied. Directives should be written with one simple and clear objective so that subordinates can work more effectively and do things right the first time. Orders must be issued in a manner that demands immediate compliance. The major reason people do or do not obey an order depends on the amount of respect that they have for you. Therefore, never issue an order that you cannot enforce. Oral orders and directives should be disguised as suggestions or requests. The requestor should ask the receiver to repeat the oral orders so that there is no misunderstanding.

Proposal managers must understand human behavior, perhaps more than functional managers. The reason for this is that proposal managers must motivate people continually toward successful accomplishment of project objectives. Motivation cannot be accomplished without at least a fundamental knowledge of human behavior.

Douglas McGregor advocated that most workers can be categorized into one of two groups. The first group, often referred to as Theory X, assumes that the average worker is inherently lazy and requires supervision. Theory X further assumes that:[5]

- The average worker dislikes work and avoids work whenever possible.
- To induce adequate effort, the supervisor must threaten punishment and exercise careful supervision.
- The average worker avoids increased responsibility and seeks to be directed.

The manager who accepts Theory X normally exercises authoritarian control over workers and allows little participation during decision making. Theory X employees generally favor lack of responsibility, especially in decision making.

Theory Y employees advocate a willingness to get the job done without constant supervision. Theory Y further assumes that:

---

[5] Douglas McGregor, *The Human Side of Enterprise,* New York: McGraw-Hill, 1960, pp. 33–34.

- The average worker wants to be active and finds the physical and mental effort on the job satisfying.
- Greatest results come from willing participation that tends to produce self-direction toward goals without coercion and control.
- The average worker seeks opportunity for personal improvement and self-respect.

The manager who accepts Theory Y normally advocates participation and a management-employee relationship. However, when working with professionals, especially engineers, special care must be exercised because these individuals often pride themselves on their ability to find a better way to achieve the end result, regardless of the cost. The risk of this happening increases with the number of professional degrees that one possesses. This poses a problem in that it is the responsibility of the functional manager to determine *how* the job will be done once the proposal manager states *what* must be done. Project and proposal management must take a vested interest in the individual who, given free rein to accomplish an objective, must understand the necessity of time, cost, and performance constraints fully. This situation holds true for several engineering disciplines where engineers consistently strive to exhibit their individuality by seeking new and revolutionary solutions to problems for which well-established solutions already exist. Under these conditions, project managers must become authoritarian leaders and change from Theory Y to Theory X. Employees must be shown how to report to two bosses at the same time. The problem occurs when the employee's line manager uses Theory Y but the project manager uses Theory X. Employees must realize that this situation can occur.

Another situation in which this problem occurs is shown in Figure 3-2. The proposal has a 12-week response period. If the response period were reduced to eight weeks, then the only place where time could be reduced would be in the time allocated to the functional managers for estimating the work. If functional managers begin complaining about not having sufficient time to estimate their efforts, then the proposal manager may have to resort to treating his people as though they were Theory X instead of Theory Y.

Many psychologists have established the existence of a prioritized hierarchy of needs that motivate individuals toward satisfactory performance. Maslow was the first to identify these needs.[6] The first level is that of the basic physiological needs: food, water, clothing, shelter, sleep, and sexual satisfaction. Put simply, one's primal desire to satisfy these basic needs motivates one

---

[6] Abraham Maslow, *Motivation and Personality,* Harper and Brothers, 1954.

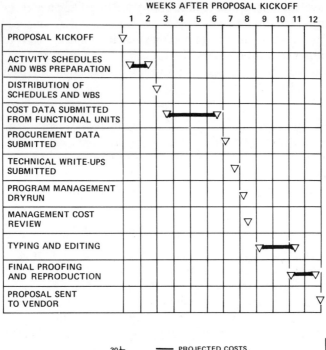

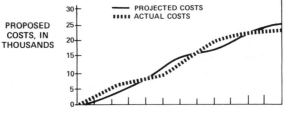

Figure 3-2. Proposal activity schedule.

to do a good job. However, once a need becomes satisfied, the motivation ceases unless there is a lower level need. Fulfilled needs are not motivators.

Once employees fulfill physiological needs, they turn to the next lower need of safety. Safety needs include economic security and protection from harm, disease, and violence. These needs must be considered on projects involving the handling of dangerous materials or anything that could cause bodily harm. Safety can also include security. It is important that project managers realize this because as a project nears termination, functional employees are more interested in finding a new role for themselves rather than giving their best to the current situation. The next level contains the social needs. This includes love, belonging, togetherness, approval, and group membership. It is at this level where the informal organization plays a dominant role. Many people refuse promotions to project management (as project managers, project office personnel, or functional representatives) because they fear that they will lose their "membership" in the informal organization. This problem can occur even on short-term projects and proposals. In a proposal environment, proposal managers generally do not belong to any informal organization and therefore tend to be viewed as external to the organization. Proposal managers consider authority and funding to be very important in gaining proposal support. Functional personnel, however, prefer friendship and work assignments. In other words, the proposal manager can use the proposal itself as a means of helping fulfill the third level for the line employees, i.e., the team spirit.

The two highest needs are esteem and self-actualization. The esteem need includes self-respect, reputation, the opinion of others, recognition, and self-confidence. Highly technical professionals are often not happy unless esteem needs are fulfilled. For example, many engineers strive to publish and invent as a means of satisfying these needs. The highest need is self-actualization and includes doing what one can do best, desiring to utilize and realize one's fullest potential, maintaining constant self-development, and striving to be truly creative. Many good proposal managers find this level as the most important and consider each new proposal as a challenge by which they can achieve this self-actualization. In addition, proposal managers can bring out the best in some of their highly technical personnel by giving them the opportunity to input some of their expertise as part of the proposal effort.

Proposal managers must motivate these temporarily assigned individuals by appealing to their desires to fulfill the highest two levels. Of course, the motivation process should not be developed by making promises that the proposal manager knows cannot be met. Proposal (and project) managers must motivate by providing:

- A feeling of pride or satisfaction for one's ego
- Security of opportunity
- Security of approval
- Security of advancement (if possible)
- Security of promotion (if possible)
- Security of recognition
- A means for doing a better job, instead of just keeping a job.

Motivating employees so that they have feeling of security on the job is not easy, especially because the project as well as the proposal has a finite lifetime. Specific methods for producing security in a project environment include:

- Informing employees why they are where they are
- Encouraging a sense of belonging
- Placing individuals in positions for which they are trained properly
- Explaining to employees how their efforts fit into the big picture.

Because proposal managers cannot motivate by promising material gains, they must appeal to each person's pride. To encourage proper motivation:

- Adopt a positive attitude
- Do not criticize management
- Do not make promises that cannot be kept
- Circulate customer reports
- Give each person the attention they require.

There are several ways of motivating project personnel. Some effective ways include:

- Providing assignments that provide challenges
- Defining performance expectations clearly
- Giving honest appraisals
- Providing a good working atmosphere
- Developing a team attitude
- Providing a proper direction (i.e., see Theory Y).

3.9 PROJECT AUTHORITY

Both project management and proposal management structures create a web of relationships that can cause chaos in the delegation of authority and the internal authority structure. Four questions must be considered in describing authority:

- What is project authority?
- What is power and how is it achieved?
- How much project authority should be granted to the project manager and proposal manager?
- Who settles project authority interface problems?

Authority is usually defined as the legal or rightful power to command, act, or direct the activities of others. Authority can be delegated from one's superiors. *Power,* on the other hand, is granted to an individual by subordinates and is a measure of their respect. A manager's authority is a combination of power and influence that subordinates, peers, and associates accept willingly.

Authority is the key to the project management process. The project manager must manage across functional and organizational lines by bringing together activities required to accomplish the objectives of a specific project. Project authority provides the required way of thinking to unify all organizational activities toward accomplishment of the project regardless of location.

The manager who fails to build and maintain alliances soon finds opposition or indifference to project requirements.

The amount of authority granted to the project manager varies according to project size, management philosophy, and management interpretation of potential conflicts with functional managers. There does exist, however, certain fundamental elements over which the project manager must have authority in order to maintain effective control. According to Steiner and Ryan,[7]

> The project manager should have broad authority over all elements of the project. His authority should be sufficient to permit him to engage all necessary managerial and technical actions required to complete the project successfully. He should have appropriate authority in design and in making technical decisions in development. He should be able to control funds, schedule and quality of product. If subconstractors are used, he should have maximum authority in their selection.

> Generally speaking, project managers should have more authority than their responsibilities call for, the exact amount usually being dependent upon the amount of risk involved. The greater the risk, the greater the amount of authority. Good project managers know where their authority ends and do not hold employees responsible for duties not under their (the project managers') jurisdiction. Some projects are directed by project managers who have only monitoring authority. These project managers are referred to as *influence project managers*.

Because time is of the essence during proposal preparation, the proposal manager must define his own authority and that of his team clearly during proposal efforts. Likewise, the proposal should delineate clearly the authority of the project manager and his team with regard to resource control, decision making, and interfacing with the customer.

---

[7] Steiner and Ryan, *Industrial Project Management,* Macmillan. Copyright © 1968 by the Trustees of Columbia University in the City of New York, 1968, p. 24.

Failure to establish authority relationships can result in

- Poor communication channels, often containing misleading information
- Antagonism, especially from the informal organization
- Poor working relationships with superiors, subordinates, peers, and associates
- Surprises for the customer

Both the project management and proposal management organizational structures are arenas of continuous conflicts and negotiations. Although there are many clearly defined authority boundaries between functional and project management responsibilities, the fact that each project can be inherently different almost always creates new areas where authority negotiations are necessary. The proposal manager does not have unilateral authority in the proposal effort. There is frequent negotiation with the functional manager. The project and proposal managers have the authority to determine the "when" and "what" of the project activities, whereas the functional manager has the authority to determine "how the support will be given." The project manager accomplishes objectives by working with personnel who are largely professional. For professional personnel, project leadership must include explaining the rationale of the effort as well as the more obvious functions of planning, organizing, directing, and controlling.

Certain ground rules exist for authority control through negotiations:

- Negotiations should take place at the lowest level of interaction.
- Definition of the problem in four basic terms must be the first priority.
  - The issue
  - The impact
  - The alternatives
  - The recommendations
- Higher level authority should be used if and only if agreement cannot be reached.

The critical stage of any project is planning, thus justifying the need for the proposal manager to have excellent communicative skills. This includes more than just planning out the activities to be accomplished, but also the anticipation and establishment of the authority relationships that must exist for the duration of the project. Because the project management environment is changing constantly, each project (and therefore each proposal) establishes its own policies and procedures, a situation that can result ultimately in a variety of authority relationships. It is therefore possible for functional personnel to have different responsibilities on different projects, even if the tasks are the same.

During the planning phase the project team develops a responsibility matrix that contains such elements as:

- General management responsibility
- Operations management responsibility
- Specialized responsibility
- Must be consulted
- May be consulted
- Must be notified
- Must approve.

The responsibility matrix is often referred to as a *linear responsibility chart* (LRC) and can be used for proposal preparation as well as project execution. Linear responsibility charts identify the participants and to what degree an activity will be performed or a decision will be made. The LRC attempts to clarify the authority relationships that can exist when functional units share common work. As described by Cleland and King:[8]

The need for a device to clarify the authority relationships is evident from the relative unity of the traditional pyramidal chart, which (1) is merely a simple portrayal of the overall functional and authority models and (2) must be combined with detailed position descriptions and organizational manuals to delineate authority relationships and work performance duties.

Figure 3–3 shows a typical linear responsibility chart. The rows indicate the activities, responsibilities, or functions required. The rows can be all of the tasks in the work breakdown structure. The columns identify either the positions, titles, or the people themselves. If the chart is given to an outside customer, only the titles should appear. Otherwise, the customer will call the employees directly without going through the project manager. It is not uncommon for both the proposal and project manager to prepare two sets of linear responsibility charts, one for the customer and one for internal control. The chart for internal control contains the names of the employees rather than their titles, and can undergo several revisions as names change and people are reassigned. The symbols indicate the degrees of authority or responsibility that exists between the rows and columns.

---

[8] From *Systems Analysis and Project Management* by David Cleland and William Richard King. Copyright © 1968, 1975 McGraw-Hill Inc. Used with permission of McGraw-Hill Book Company, p. 271.

Figure 3–3. Linear responsibility chart.

Another example of an LRC is shown in Figure 3–4. In this case, the LRC is used to describe how internal and external communications should take place. This type of chart can be used to eliminate communications conflicts. Consider a customer who is unhappy about having all of his information being filtered through the project manager, and requests that his line people be permitted to talk to your line people on a one-on-one basis. You may have no choice, but you should make sure the customer understands that:

- Functional employees cannot make commitments for additional work or resources[9]

---

[9] Further comments on this subject appear in Section 3.15.

| | REPORTED TO | | | | | | | | | | | | | |
| --- | INTERNAL | | | | | | | EXTERNAL (CUSTOMER)** | | | | | | |
INITIATED FROM	PROJECT MANAGER	PROJECT OFFICE	TEAM MEMBER	DEPARTMENT MANAGERS	FUNCTIONAL EMPLOYEES	DIVISION MANAGER	EXECUTIVE MANAGEMENT	PROJECT MANAGER	PROJECT OFFICE	TEAM MEMBER	DEPARTMENT MANAGER	FUNCTIONAL EMPLOYEES	DIVISION MANAGER	EXECUTIVE MANAGER
PROJECT MANAGER	▨	O	◆	△	▲	▲	◆	O	O	■	■	■	■	△
PROJECT OFFICE	O	▨	O	O	▲	▲	▲	O	O	△	△	■	■	△
TEAM MEMBER	◆	O	▨	◆	⬡	■	■	■	■	▲	▲	▲	■	■
DEPARTMENT MANAGER	▲	△	O	▨	O	◆	■	△	△	△	△	△	■	■
FUNCTIONAL EMPLOYEES	▲	▲	O	O	▨	■	■	▲	▲	▲	▲	▲	■	■
DIVISION MANAGERS	△	▲	▲	▲	▲	▨	△	■	■	■	■	■	△	△
EXECUTIVE MANAGEMENT	△	▲	▲	▲	▲	▲	▨	△	△	▲	▲	■	△	△

*CAN VARY FROM TASK TO TASK AND CAN BE WRITTEN OR ORAL
**DOES NOT INCLUDE REGULARLY SCHEDULED INTERCHANGE MEETINGS

LEGEND

O	DAILY
◆	WEEKLY
O	MONTHLY
▲	AS NEEDED
△	INFORMAL
■	NEVER

Figure 3-4. Communications responsibility matrix.*

- Functional employees give their own opinion and not that of the company. Company policy comes through the project office. Linear responsibility charts can be used to alleviate some of these problems.

The responsibility matrix attempts to answer such questions as: Who has signature authority? Who must be notified? Who can make the decision? These questions can only be answered by clear definitions of authority, responsibility, and accountability:

- *Authority* is the right of an individual to make the necessary decisions required to achieve objectives or responsibilities.
- *Responsibility* is the assignment of a specific event or activity until completion.
- *Accountability* is the acceptance of success or failure.

The linear responsibility charts, although a valuable tool for management, do not describe fully how people interact within the program. The LRC must be combined with the organization to understand how interactions between individuals and organizations take place. As described by Karger and Murdick, the LRCs have merit:[10]

Obviously the chart has weaknesses, of which one of the larger ones is that it is a mechanical aid. Just because it says that something is a fact does not make it true. It is very difficult to discover, except generally, exactly what occurs in a company and with whom. The chart tries to express in specific terms relationships that cannot always be delineated so clearly; moreover, the degree to which it can be done depends on the specific situation. This is the difference between the formal and informal organizations mentioned. Despite this, the Linear Responsibility Charts is one of the best devices for organization analysis known to the authors.

Linear responsibility charts can result from customer-imposed requirements above and beyond normal operations. For example, the customer may require that, as part of quality control requirements, a specific engineer supervise and approve all testing of a certain item or that another individual approve all data released to customer over and above program office approval. Customer requirements similar to these require LRCs and can cause disruptions and conflicts within an organization.

There are several key factors that affect the delegation of authority and responsibility both from upper-level management to project management, and from project management to functional management. These key factors include:

- The maturity of the project management function
- The size, nature, and business base of the company
- The size and nature of the project
- The life cycle of the project
- The capabilities of management at all levels.

Once agreement has been reached on the project manager's authority and responsibility, the results must be documented to delineate clearly that role regarding:

- Focal position
- Conflict between the project manager and functional managers

---

[10] Karger, D. W., and Murdick, R. G., *Managing Engineering and Research,* Industrial Press, New York, 1963, p. 89.

- Influence to cut across functional and organizational lines
- Participation in major management and technical decisions
- Collaboration in staffing the project
- Control over allocation and expenditure of funds
- Selection of subcontractors
- Rights in resolving conflicts
- Input in maintaining integrity of project team
- Establishment of project plans
- Provisions for leadership in preparing operational requirements
- Provisions for a cost-effective information system for control
- Maintenance of prime customer liaison and contact
- Promotion of technological and managerial improvements
- Establishment of project organization for the duration
- Elimination of red tape.

Documenting the project manager's authority as part of the proposal effort is necessary because:

- All interfacing must be kept as simple as possible.
- The project manager must have the authority to "force" functional managers to depart from existing standards and incur possible risk.
- Gaining authority over the elements of a program that are not under the project manager's control is essential. This is normally achieved by earning the respect of the individuals concerned.
- The project manager should not attempt to describe fully the exact authority and responsibilities of the project office personnel or team members. Problem solving rather than role definition should be encouraged.

There exists a variety of relationships (although not always clearly definable) between power and authority. This relationship is usually measured by "relative" decision power as a function of the authority structure, and is strongly dependent upon the project organizational form.

3.10 INTERPERSONAL INFLUENCES

Consider the following two expressions made by a project manager:

- *"I've had good working relations with Department A. They like me and I like them. I can usually push through anything ahead of schedule."*
- A research scientist was temporarily promoted to project management for an advanced state-of-the-art effort. He was overheard making the following remark to a team member: *"I know it's contrary to depart-*

ment policy, but the test must be conducted according to these criteria or else the results will be meaningless."

These two statements reflect the way that some project and proposal managers get the job done.

Project managers are generally known for having a lot of delegated authority but very little formal power. Project managers must therefore get the job done through the use of interpersonal influences. There are five such interpersonal influences:

- *Formal authority.* The ability to gain support because project personnel perceive the project manager as being officially empowered to issue orders.
- *Reward power.* The ability to gain support because project personnel perceive the project manager as capable of directly or indirectly dispensing valued organizational rewards (i.e., salary, promotion, bonus, future work assignments).
- *Penalty power.* The ability to gain support because the project personnel perceive the project manager as capable of directly or indirectly dispensing penalties that they wish to avoid. Penalty power usually derives from the same source as reward power, with one being a necessary condition for the other.
- *Expert power.* The ability to gain support because personnel perceive the project manager as possessing special knowledge or expertise that functional personnel consider as important.
- *Referent power.* The ability to gain support because project personnel feel personally attracted to a particular project.

The following six situations are examples of referent power (the first two are also reward power):

- The employee might be able to get personal favors from the project manager.
- The employee feels that the project manager is a winner and that the rewards will be passed down to the employee.
- The employee and the project manager have strong ties, such as the same foursome for golf.
- The employee likes the project manager's manner of treating people.
- The employee wants identification with a specific product or product line.
- The employee has personal problems and believes that the project manager can give empathy or understanding.

Figure 3-5 shows how project managers perceive their influence style.[11] Figure 3-5 represents the results of a survey taken in the early 1970s. A 1980 survey conducted by the authors showed that the first three responses were the same, except that work challenge was first and expertise was lowered to third.

As was the case with relative power, these interpersonal influences can also be identified with various project organizational forms as to their relative value. This is shown in Figure 3-6.

For any temporary management structure to be effective, there must be a rational balance of power between functional and project management or else the best proposals may fail during execution. Unfortunately, such a balance of equal power is often impossible to obtain because each project is inherently different and each project manager possesses a different leadership ability. Organizations, nevertheless, must attempt to obtain this balance so that trade-offs can be accomplished effectively according to the individual merit and not as a result of some established power structure.

Achieving this balance is a never-ending challenge facing management. If time and cost constraints on a project cannot be met, the project influence in decision making is increased, as can be seen in Figure 3-6. If the technology or performance constraints need reappraisal, then the functional influence in decision making will dominate. First, proposal managers must work closely with executives and functional managers to select the organizational structure for the customer's proposal.

Regardless of how much authority and power a project manager develops over the course of the project, the ultimate factor in one's ability to get the job done is usually leadership style. Project managers, because of the inherent authority gaps that develop at the project functional interface, must rely heavily upon supplementary techniques for getting the job done. These supplementary techniques include facets that affect the leadership style directly, and include such items as developing bonds of trust, friendship, and respect with the functional workers. Of course, the relative importance to these techniques can vary, depending upon the size and scope of the project.

3.11 TOTAL PROJECT PLANNING

The difference between the good proposal manager and poor proposal manager is often described in one word: planning. Unfortunately, people have a poor definition of what project planning actually involves. Project planning involves planning for

- Schedule development
- Budget development

---

[11] *Seminar in Project Management Workbook* Copyright © 1979 by Hans J. Thamhain. Reproduced by permission.

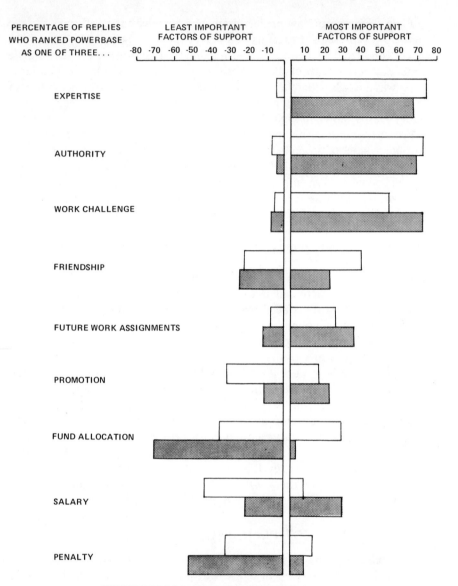

SIGNIFICANCE OF FACTORS IN SUPPORT TO PROJECT MANAGEMENT
FIGURE 3-5

☐ SUPPORT FROM ASSIGNED PROJECT PERSONNEL
▓ SUPPORT FROM SUBORDINATES

Figure 3–5. Significance of factors in support to project management.

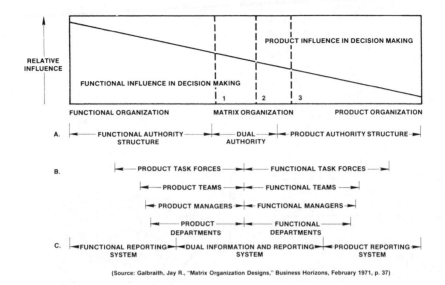

(Source: Galbraith, Jay R., "Matrix Organization Designs," Business Horizons, February 1971, p. 37)

Figure 3-6. The range of alternatives.

- Project administration
- Leadership styles (interpersonal influences)
- Conflict management.

The first two items involve the quantitative aspects of planning. Planning for project administration includes the development of the linear responsibility chart. Leadership styles refer to the interpersonal influence modes that a project and proposal managers can use. Project managers may have to use several different leadership styles depending upon the make-up of the project personnel. Conflict management is important because, if the project manager can predict what conflicts will occur and when they are most likely to occur, then the project manager may be able to plan for the resolution of the conflict through project administration and the linear responsibility charts.

Figure 3-7 shows the complete project planning phase for the quantitative portions[12] The object, of course, is to develop a project plan which shows complete distribution of resources and the corresponding costs. The figure represents an iterative process. The project manager begins with a coarse (ar-

---

[12] Figure 3-7 is described in more depth in Chapter 6. The intent here is to provide a rough framework to show how complex good planning actually is.

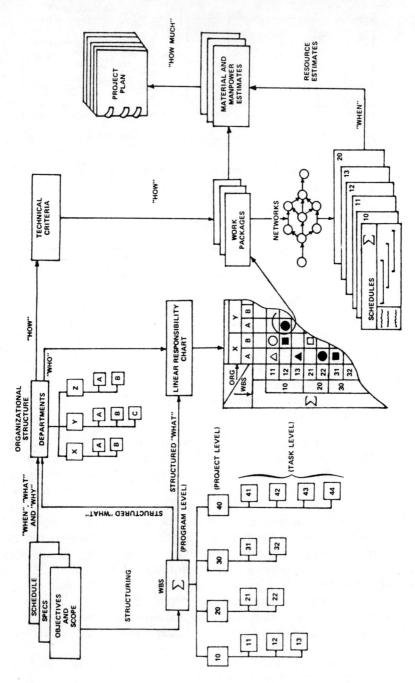

Figure 3–7. Complete project planning.

row diagram) network and then decides upon the work breakdown structure. The WBS is essential to the arrow diagram and should be constructed such that reporting elements and levels are easily identifiable. Eventually, there will be an arrow diagram and detailed chart for each element in the WBS. If there is too much detail, the project manager can refine the diagram by combining all logic into one plan and then deciding upon the work assignments. There is a risk here that, by condensing the diagrams as much as possible, there may be a loss of clarity. Finally, as shown in Figure 3-7, all the charts and schedules can be integrated into one summary level figure. This can be accomplished at each WBS level until the desired plan is achieved.

Finally, proposal, project, line, and executive management must analyze other internal and external variables before finalizing these schedules. A partial list of these variables would include:

- Introduction or acceptance of the product in the marketplace
- Present or planned manpower availability
- Economic constraints of the project
- Degree of technical difficulty
- Manpower availability
- Availability of personnel training
- Priority of the project.

3.12 MANAGEMENT PITFALLS

The project and proposal environments offer numerous opportunities for project managers and team members to get into trouble. Activities that create problems readily are referred to as *management pitfalls*. The lack of planning, for example, can be considered as a management pitfall. Other common management pitfalls are:

- Lack of self-control ("knowing oneself")
- Activity traps
- Managing versus doing
- People versus task skills
- Ineffective communications
- Time management
- Management bottlenecks.

Knowing oneself, especially one's capabilities, strengths, and weaknesses, is the first step toward successful project management. Too often, managers assume that they are "jack-of-all-trades" and indispensible to the organization. The ultimate result is that such managers tend to "bite off more than they can chew," and then find that insufficient time exists for training additional personnel. This, of course, assumes that the project budget provided sufficient funding for additional positions that were never utilized.

Activity traps result when the means becomes the end, rather than the means to achieve the end. The most common activity traps are team meetings and customer technical interchange meetings. Another common activity trap is the development of special schedules and charts that cannot be used for customer reporting, but are used to inform upper-level management of project status. Managers must always evaluate whether or not the time spent to develop these charts is worth the effort. Sign-off documents, such as manufacturing plans, provide yet another activity trap by requiring that the project manager and/or several key project team members sign off all documentation. Proper project planning and the delegation of authority and responsibility can reduce this activity trap.

Previously, we defined one of the characteristics of poor leadership as the inability to obtain a balance between the management functions and the technical functions. This can easily develop into an activity trap where the individual becomes a doer rather than a manager. Unfortunately, there often exists a very fine line between managing and doing. As an example, consider a project manager who was asked by one of his technical people to make a telephone call to assist in solving a problem. Simply making the phone call is doing work that should be done by the project team members or even the functional manager. However, if the person being called requires that someone in absolute authority be included in the conversation, then the project manager is managing instead of doing.

There are several other cases where one must become a doer in order to be an effective manager and command the loyalty and respect of subordinates. Assume a special situation where you must schedule subordinates to work overtime, say on special holidays or even weekends. By showing up at the plant during these times, just to make a brief appearance before the people in question, you can create a better working atmosphere and understanding with the subordinates.

Another major pitfall is the decision to utilize either people skills or task skills. Is it better to utilize subordinates with whom you can obtain a good working relationship, or to employ highly skilled people simply to get the job done? Obviously, the project manager would like nothing better than to have the best of both worlds. Unfortunately, this is not always possible. Consider the following situations:

- There exists a task that takes three weeks to complete. John has worked for you before, but not on such a task as this. John, however, understands how to work with you. Paul is very competent but likes to work alone. Paul can get the job done within constraints. Should you employ people or task skills? (Would your answer change if the task were three months instead of three weeks?)

- There exist three tasks, each requiring two months of work. Richard has the necessary people skills to handle all three tasks, but will not be able to perform as efficiently as a technical specialist. The alternate choice is to utilize three technical specialists.

In both situations, there should be more information made available to assist in the final decision. However, based upon the amount of information given, the authors prefer task skills so as not to hinder the time or performance constraints on the project. Generally speaking, for long-term projects that require constant communications with the customer, it might be better to have employees assigned permanently to perform a variety of tasks. Customers dislike a steady stream of new faces.

Highly technical industries are modifying the marketing function because of this distinction between people and task skills. In the past, people skills were considered extremely important in marketing technology. Today, the trend is toward giving more importance to the task skill. The result has been that the project manager and project engineer must undertake marketing efforts in addition to their everyday duties. The marketing function has therefore moved down to middle management.

It is often said that a good project manager must be willing to work 60 to 80 hours a week to get the job done. This might be true if fire fighting continually or budgeting constraints prevent employing additional staff. The major reason, however, is the result of ineffective time management. Prime examples might include a continuous flow of paperwork, unnecessary meetings, unnecessary phone calls, and acting as a tour guide for visitors. Improper time management becomes an activity trap where the project manager becomes controlled *by* the job rather than controlling the job. The final result is that the project manager must work long, arduous hours in order to find time for creative thinking.

To be effective, the project manager must establish time management rules and then ask himself four questions:

- Rules for Time Management
  - Conduct a time analysis (time log)
  - Plan solid blocks for important things
  - Classify your activities
  - Establish priorities
  - Establish opportunity cost on activities
  - Train your system (boss, subordinate, peers)

- Practice delegation
- Practice calculated neglect
- Practice management by exception
- Focus on opportunities, not on problems
- Questions
  - What am I doing that I don't have to be doing at all?
  - What am I doing that can be done better by someone else?
  - What am I doing that could be done sufficiently well by someone else?
  - Am I establishing the right priorities for my activities?

This type of time management analysis can reduce greatly the proverbial "time robbers," such as:

- Incomplete work
- A poor job that must be done over
- Delayed decisions
- Poor communications channels
- Uncontrolled telephone calls
- Casual visitors
- Waiting for people
- Failure to delegate
- Poor retrieval system.

3.13 COMMUNICATIONS: GENERAL

Proper communications is vital to the success of the project. *Communications* is the process by which information is exchanged. Communications can be

- Written formal
- Written informal
- Oral formal
- Oral informal.

Noise tends to distort or destroy the information within the message. Noise results from *personality screens* that dictate the way we present the message, and *perception screens* that may cause us to "perceive" what we thought was said. Noise can therefore cause ambiguity.

- Ambiguity causes us to hear what we want to hear.
- Ambiguity causes us to hear what the group wants.

- Ambiguity causes us to relate to past experiences without being discriminatory.

Communications is more than simply conveying a message; it is also a source for control. Proper communications inform employees because employees need to know and understand. Communication must convey both information and motivation. The problem, therefore, is how to communicate. Below are six simple steps:

- Think through what you wish to accomplish.
- Determine the way you communicate.
- Appeal to the interest of those affected.
- Give playback on ways others can communicate to you.
- Get playback on what you communicate.
- Test effectiveness through reliance on others to carry out your instructions.

Knowing how to communicate does not guarantee that a clear message is generated. Techniques that can be used to improve communications include:

- Obtaining feedback, possibly in more than one form
- Establishing multiple communications channels
- Using face-to-face communications, if possible
- Determining how sensitive the receiver is to your communications
- Being aware of symbolic meanings as expressions on people's faces
- Communicating at the proper time
- Reinforcing words with actions
- Using a simple language
- Using redundancy (i.e., saying it two different ways) whenever possible.

With every effort to communicate, there are barriers. These barriers include:

- Hearing what they want to hear. This results from people doing the same job so long that they no longer listen.
- Sender and receiver having different perceptions. This is vitally important in interpreting contractual requirements, statements of work, and proposal information requests.
- Receiver evaluating the source before accepting the communications.
- Receiver ignoring conflicting information and doing as he pleases.
- Jargon meaning different things to different people.
- Ignoring nonverbal cues.
- Receiver being upset emotionally.

The scalar chain of command can also become a barrier with regard to in-house communications. The project manager must have the authority to go to the general manager or counterpart to communicate effectively. Without direct upward communication, it is possible that filters can develop so that the final message gets distorted.

Three important conclusions can be drawn from communications techniques and barriers:

- Don't assume that the message you sent will be received in the form you sent it.
- The swiftest and most effective communications take place among people with common points of view. The manager who fosters a good relationship with associates has less difficulty in communicating with them.
- Communications must be established early in the project.

Communications is also listening. Good project managers must be willing to listen to their employees, both professionally and personally. The advantages of listening properly are that:

- Subordinates know you are sincerely interested.
- You obtain feedback.
- Employee acceptance is fostered.

The successful manager must be willing to listen to a man's story from beginning to end, without interruptions. The manager must be willing to see the problem through the eyes of the subordinate. Finally, before making a decision, the manager should ask the subordinate for his solutions to the problem.

Project managers should ask themselves four questions:

- Do I make it easy for employees to talk to me?
- Am I sympathetic to their problems?
- Do I attempt to improve human relations?
- Do I make an extra effort to remember names and faces?

3.14 CONDUCTING EFFECTIVE TEAM MEETINGS

Team meetings are supposedly meetings of the minds where information giving, receiving, and listening take place. Team meetings must be effective or else they become time management pitfalls. It is the responsibility of the project manager to insure that meetings are valuable and necessary for the exchange of information. The following are general guides for conducting a more effective meeting:

- Start on time. If you wait for people, you reward tardy behavior.
- Develop agenda "objectives." Generate a list and proceed. Avoid getting hung up on the order of topics.
- Conduct one piece of business at a time.
- Allow each member to contribute. Support, challenge, and counter. View differences as helpful. Dig for reasons or views.
- Silence does not always mean agreement. Seek opinions: "What's your opinion on this, Peggy?"
- Be ready to confront the verbal member: "Okay, we've heard from Mike on this matter, now how about some other views?"
- Test for readiness to make a decision.
- Make the decision.
- Test for commitment to the decision.
- Assign roles and responsibilities (only after decision making).
- Agree on follow-up or accountability dates.
- Indicate the next step for this group.
- Set the time and place for the next meeting.
- End on time.
- Was the meeting necessary?

Team meetings quite often provide individuals with means of exhibiting suppressed ideas. The following three humorous quotations identify these:

- *"In any given meeting, when all is said and done, 90 percent will be said—10 percent will be done."*——Orben's *Current Comedy*
- *"A committee meeting provides a great chance for some people who like to hear their own voices talk and talk, while others draw crocodiles or lady's legs. It also prevents the men who can think and make quick decisions from doing so."*——Lin Yutang, *The Pleasures of a Nonconformist (World)*
- *"Having served on various committees, I have drawn up a list of rules: Never arrive on time or you will be stamped a beginner. Don't say anything until the meeting is half over; this stamps you as being wise. Be as vague as possible; this prevents irritating the others. When in doubt, suggest that a subcommittee be appointed. Be the first to move for adjournment; this will make you popular—it's what everyone is waiting for."*——Harry Chapman, quoted in *Think*.

Many proposal managers do not understand when and how to use team meetings effectively. Team meetings are used to:

- Communicate project/proposal status to all employees in a reasonable manner
- Provide a common basis for decision making.

Team meeting communications is a two-way street. The proposal manager provides proposal status information to the team members and seeks out necessary functional information. As an example, team meetings are a fast, effective means of updating and revising schedules and providing the information to all other employees on an equal basis.

Decision making poses a problem for the proposal manager because not all project team members have the authority to make decisions. Team meetings cannot be effective for decision making unless the team members have the delegated authority to commit functional resources and make decisions. In this case, the proposal manager should send team meeting agenda items to the functional managers, together with a list of potential problems and decisions. This should indicate to the functional managers that someone with authority to commit resources is required to attend the team meeting. It is always a good policy to send out meeting agendas and an approximate time that each item will be discussed. This usually works well because line managers do not have the time to sit through a two-hour team meeting simply to discuss a 15-minute agenda item. If employees do not have the right to make decisions, then the proposal manager may find that his team will flood the agenda with irrelevant items simply to avoid decision making. Finally, proposal managers, as well as project managers, must be aware that it is possible to conduct too few team meetings as well as too many team meetings. The proposal manager may also find the following problems:

- People tend to resist the exploration of new ideas.
- People tend to protect themselves.
- People tend to look at day-to-day activities rather than long-term efforts.
- People tend to create win or lose positions.
- People look for individual rather than group recognition.
- Because of superior, subordinate relationships (i.e., pecking orders), creativity is inhibited.
- Criticism and ridicule have a tendency to inhibit spontaneity.
- Pecking orders, unless adequately controlled, can inhibit team work and problem solving.
- All seemingly crazy or unconventional ideas are ridiculed and eventually descarded. Contributors do not wish to contribute anything further.
- Many lower-level people, who could have good ideas to contribute, felt inferior and therefore refused to contribute.
- Meetings were dominated by upper-level management personnel.

- The meetings were held at an inappropriate place and time.
- Many people were not given adequate notification of the meeting time and subject matter.

3.15 PROJECT MANAGEMENT BOTTLENECKS

Poor communications can produce communication bottlenecks. These bottlenecks occur in both the parent and customer organizations. The most common bottleneck occurs when all communications between the customer and the parent organization must flow through the project office. There are two major disadvantages to this type of arrangement. First, this requirement may be a necessity but develops slow reaction times. Second, regardless of the qualifications of the project office members, the customer always fears that information received this way is "filtered" prior to disclosure.

Techniques can vary from project to project. For example, on one project, the customer may require that all test data be made available, in writing, as soon as testing occurs and possibly before your own people have had a chance to examine the results. This type of clear and open communication cannot exist indefinitely because the customer might form his own opinion of the data before hearing the project office position. Similarly, project managers should not expect functional managers to provide them with immediate raw test data until functional analysis is conducted.

Customers not only like first-hand information, but also prefer that their technical specialists be able to communicate directly with the parent's technical specialists. Many project managers dislike this arrangement, for they fear that the technical specialists may say or do something contrary to project strategy or thinking. These fears can be allayed by telling the customer that this situation will be permitted if and only if the customer realizes that the remarks made by the technical specialists do not in any way, shape, or form reflect the position of the project office or company. Furthermore, only the project office can authorize resource commitment or the release of information for a customer request. This alleviates the necessity of having a project representative present during all discussions, but requires that records be provided to the project office of all communications with the customer.

For long-term projects, the customer may require that the contractor have an established customer representative office in the contractor's facilities. This idea is sound in that all information to the customer must flow through the customer's project office at the contractor's facility. This creates a problem in that it attempts to sever direct communications channels between the customer and contractor project managers. The result is that in many situations, the establishment of a local project office is merely an "eyewash" situation to satisfy contractual requirements, whereas actual communications go from customer to contractor as though the local project office did not exist. This creates an antagonistic local customer project office.

The last bottleneck to be discussed occurs when the customer's project manager assumes a higher position than the contractor's project manager and therefore seeks some higher authority to which to communicate. As an example, the customer has a $130 million program and subcontracts $5 million out to you. Even though you are the project manager and report to either the vice president and general manager or the director of program management, the customer's project manager may wish to communicate directly with the vice president or one of the directors. Project managers who seek status can often jeopardize the success of the project by creating rigid communications channels.

Figure 3–8 identifies why communications bottlenecks such as these occur. There almost always exist a minimum of two paths for communications flow to and from the customer. Many times, strategic project planning is accomplished between the customer and contractor at a level above the respective project managers. This type of situation can have a strongly demoralizing effect. Proposals should identify all paths for communications between the customer and contractor. This includes communications at the project sponsor level.

There is a hidden bottleneck in proposals which could have severe implications downstream. If a situation of mistrust develops between the customer and contractor, then the following sequence of events can take place:

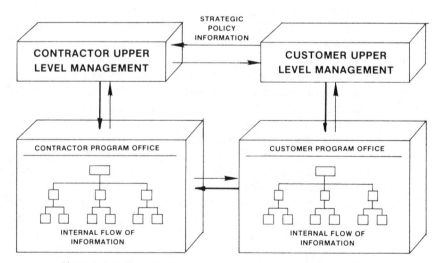

Figure 3–8. Information flow pattern from contractor program office.

- Increased documentation
- More technical interchange meetings
- Customer representation at your site.

Mistrust can cause each of these three events to take place in the order given and, in each case, can cause a tremendous amount of grief, aggravation, and additional work (especially paperwork) for the project manager. Mistrust can result from a poorly prepared proposal and then, downstream, the project manager finds himself severely handcuffed.

3.16 EFFECTIVE MANAGEMENT PROVERBS

The following list of proverbs apply to both proposal managers as well as project managers:[13]

1. You cannot produce a baby in one month by impregnating nine women.
2. The same work under the same conditions will be estimated differently by ten different estimators or by one estimator at ten different times.
3. The most valuable and least used word in a project manager's vocabulary is "no."
4. You can con a sucker into committing an unreasonable deadline, but you can't bully him into meeting it.
5. The more ridiculous the deadline, the more it costs to try to meet it.
6. The more desperate the situation, the more optimistic the person providing the estimate.
7. Too few people on a project can't solve the problems. Too many create more problems than they solve.
8. You can freeze the user's specs but he won't stop expecting.
9. Frozen specs and the abominable snowman are alike: they are both myths and they both melt when sufficient heat is applied.
10. The conditions attached to a promise are forgotten and the promise is remembered.
11. What you don't know hurts you.
12. A user will tell you anything you ask about—nothing more.
13. Of several possible interpretations of a communication, the least convenient one is the only correct one.
14. What is not on paper has not been said.
15. No major project is ever installed on time, within budget, with the same staff that started it.

---

[13] Source unknown.

16. Projects progress quickly until they become 90% complete; then remain at 90% complete forever.
17. If project content is allowed to change freely, the rate of change will exceed the rate of progress.
18. No system is ever completely debugged; attempts to debug a system inevitably introduce new bugs that are even harder to find.
19. Project teams detest progress reporting because it vividly demonstrates their lack of progress.
20. Parkinson and Murphy are alive and well—in your project.

Chapter 4

Planning and Organizing the Proposal

4.0 INTRODUCTION

Proposal inquiries usually begin with either a request brought in by a sales representative or through the formal soliciting of bids by the owner. The first step taken for any proposal request is to get authorization to go ahead. The procedure for obtaining authorization can be formal or informal, and in most cases it is done through a committee made up of upper management. An authorization form is prepared; it contains the type of information shown in Figure 4-1, including the man-hours and cost required to prepare the proposal.

Through normal, continued communication channels with sales, the proposal manager or manager of proposals is often aware of a forthcoming proposal before authorization is given to proceed with the actual work.

Work within the proposal department starts when authorized by the manager of proposals. This follows receipt of the proposal notice, or notification from sales administration that a proposal number has been issued. The proposal number is logged in the department's proposal listing book and a file is created in the department's proposal files by the secretary to the manager of proposals.

A proposal manager is selected and assigned the responsibility of carrying the proposal effort to completion by establishing a working proposal file. When the effort is complete, the working file is transferred to the permanent proposal files.

Generally, planning and organizing the proposal consists of:

DATE: _____

NO.: _____

1. CLIENT   —

2. PROJECT   —

3. UNITS & CAPACITIES   —

4. LOCATION   —

5. SCOPE OF WORK   —

6. VALUE OF PROJECT   —

7. TYPE OF CONTRACT   —

8. TYPE OF PROPOSAL   —

9. PROPOSAL COST   —

10. DUE DATE OF PROPOSAL   —

11. % PROB. TO GO AHEAD   —
     % PROB. FOR AWARD TO COMPANY   —

12. OTHER FACTORS   —

    a. TIMING OF AWARD   —
       (if long range)

    b. FINANCING   —
       (if Financing involved)

    c. SOURCE OF KNOW—HOW   —
       (if other than Company)

    d. SPECIAL CONTRACT CONDITIONS   —
       (if not Company Standard)

    e. MANPOWER AVAILABILITY   —
       (if not readily available)

    f. SECRECY CONDITIONS   —
       (if any)

    g. COMPETITION   —
       (if known)

    h. UNUSUAL FACTORS   —
       (if any)

Management Review Committee

Approved By: _____   Date: _____

2

Figure 4-1. Request for approval of bid preparation.

- Setting up the proposal preparation mechanism
- Planning the proposal effort
- Coordinating the team effort
- Insuring a good finished product
- Conducting an internal evaluation.

To insure that the proposal contains the required information in the proper format, once the decision to bid has been made, the proposal manager must take these steps:

1. Thoroughly acquaint himself with the owner's bid specification
2. Distribute all pertinent client documents to the proper persons
3. Organize a planning meeting to determine the basis of proposal
4. Detail all responsibilities and assignments, and state overall schedule dates
5. Prepare and distribute a detailed proposal schedule
6. Prepare a proposal man-hour budget with the participating departments
7. Coordinate engineering, estimating, purchasing, and sales in selecting vendors for major items
8. Set up controls and checklists for the proposal work
9. Obtain reviews, comments, and approvals
10. Exercises control over the total proposal effort
11. Distribute preliminary proposal to member of top management and key people for review
12. Distribute draft sales letter, guarantees, and contract terms for review
13. Conduct final review meeting before submission to client
14. Transmit all proposal documents to client in quantity specified.

This chapter covers the major items enumerated above.

4.1 IMPLEMENTING THE SYSTEM

Upon obtaining the approved authorization form, the proposal manager starts to get the preparation machinery moving.

The first phase begins with a preliminary review of the owner's bid specification to determine what the owner is looking for, what type of information must be provided, and in how much detail. The proposal manager must determine the size and scope of effort required for the proposal. While reviewing the owner's documents, the proposal manager must consider the company's intermediate and long-range objectives, as well as the prime concerns of the moment.

If the company is anxious to move into a new area or to gain a larger share of an existing area, then a reduction in profit may be necessary in order to get the job. Another reason for reducing profit might involve a "showpiece" plant, such as a government-agency facility that will be visited by many foreign business persons. If the profit picture is already tight, then possibly an all-out effort to do a superior job may be the answer.

The opposite side of the coin would be where management, for economic reasons, has decided to reduce the overhead costs of the proposal, thereby imposing only a minimum manpower effort, and using off-the-shelf designs as much as possible. Also to be considered are possible political implications, such as U.S. requirements when dealing with Communist-bloc countries, countries that have unstable governments, and even state restrictions that give a rival company from that area a competitive edge.

More usually, the prime considerations are in the areas of personnel scheduling and the competitive situation. If a contractor is exceptionally busy, with many projects being done simultaneously, there may not be enough personnel available to complete the proposal-development work in time to meet the bid submission date. Only a foolish contractor tries to bid on every job. Not finishing in time to submit a bid, or submitting a hastily written incomplete proposal, may preclude the contractor from future bid lists.

Therefore, an analysis is made of every incoming bid request to determine the likelihood of getting the job as compared to other contractors who are bidding. If a choice must be made between two projects to bid on, the contractor is less likely to choose a project in which some other contractor is the owner's favorite.

If the objectives are not defined sufficiently by client correspondence or the inquiry document, the manager of proposals sets up an informational meeting with the sales representative and proposal manager to define the purpose and intent of the proposal. The client's requirements and behind-the-scenes activities are discussed to determine what approach would be most successful. Agreement is reached on the type of proposal and its format and contents, if these requirements are not already obvious from the nature of the inquiry.

The manager of proposals and Proposal Manager review the inquiry documents to determine which departments are to participate in the effort. As soon as possible, the work is completely defined and work assignments are made. A schedule is prepared, indicating when important portions of the work must be done. A man-hour budget for the proposal work is developed, reviewed, and finalized. The proposal manager determines the number of people required for the proposal staff in accordance with the defined scope of work, the schedule, and the man-hour budget. Pertinent documents are distributed to everyone working on the project. A kick-off notice is written by the proposal manager. This notice summarizes the purpose of the proposal, the plan of approach, the specific duties of individuals, the proposal schedule, and additional details. For a major proposal, a kick-off meeting is held.

After the initial conceptualization of the proposal's scope and the types of personnel needed to implement it, the proposal manager distributes copies of the client's inquiry documents to the supervisors who are to be involved with the proposal, and who make the actual personnel assignment.

After allowing a few days for review, the proposal manager schedules a meeting that includes the managers of project engineering, estimating, and sales, as well as any specialists required to cover unusual requirements the owner may have included in his bid request. At this in-depth proposal-review meeting, the proposal manager provides background information, defines the scope and requirements, indicates any special considerations, and recommends the approach to be taken in preparing the proposal. The proposal manager leads the participants in covering such areas as:

- Amount of bidding time allowed
- Process schemes and number of options
- Amount of detailed engineering information required for the proposal specifications and for the estimate
- Amount of time required to prepare the engineering information
- Special requirements of the client, e.g., standard specifications, required vendors
- Major equipment to be sent out for quotation
- Schedule of work
- Special legal, guarantee, royalty, etc., problems to be investigated
- Additional information required from client
- Necessity of a site or installation survey.

The proposal manager must provide enough definition at this proposal review meeting to enable the managers of the participating departments to assign staff members as quickly as possible to avoid delays in performing the proposal work.

At the conclusion of this meeting, the proposal manager prepares a scope memorandum recording the results of the meeting, establishing the scope of work, and containing the proposal work-schedule on a group-by-group basis, as agreed to by the participants.

4.2 THE KICK-OFF MEMO/MEETING

Soon after the decision to bid has been made, a preliminary *proposal kick-off meeting* or *proposal strategy planning meeting* should be held. This meeting, chaired by the proposal manager, consists of the heads of the various contributing departments, the sales representative, and possibly senior management. Because there is a limited amount of time available for preparation of a proposal, it is mandatory that the proposal effort be planned in all aspects to make the most use of that time. A plan produces the best effort and response to a client's request that the time period allows. To be time-effective, no work should commence without first having a proposal strategy planning meeting.

After the strategy planning meeting and development of a preliminary proposal plan, the proposal manager calls a kick-off meeting. This meeting is attended by all participants working on the proposal or their representatives. The proposal manager writes a kick-off memo or notice to inform the participating departments what is required to be discussed at the meeting regarding the proposal effort. The kick-off memo and meeting are also referred to as the proposal coordination memo and meeting. The purpose of the kick-off meeting is to inform all participants of the proposal plan and objectives. The kick-off meeting gives you an excellent opportunity to brief and obtain feedback from a large number of contributing people at one session. It is crucial to success that all personnel contributing to the proposal understand the overall objectives and requirements of the proposal so that it meets the client's project needs. It is always helpful to look at the proposal response and organization from the client's point of view.

Kick-off memos are satisfactory for most proposals, and are preferred over kick-off meetings. Meetings are time-consuming, and are normally held for the more complex efforts with relatively long schedules. A kick-off memo from the proposal manager to the managers of the participating departments or the proposal staff members, if assigned at this point, is adequate for starting the work in most cases. The memo informs the participants to begin work and transmits to them the information they need. The memo is sent shortly after work authorization has been received and commercial objectives have been established.

Topics that should be covered in every kick-off meeting or memo to insure a good start on the work are illustrated in the following outline:

• *Project Scope.* The type of plant or unit, the client, the project location, the order of magnitude total installed cost (if known), the job or proposal number, and any other general identification plus designation of proposal manager and other key personnel.

• *Commercial Objectives.* The type of proposal required is discussed as well as the management philosophy to be incorporated into the proposal. The sales representative provides background on the client's requirements, exceptions to be taken, and the client's budget, if known.

• *Proposal staffing.* Three factors—the proposal schedule, man-hour budget, and the type of proposal desired—determine which departments will participate and also set the proposal staffing requirements. Staffing should be settled soon after the kick-off meeting or issuance of the kick-off memo.

• *Assignments of participants.* Work assignments with clear areas of responsibility shall be made. Relationships between participating departments should be spelled out. Because the proposal manager may be on loan from another department, the role of coordinator of the work shall be defined clearly.

• *Proposal dates, schedule, and budget.* The key dates for issuance of proposal documents and completion of important portions of the work should be discussed and the participants advised of the available man-hour budget. Cautionary measures should be taken to be sure that the schedule is realistic. If not, the sales representative has to notify the client and seek an extension of the due date.

• *Qualifications.* On occasion, the proposal may have to be tailored to sell the client on your qualifications and capabilities in some area covered by the proposed project. The desired slant to accomplish this should be considered and made known to all involved.

• *Type of estimate.* The type of estimate to be submitted with the proposal may already have been decided on the basis of the client's requirements. If not, the proposal manager defines clearly the requirements. The type of estimate determines the quality and quantity of estimating information that must be generated by the participants in the proposal effort. The proposal manager specifies what is required for proper support of the estimate.

• *Final proposal contents.* The type of proposal determines to some extent what must be included in the final documents sent to the client. Specific requirements for the contents should be brought to everyone's attention. The proposal manager develops and includes a tentative table of contents for the proposal documents under discussion. Definite assignments for preparation of the draft write-ups for each section of the proposal are also made.

• *Working information.* Copies or a summary of the inquiry documents are distributed before or with the kick-off memo. Any other information from the client that is to be used in preparing the proposal is also distributed and discussed. If the information is inadequate, the proposal manager arranges to obtain additional information from the client. Preferably, the technical basis for design should be summarized in a standard project design questionnaire. Useful information from other proposals or projects should be called to everyone's attention. Its validity for use in the proposal work should also be settled.

The contents of the memo are divided into five main sections, as are the minutes of kick-off meetings.

• *Purpose.* Type of proposal and estimate to be prepared
• *Plan of approach.* Explains methods to be used
• *Action.* Specific duties of individuals and groups

- *Proposal schedule.* Indicating key dates for internal submission of parts of the work
- *Details.* Any information in addition to that outlined above.

Kick-off memos are distributed in accordance with a standard distribution schedule as described in Section 4.11.

The kick-off meeting is the preferred device for starting the proposal work only for complex efforts. It is held shortly after work authorization has been received and sales objectives have been established. Production work on the proposal begins after the kick-off meeting.

The proposal manager sets the meeting time and place. Attendance is limited to those who actually contribute to the definition and initiation of the proposal effort, such as the following persons:

- Sales representatives responsible for the inquiry
- Heads of departments and groups responsible for any of the proposal work
- Key personnel from departments and groups responsible for any of the proposal work, if they have been selected
- The general manager of operations and a member of the legal department responsible for proposal review are notified of the meeting so they may attend if they wish.

There are no strict rules for the agenda of a kick-off meeting because of the wide variations in the nature of the inquiries received and the proposals developed in reply to them. Topics that should be covered in every meeting to insure a good start on the work are the same as those described for the kick-off memo.

In addition to covering the elements of the client's request and the proposal response to them, the kick-off meeting also provides to:

- Outline the marketing strategy behind the proposal
- Establish management's interest in the project
- Introduce team members to each other
- Create interchange of ideas and suggestions early
- Obtain overall agreement of work assignments and timing
- Develop a winning attitude in the proposal effort.

For lump sum bids, it is especially important that a kick-off meeting be held as soon as possible following receipt of inquiry, allowing sufficient time for personnel who are involved in the bid to familiarize themselves with the bidding specifications. The objectives of this meeting should be to:

- Allow time for a pricing strategy to be developed and approved
- Establish a schedule of latest dates whereby engineering issues bills of materials and specifications to purchasing, purchasing goes out for inquiries, inquiries must be received back, bid tabs completed and recommended suppliers furnished to estimating
- Discuss any special problems concerning the project or preparation of the proposal
- Complete any engineering or design that may be required in order to go out for competitive bids or for preparation of the estimate.

The proposal manager is responsible for preparing the minutes of the kick-off meeting, which are issued no later than the second working day after the meeting. The contents are divided into five main sections in the same fashion as the kick-off memo.

4.3 THE PROPOSAL OUTLINE

The final outcome of the kick-off meeting is the development of the *proposal outline*. It is the guiding document for preparation of the proposal. The outline is an organized list of subject items that are to be included in the proposal, and it divides them into their logical components. The outline is necessary in order that the participants have a clear definition and direction to the generation and collection of data. It guides the entire preparation of the proposal and becomes the basic control tool or checklist against which progress of the proposal is measured. The importance of the proposal outline in preparing a proposal cannot be overemphasized.

It is the purpose of this document to list and outline all required activities and functions to be performed from the start date until the final delivery and submitting of the proposal. Each of the functions is itemized together with the description, due date, and name of the individuals of assigned responsibility.

Basically, the proposal outline provides the following information:

- Organizes your response in a sequential and logical manner
- Specifies information to be generated by different groups
- Identifies subjects to be required for the proposal
- Creates a subject checklist or control sheet against which progress is measured
- Lists suggestions to aid the proposal effort
- Establishes priority requirements.

A proposal outline should be prepared and distributed prior to the start of any proposal effort. It is the basis upon which the various assignments for the preparation of the proposal are made. It allows the proposal manager to coordinate control, integrate the various inputs, and assure that all essential elements of the proposal are prepared. For a small proposal, a proposal outline can be helpful. For a large proposal, the outline is mandatory to success. Although time and cost are always the ultimate consideration in the final proposal, the outline can make the difference. Except where time and conditions do not permit or do not warrant, a proposal coordination memo should always be prepared and issued to all affected parties.

The proposal outline conveys the following information to the proposal team:

- Defines and describes project and services to be furnished
- Establishes proposal responsibility and distribution
- Establishes contents and organization of the proposal in sufficient detail to define clearly what the bid should include
- Assigns responsibility for preparation of specific parts of the proposal together with the latest deadline by which these parts can be received in typed, draft form
- Identifies components that are already defined or available in other documents
- Identifies any special technology or design features that are required
- Identifies outside consultants or subcontractors to be used and their contribution.

The outline also provides publication information such as:

- Ordering of covers and tabs
- Typing and proofing of normal proposal documents
- Identifying of the proposal number, due date, page numbering system, and printing requirements.

The outline provides a list of specific tasks or data that the proposal team must develop or obtain for the proposal. Once the outline has been agreed upon and finalized, all members of the team or other contributors must be informed of the need to adhere to it strictly.

Key segments of the inquiry could also be attached to the outline for more detailed review by the proposal team. The outline references these excerpts and the reason for their inclusion.

The actual subject heading that is included in your proposal varies with the scope and content of the proposal, and with the individual requirements specified by the inquiry. Chapter 5 discusses the major subject headings that appear in most proposals.

Figure 4–2 illustrates a typical proposal outline that would be used for preparing a proposal.

The following are typical headings or subject areas you would find in a proposal.

Proposal No. . . . .   Issue No. . . . .   Date . . . .

Proposal Schedule

ITEM	START DATE	COMPLETION RESPONSIBILITY DATE

All Departments

Written questions regarding client's specifications
    and requirements

Financial and Legal

Comments on legal and financial terms

Process Engineering

Equipment list
Major equipment specifications for use in obtaining
    price quotations
All remaining equipment specifications to be
    estimated
Process flow diagrams
Motor list
Engineering flow diagrams
Assist plot plan preparation
Process description
Operating requirements (raw material and utility)
Steam-condensate power balance
Guarantees
Review proposal volume

Electrical Engineering

One-line diagram
Description of electrical system for use in proposal
Furnish other data to Estimating Department

Water Engineering

Provide technical assistance as required
Design process-waste and storm-drainage system

Figure 4–2. Schedule for typical plant proposal.

(continued)

Proposal No. . . . .   Issue No. . . . .   Date . . . .

Proposal Schedule

ITEM	START DATE	COMPLETION DATE	RESPONSIBILITY

Purchasing

Data sheets for quotes
Furnish firm price quotation on selected items of
    major equipment

Contract Administration

Review technical proposal volume
Review contract

Planning and Scheduling

Prepare project schedule including erection and
    start-up

Estimating

Equipment estimate
Piping, insulating, and painting estimate
Civil estimate
Buildings estimate
Engineering and drafting manhours
Other costs

Civil Engineering

Description of civil work
Paving and draining plan
Structural design information for use in
    estimating

Construction

Plantsite survey
Report on survey
Field-labor estimate
Material take-off completed and priced

Piping Engineering

Size lines and provide necessary valving
Furnish underground piping plan

Instrument Engineering

Instrument list
Instrument flow diagram
Description of instrumentation
Instrument cost estimate

Figure 4–2. (*Cont.*)

Technical Proposal

- Introduction
- Scope of Work
- Project Organization
- Project Execution Plan
- Project Task Breakdown
- Project Schedule
- Manpower Resources and Availability
- Resumés of Project Team
- Reporting and Control Methods

Cost Proposal

- Introduction
- Scope of Work
- Basis of Estimate (Technologies)
- Commercial Offer
  - Charges at a Mark-Up
  - Charges at Cost
  - Fees
  - Payment Terms
- Taxes, Licensing, and Royalties
- Contract Terms and Conditions
- Proprietary Ownership
- Other Requirements

Management Proposal

- Introduction
- Project Management Approach
- Company Organization and Background
- Company Administrative Information
- Philosophy and Policies
- EEO and Affirmative Action
- Accounting Methods
- Medical Benefits
- Community Relations Program
- Related Experience (past and present)
- Any Special Equipment or Facilities

The more carefully organized and complete a proposal is in response to a specific inquiry, the more chance it has winning. As is the case in most writing activities, the best way to be complete and organized is first to develop an outline.

4.4 SELECTING THE PROPOSAL TEAM

A successful proposal is usually the result of an intensive, well-coordinated team effort, with strong leadership and clearly defined duties and responsibilities. Regardless of the size of the organization, a successful proposal effort requires the cooperation of individuals from many different areas of the company, including upper management. These individuals may be a permanent group or just a temporarily assigned team. If a temporarily assigned team, the individuals involved will change from proposal to proposal. The size of the group also varies depending upon the size or complexity of the proposal effort required.

The proposal team generally consists of the proposal manager, the proposal office (whose members report directly to the proposal manager), and the functional or interface members (who must report to both horizontal and vertical levels).

The proposal office is an organization development to support the proposal manager in carrying out his duties. Proposal office personnel must have the same dedication toward the proposal as does the proposal manager, and must have good working relationships with both the proposal and functional managers. The responsibilities of the proposal office include:

- Acting as the focal point of information for both in-house and outside support
- Controlling time, cost, and performance established for proposal
- Insuring that all work required is documented and distributed to all key personnel
- Insuring that all work performance is both authorized and required.

The major responsibility of the proposal manager and the proposal team personnel is the integration of work across the functional lines of the organization. Functional units, such as engineering, cost, R&D, and manufacturing, together with extra-company subcontractors, must work toward the same specifications, designs, and even objectives. The lack of proper integration between these functional units is the most common cause of proposal failure. The team members must be dedicated to all activities required for proposal success, not necessarily their own functional responsibilities. The problems resulting from lack of integration can best be solved by full-time membership and participation of proposal office personnel. Not all team members need to be part of the proposal office. Functional representatives, performing at the interface position, also act as integrators but at a closer position to where the work is finally accomplished.

One of the biggest challenges facing proposal managers is determining the size of the proposal office. The optimal size is determined by a trade-off between the maximum number of members necessary to assure compliance with requirements, and the minimum number so that total administrative costs can be reduced. Membership is determined by factors such as proposal size, internal support requirements, type of project (i.e., R&D, qualification, production), level of technical competency required, and customer requirements. Membership size can also be susceptible to how strategic management views this proposal. There is a tendency to enlarge proposal offices if the proposal is considered strategic, and especially if follow-on work is possible.

Functional team members can be full-time or part-time for either the entire duration of the proposal or only during specific phases. Functional managers must develop a positive attitude toward project success. This is best achieved by inviting their participation in the early activities of the planning phase.

Ideally, proposal managers would like to have a permanent, full-time proposal staff. While some personnel can be assigned permanently to a proposal department, most technically trained people prefer to work in a group that is devoted to their area of specialization with a manager with the same background and expertise. All factors favor keeping the proposal team office as small as possible and dependent upon established functional departments and specialized staffs to the greatest extent posssible for performance of the various tasks necessary for proposal completion. This approach places great emphasis on the planning, scheduling, control, and administrative support procedures used on the proposal.

Under ideal conditions, each member of the proposal office should have a working knowledge in all areas, with expertise in perhaps two or three. Unfortunately, this is almost never the case, except in the responsibilities of the proposal manager and the technical proposal leader. In any event, both the proposal manager and team members must understand fully the responsibilities and functions of each other team member to such a degree that total integration can be achieved as rapidly and effectively as possible.

The selection process for both the functional team member as well as the proposal office must include evaluation of any special requirements. The most common special requirements develop from:

- Technical specifications and requirements
- Special customer requests
- Organization manpower availability.

Each of these has a direct impact on whether an individual is assigned to the proposal office or to a functional interface.

Upper-level management must have an input into the selection process for functional members just as with proposal office membership. Functional management must be represented at all staffing meetings. Functional staffing is directly dependent upon proposal (project) requirements and must include functional management because they generally have more expertise and can identify problem areas better.

For large proposals, it is desirable to have a full-time functional representative from each major division or department assigned to the proposal office. Such representation might include:

- Project engineering
- Engineering operations
- Manufacturing/production
- Procurement
- Cost estimating
- Construction
- Sales/marketing
- Publications.

Whether there is a permanently staffed proposal department, or a proposal manager working alone and drawing upon input from other departments, or an organization that falls somewhere in between, the make-up of the proposal team usually draws upon the services of the following participants.

The *proposal manager* has total authority and responsibility for carrying out the following work in preparing a proposal:

- Establishes the proposal team and the ground rules by which they operate
- Coordinates and monitors all areas of input involved
- Approves the finished written product
- Reviews, evaluates, accepts, and edits all material to be used
- Is responsible to upper management for the output of each participant
- Develops the proposal plan
- Gives direction to the team
- Makes the critical decisions
- Controls all aspects of the work.

The management of a proposal is not a simple task and requires perseverance, strength, and competence. The proposal manager must be able to work well under pressure, and must be prepared to disrupt personal obligations to work substantial overtime hours for several consecutive days, including weekends. As discussed in Section 2.2, the proposal manager must be an outstanding leader and manager. The proposal manager should know the company's organization and capabilities, should be aware of time-saving shortcuts that can be taken when necessary, and should have a good working relationship with others in the company to call upon personal favors to get things done more quickly. Most important, the proposal manager must know what it takes to have a winning proposal.

The above characteristics of a proposal manager can best be found in a project manager. In many companies, the individuals selected to be proposal managers come from the project management area.

A typical position description of a proposal manager can be found in Section 2.10.

In general, on most proposal efforts, the proposal manager does the following:

- Reviews all work performed by the proposal staff
- Insures good communications among the staff
- Coordinates the efforts of all participants
- Insures that the proposal objectives are being met in the work prepared
- Insures that the proposal schedule is maintained
- Monitors progress continually in all areas of the effort to provide detailed feedback for close control and for earliest possible indications of problems
- Anticipates delays and discuss corrective action with management
- Takes such corrective measures as are necessary to modify the plan of implementation, should this become necessary to meet schedule/cost targets
- Provides ideas and concepts to keep the effort moving
- Insures protection of confidential information, and observes secrecy agreements and applicable federal regulations
- Makes changes and corrections in the work as necessary
- Establishes procedures and controls for the finished product.

On a small proposal, the proposal manager may work alone; on a large proposal, as a manager and publisher. The proposal manager is directly responsible for the final form of all proposals, but receives write-ups of technical sections from other groups. A large proposal represents many man-hours of work. The effort requires the coordination of specialized groups: process and project engineering, design and drafting, estimating, purchasing, construction, and others. The advice of engineering specialists, with a thorough knowledge of technical developments, is incorporated. Figure 4–3 shows in simple form a typical organizational structure for a proposal effort.

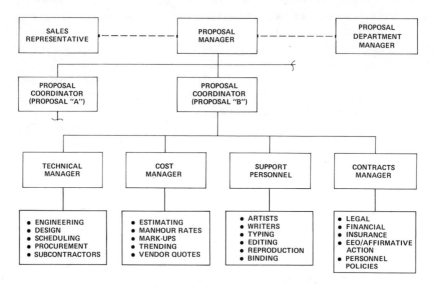

Figure 4-3. Proposal team organization chart.

The primary members of a proposal team and their functions are the following:

- Marketing or Sales Representative
  - Identifies the projects that are of value to the company
  - Reviews inquiry, presents an interpretation, and makes suggestions regarding the proposals response
  - Passes along to proposal manager any unwritten knowledge or insight regarding client's objectives, technical approach, pricing, commercial terms, and other key client concerns
  - Maintains liaison with the client to have answers provided to any questions that may come up during preparation of the proposal
- Proposal Coordinator
  - Assists the proposal manager in coordinating and managing the overall effort and meeting the required deadlines
  - Serves as a single point of collection for write-ups being prepared by each specialized area
  - Develops the arrangement of proposal information in a format that is most responsive to the client's request
  - Helps prepare and monitor the proposal schedule and budget
  - Obtains and writes sections on company's experience, capabilities, and other boilerplate information

- Prepares or obtains most of the information in the management section of the proposal
- Arranges for publication services including cover design, tabbing, typing, reproduction, and binding
- Does most of the final editing and proofreading
- Writes the introduction, summary, or abstract sections of the proposal
- Engineering or Technical Specialist
  - Develops scope of work description and task breakdown
  - Develops man-hour estimates
  - Selects the staffing for the technical portion of the proposal work
  - Directs the write-up preparation for the technical portion of the proposal
  - Insures the completeness and accuracy of the technical response
  - Reviews the cost estimate to see that it matches the work breakdown structure
  - Assists proposal manager in coordinating technical sections of the proposal
  - Nominates candidates for the technical work
  - Directs the development of the project schedule for the proposal
  - Directs the effort of the design and drafting group.
- Cost Estimator
  - Develop the cost estimate of the work
  - Insures costs are consistent with company pricing policy
  - Prepares the basis of estimate section of the cost proposal
  - Establishes standard rates to be used for estimating
  - Maintains items of direct charges and other overhead items and rates
  - Checks that the estimate is consistent with the scope of work
  - Responsible that the cost information is in a form consistent with the client's request
  - Prepares trend analysis when required
  - Prepares confidential quoting calculations for internal use.
- Contract or Legal Specialist
  - Reviews the entire inquiry from a legal or contractual standpoint
  - Reviews and comments on the terms and conditions of the contract portion of the proposal
  - Has final approval over the contract portion of the proposal
  - Reviews the entire proposal to insure that it is consistent with company policy and procedure
  - Recommends contractual terms and conditions language that may be required for proposal
  - Maintains file on past contracts to insure similar agreements from job to job

- Participates in contract negotiations as follow-up to the proposal submittal.
- Other Specialized Groups: Examples of the services or inputs that would be provided by other specialized support groups in the company are the following:
  - The procurement department obtains pricing and deliveries for equipment as requested by the Proposal Manager.
  - The construction department provides consultation on construction methods and sequence. They provide write-ups on field execution and staffing. They also prepare site reports and make productivity assessments.
  - The scheduling department prepares schedules, planning documents, and time control write-ups.
  - The personnel department provides information on labor breakdown, EEO and affirmative action, personnel salary, and benefit policies.
  - The design and drafting department prepares the drawings, illustrations, elevations, and plot plans.

The proposal manager has complete responsibility for publishing the proposal. To assist in publishing the proposal, there may be a proposal services group to do the typing, graphic arts work, collating, and assembly. The reproduction section plays an essential part in the proposal effort. The appearance of the completed work testifies to the need for quality procedures. Large companies, such as in the aerospace industry, especially when bidding on big projects, may have a permanent staff of technical writers to rewrite the individual sections of the proposal. This group is also used for editing, proofreading, and organizing. Figure 4–4 shows a graphical representation of the interaction between the proposal manager and the other disciplines in an organization. This representation shows the proposal manager as the focal point of the proposal effort.

A proposal function or department can be organized either as a full-time activity with a permanent staff or as an ad hoc team pulled together for a specific proposal. The choice of organization and size of staff, if permanent, depends on the size of the firm, its budget, philosophy, and the availability of resources. For companies that do a lot of bidding work, it would be necessary to have a proposal department, headed by a manager of proposals, with several proposal managers and proposal coordinators. If personnel are assigned on a temporary basis, a usual source of proposal managers is from the project management group. If a large or complex proposal effort is required, no matter what type of organization is employed, the staffing needed for the proposal would be sizable.

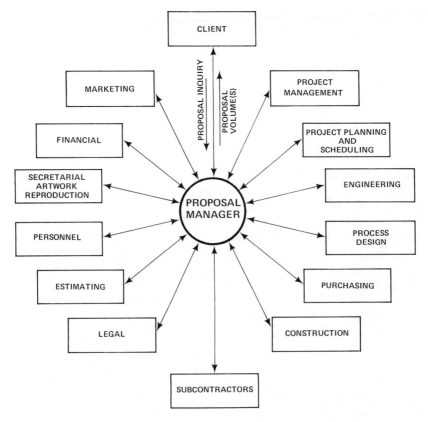

Figure 4-4. A graphic representation of proposal management.

4.5 BRIEFING THE PROPOSAL TEAM

One of the earliest activity of the proposal manager is to put together a successful proposal team. This is usually done jointly with the respective department managers who are in the best position to select the most qualified people from their departments. Besides selecting the individuals who have the needed capabilities and experience for the proposal, they also know who is available or who can be made available if required. The selection criteria of the proposal team, their management, and the problems that must be overcome are discussed in Chapter 2. As we have discussed in Section 4.4, the staffing size and make-up of any specific proposal depends on the nature of the proposal being prepared and the availability of your personnel.

Once selection of the specialists needed for the proposal team have been made, the next step is to allocate work to these specialists. This begins with the kick-off meeting and ends with specific assignments being made through the coordination memo and its proposal outline. If specific individuals are known at the time of the kick-off meeting, their names can be placed right in the memo. If specific individuals are not known, their department designation is placed next to the work item. It then becomes the department heads' responsibility to assign someone and get the work done.

The proposal manager, as proposal leader, is faced with the challenge of directing and managing a team that has been assembled quickly for a short duration, yet must produce at its very best. While the proposal effort is demanding on the team, its output must remain high and creative. It is also important that no matter if the proposal is done by a part-time or full-time staff, it must be written cohesively and maintain continuity from one proposal to another. In directing the proposal preparation, the proposal manager, like the project manager, strives to get the most out of his team. One way is to establish a clear chain of command and a central point of responsibility and coordination. In addition, each team member should have as much guidance and knowledge about the task requirements as possible to do a more effective and timely job. Each member should also know the depth of effort that is required in performing the task. Any past proposal, background information, sales documents, or other source should be referenced.

The proposal manager points the proposal team in the proper direction, beginning with the kick-off meeting and continuing at subsequent follow-up meetings. The proposal manager briefs all team members carefully on the requirements of the inquiry and reviews the proposal outline, including the scope of work, task breakdown, and proposal schedule. The importance of the proposal effort and its value to the company's long-range plans are stressed. The importance placed on the project is also discussed. The proposal budget, manpower, and time constraints are discussed to encourage the proper team cooperation and attitude. The proposal manager describes the tasks required to satisfy the inquiry and defines the team or department responsibilities assigned to accomplish these tasks. The briefing session is also a good opportunity for team members to meet one another. The proposal manager, who is totally responsible for securing inputs from team members and outside departments, must also plan, coordinate, monitor, and integrate all aspects of the proposal effort. To insure proper control, the proposal manager should schedule meetings with the proposal team on a regular basis throughout the proposal preparation time period.

4.6 PROPOSAL SCHEDULING

The proposal manager is responsible for planning the proposal and for scheduling, budgeting, coordinating, and controlling all of the work. We have already discussed how the proposal is planned by defining the proposal objectives, determining the proposal format, and defining the scope of work for each participating department. In this section, we review how a detailed proposal schedule is established with the participating departments, which is very critical to proposal success because of the short time span of proposal preparation. The schedule is used to budget both the time and cost of proposal preparation.

Proposal schedules consist basically of the dates of specific meetings and milestone events that are critical to proposal completion. Typical major milestone events which would be included in the proposal schedule are:

- Kick-off meeting
- Completion dates for the first draft
- First draft review and approval
- Completion dates for additional drafts as may be required
- Status or progress review meetings on at least a weekly basis
- Completion date for the proposal final draft
- Final draft review and approval
- Final integrating and editing of the complete proposal
- Management review and approval
- Pricing strategy meeting
- Final artwork, typing, and proofreading
- Proposal reproduction, binding, and delivery schedule
- Proposal submission date.

To insure that the proposal can be delivered at the place and time designated in the inquiry, it is necessary that a schedule be prepared, indicating all details of the final collection, transmittal, and delivery of the proposal documents together with adequate alternate paths to insure success in case of unknown or unexpected events of a delaying nature, such as strikes and weather. As soon as the proposal work has been assigned and the date set for transmitting the proposal to the client, the proposal manager prepares an outline or draft proposal schedule for discussion at the kick-off meeting. This should at least include approximate due dates for key items of the proposal work.

The detailed proposal schedule is prepared with the participating departments as soon as their scopes of work have been developed. This is done during the kick-off meeting, or shortly thereafter. Key dates must be shown on the detailed schedule.

In the event of a small proposal effort, adequate scheduling may consist simply of publicizing the overall completion date. This is a matter of judgment between the manager of proposals and the proposal manager. For many proposals, it is adequate to place the required due dates only in the coordination or kick-off memo. These due dates can be extremely important. Some defense-related proposals are timed with a stopwatch on the due date.

The schedule for the proposal can be submitted on a form similar to Figure 4-1, which indicates when various information is required, as well as the overall completion dates. In establishing the schedule, the proposal manager considers two critical requirements that are often conflicting: (1) to expedite the proposal so that it is completed on time, and (2) to stay within the proposal budget.

This requires the careful budgeting of time (e.g., via a network-diagram approach) so that work done by one group that is crucial to a second group, is completed and given to the second group with enough time left for that group to complete its portion of the work, and possibly pass it on to still another group. In addition, sufficient time must be included in the schedule for complete rewrites of drafts that are unacceptable. The proposal manager must avoid spending too much time on the technical section at the expense of the other sections of the proposal. All sections and all events or activities are crucial to the completion of a winning proposal.

The proposal manager may find that extra effort is required from the participating departments to meet the schedule. With the approval of management, additional help may be sought. Overtime and weekend work may be authorized, but this should be considered as exceptional rather than normal procedure.

The proposal manager must make sure the overall proposal schedule is flexible but realistic. The schedule must provide enough time for the proper preparation of the proposal. This is best handled by discussion at the kick-off meeting.

If the desired schedule is not realistic, the sales representative should be advised of the minimum time requirements and should arrange with the client for an extension.

While very large and complex proposal efforts, such as those done for the aerospace or military industries, may require a network (PERT/CPM) schedule, most other proposal efforts can be controlled adequately with a milestone or bar chart schedule.

Most proposals are small enough to be scheduled on a *proposal progress chart,* as in Figure 4–5. In these cases, where only the key dates are significant, enough detail can be put on the form to make it an adequate schedule as well as a budget record and control for the proposal. On the other hand, a *proposal detailed schedule,* as in Figure 4–6, is used for complex, detailed proposals. This form shows all of the specific items that must be scheduled for this kind of effort.

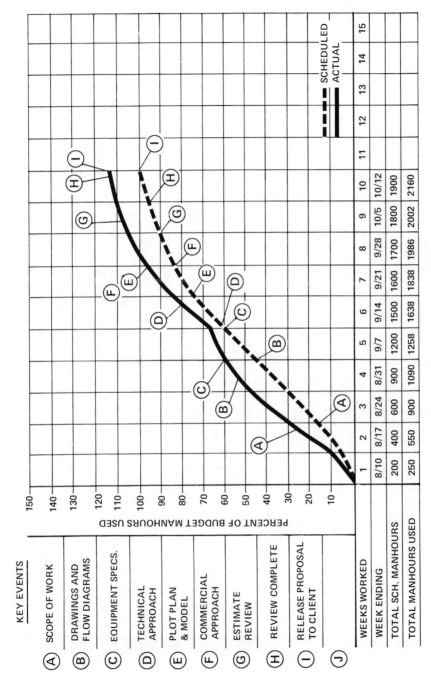

Figure 4-5. Progress chart.

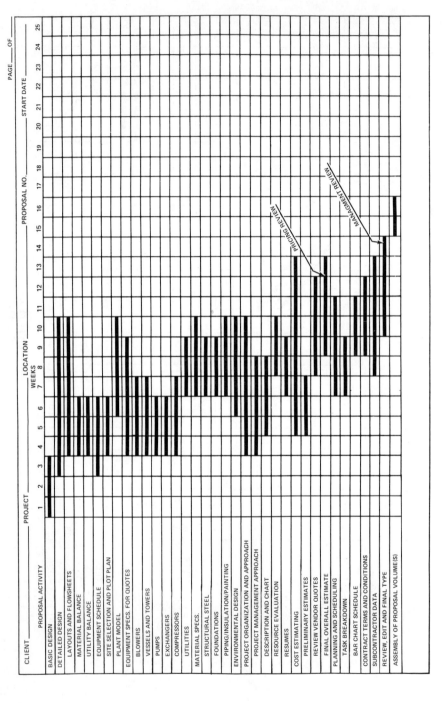

Figure 4–6. Detailed proposal schedule.

In addition, a highlighted schedule showing key dates for each proposal is maintained on an overall proposal department schedule board. This composite schedule is for all work in progress and is used as a control tool to anticipate possible conflicts among all proposal efforts, and helps to even out the flow of activities. Such conflicts may include typing, reproduction, proposal assembly, reviews and approvals, and so forth. A representation of a schedule board is given in Figure 4–7.

The proposal schedule must be followed strictly and is monitored weekly. Man-hour reports are received weekly by the proposal manager, who compares them to the budgeted man-hours and progress. Failure to adhere to the schedule results in a breakdown in the flow of activities and a panic situation toward the end of the proposal preparation effort. To aid in enforcing adherence to the schedule, status meetings are held throughout the proposal period, starting with the kick-off meeting. The main theme for each subsequent meeting is noted in the proposal schedule.

The proposal manager must recognize that proposal schedules are generally tight, and that certain parts of any proposal effort are inherently time-consuming. Each of these parts must be initiated early enough in the schedule to avoid delays. They include:

- Adequate time to find data and prepare the written material
- Reviews and critique of work in progress, with final review before the proposal goes to the client

PROPOSAL NUMBER	CLIENT	PROJECT AND LOCATION	CURRENT MONTH (By days)	FOLLOWING MONTH By Days)	PROPOSAL MANAGER	PROJECT MANAGER	REMARKS

Figure 4–7. Proposal department schedule.

- Special approvals required by certain aspects of the proposal, such as licensing, unusual commercial terms, third-party relationships, and so on
- Editing, corrections, and changes
- Typing and reproduction
- Preparing special artwork, charts, graphs, and so on
- Obtaining materials for proposal books, such as embossed hard covers, printed index tabs, title sheets, and so on
- Assembling and binding proposal books
- Adequate time to mail or hand deliver books.

The progress chart in Figure 4–5 is used in the following manner. To establish the progress chart, the proposal manager draws the schedule man-hours used curve by totaling week-by-week personnel assignments that are obtained from the participating departments with their man-hour budgets. He draws the actual man-hours used curve by entering the total cumulative hours week by week from the tabulation on the proposal man-hour report. Dates for key events, that are always listed in the column to the left of the progress chart, are indicated by attaching the corresponding encircled letters to the man-hours used curves. Both schedule and actual dates must be so indicated. A substantial number of key events should be used in order to assess proposal progress properly.

If the proposal effort is small in size or under four weeks in duration, a progress chart is not necessary. But the proposal manager may still want to list key events as a checklist for monitoring progress.

4.7 PROPOSAL BUDGET AND COST CONTROL

All new business development activities, especially proposals, should be accounted for by a cost budget. The sum of these individual budgets approximate the total budget allocated to the bidding effort by upper management. The proposal manager, assisted at times by a project manager, is responsible for determining the cost or budget for each proposal. Once established, the proposal manager is responsible for monitoring and controlling the expenditures logged against the budget.

The proposal manager should prepare the proposal budget and maintain cost control records in terms of man-hours, rather than dollars. This method provides a quick means of evaluating the status of the effort without unnecessary dissemination of confidential or sensitive information.

As with any work effort, if you can control the end product, then you can control the work (including cost) required to produce that product. Relating this to the proposal preparation effort, the first step toward producing the end product, the proposal, is to establish the format and content and then to develop a comprehensive, detailed plan. To implement the plan, it is essential that all members of the project team understand the proposal plan. A substantial effort should be made before starting on a proposal to define the work required from each participant. As discussed earlier, the major means of informing the entire team is the kick-off meeting. All team members must attend this meeting so that they can be briefed properly. This meeting insures that each member of the team fully understands what is required. This results in the development of a better man-hour estimate and therefore a better and more realistic budget. The plan is published as the kick-off or coordination memo.

Immediately following the kick-off/coordination meeting, the proposal manager and/or the project manager assigned to the effort develops a budget for the activity. A budget should be developed for each major step. For example, if you need to make a presentation to qualify for a project before submitting a proposal, separate budgets should be prepared for the presentation and the proposal effort. The budget for the proposal should then include, as best as can be determined, the actual cost of the presentation, assuming you use the same assignment number in both cases.

Figure 4–8 shows a sample format for a proposal budget. This budget can be prepared solely by the proposal manager, but usually requires some man-hour input from the participating departments.

DEPARTMENT	MAN-HOURS	RATE	AMOUNT $
PROJECT MANAGEMENT			
PROCESS/BASIC DESIGN			
ENGINEERING			
ESTIMATING, COST CONTROL & SCHEDULING			
PURCHASING			
CONSTRUCTION			
LEGAL/TAX/INSURANCE			
SALES & PROPOSALS			
COMMERCIAL DEVELOPMENT			
RESEARCH & DEVELOPMENT			
MARKETING COMMUNICATIONS			
ACCOUNTING			
SECRETARIAL/CLERICAL			
TOTALS S & W			
FRINGES @ % OF S & W			
OTHER OUT OF POCKET			
TRAVEL			
TOTAL BUDGET			

Figure 4–8. Proposal Budget.

Once a detailed task breakdown has been developed for each participating department, the proposal manager has each department provide a man-hour budget estimate for their portion of the work. If the proposal extends over several weeks, the department will also provide an estimate of personnel assignments week by week. This information is used by the proposal manager in setting up a proposal progress chart. On large proposals, it is necessary to turn the departmental man-hours over to the estimating department so that they can apply appropriate factors and other support costs to develop the final total proposal cost. Proposals of this size require upper management approval of the final proposal budget.

The approach to control of costs of proposal activities must allow for a wide range of both costs and time of performance that can be encountered on such activities. Effective cost control begins at the very start of a proposal effort and is continued throughout its life until the proposal is submitted to the client or conclusion of all chargeable activities. To accomplish this, it is necessary to use a formal system or procedure. One method of effective control is to record the time charges applied to a proposal effort from start to finish. This is normally done by opening or assigning a charge number at the beginning of a proposal activity and closing it out at its completion. All persons working on the proposal can charge their time to the number. Therefore, all time charged against the proposal is recorded. Charge numbers can be opened and closed as many times as necessary, but to keep down overhead costs, this should be done only when required for project continuity.

Control of labor costs requires real-time reporting of time charges, either on a daily report giving man-hours charged by each person or a weekly report that provides total hours charged by each department or section. Other information that can be reported is payroll costs for the week, year to date, and total to date. The proposal manager and the project manager (or a designee) should monitor both reports for all proposal activities. Another report is the *monthly cost report* that covers payroll, travel, long-distance telephone calls, telex, and out-of-pocket expenses. Control out-of-pocket, travel, and other miscellaneous charges are more difficult on labor charges, because of the much longer lag time for their reporting. Certain charges for other costs are subject to prior approval of the manager of proposals or operations manager as follows:

- Travel by all personnel working on the activity—approval of expense accounts
- Costs invoiced by other offices—approval of invoice
- Costs invoiced by subcontractors or outside consultants—approval of invoice.

All questionable charges should be reviewed and appropriate action immediately taken on all mischarges.

The principal tools for controlling proposal labor costs are:

- The man-hours budget for the effort
- The proposal schedule
- The weekly accounting department reports of man-hours charged against the proposal effort.

From these principal tools, the proposal manager can prepare a proposal man-hour report and/or progress chart to provide a unified record and control for the proposal effort. The proposal manager sets up the record and chart for the proposal as soon as the budget and schedule are established. The record and chart enable the proposal manager or others to make quick comparisons of progress, budgets, costs, and schedule, including dates for key proposal events.

Each week, the proposal manager can update the report and chart, using information from the accounting department as input. With the dates for key events as guideposts, progress, budget, costs, and schedule can be reviewed to determine whether or not the effort is proceeding properly. Management receives a copy of the update report and chart and reviews with the proposal manager any actual or potential problems.

The proposal man-hour report, Figure 4–9, is used in the following manner. To establish the man-hour report, the proposal manager first enters the budgeted man-hours for each department on the form. On a weekly basis, the accounting department issues reports of man-hours charged to the proposal by all departments. The proposal manager enters these man-hours on the form, and then enters the cumulative totals. This provides a continuous record of man-hour expenditures on the proposal.

In reviewing the accounting department reports to obtain input for the report and chart, the proposal manager makes sure that individuals who charge time to the proposal have actually been working on it, in order to reduce excessive individual man-hour charges. If mischarges are evident, the departments concerned will transfer the charges to other accounts.

To provide for the practical control of costs over the wide range of expenditures that may be encountered for various proposal activities, it may be worthwhile to set up different levels of budgets. These levels would have different preparation, approval, and monitoring procedures. A typical set of budget levels could be the following:

Level I.   This is normally a minor effort, taking less than two weeks, costing under $3,000, and requiring minimal upfront planning and coordination.

Level II.   This effort usually takes 2 to 4 weeks, costs from $3,000 to $25,000, and requires good upfront planning, budgeting, and

CLIENT __NEW ENERGY RESOURCES__
PLANT __OIL SHALE FACILITY__
LOCATION __COLORADO__

PROPOSAL NUMBER __S-522__
BY __M. BAKER__　DATE __9/4/81__
PROPOSAL DUE DATE __11/2/81__

WEEKS	WEEK ENDING	PROJECT MANAGEMENT	ENGINEERING	DESIGN & DRAFTING	PURCHASING	CONSTRUCTION	SCHEDULING	ESTIMATING	PROPOSAL	LEGAL/TAX/ INSURANCE	ACCOUNTING	SECRETARIAL & CLERICAL	MISC.	TOTAL	PERCENT OF TOTAL BUDGET	REFERENCE
1	9/12	40	14	18	–	–	–	–	42	–	4	11	–	129		Coord.
	CUM. TOTAL	40	14	18	–	–	–	–	42	–	4	11	–	129		Memo
2	9/19	40	35	49	10	6	–	12	38	16	6	26	2	224	5.6	
	CUM. TOTAL	80	49	67	10	6	–	12	80	16	10	37	2	353	15.3	
3	9/26	15	62	88	18	12	16	22	23	16	6	37	7	322		
	CUM. TOTAL	95	111	155	28	18	16	34	103	16	16	74	9	675	29.3	
4	10/3	22	64	81	32	10	26	34	46	29	13	42	–	399		
	CUM. TOTAL	117	175	236	60	28	42	68	149	45	29	116	9	1,074	46.7	
5	10/10	18	76	72	29	39	18	48	51	10	28	58	15	462		Rev. 1
	CUM. TOTAL	135	251	308	89	67	60	116	200	55	57	174	24	1,536	66.8	
6	10/17	21	48	28	14	48	18	41	42	32	27	51	6	376		
	CUM. TOTAL	156	299	336	103	115	78	157	242	87	84	225	30	1,912	83.1	
7	10/24	10	40	15	2	14	6	18	48	9	22	62	–	246		
	CUM. TOTAL	166	339	351	105	129	84	175	290	96	106	287	30	2,158	93.8	
8	10/31	10	12	5	–	4	–	12	58	4	18	53	8	184		
	CUM. TOTAL	176	351	356	105	133	84	187	348	100	124	340	38	2,342	101.8	
9	CUM. TOTAL															
19	CUM. TOTAL															
20	CUM. TOTAL															
	PROJECTED TOTAL	176	351	356	105	133	84	187	348	100	124	340	38	2,342	101.8	
	BUDGET	180	300	400	90	120	80	160	340	120	130	380	–	2,300	100.0	

Figure 4-9. Proposal man-hour report.

close coordination of the effort. The majority fall into this category.

Level III. This type of effort usually takes 1 to 3 months, costs between $25,000 to $100,000, and requires the best in planning, budgeting, and coordination of the effort. This is a major effort such as bidding a large project or a lump-sum bid.

Level IV. This level of expenditure occurs only occasionally and involves a turnkey, lump-sum bid, or a super project. The time from receipt of inquiry to proposal submission usually exceeds three months and costs over $100,000. This level of effort requires project execution quality planning, budgeting, and coordination of execution.

In certain cases when actual cost underruns or overruns are significant, the proposal manager and/or project manager shall conduct a post mortem to ascertain the cause(s) for the difference. The post mortem should be done immediately following completion of the proposal activity, essentially when all charges have been submitted. The proposal manager compares actual versus planned cost and time performance. A written report analyzing the activity and explaining the reason(s) for any deviation in expenditure is submitted to management for review. The post mortem itself must not become a major activity and cost and time spent on it should be held to a minimum.

4.8 PULLING IT ALL TOGETHER

Once the scope has been defined, schedule and budget established, and the proposal outline distributed, Phase II begins for the proposal manager. Phase II involves the monitoring, appraisal, and control of the entire proposal effort. Unless the project manager keeps a close watch on the progress of the proposal and evaluates the performance of the personnel assigned to work on it, the various groups can lose direction and either overlap each other's efforts or engage in a "let's do the easy part first" philosophy that can lead to a workload crisis at deadline time. For small and medium-sized proposals, the proposal manager alone is responsible for controlling the proposal input. On large proposals, major section leaders assist the proposal manager in maintaining control over proposal inputs.

One method of control is to have all proposal information, drawings, instructions, data, schedule revisions, and so on, flow through the proposal manager (or a technical representative), who examines the work performed by one group for completeness and accuracy before forwarding it to the next group.

Another method of overall control is to have a checklist of areas of primary consideration that can be checked against a proposal to identify any missing area. Some people use mental checklists, but experience has shown that written checklists are more valuable in preventing oversights.

Carrying out the proposal work may involve essentially the proposal manager just working alone or a large staff of people from many departments. The most common situation is the proposal manager doing the work with the help of a few part-time people. The proposal manager's functions vary with the size of the staff, but responsibility for the effort, regardless of size, and the finished product, typed, bound, and published.

Although the proposal manager may work alone, or virtually alone, on small proposals, the overall responsibilities are no different than on larger proposals. On a small proposal, the proposal manager must perform many tasks that would be handled by someone else on a large proposal. On a large proposal, the proposal manager's functions are primarily those of manager and publisher.

Whatever size the proposal may be, the participants from each department provide the same kind of services that they do on projects. How much information or documentation they provide depends on the size or the proposal and the type of estimate the client wants.

For a large proposal effort, typical information that would be prepared for the technical proposal would include the following:

- Basis for design
- Specification and description
- Material and energy balances
- Flow diagrams
- Equipment data sheets
- Utilities summaries and balances
- Plot plan and layouts
- Mechanical design considerations
- Building design and layout
- Single-line electrical diagrams
- Vessel and tank schedules
- Instrument lists
- Warrantees and guarantees.

The extent of information that is included in a proposal depends on the scope of work or services required for the project, the type of estimate accuracy requested, and whether the bid is fixed or cost-plus. The amount of information required to be responsive is usually explained in the client's inquiry. Typical of the additional information that could be required for the proposal is the following:

- Procurement procedures and techniques
- Construction procedures and methods, including direct hire or subcontract plan
- Site reports and labor productivity assessments
- Schedules and time control procedures
- Estimating and cost control procedures
- Project cost estimates, which could include home office costs, field costs, equipment and commodities costs, and estimates of total project cost
- Management and project organizations
- Project execution plan
- Subcontractor plan
- Employee relations program
- EEO and affirmative action plan
- Construction safety program
- Other variables.

Because the proposal information is prepared by personnel from many different departments and specialties, it is challenging for the proposal manager to coordinate, edit, and integrate these separate and differently written sections of the proposal. While the drafts may be written by people knowledgeable about their specialty, they are usually not proficient writers. It is the proposal manager's job to put all the proposal sections into the right language and style for the proposal. Depending on the size and complexity of the proposal, rewriting and organizing the input material can be tough and time-consuming.

In general, a proposal must convey the ideas, data, and know-how that qualify the contractor to perform the work specified by the owner. The proposal must be prepared in a way to adequately reflect the owner's specification, scope of work and, where possible, alternative approaches that will demonstrate to the owner that this proposal will save him time and money. The proposal must be clearly written and in a style and format that convinces the client that you are the best one for the job. Because the proposal is in all aspects a sales tool, it should look professional and be written as a sales document.

The proposal manager's job of editing and restructuring the input material is made even more difficult because of the diverse make-up of the people who read the proposal. These individuals include:

- Engineers and other technical personnel
- Cost and accounting personnel
- Procurement specialists

- Legal and contractual personnel
- Client managers and executives
- Many others.

It is for this reason that specific sections are prepared and written for those individuals who would be most interested in reading them. Examples of this would be:

- The technical section for technical personnel
- The cost section for cost and accounting personnel
- The summary for the client's executives.

To help make the proposal manager's job somewhat easier, the establishment of a clear outline of what to include in the initial or first draft and the format to follow should be given to each contributor.

4.9 WRITING THE FIRST DRAFT

Creating the first draft is usually the most difficult part of the proposal writing effort because it is least understood by the people writing it. After the first draft has been reviewed and returned for rewrite, the scope of what needs to be done is better defined. The information supplied for the rewrite must be complete because the proposal time span rarely allows for more than a second or third draft. The proposal manager and the team must be aware of the fact that although the first draft should be as complete as possible, it could change substantially from its original form. One time-honored method used to re-structure a draft write-up is to "cut and paste". This method means literally to cut up a copy of the draft write-up and, after rearranging, paste it back together. A copy is used so that you can retain a complete, untouched original draft for your files. This method saves the writer a lot of rewriting time. To aid in the preparation and review of the first draft, the following should be considered:

- Label, date, and number all drafts.
- Organize each part with section headings.
- Begin each section with a new page number.
- Provide captions or heading and numbers for all figures and tables.
- Use small words and short sentences.
- Use the active voice and avoid slang, company jargon, and complicated sentences.
- Identify all abbreviations and acronyms the first time you use them.
- Don't overkill with too many details or examples.
- Submit drafts typed and double-spaced.

The proposal manager places all draft write-ups in a three-ring looseleaf binder in the same order as the outline or final proposal. This "mock-up" of the proposal gives a visual check of the status of the proposal and a good preliminary idea of how the completed product should appear. It should show an up-to-date version of all the inputs, to help to prevent portions of the proposal from being misplaced. It can also be used as a control tool in gathering the various parts of the proposal. Page numbering, if used, should only be done at the very end, when all typing has been completed. The proposal manager also uses a checklist, as in Figure 4–10, to keep track of the individual proposal items as they go through the publication production process.

4.10 TYPE OF ESTIMATING DETAIL

Projects can range from a feasibility study, through modifications of existing facilities, to the complete design, procurement, and construction of a multiplant complex. Many times, the design and engineering has been done by the owner, and the project is primarily a procurement and construction effort; sometimes, just a pure construction job. Whatever the project may be, the bid request and type of information desired may differ radically.

Bids are solicited for a variety of reasons, such as for plant feasibility evaluation, as an aid in capital expenditure planning, or for a firm commitment to build. For the purpose of defining the work to be performed by their staff, contractors categorize the incoming request according to the amount of information and the accuracy desired.

An *order-of-magnitude bid* or estimate is made without detailed engineering data, and has an accuracy of ± 25% within the scope of the project. This type of estimate may make use of cost-capacity curves, approximations of past estimates (not necessarily similar), or scale factors.

Next, there is the *approximate estimate,* which is also made without detailed engineering data, but is prorated from previous projects that are similar in scope and capacity. This type of estimate has an accuracy of ± 15%.

A *definitive estimate* is prepared from defined engineering data including (as a minimum) fairly complete plot plans and elevations, piping and instrument diagrams, one-line electrical diagrams, equipment data sheets and quotations, structural sketches, soil data and sketches of major foundations, building sketches, and a complete set of specifications. This type of estimate is accurate within ± 5%, depending on basic information.

The soliciting of vendors' quotations is a critical input to a good proposal, especially if it is for a lump-sum job. Depending on the company's estimating set-up and on the amount of effort going into the proposal (i.e., order of magnitude versus all-out effort), bids are usually obtained on 50 to 90% of the equipment. One method of insuring proper use of vendors' quotations is for the proposal manager to indicate on an equipment list released by the

CLIENT _____   PAGE ____ OF _____

PROJECT _____

LOCATION _____

PROPOSAL NO. _____ DATE _____

SECTION NUMBER	TITLE OF SECTION (AND DESCRIPTION, IF NECESSARY)	SOURCE					STATUS							
		RESPONSIBLE FOR INITIAL/DRAFT	WRITE NEW	REVISE/MODIFY BOILER PLATE	USE BOILER PLATE AS IS	PREPARED BY OTHERS (OUTSIDE COMPANY)	DATE REQUIRED	REVIEW	EDIT/REVISE	FINAL TYPING	PROOF/CORRECT	REPRODUCTION	NUMBER OF COPIES	READY FOR BINDING
	INTRODUCTION													
	SCOPE OF WORK/SERVICES													
	PLANT DESCRIPTION													
	BASIS OF DESIGN													
	DESIGN CONSIDERATIONS													
	CONTROL PROCEDURES													
	PROJECT ORGANIZATION													
	STAFFING													
	ORGANIZATION CHART													
	RESUMES – KEY PERSONNEL													
	SCHEDULING													
	BAR CHART SCHEDULE													
	QUALIFICATIONS													
	GENERAL													
	RELATED EXPERIENCE													
	BASIS OF ESTIMATE													
	CONTRACT COMMENTS													
	PERSONNEL POLICIES													

Figure 4–10. Proposal work checklist.

engineering group the dates by which each group must complete a certain item, and the deadline for receiving a quotation.

The actual items to be sent for quotes are decided upon by the proposal manager, the project estimator, the process and project engineers, the purchasing manager, and other key individuals for specialty items. The proposal manager, as part of his progress monitoring, makes sure that verbal quotations are followed by a written confirmation, and that the quotations are complete to the point of including prices, expiration dates, escalation requirements, and delivery terms.

If the client has asked for a type of estimate that is inconsistent with the available supporting information or with the nature of the proposal, the sales representative should inform the client and seek an adjustment. Such matters as the use of quotations versus in-house pricing of equipment, use of factoring versus complete take-offs for estimates of bulk materials, and similar topics also should be explored where appropriate.

The type of estimates and the detailed procedures required for preparing the cost proposal are discussed in Chapter 8.

4.11 FINAL REVIEW AND APPROVAL

After the proposal preparation has reached its endpoint and a draft copy has been put together (but before the proposal is released for management's approval), a final review meeting is held. There, the various aspects of the proposal are checked for validity, and the design is completely reviewed.

Although each proposal section is normally reviewed by the originator and his department head, there still remains a need for a detailed review of the entire proposal package before it is given to the client. Attention must be given during the proposal preparation because there will not be enough time to review all aspects of the proposal closely at the final review. If at the final review meeting it is determined that changes must be made, the proposal schedule dictates that these changes be made quickly. To help insure that only minor revisions and adjustments will be made during the final review, proposal drafts should be as thoroughly prepared as possible.

While it is usually the intention of a company to be completely responsive to any and all requirements of the inquiry, it is possible that some exceptions may be necessary. These exceptions may be for reasons such as they are contrary to company practices or policies, that they may be considered impractical, or you believe you have a sufficiently better idea to warrant such an exception. Upon reading the inquiry, if the proposal team identifies any exceptions, they should make them known at the kick-off meeting. If the exceptions are adopted, they should be reviewed by management for their validity before being submitted to the client.

Along with the interdepartmental final review, there may be separate departmental ones, such as a cost or estimating review, a proposal management or commercial review, an engineering review, and so on.

As part of the proposal manager's final review, a check is made to see that the owner has signed a secrecy agreement, if any proprietary information is included in the proposal.

At the completion of the final review meeting, a draft copy is sent to key management people in the organization for their comments and approval. This is the final hurdle to overcome and, if the proposal manager has done his job well, involves only minor changes such as deletion or rewording of a paragraph, addition of a table or figure, or possibly a rearrangement of the proposal contents.

Once the proposal manager has obtained final approval from management to complete the proposal and to print copies, the proposal must be complete technically, aesthetically, and commercially. Phase III in the development of a proposal is the actual assembly of the information. Writing a complete and reliable proposal requires many inputs, all of which are important. A well-organized proposal, free from unclear or sloppy data sheets and flow diagrams and with an orderly arrangement of information, may indicate to a prospective owner that information transmitted during the job phase will be equally well organized.

Obtaining reviews and approvals is naturally a time-consuming process. The proposal manager should circulate and review copies of each completed part instead of waiting for all sections. Because the publishing effort is also a lengthy one, each section of a proposal should be printed as soon as it is approved. To expedite the effort, the proposal manager starts publishing as soon as practical, after the desired format for the proposal documents has been established. Proposal delivery should be arranged and coordinated with the sales representative on the project. The U.S. mail, parcel post, air freight, and so on should be used only where sufficient time is available to insure delivery of the proposal to the client by the specified due date.

4.12 STANDARD DISTRIBUTION OF DOCUMENTS

As part of an internal communication plan, a formal distribution of proposal documents should be established. In general, especially regarding cost data, proposal distribution within your own organization should be limited to a need-to-know basis. Specifically, the following people should review a copy of the proposal:

- Sales representative
- Project manager assigned to job
- Estimating department
- Operations or engineering department
- Senior P&L manager
- Manager of proposals (proposal file)
- Other concerned departments.

Table 4-1. Correspondence/Document Distribution

LEGEND
X — RECEIVES COPY
O — SEND COPY IF AFFECTED
P — PRICED COPY
U — UNPRICED COPY

CORRESPONDENCE OR DOCUMENT	EXECUTIVE VICE PRESIDENT	DIV. V.P./SALES MANAGER	DIVISION VICE PRESIDENT	SALES MANAGER	ENGINEERING MANAGER	OPERATIONS MANAGER	EASTERN REGION SALES OFFICE	SOUTHERN REGION SALES OFFICE	WESTERN REGION SALES OFFICE	CORPORATE ACCOUNTING	SALES REPRESENTATIVE	PROJECT MANAGER	PROPOSAL MGR./PROPOSAL FILE	PROPOSAL MGR./SALES FILE	PROPOSAL COORDINATOR	ESTIMATING DEPARTMENT	ROUTE COPY/SALES FILE	SALES FILE	SCHEDULING	PROCUREMENT	CONSTRUCTION
A. PROPOSAL COORDINATION																					
INQUIRY SCREENING		X	X	X							X		X		X			X			
COORDINATION MEMOS	X	X		X	O						X	X	X		X			X	O	O	O
PROPOSAL BUDGETS		X	X	X	O						X	X	X		X	O		X	O	O	O
NEW ISSUES/CLOSE-OUTS	X	X		X	X					X	X	X	X		X	X		X	O	O	O
B. PROPOSALS																					
COMMERCIAL OFFER	P	P			OU	OU					P	U	P		P	U	P			OU	OU
QUALIFICATIONS		X					O	O	O		X		X		X						
PRESENTATION MATERIAL		X				O					X		O		X		X	X			
C. CONTRACT DOCUMENTS																					
CONTRACTS/LETTERS OF INTENT/PURCHASE ORDERS	X	X			X						X	X			X						
CONTRACT NO. ASSIGNMENT	X		X	X	X					X	X	X	X		X	X	X		O	O	O
D. REPORTS																					
SALES REPORTS		X	X	X	X	X	X				X		X		X						
NEW BUSINESS PROSPECTS REPORT		X	X	X	X	X	X	X	X		X		X				X				
NEW JOB REPORTS	X	X	X	X						X	X		X				X				
QUARTERLY PROPOSAL COST REPORTS	X	X	X				X	X	X				X				X				
E. NEW BUSINESS COORDINATION MEETING MINUTES		X	X	X	X						X	X	X				X	X	X	X	X

The originals, or when not available, a legible copy of all documentation pertinent to the proposal, should be placed in the proposal file. Because it is very useful in proposal preparation to refer to past proposals, particularly in the case of the same client, you should maintain a separate parallel file to the sales file. This eliminates the need to borrow documents continuously from the sales file thereby maintaining the integrity of this file.

In general, you should keep extra copies for the proposal file on lump-sum bids and one extra copy on reimbursable bids. You should also try to print sufficient material to prepare an additional two copies on lump-sum bids, leaving this material loose, not collated or assembled. Distribution of completely priced proposals should be limited to the sales representative, estimating, the proposal file, and generally, keep a copy for reference in negotiations or for future proposals. Pricing data, that is lump-sum prices, percentage fees, fixed fees, salary ranges, overlays for extra work, and so on should be cut out of the copies distributed to all other parties.

Table 4-1 is representative of a typical standard document distribution. The actual distribution of documents depends on the organizational structure under which a company operates.

Chapter 5

Elements of a Proposal

5.0 INTRODUCTION

A proposal is a written or verbal formal offer to perform a service, supply a product, or sell a concept. In some cases, the proposal offers a combination of things like services and a product. Some proposals require developing data or concepts while others are just an offer to provide off-the-shelf material, using catalog information. The proposal can take on various forms, going from a brief two-page letter all the way to a multivolume document containing thousands of pages and professionally prepared artwork. Translating this into dollars, a proposal can cost anywhere from a few dollars for the time it takes to type a letter to several hundred thousands of dollars, and occasionally into the million dollar range.

The basis function of a proposal is to sell the unique capabilities of an organization to do something for a fee. It is an official document that explains what the company has to offer, why it is better than the competition, and the cost to the client. It is also a quasilegal document that sets the foundation for later contract negotiations. All too often, people concentrate their efforts exclusively on the technical aspects of a proposal. But a proposal is much more. To be complete and to win contracts successfully, a proposal must address more than just the technical details of an offer. The proposal must convince the client that the offeror holds something that is better or cheaper than they can obtain elsewhere. It must singlehandedly convince the client that the company is sound: having the proper organization and facilities to do the job or make the product. In addition, the proposal must convince the client that it can be done in the time and cost specified.

5.1 PROPOSAL TYPES

The majority of proposals that are prepared by companies are based on inquiries received from prospective clients. The inquiry stipulates the conditions under which the clients wish the work to be done. The responses we make to inquiries received from clients are termed "proposals," even though in many cases no commitment is proposed. Our proposals can be classified broadly in two major categories: *qualification proposals* and *commercial proposals*

The qualification proposal generally gives information about company organization, qualifications, working procedures, or information for a specific area of technology. Qualification proposals make no offer to perform services and make no commitments of a general or technical nature. These are also called *informational* proposals if the contents relate to company organization, general qualifications, and procedures. They are sometimes called *technical presentations* or *technical volumes* if technical and economic data are provided for a specific area of technology. A special form of the qualification proposal is the *presentation*.

The commercial proposal offers a definite commitment by the company to perform specific work or services, or to provide equipment in accordance with explicit terms of compensation. A commercial proposal may also contain the type of information usually found in qualification proposals.

Both qualification and commercial proposals may be presented to the client in various forms under a wide variety of titles, depending on the situation, e.g., the client's requirements and your firm's willingness to commit its resources under the specific circumstances involved. The most common forms are:

- Letter proposals
- Preliminary proposals
- Detailed proposals
- Presentations.

There are no sharp distinctions among these on the basis of content. Differentiation is mainly by the extent of the work required to prepare them. Included in the following paragraphs are definitions of these most common forms.

Letter proposals are either qualification or commercial proposals. They are brief enough to be issued in letter form rather than as bound volumes.

Preliminary proposals are either qualification or commercial proposals and are large enough to be issued as bound volumes. They may be paid technical and/or economic studies, bids to furnish services, or other offerings of this kind.

Detailed proposals are most often commercial proposals, generally including the preparation of a detailed estimate. They are the most complex and inclusive proposals. Because of the high cost of preparation and the high stakes involved in the commitments offered, organization and contents of the documents are defined and detailed to a much greater degree than other kinds of proposals. Refer to Table 5-1 for the typical contents of the different proposal types.

Presentations are generally in the nature of oral qualification proposals. Selected personnel, specialized in various areas, describe their subjects verbally to client representatives in time periods varying from an hour to an entire day. To aid in the success of a presentation, audio-visual aids are encouraged. Many companies maintain a library of photographic slides developed just for this purpose.

5.2 STANDARD PROPOSAL ORGANIZATION

While every individual proposal is different, the basic composition of each proposal has similar features. In general, the three principal elements of a proposal are:

- The technical section
- The management section
- The cost section.

Each of these sections is equally important, and must stand on its own because the client evaluates each separately. Even though there are three principal sections, proposals are usually assembled on a modular basis. In most cases, modular construction consists of the following distinct, self-contained components:

- Technical approach and details
- Management structure and qualifications
- Cost estimates and pricing details
- Company qualifications and background
- Contractual terms and conditions.

The technical component describes the approach that the company will take to meet the client's project requirements, including the techniques, system, and tools used to do the job as well as the schedule developed for the project.

The management component describes the organization, staffing, and special capabilities of the firm to perform the work satisfactorily. Any directly related experience can also be included in this section.

Table 5-1. Guide to Typical Proposal Contents

TYPE	COMMERCIAL OFFER			QUALIFICATIONS		
FORM / ITEM	LETTER	BASIC	DETAILED	LETTER	BASIC	DETAILED
TABLE OF CONTENTS			●		●	●
INTRODUCTION OR SUMMARY		■	■		■	■
SCOPE OF SERVICES	●	●	●			
TERMS OF COMPENSATION	●	●	●			
GUARANTEES	▲	▲	●			
INVESTMENT COSTS	▲	▲	■			▲
ELEMENTS OF PRODUCTION COSTS	▲	▲	▲			▲
COMPANY/DIVISION ORGANIZATION AND BACKGROUND — EXPERIENCE		■	■	▲	■	■
PROJECT ORGANIZATION AND EXECUTION	▲	●	●			▲
RESUMES		■	■			▲
MASTER PLANNING		▲	●			▲
DETAILED ESTIMATE		■	●			
PROCESS DESCRIPTION AND DESIGN CRITERIA	▲	●	●			▲
FLOW DIAGRAMS AND PLOT PLANS		■	●			▲
EQUIPMENT LIST	▲	■	●			▲
DETAILED EQUIPMENT DATA			●			▲
PROJECT STAFFING		■	■		▲	▲
PROJECT SCHEDULE		■	■			▲
CONTRACT COMMENTS	■	■	●			
DRAFT AGREEMENT	▲		●			

● = MANDATORY
▲ = OPTIONAL
■ = RECOMMENDED

The cost component describes the details used in estimating the cost of doing the work and includes enough back-up to give the client a high degree of confidence in its accuracy. Past cost performance can also be included.

The company qualifications and background describe the company's structure and overall capabilities and experience, including its policies, procedures, and financial status.

The contractual component contains the terms and conditions under which the company will perform the work, including contract agreement, contract comments, secrecy agreements, proprietary data, and other matters.

Depending upon the type or size of the proposal required to be responsive, the proposal elements can be arranged in different ways. If the proposal is a small effort, the technical, management, and cost sections can be combined within one cover, but are separated physically by organization. If a large proposal effort is required, each individual module could be organized into separate volumes. The usual organization of proposals is into two volumes, one technical and one commercial or cost/management.

To provide clarity and continuity of approach, the technical, management, and cost sections of the proposal should follow the same general format. The introduction should summarize the pertinent points of all three sections. While each proposal is different, the overall format and individual sections should be similar. By standardizing the format, much information can be revised, and it gives you a starting point. While large proposals may require an extensive multipage write-up, a small proposal requiring only a few paragraphs can be extracted for the larger write-up. Sometimes the client requests a specific format to follow to aid in his own evaluation of the proposal. This also aids your organization when putting the proposal together. Table 5-2 presents an example of the type of information that would be included in a proposal for a large project.

5.3 THE SINGLE-VOLUME PROPOSAL

For both small and large projects, a single-volume proposal may suffice. In such a case, the front matter should contain:

- The transmittal letter
- Title page
- Disclosure protection statement, if any
- Table of contents
- List of illustrations and tables
- Summary, abstract, and/or introduction.

Table 5-2. Proposal Bid Package

The bid package basically consists of these items, which can be divided into three main headings:

1. TECHNICAL PROPOSAL	2. MANAGEMENT	3. COST PROPOSAL
Introduction and background to contractor's company	Process schedule	Price for services offered in proposal
Organization of contractor's company	Process description	Breakdown of price (materials, labor, etc.)
Schedule of professional personnel	Operating requirements	Escalations (lump sum contract)
Resume of key personnel or a resume summary	Plot plans and elevations	Amount for subcontract work
Project-management policy or philosophy	Process flow diagrams	Amount of offsite facilities
Description of contractor's Engineering Department	Engineering flow diagrams	Taxes
	Utilities flow diagrams	Royalty payment
Description of contractor's Procurement Department	Heat and material balance	Alternative systems
Description of contractor's Financial Controls Department	Equipment list	Optional equipment
	Equipment data sheets	Price adjustments (labor efficiency, etc.)
Experience List of similar plants built	General facilities, such as piping, instrumentation, electrical, civil, construction, etc.	Schedule of payments
Experience List of large complexes built	Contractor's or client's specifications or standards	
Experience List of all plants built by contractor	Services provided by contractor	
Experience List of using a client's process	Services provided by client	
Photographs of plants built by contractor	Model and/or rendering of proposed plant	
Draft contract		

The main body of the proposal should contain:

- Opening statement
- Reference to inquiry document
- Description of project
- Statement of work plan
- End result of proposed plan
- Participation in related activities
- Company objectives and qualifications.

5.4 THE TECHNICAL VOLUME

The technical volume is usually the most difficult to prepare in both time and complexity. As a minimum, the technical volume should contain:

- *Statement of problem.* This should be your interpretation of the statement of the problem, in order to show the customer that you understand fully the work to be accomplished.

- *Technical discussion.* This is a detailed discussion of your intended technical approach to achieve the objectives.
- *Program plan.* The program shows the logical steps that you plan to follow to achieve the objective. For complex projects, you may wish to include a detailed program plan for such items as procurement, management, accounting, logistics, configuration management, quality assurance, and so on.
- *Description of facilities.* This section, if not already included in the management volume, describes the facilities that will be used for the project.
- *Exceptions, deviations, and assumptions.* This section delineates any exceptions, deviations, or assumptions that may differ from the customer's contract, statement of work, schedule, or specifications.
- *Background or supplemental information.* This section should contain the background or supplemental technical information and should not be a duplication of the management volume.

Chapter 6 contains a detailed description of the technical volume of a proposal.

5.5 THE MANAGEMENT VOLUME

When separately bound volumes are required, the management volume is usually the easiest because it may be a simple "boilerplate" from previous proposals. The following sections appear frequently in management volumes:

- *Administrative management capability.* This includes such items as the organizational structure of the company, the financial stability, the accounting system, employee compensation policies, EEO and Affirmative Action plans, employee safety and health programs, small business and labor surplus, quality assurance and control plans, and security.
- *Program management.* This describes your exact method for managing the project, including the organizational charts for the project, a definition of the project managers authority and responsibility, and interface mechanisms with the customer.
- *Facilities.* This describes briefly the facilities that will be utilized on the project and may also include the utilization rate of the facilities for all ongoing activities.
- *Cost and schedule controls.* This is merely a management summary of the detailed sections of the cost proposal, assuming that the cost proposal contains an indepth description. This includes the methods for

authorizing costs, tracking costs, comparing actual to planned expenditures, variance analyses, and reporting.
- *History and experience.* This describes briefly the history of your company and both your related and nonrelated experiences with emphasis, of course, upon the related activities.

Chapter 7 contains a detailed description of the management volume of a proposal.

5.6 THE COST VOLUME

The actual content of the cost volume depends upon the type of contract and the nature of the product or services rendered. The following items may be included as part of the cost volume:

- *Basic material.* This includes the abstract or title page, table of contents, introduction, and perhaps a summary.
- *Statement of work.* This may be customer furnished or developed in-house, and may simply be rewritten in the contractor's own language to show that the contractor understands the work required fully.
- *Cost summary.* This is an overall picture of the total cost for the project, perhaps broken down to one level of reporting.
- *Supporting schedules.* These may very well be the same schedules that appear in the technical and management proposals.
- *Fee or profit statement.* This is the supporting data to justify either the fee or profit.
- *Government or customer-furnished equipment.* The proposal must state the equipment that you expect to be furnished to you, usually free of charge (except for refurbishment).
- *Elements of cost/cost breakdown.* This is the basis against which costs are measured, controlled, and accumulated.
- *Cost format.* This is a further clarification of the cost breakdown, identifying the exact methods by which the costs are shown to the customer, either before or after accumulation.
- *Cost estimating techniques used.* This describes the company's policy and procedures for estimating the work, whether manual or by estimating manuals.
- *Supporting data.* This section, if required, contains the supporting data for labor, material, and overhead estimates.

Chapter 8 contains a detailed description of the cost volume of a proposal.

Chapter 6
The Technical Proposal

6.0 INTRODUCTION

Large, complex projects generally require at least three volumes as part of the proposal project: cost, management, and technical. The technical volume is the most complex and can contain several parts. The management volume of the proposal is usually a boilerplate of previous management volumes. The cost volume is usually loaded with computer printouts and may require very little maintenance from proposal to proposal.

The technical volume, on the other hand, changes from proposal to proposal. No two technical volumes are ever the same, even for a follow-on effort. The technical volume summarizes the technical capabilities of the company as well as the technical approach to be employed, and can utilize information provided by subcontractors and consultants. The technical volume is often considered to be the most important part of a proposal because it illustrates the contractor's understanding of the problem and the proposed methods of solution. This does not imply that the management and cost volume are unimportant. Successful proposals require that all three volumes complement one another in a logical fashion.

The technical volume should provide a complete analysis of the problem, including such items as a complete description of work required, specification identification, equipment to be utilized, and the detailed schedules. The proposal's technical content should discuss the base case approach as well as the alternatives considered. All assumptions should be clearly defined together with a good description of any technology requirements that may be beyond the current state-of-the-art. The base case, as well as the alternatives, should be designed to meet, rather than to exceed, the customer's requirements unless it can be shown that the additional effort is cost-justified.

Illustrations, charts, tables, sketches, and drawings should be used to explain how the desired results are to be accomplished. Proposals (especially follow-on types) are often awarded based upon the communication that takes place between the customer and contractor. Illustrations provide a vital link in the communication process.

The technical volume should also contain discussions on effectiveness. This includes technical effectiveness, cost effectiveness, and time/cost/performance trade-offs. This volume should also describe the mechanisms for tradeoffs to be implemented as well as the roles and relationships of the customer and contractor in the decision-making process.

For small proposals (and even some larger ones), the following would be a "bare minimum" outline for a technical volume:

- Introduction or overview
- Statement of the problem
- Technical discussion
- Program plan
- Description of facilities
- Exceptions, deviations, and assumptions
- Background or supplemental information.

For the remainder of this chapter, we refer to the technical *proposal,* rather than the technical *volume,* simply to concentrate on its organization and contents.

6.1 SCOPE OF WORK

As part of the technical proposal, the contractor must prepare a statement of the problem that verifies the company's understanding of the problem at hand. This statement of the problem includes such topics as the:

- Nature of the problem
- Background of the problem
- Details of the proposed solution
- Alternate solutions
- Solution approach selected (i.e., base case).

The first step, the nature of the problem, requires that the contractor have a complete understanding (or definition) of all the work necessary to complete the effort.

Effective planning and implementation of projects cannot be accomplished without a complete definition of the requirements. For projects internal to the organization, the project and proposal managers work with the project sponsor and user (whether they be executives, functional managers, or employees) in order for the work to be defined completely. For these types of in-house projects, the project manager may wear multiple hats as project manager, proposal manager, and project engineer on the same project.

For projects funded externally to the organization, the proposal manager (assisted by the project manager and possibly the contracts administrator) must work with the customer to make sure that all of the work is defined completely and that there is no misinterpretation of the requirements. In many cases, the customer simply has an idea and needs assistance in establishing the requirements. The customer may hire an outside agency for assistance. If the activity is sole-source or perhaps part of an unsolicited effort, then the contractor may be asked to work with the customer in defining the requirements even before soliciting is attempted.

A complete definition of project requirements must include:

- Scope (or statement) of work
- Specifications
- Schedules (gross or summary)
- Work breakdown structure.

The scope of work or statement of work (SOW) is a narrative description of all of the work required to perform the project. The statement of work identifies the goals and objectives that are to be achieved. If a funding constraint exists, such as "this is a not-to-exceed effort of $250,000," this information might also appear in the SOW.

If the customer supplies a well-written statement of work, then the project and proposal managers will supply this SOW to the functional managers for dollar and man-hour estimates. Unless the customer maintains a staff of employees to provide a continuous stream of requests for proposals/requests for quotations, (RFPs/RFQ's), the customers may ask potential bidders to assist them in the preparation of the SOW. As an example, Alpha Company wishes to build a multimillion dollar chemical plant. Because Alpha does not erect such facilities on a regular basis, Alpha Company would send out inquiries instead of a formal RFP. These inquiries are used not only to identify potential bidders, but also to identify to potential bidders that they have to develop an accurate SOW as part of the proposal process. This is quite common, especially on large dollar-value projects in which contractors are willing to risk the additional time, cost, and effort as part of the bidding process. If the proposal is a sole-source effort, then the contractor may pass this cost on to the customer as part of the contract.

The statement of work is vital to proposal pricing and should not be taken lightly. All functional managers involved should be given the opportunity to review the SOW during the pricing process. Functional managers are the true technical experts in the company and are best qualified to identify high-risk areas and prevent anything from "falling through the cracks." Misinterpretations of the statement of work can lead to severe cost overruns and schedule slippages.

The statement of work might be lumped together with the contractual data as the terms and conditions. The proposal manager may then have to separate the SOW data from the RFP data. This is vital for the pricing effort. As part of the technical proposal, it is recommended that the proposal and program managers include, in their own words, the major elements of the technical portion of the statement of work as part of the technical proposal. This is essential to make sure that nothing has "fallen through the cracks."

This reiterative process is essential because misinterpretation of the statement of work can cause severe cost overruns. As an example, consider the following two situations:

- Acme Corporation won a Navy contract in which the government RFP stated that "this unit must be tested in water." Acme built a large pool behind their manufacturing plant. Unfortunately, the Navy's interpretation was the Atlantic Ocean. The difference was $1 million.
- Ajax Corporation won a contract to ship sponges across the United States using aerated boxcars. The project manager leased boxcars that had doors on the top surface. The doors were left open during shipping. The train got caught in several days of torrential rainstorms and the boxcars eventually exploded, spreading sponges across the countryside. The customer wanted boxcars aerated from below.

The amount of money and time spent in rewording the technical data in the SOW of the technical proposal is minimal compared to cost of misinterpretation.

6.2 SPECIFICATIONS AND STANDARDS

The second major item in the definition of the requirements is the identification of the specifications, if applicable. Specifications form the basis from which man-hours, equipment, and materials are priced out. The specifications must be identified in the proposal, possibly in a format as shown in Table 6-1, so that the customer understands the basis for the man-hour,

Table 6-1. Specification for Statement of Work

DESCRIPTION	SPECIFICATION No.
Civil	100 (Index)
• Concrete	101
• Field equipment	102
• Piling	121
• Roofing and siding	122
• Soil testing	123
• Structural design	124
Electrical	200 (Index)
• Electrical testing	201
• Heat tracing	201
• Motors	209
• Power systems	225
• Switchgear	226
• Synchronous generators	227
HVAC	300 (Index)
• Hazardous environment	301
• Insulation	302
• Refrigeration piping	318
• Sheetmetal ductwork	319
Installation	400 (Index)
• Conveyors and chutes	401
• Fired heaters and boilers	402
• Heat exchangers	403
• Reactors	414
• Towers	415
• Vessels	416
Instruments	500 (Index)
• Alarm systems	501
• Control valves	502
• Flow instruments	503
• Level gages	536
• Pressure instruments	537
• Temperature instruments	538
Mechanical Equipment	600 (Index)
• Centrifugal pumps	601
• Compressors	602
• High-speed gears	603
• Material handling equipment	640
• Mechanical agitators	641
• Steam turbines	642

(continued)

Table 6-1. (cont.)

DESCRIPTION	SPECIFICATION No.
Piping	700 (Index)
• Expansion joints	701
• Field pressure testing	702
• Installation of piping	703
• Pipe fabrication specs	749
• Pipe supports	750
• Steam tracing	751
Project Administration	800 (Index)
• Design drawings	801
• Drafting standards	802
• General requirements	803
• Project coordination	841
• Reporting procedure	842
• Vendor data	843
Vessels	900 (Index)
• Fireproofing	901
• Painting	902
• Reinforced tanks	948
• Shell and tube heat exchangers	949
• Steam boilers	950
• Vessel linings	951

equipment, and materials estimates. Small changes in a specification can cause large cost overruns.

Another reason for identifying the specifications is to make sure that there are no surprises for the customer downstream. The specifications should be the most current revision. It is not uncommon for a customer to hire outside agencies to evaluate the technical proposal and to make sure that the proper specifications are being used.

Specifications are, in fact, standards for pricing out a proposal. If specifications either do not yet exist or are not necessary, then work standards should be included in the proposal. The work standards can also appear in the cost volume of the proposal. Labor justification back-up sheets may or may not be included in the proposal, depending upon RFP/RFQ requirements.

For R&D proposals, standards may not exist and the proposal team may have to use educated guesses based upon the estimated degree of difficulty, such as:[1]

- Task 02-15-10 is estimated to be 25% more difficult than a similar task accomplished on the Alpha Project which required 300 man-hours. Hours needed for Task 02-15-10 are therefore 375.

---

[1] Further explanations of this procedure appear in Chapter 8.

- Task 03–07–02 is estimated at 450 hours. This is 20% more than the standard because of the additional reporting constraints imposed by the customer.

The standards mentioned here are usually the technical standards only. The technical standards and specifications may be called out by the customer or, if this is a follow-on project, the customer will expect you to perform the work with the estimates on the previous activitiy. If the standards or specifications are different, then an explanation should appear in the proposal or else the customer may feel cheated. Customers have the tendency of expecting standards to be improved on follow-on because the employees are expected to be performing at an improved position on the learning curve.

The key parameter in explaining the differences is the time period between the original proposal and the follow-on or similar proposal. the two most common reasons for having standards change are:

- New technology requiring additional effort
- Key employees with the necessary skills or expertise either leaving the organization or being unavailable.

In either event, justifications of the changes or modifications must be made so that the customer understands the new ground rules.

6.3 GROSS SCHEDULING

The third item in the identification of the requirements is the gross schedule. In summary, the gross schedule identifies the major milestones of the project and includes items such as:

- Start date
- End date
- Other major activities
- Data items and reports.

If possible, all gross schedules should contain calendar start and end dates. Unfortunately, some projects do not have definable start and end dates and are simply identified by a time spread. Another common situation is where the end date is fixed and the proposal must identify the start date. This is a common occurrence because the customer may not have the expertise to determine accurately how long it takes to accomplish the effort.

Identifying major milestones can also be a tedious task for a customer. Major milestones include such activities as long-lead procurement, prototype testing, design review meetings, and any other critical decision points. The proposal manager must work closely with the customer or in-house sponsor to either verify the major milestones in the RFP or to identify additional milestones.

Major milestones are often grossly unrealistic. In-house executives of the customer and contractor occasionally identify unrealistic end dates either because resources will be idle without the completion at this point in time, not enough money is available for a longer project, or management wants the effort completed earlier because it affects management's Christmas bonus.

All data items should be identified on the gross schedule. Data items include written, contractual reports and can be extended to include hand-out material for customer design review meetings and technical interchange meetings. Data items are not free and should be priced out accordingly. There is nothing wrong with including in the proposal a separate contingency fund for "unscheduled or additional" interchange meetings.

6.4 REQUIREMENTS AND BACKGROUND ON PROJECT

The proposal and project managers must now determine how much information their company has in the way of experience on this type of project. If this is a new R&D effort, have we done anything like this before? Do we have employees with the necessary expertise? If not, are there people available for hiring with this level of expertise? How much time is available to find these people? Are consultants available?

This step is merely an assessment of the company's competitive posture with regard to its technology base, knowledge, and state-of-the-art expertise. This step can also include assessing gross risks in meeting the customer's schedules and major milestones. It is better to assess these risks early with an analysis of the project requirements rather than waste the company's bid and proposal dollars just to be considered nonresponsive.

This step often leads to the bid or no-bid decision. If the company does not have the necessary expertise, then the company may wish to submit a "token" bid just to keep its name on the bidder's list. There is also the possiblity that the company has the expertise but cannot compete effectively with one or two of the other competitors and therefore does not wish to assume the cost burden of preparing a formal proposal.

6.5 TECHNICAL APPROACH SELECTED

Once a decision is reached either to undertake the project or to prepare a proposal, the base-case technical approach must be selected. Two questions must be answered:

- How should we organize to get the job accomplished?
- What kind of life-cycle phases should be considered?

Answering these questions and determining the best technical approach are not easy tasks. Time, cost, and performance trade-offs must be considered. Should we go with our low-risk, present state-of-the-art technology where we have expertise or should we contemplate a high-risk, advanced state-of-the-art program? Should we make the entire product or buy components from elsewhere (i.e., the make-or-buy decision)? Should we hire outside subcontractors? If so, how much work should be subcontracted out and what role does the customer or management sponsor play in subcontractor selection?

Once the work and technical organization are defined, all major and minor activities should be categorized into clear, meaningful life-cycle phases. Every program and project has certain phases in development. A clear understanding of these phases permits both customer and contractor managers and executives to control and understand the required resources needed to achieve the desired goals. These phases of development are known as *life-cycle phases*.

The breakdown of these life-cycle phases varies from company to company and even project to project. There is no agreement among industries about the various life-cycle phases. This is understandable because of the complex nature and diversity of projects. Table 6–2 shows the life-cycle phases for a variety of industries.

To illustrate the work that may be categorized in each life-cycle phase, consider a project that is structured as:

- Feasibility phase
- Planning phase

Table 6-2. Life-Cycle Phase Definitions

ENGINEERING	MANUFACTURING	CONSTRUCTION	COMPUTER PROGRAMMING
• Start-up • Definition • Main • Termination	• Formation • Build-up • Production • Phase-out • Final audit	• Planning, data gathering, and procedures • Studies and basic engineering • Major review • Detail engineering • Detail engineering/ construction overlap • Construction • Testing and commissioning	• Conceptual • Planning • Definition and design • Implementation • Conversion

- Start-up phase
- Main phase
- Termination.

The feasibility phase, just as the title implies, includes the feasibility study and a cost/benefit analysis. Most important in this phase is the preliminary analysis of the risks and the resulting impact on time, cost, and performance, together with the impact on corporate resources.

The feasibility phase is used predominantly for in-house projects but can be used for external projects. As an example, a customer wishes to build a manufacturing plant but does not have a good grasp on the cost or time. In this case, the customer might be willing to pay $200,000 to $300,000 for a feasibility study rather than to authorize several million dollars and then see a large cost overrun. The customer has the right to cancel the project based upon the results of the feasibility study.

The second phase, planning, involves the development of detailed plans in order to develop costs and a detailed program plan. Figure 6–1 shows the steps in the planning process. The planning phase can also include the development of the formal statement of work, if not customer-supplied.

In the third phase, start-up, the project manager negotiates with functional managers and begins bringing resources onboard the project. The project team also begins formatting data items in accordance with customer requirements. In the main phase, the bulk of the work is generally accomplished, and in the termination phase, work is being completed, hopefully within contractual requirements.

Proposals should describe detailed planning for termination as well as start-up. Termination planning should include items such as:

- Disposition of materials
- Review of contract requirements/data items
- Closing out work orders
- Disposition of personnel
- Review customer/contractor financial payment plans.

Poor termination planning can lead to severe cost overruns. Good proposals describe project termination procedures.

Figure 6–2 shows how total resources can be identified per life-cycle phase. The peak could shift to the left or right. Figure 6–2 represents the life-cycle phases for a computer project where PMO represents the *present method of operations* and PMO′ is the new present method of operations.

Figure 6–2 illustrates two key points. First, by structuring the project into life-cycle phases, the project can be easily cancelled at the completion of any

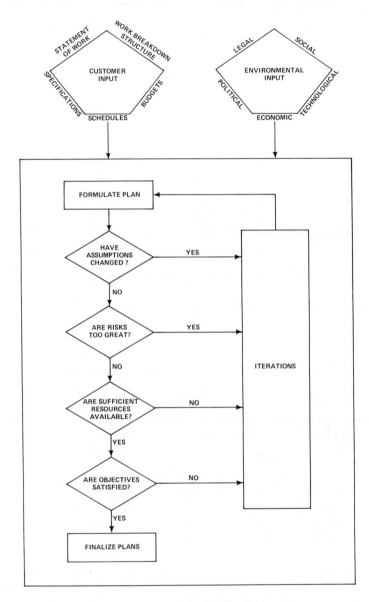

Figure 6–1. Iterations for the planning process.

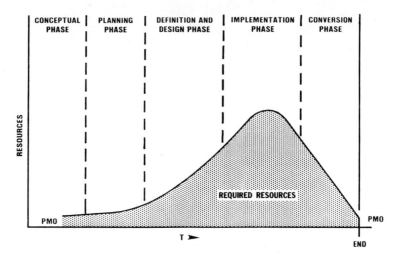

Figure 6–2. Definition of a project life cycle.

phase if performance or costs have not been satisfactory. Second, top-level management involvement can be identified more easily. For example, top executives are involved actively in the planning and conceptual stages, but take on a more passive role during the other phases. Thus, the life cycles can be used as the framework for internal and external communications and reporting procedures.

The life-cycle phases form the basis for the proposed technical approach and, therefore, for the technical discussion in the technical approach section of the proposal. The technical discussion includes:

- Description of solution
- How solution satisfies the problem
- How solution fits into the existing environment
- Detailed characteristics
- Problems to overcome
- Alternatives considered.

The objective of the technical approach section is to state briefly, concisely, and exactly what is being proposed. The life-cycle approach provides a well-structured means of identifying that all of the requirements are being met, as well as the proposed solution to any anticipated problems. The following questions must be answered as part of the discussion:

- What will be the capabilities of the end product?
- What will be the limitations of the end product?

- What potential problems will be encountered during development and what steps will be taken to overcome them?
- How will the item function in the operational environment?
- If applicable, how well will the item interface with other interrelated items?

The technical approach section must demonstrate your company's knowledge and understanding of the problem. This includes state-of-the-art information as well as the company's sponsorship of any type of related work. The technical approach section should demonstrate clearly that you have considered all reasonable alternatives. There are several benefits from showing the alternatives considered. First, it demonstrates vividly your clear understanding and appreciation for the problem. Second, it provides the customer with the option of considering one of the alternatives. And third, it provides you with the opportunity to discuss the disadvantages of your alternatives, which may just be your competition's base case choice.

6.6 WORK BREAKDOWN STRUCTURE

The successful accomplishment of both contract and corporate objectives requires a plan that defines all of the effort to be expended, assigns responsibility to a specially identified organizational element, and establishes schedules and budgets for the accomplishment of the work. The preparation of this plan is the responsibility of the program manager who is assisted by the program team (and proposal manager) assigned in accordance with program management system directives. Detailed planning is also established in accordance with company budgeting policy before contractual efforts are initiated.

The *work breakdown structure* (WBS) is the single most important element because it provides a common framework from which:

- The total program can be described as a summation of subdivided elements.
- Planning can be performed.
- Costs and budgets can be established.
- Time, cost, and performance can be tracked.
- Objectives can be linked to company resources in a logical manner.
- Schedules and status reporting procedures can be established.
- Network construction and control planning can be initiated.
- The responsibility assignments for each element can be established.

The work breakdown structure acts as a vehicle for breaking the work down into smaller elements, thus providing a greater probability that every major and minor activity is taken into account. Although a variety of work breakdown structures exist, the most common is the five-level indentured structure shown below:

Level	Description
1	Total Program
2	Project
3	Task
4	Subtask
5	Work Package

Level 1 is the total program and is composed of a set of projects. The summation of the activities and costs associated with each project must equal the total program. On the other hand, each project can be broken down into tasks, where the summation of all tasks must equal the summation of all projects which, in turn, must comprise the total program. The reason for this subdivision of effort is simple: projects are subdivided for control. Program management therefore becomes synonymous with the integration of activities in which the project manager acts as the integrator using the work breakdown structure as the common framework.

The upper three levels of the WBS are normally specified by the customer (if part of an RFP/RFQ) as the summary levels for reporting purposes. The lower levels are generated by the contractor for in-house control. Each level serves a vital purpose: level 1 is generally used for the authorization and release of all work; budgets are prepared at level 2; and schedules are prepared at level 3. Certain characteristics can now be generalized for these levels:

- The top three levels of the WBS reflect integrated efforts and should not be related to one specific department. Effort required by departments or sections should be defined in subtasks and work packages.
- The summation of all elements in one level must be the sum of all work in the next lower level.
- Each element of work should be assigned to one and only one level of effort. For example, the construction of the foundation of a house should be included in one project (or task), not extended over two or three.
- The WBS must be accompanied by a description of the scope of effort required or else only those individuals who issue the WBS will have a complete understanding of what work has to be accomplished. It is common practice to reproduce the customer's statement of work as the description for the WBS.
- Each lowest element of the WBS must have a clearly definable start and end date. Figure 6–3 and 6–4 show this. Note that a separate detailed schedule exists for each element of the WBS.

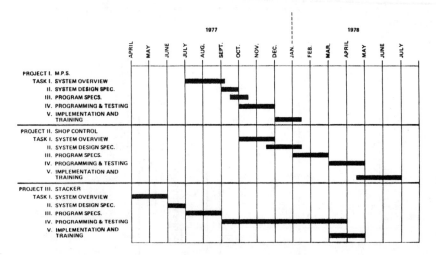

Figure 6-3. Work breakdown structure.

- Each element must be able to be used as a communicative tool by which you can communicate the results and progress that are expected.
- Each element should be estimated on a "total" time duration, not necessarily when each element must start or end.
- The total WBS should be structured so that a minimum of project office control and documentation (i.e., forms) are necessary.
- All elements must be manageable to a degree that specific authority and responsibility can be assigned.
- Whenever possible, the work should be structured into small elements that are independent or that require minimum interfacing and dependence on other ongoing elements.

Table 6-3 shows a simple work breakdown structure with the associated numbering system. The numbering system follows the work breakdown structure: the first number represents the total program (in this case, it is represented by 01); the second number represents the project, and the third number identifies the task. Therefore, number 01-03-00 represents project 3 of program 01 while 01-03-02 represents task 2 of project 3. This type of numbering system is not unique: each company may have its own system depending on how costs are to be controlled.

The preparation of the work breakdown structure is not easy. Because the WBS is a communications tool, it must provide detailed information to different levels of management. If the WBS does not contain enough levels, then the integration of activities may prove difficult. If too many levels exist, then

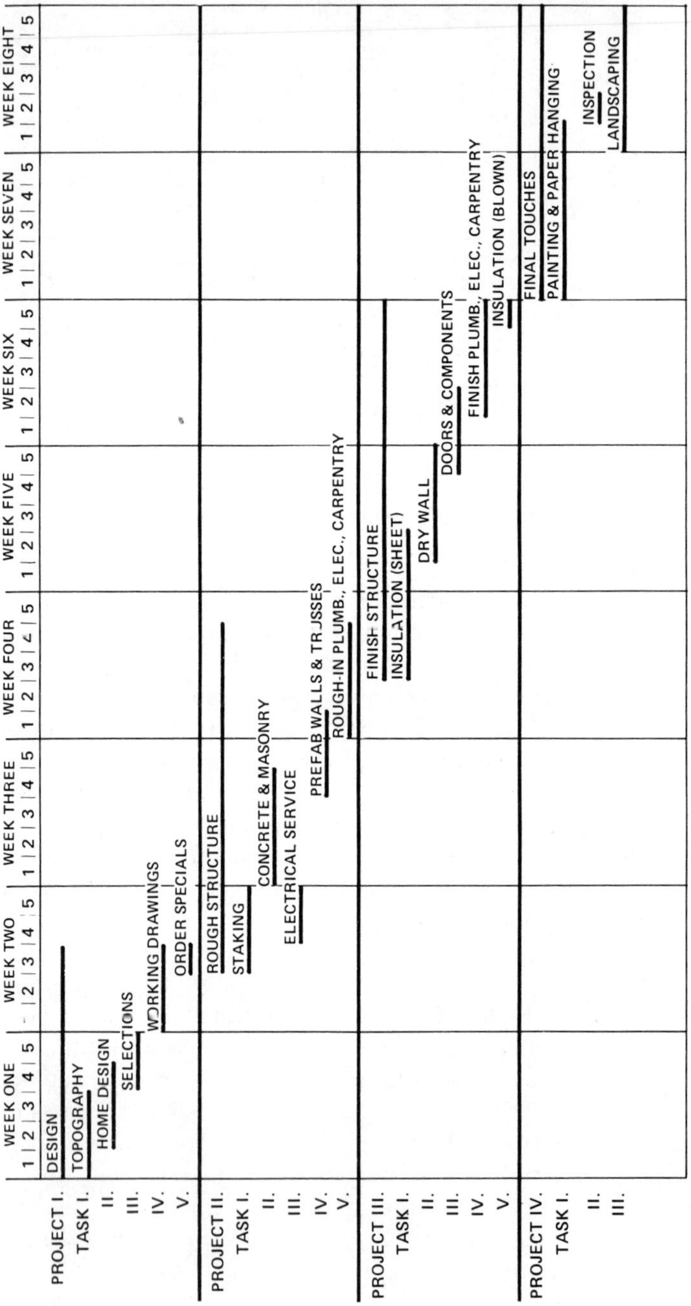

Figure 6–4. Gantt chart for the work breakdown structure.

Table 6-3. Work breakdown structure for new plant construction and start-up

Program: New Plant Construction and Start-up	01-00-00
Project 1: Analytical Study	01-01-00
Task 1: Marketing/Production Study	01-01-01
Task 2: Cost Effectiveness Analysis	01-01-02
Project 2: Design and Layout	01-02-00
Task 1: Product Processing Sketches	01-02-01
Task 2: Product Processing Blueprints	01-02-02
Project 3: Installation	01-03-00
Task 1: Fabrication	01-03-01
Task 2: Set-up	01-03-02
Task 3: Testing and Run	01-03-03
Project 4: Program Support	01-04-00
Task 1: Management	01-04-01
Task 2: Purchasing Raw Materials	01-04-02

unproductive time will be incurred, followed by additional cost and paper-work. No attempt should be made to have the same number of levels for all projects, tasks, and so on. Each major work element should be considered by itself. Remember, the work breakdown structure establishes the number of required networks for cost control.

For many programs, the work breakdown structure is established by the customer. If the contractor is required to develop a WBS, then certain guidelines must be considered: A partial list is identified below:

- The complexity and technical requirements of the program (i.e., the statement of work)
- The program cost
- The time span of the program
- The contractor's resource requirements
- The contractor's and customer's internal structure for management control and reporting
- The number of subcontracts.

Applying these guidelines serves only to identify the complexity of the program. This complexity of information must then be subdivided and released together with detailed information, to the different levels of the organization. The WBS should follow a specified criterion, because, although preparation of the WBS is performed by the program office, the actual work is performed by the doers, not the planners. Both the doers and the planners must be in agreement as to what is expected. A sample criteria listing for developing a work breakdown structure is shown below:

- The WBS and work description should not be difficult to understand.
- All schedules should follow the WBS.
- No attempt should be made to subdivide work arbitrarily to the lowest possible level. The lowest level of work should not end up being a ridiculous cost in comparison to other efforts.
- Because scope of effort can change during a program, every effort should be made to maintain flexibility in the WBS.

From a cost control point of view, cost analysis down to the fifth level is advantageous. However, it should be noted that the cost required to prepare cost analysis data to each lower level may increase exponentially, especially if the customer requires data to be presented in a specified format that is not part of the company's standard operating procedure. The level-five work packages are normally for in-house control only.

The WBS can be subdivided into subobjectives with finer divisions of effort as we go lower into the WBS. By defining subobjectives, we add greater understanding and clarity of action for those individuals who are required to complete the objectives. Whenever work is structured, understood, easily identifiable, and within the capabilities of the individuals, then there will almost always exist a high degree of confidence that the objective can be reached.

Work breakdown structures can be used to structure work for reaching such objectives as lowering costs, reducing absenteeism, improving morale, and lowering scrap factors. The lowest subdivision now becomes an end item or subobjective, not necessarily a work package as we have described it here. However, because we are describing project management, for the remainder of the text we consider the *work package* as the lowest level.

Each work package has discrete, scheduled start and completion points. The responsibility for the work to be accomplished is assigned to a single organization unit. All work packages are identified uniquely so that all resources budgeted can be traced to one and only one organizational unit.

Work packages are identified in dollars, hours, or other measurable units, which have assigned values or budgets and reflect the contractor's estimate of the total cost to be incurred for that unit of work. The sum of the work package budgets is published in both dollars and hours. Once a work package is initiated, the assigned budget and schedule must not be changed because they form the baseline against which actual work accomplishment and expenditures are compared for performance measurement purposes. The sum of these budgets plus management reserve must always equal the total contract target cost, plus the estimate for authorized, but not yet negotiated work.

Each month after contract award, the budgets for all work scheduled to have been completed, and the value for the work actually accomplished, are compared to determine schedule variances. A comparison of actual costs to date with the value planned for the work accomplished provides the contractor with a cost variance—either an overrun or an underrun. Cost and schedule variances in labor and materials are tabulated for comparison purposes. By summarizing all data elements up through the work breakdown structure, overall contract performance can be evaluated with respect to cost and schedule. Technical performance can also be assessed and related to cost and schedule. By summarizing through the organizational structure, performance of functional organizations can be evaluated.

One of the most important functions of the work breakdown structure is to provide a disciplined framework from which actual network plans can be prepared. The definition provided by the work breakdown structure builds this framework by providing a basic list of the networks required to fulfill contractual requirements, a description of the items needed in each of the networks (needed to select the work packages), and a composite picture of the basic milestone and interface events. Milestones are specific events related directly to certain points in time against which dollar or performance tracking is accomplished. Typical milestones might be the completion of a finished product, the testing of a piece of equipment, or the purchase of an item. Interface events occur between milestones, usually requiring a change in responsibility. Typical interface events might require the contractor to obtain customer approval on blueprints or designs, obtain authorization for procurement funds, or determine facility availability.

Careful consideration must be given to the design and development of the work breakdown structure. From Figure 6–5, the work breakdown structure through work packages, provides the basis for:

- The responsibility matrix
- Network scheduling
- Costing
- Risk analysis
- Organizational structure
- Objective coordination
- Control (including contract administration).

Once the WBS is established and the program is "kicked off," it becomes a very costly procedure to either add or delete activities, or change levels of reporting because of cost control. Many companies do not give careful forethought to the importance of a properly developed WBS and ultimately risk cost control problems downstream. One important use of the WBS is that it serves as a cost control standard for any future activities that may follow on or just may be similar. One common mistake made by management is combin-

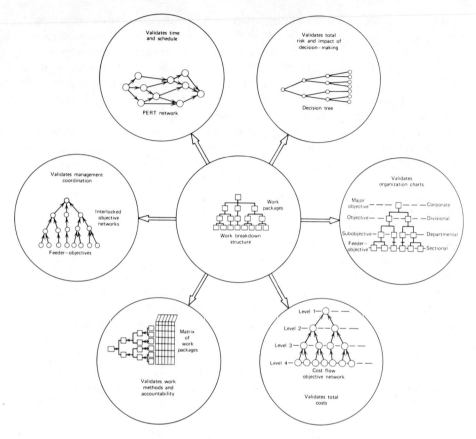

Figure 6-5. Work breakdown structure for objective control and evaluation. (*Source:* Mali, Paul, *Managing By Objectives,* John Wiley and Sons, 1972, p. 163)

ing direct support activities with administrative activities. For example, the department manager for manufacturing engineering may be required to provide administrative support (possibly by attending team meetings) throughout the duration of the program. By spreading the administrative support over each of the projects, a false picture of the actual hours needed to accomplish each project in the program is obtained. If one of the projects should be cancelled, then the support man-hours for the total program will be reduced, when in fact the administrative and support functions may be constant, regardless of the number of projects and tasks.

Quite often, work breakdown structures accompanying customer RFPs contain much more scope of effort as specified by the statement of work (SOW) than there exists funding. This is done intentionally by the customer in hopes that a contractor may be willing to "buy in." If the contractor's price exceeds the customer's funding limitations, then the scope of effort must be reduced by eliminating activities from the WBS. By developing a separate project for administrative and indirect support activities, the customer can modify costs easily by eliminating the direct support activities of the cancelled effort.

Before proceeding, there should be a brief discussion concerning the usefulness and applicability of a WBS system. There are many companies and industries that have been successful in managing programs without the use of work breakdown structures, especially on repetitive kinds of programs. However, even as you read this text, more and more companies are entering in diversified project areas where some fundamentally common basis is needed for organizational synergy. The development of the WBS system fulfills this need.

As a final note, proposal managers must exercise extreme caution in how to include management support as part of the WBS. It is highly recommended that all management support, which includes project office personnel, functional team meeting time, and so on, be included in one WBS element, not spread over several. Management support is time-dependent, not necessarily quantity-dependent. Occasionally, customers provide the WBS for proposal comparison. It is not uncommon for customers to include WBS elements for which they know that sufficient funding is not available. In this case, the customer hopes that some contractors will buy in. If no contractor buys in, then the customer will delete these activities from the project. If the contractor makes the mistake of spreading all management support arbitrarily over the entire WBS, then the cancellation of just one WBS element will cause the contractor to lose management support hours that are necessary for other elements.

6.7 DETAILED SCHEDULING

One of the most important functions of the proposal manager is to develop *detailed schedules*. The purpose of detailed scheduling is to identify to the customer that the contractor has thoroughly thought out all of the work necessary to accomplish the objectives. Unless the activity is part of sole source procurement or an in-house project, the detail schedules are based upon unlimited resources because

- The start and/or end date may as yet be undefined
- Facility/equipment requirements are not defined
- Human resources may not be available at the date required
- The contractor may not win the contract, thus adding to the degree of uncertainty.

As part of the proposal effort, the proposal manager must identify to the customer the methods by which schedules will be updated. Depending on program size and contractual requirements, it is not unusual for the program office to maintain, at all times, a program staff member whose responsibility is that of a scheduler. This individual develops and updates activity schedules constantly to provide a means of tracing program work. The resulting information is then provided to the program office personnel, functional management, and team members and, last but not least, presented to the customer.

Activity scheduling is probably the single most important tool for determining how company resources should be integrated so that synergy is produced. Activity schedules are invaluable for projecting time-phased resource utilization requirements as well as providing a visual basis for tracking performance. Most programs begin with the development of the schedules in order that accurate cost estimates can be made. The schedules serve as master plans for which both the customer and management have an up-to-date picture of operations.

Certain guidelines should be followed in the preparation of schedules, regardless of the projected use or complexity:

- All major events and dates must be identified clearly. If a statement of work is supplied by the customer, then those dates shown on the accompanying schedules must be included. If for any reason the customer's milestone dates cannot be met, then the customer should be notified.
- The exact sequence of work should be defined through a network in which interrelationships between events can be identified.
- Schedules should be directly relatable to the work breakdown structure. If the WBS is developed according to a specific sequence of work, then it becomes an easy task to identify work sequences in schedules using the same numbering system as in the WBS. The minimum requirement should be to show where each task starts and finishes, and when all tasks start and finish.
- All schedules must identify the time constraints and, if possible, should identify those resources required for each event.

Although these four guidelines serve as reference for schedule preparation, they do not define how complex schedules should be. Before preparing the schedules, three questions should be considered:

- How many events or activities should each network have?
- How much of a detailed technical breakdown should be included?
- Who is my intended audience for this schedule?

Most organizations develop multiple schedules: summary schedules for management and planners, and detailed schedules for the doers and lower-level control. The detailed schedules may be strictly for interdepartmental activities. Program management must approve all schedules down through the first three levels of the work breakdown structure. For higher-level schedules, i.e., detailed interdepartmental schedule, program management may or may not request sign of approval.

The necessity for two schedules is clear. According to Martin;[2]

In larger complicated projects, planning and status review by different echelons are facilitated by the use of detailed and summary networks. Higher levels of management can view the entire project and the interrelationships of major tasks without looking into the detail of the individual subtasks. Lower levels of management and supervision can examine their parts of the project in fine detail without being distracted by those parts of the project with which they have no interface.

One of the most difficult problems to identify in schedules is a *hedge position*. A hedge position is a situation in which the contractor may not be able to meet a customer's milestone date without incurring a risk, or may not be able to meet activity requirements following a milestone date because of contractual requirements. To illustrate a common hedge position, consider Example 6-1 below:

Example 6-1: Hedge Position

Condor Corporation is currently working on a project that includes three phases: design, development, and qualification of a certain component. Contractual requirements with the customer specify that no components will be fabricated for the development phase until the design review meeting is held following the design phase. Condor has determined that if they do not begin component fabrication prior to the design review meeting, then the second and third phase will slip to the right. If Condor is willing to accept the risk that the specifications are not acceptable during the design review meeting, then Condor will incur the costs associated with preauthorization of fabrication. How should this be shown on a schedule? (The problems associated with performing unauthorized work are not considered here.)

The solution to Example 6-1 is not an easy one. Condor must play an honest game and identify on the Master Production Schedule that component

---

[2] Charles Martin, *Project Management: How to Make it Work*. New York: AMACOM, a division of American Management Associations, 1976, p. 137.

fabrication will begin early, at the contractor's risk. This should be followed by a contractual letter in which both the customer and contractor understand the risks and implications.

Example 6-1 also brings up the question as to whether this hedge position could have been eliminated with proper planning. Hedge positions are notorious for occurring in research and development or design phases of a program. Condor's technical community, for example, may have anticipated that each component could be fabricated in one week based on certain raw materials. If new raw materials were required or a new fabrication process had to be developed, then it is possible that the new component fabrication time could increase from one week to two or three, thus creating an unanticipated hedge position.

Detailed schedules are prepared for almost every activity. It is the responsibility of the program office to marry all of the detailed schedules into one master schedule to verify that all activities can be completed as planned. The preparation sequence for schedules (and also for program plans) is shown in Figure 6-6. The program office submits a request for detailed schedules to the functional managers. The request may be in the form of a planning work authorization document. The functional managers then prepare summary schedules, detailed schedules, and if time permits, interdepartmental schedules. Each functional manager then reviews the schedules with the program office. The program office, together with the functional program team members, integrate all of the plans and schedules and verify that all contractual dates can be met.

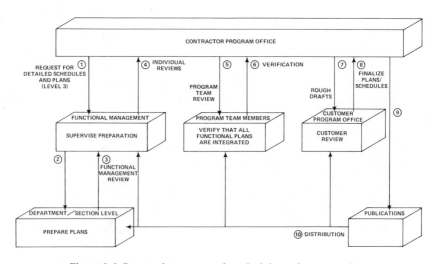

Figure 6-6. Preparation sequence for schedules and program plans.

Before submitting the schedules to publications, rough drafts of each schedule and plan should be reviewed with the customer. This procedure accomplishes the following:

- Verifies that nothing has "fallen through the cracks"
- Prevents immediate revisions to a published document and can prevent embarrassing moments.
- Minimizes production costs by reducing the number of early revisions.
- Shows the customer, early in the program, that you welcome his help and input into the planning phase.

After the document is published, it should be distributed to all program office personnel, functional team members, functional management, and the customer.

The exact method of preparing the schedules is usually up to the individual performing the activity. All schedules, however, must be approved by the program office. Normally the schedules are prepared in a manner that is suitable to both the customer and contractor. If the schedules are prepared in such a manner as to be easily understood by all, then the schedules may be used both in-house as well as for customer review meetings, in which case the contractor can "kill two birds with one stone" by tracking cost and performance on the original schedules.

In addition to the detailed schedules, the program office, with input provided by functional management, must develop organizational charts. The organizational charts provide information to all active participants of the project as to who has responsibility for each activity. The organizational charts display the formal (and often informal) lines of communication.

The program office may also establish linear responsibility charts (LRCs). Regardless of the best attempts by management, many functions in an organization can overlap between more than one functional unit. Also, management might wish to have the responsibility for a certain activity given to a functional unit that normally would not have this responsibility. This is a common occurrence on shortterm programs where management desires to cut costs and red tape.

Detailed scheduling should also make some mention of PERT/CPM techniques, if applicable.[3] The prime advantage of PERT/CPM is that it shows the customer that the contractor has looked at all of the activities of the pro-

---

[3] A description of PERT/CPM techniques can be found in any text on operations research or production management.

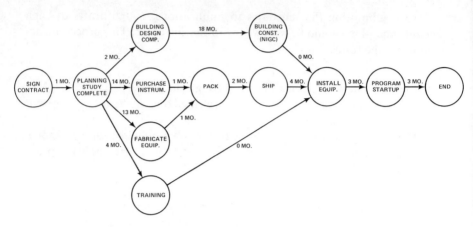

Figure 6–7. Critical path method.

ject, as well as their interrelationship. Figure 6–7 shows a simple PERT network. PERT networks also provide the basis for pricing out the work, as shown in Figure 6–8. In general, the PERT/CPM network identifies to the customer that the contractor has the following:

- Ability to plan for the best use of resources to achieve a given goal within time and cost limitations
- Ability to control one-of-a-kind projects as opposed to repetitive situations
- Ability to handle uncertainties involved in programs by answering such questions as to how time delays in certain elements influence project completion, where slack time exists between elements, and what elements are crucial to meet the completion date. This provides management with a valuable tool for evaluating alternatives
- Good basis for obtaining the necessary facts for decision making
- Time network analysis method that can be used as the basis for determining manpower, material, and capital requirements as well as providing a means for checking progress.
- Basic structure for reporting information

Figure 6–9 shows the importance of PERT/CPM to the total planning process. Although PERT/CPM does not necessarily permit easy rescheduling of resources, it does show the customer your ability to analyze the total problem. These types of PERT/CPM charts can be drawn at level 2 or level 3 of the work breakdown structure and do not have to be loaded with details.

Figure 6–8. Program bar chart.

Column headings: First 12 month columns are **1977** (JAN–DEC); the remaining columns (JAN–SEPT) are **1978**.

PROJECTS / TASKS	JAN	FEB	MAR	APR	MAY	JUNE	JULY	AUG	SEPT	OCT	NOV	DEC	JAN	FEB	MAR	APR	MAY	JUNE	JULY	AUG	SEPT
I. PROGRAM PLANS & BUILDING DESIGN																					
1. PROGRAM MANAGEMENT	102	50	48																		
2. ENGINEERING	20	174	283																		
II. EQUIPMENT PURCHASE																					
1. PROGRAM MANAGEMENT		52	40	40	30	30	30	30	30	30	20	20	20	20	20						
2. ENGINEERING		267	232	200	165	131	95	60	40												
3. TESTING & INSPECTION								154	154	266	266	266	154	112							
4. SHIPPING												154	154	308	308						
5. PROCUREMENT				154	154	154	154	77	77												
III. EQUIPMENT CONSTRUCTION																					
1. PROGRAM MANAGEMENT			20	20	30	30	30	30	30	30	20	20	20	20							
2. ENGINEERING			154	154	154	154	154	154	154	308	308	308	308	308	154						
3. PROCUREMENT				308	308	308	308	308	308	308	77										
4. SHIPPING												47	100	154							
5. FABRICATION				154	308	462	616	770	924	1078	1386	1848	1848	1848	154						
IV. TRAINING																					
1. PROGRAM MANAGEMENT											20	20	20	20							
2. ENGINEERING											60	60	60	60							
3. TRAINING											154	154	154	154							
V. PLANT START-UP																					
1. PROGRAM MANAGEMENT														5	5	5	5	5	5	20	
2. FIELD ENGINEERING														154	154	308	154	154	154	154	

II. OTHER COSTS:

PURCHASED GOODS:	$121,981.
FREIGHT:	1,988.
OTHER:	3,049.
OVERSEAS PACKING:	6,242.
	$133,260.

III. OTHER COSTS:

PURCHASED MAT'LS:	39,527.
SUBCONTRACTS:	28,082.
OVERSEAS PACKING:	3,520.
FREIGHT:	2,598.
	$ 73,727.

IV. OTHER COSTS:

SUPPLIES:	$ 980.

	RATE	OH	
PROGRAM MANAGEMENT	11.00	120%	
ENGINEERING	10.00	120%	
TESTING	8.00	117%	⎱ 125%
PROCUREMENT	8.00	110%	
SHIPPING	5.70	100%	
FABRICATION	10.00	125%	
TRAINING	10.50	120%	⎱ 12%
FIELD ENGINEERING	9.00	80%	

INDIRECT COSTS	14%
CORPORATE COSTS	1%
PROFIT:	12%

RAW MATERIALS ESCALATION	10%
DEMANNING RATIO	10%
TERMINATION LIABILITY	0%
SALARY INCREASES	6%

NOTE: ONE MAN MONTH = 154 MAN HOURS

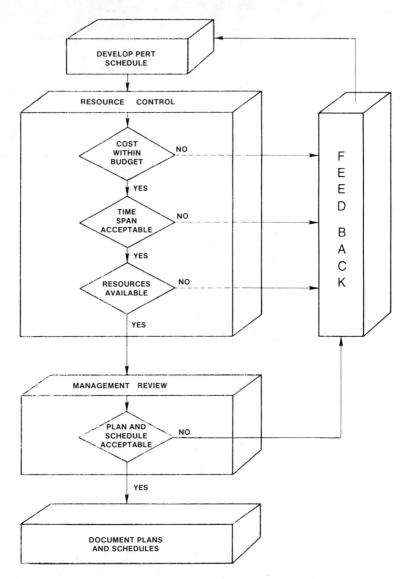

Figure 6–9. Iteration process for PERT schedule development.

6.8 PROGRAM PLANS

Fundamental to the success of any project is documented planning in the form of a *program plan*. In an ideal situation, the program office can present the functional manager with a copy of the program plan and simply say: "Execute it." The concept of the program plan came under severe scrutiny during the 1960s when the Department of Defense required all contractors to submit detailed planning. This requirement went to such extremes that many organizations were wasting talented people by having them serve as writers instead of doers. Since then, because of the complexity of large programs, program plan requirements have been eased.

For large and often complex programs, customers may require a program plan that documents all activities within the program. The program plan then serves as a guideline for the lifetime of the program and may be revised as often as once a month, depending upon the circumstances and the type of program. (i.e., research and development programs require more revisions to the program plan than manufacturing or construction programs.) The program plan provides the following framework:

- Eliminates conflicts between functional managers
- Eliminates conflicts between functional management and program management
- Provides a standard communicative tool throughout the lifetime of the program (should be geared to the work breakdown structure)
- Provides verification that the contractor understands the customer's objectives and requirements
- Provides a means for identifying inconsistencies in the planning phase
- Provides a means for early identification of problem areas and risks so that no "surprises occur downstream."
- Contains all of the schedules defined in Section 8.6 as a basis for progress analysis and reporting.

Development of a program plan can be time-consuming and costly. The input requirements for the program plan depend on the size of the project and the integration of resources and activities. All levels of the organization participate. The upper levels provide summary information and the lower levels provide the details. The program plan, as with activity schedules, does not preclude departments from developing their own planning.

The program plan must identify how the company resources are to be integrated. Finalization of the program is an iterative process similar to the sequence of events for schedule preparation, as shown in Figure 6–10. The ultimate objective of Figure 6–10 is to develop a detailed project plan that both the customer and contractor can look at during any time period and predict the activities that will be taking place. Obviously, the entire process is iterative. For example, if sufficient resources are not available when needed, the entire process of Figure 6–10 may have to be accomplished again. It is not uncommon to go through 10 to 20 iterations in the planning process just to develop the alternatives and the optimal base case program plan.

The program plan is a standard from which performance can be measured,

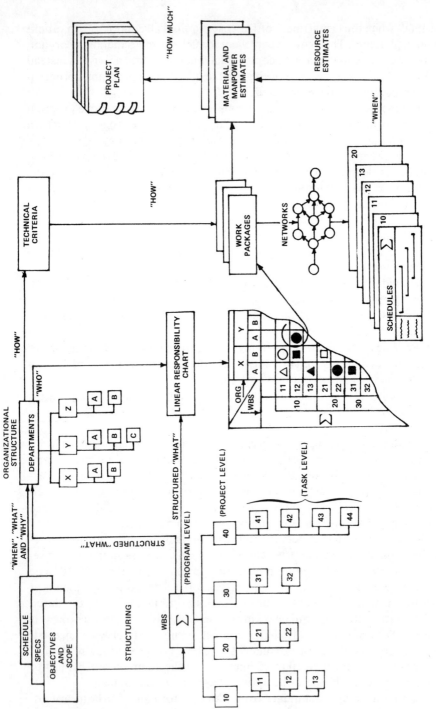

Figure 6-10. Project planning.

not only by the customer, but by program and functional management as well. The plan serves as a cookbook for the duration of the program by defining for all personnel identified with the program:

- What will be accomplished
- How it will be accomplished
- Where it will be accomplished
- When it will be accomplished
- Why it will be accomplished

These definitions force both the contractor and the customer to take a hard look at:

- Program requirements
- Program management
- Program schedules
- Facility requirements
- Logistic support
- Financial support
- Manpower and organization.

The program plan is more than just a set of instructions. It is an attempt to eliminate crisis by preventing anything from "falling through the cracks." The plan is documented and approved by both the customer and the contractor to determine what data, if any, are missing, and the probable resulting effect. As the program matures, the program plan is revised to account for new or missing data. The most common reasons for revising a plan are:

- "Crashing" activities to meet end dates
- Trade-off decisions involving manpower, scheduling, and performance
- Adjusting and leveling manpower requests.

Maturity of a program usually implies that the number of crises decreases. Unfortunately, this is not always the case.

The make-up of the program plan may vary from contractor to contractor.[4] Most program plans can be subdivided into four main sections: introduction, summary and conclusion, management, and technical. The com-

---

[4]Cleland and King define 14 subsections for a program plan. The detail appears more applicable to the technical and management volumes of a proposal. They do, however, provide a more detailed picture than presented here. See Cleland and King, *Systems Analysis and Project Management,* New York: McGraw-Hill, 1975, pp. 371–380.

plexity of the information is usually up to the description of the contractor provided that customer requirements, as may be specified in the statement of work, are satisfied.

The introductory section contains the definition of the program and the major parts involved. If the program is a follow-on to another program, or an outgrowth of similar activities, this also is identified together with a brief summary of the background and history behind the project.

The summary and conclusion section identifies the target and objectives of the program and includes the necessary "lip service" as to how successful the program will be and how all problems can be overcome. This section must also include the program master schedule showing how all projects and activities are tied together. The total program master schedule should include the following:

- An appropriate scheduling system (bar charts, milestone charts, network, and so on)
- A listing of activities at the project level or lower
- The possible interrelationships between activities, accomplished by logic networks, critical path networks, or PERT networks.
- Activity time estimates (a natural fallout from the item above).

The summary and conclusion is usually the second section in the program plan so that upper-level customer management can have a complete overview of the program without having to search through the technical information.

The management section of the program plan contains procedures, charts, and schedules for the following:

- *Assignment of key personnel to the program.* This usually calls out only the program office personnel and team members because, under normal operations, these are the only individuals interfacing with customer.
- *Manpower, planning, and training.* This is discussed so as to assure the customer that qualified people will be available from the functional units.
- *Linear responsibility charts.* These might also be included to identify to the customer the authority relationships that exist in the program.

There exist situations where the management section may be omitted from the proposal. For a follow-on program, the customer may not require this section if management's positions are unchanged. Management sections are also not required if the management information was previously provided in the proposal or if the customer and contractor have continuous business dealings.

The technical section may include as much as 75 to 90 percent of the program plan, especially if the effort includes research and development. The technical section requires constant updating as the program matures. The following items can be included as part of the technical section:

- A detailed breakdown of the charts and schedules used to comprise the program master schedule, possibly including schedule/cost estimates
- A listing of the testing to be accomplished for each activity (including the exact testing matrices)
- Procedures for accomplishment of the testing (including system specifications)
- Although uncommon, some program plans attempt to identify the risks associated with specific technical requirements. This has the tendency to scare management personnel who are unfamiliar with the technical procedures. These risks should therefore be omitted if at all possible.

The program plan, as used here, contains a description of all phases of the program. For many programs, especially large ones, detailed planning is required for all major events and activities. Table 6-4 identifies the type of individual plans that can be required in place of a (total) program plan. However, care must be taken in that too much paperwork can easily inhibit successful management of a program.

The program plan, once agreed upon by the contractor and customer, is then used to provide program direction. This is shown in Figure 6-11. If the program plan is written clearly, then any functional manager or supervisor should be able to identify what is expected.

The program plan should be distributed to each member of the program team, all functional managers and supervisors interfacing with the program and all key functional personnel. The program plan does not contain all of the

Table 6-4. Types of Plans

Budget
Configuration Management
Facilities
Logistics Support
Management
Manufacturing
Procurement Plan
Quality Assurance
Research and Development
Scheduling
Tooling
Training
Transportation

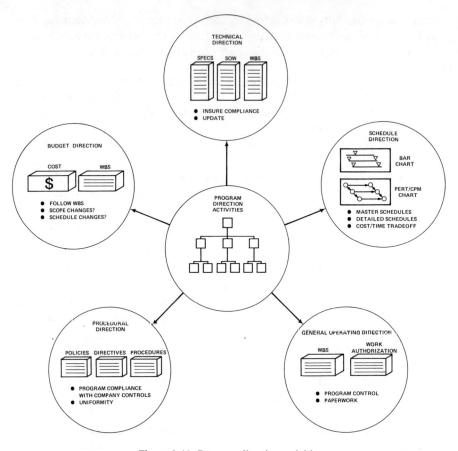

Figure 6-11. Program direction activities.

answers, for if it did, there would be no need for a program office. The plan serves merely as a guide.

One final note needs to be mentioned concerning the legality of the program plan. The program plan may be specified contractually to satisfy certain requirements as identified in the customer's statement of work. The contractor retains the right as to how to accomplish these requirements, unless a specific procedure is identified in the SOW. If the statement of work specifies that quality assurance testing be accomplished on 15 end items from the production line, then 15 is the minimum number that must be tested. The program plan may show that 25 items are to be tested. If cost overrun problems develop, the contractor may wish to revert to the SOW and test only 15 items. Contractually, this may be done without informing the customer. In most cases, however, the customer is notified and the program revised.

For large, complex projects, contractors may be required to submit individualized program plans as identified in Table 6-4. Shown below is a representation of the various information that would be included in such plans.

- Budget Plan
    - How much money is allocated to each event or activity? (The events and activities should follow the WBS.)
    - What are my monthly and yearly cash flow requirements?
    - How was the budget established?

It is often best to show the customer the procedures that you use for establishing labor and material budgets. Figures 6-12 and 6-13 serve this purpose. The system illustrated in these figures identify to the customer that your company has a systematic methodology for establishing a realistic budget.

- Configuration Management Plan
    - How will you manage the final configuration?
    - How will engineering changes be made and documented?
    - What will be the voting procedure, both with the customer as well as the contractor?
- Facilities Plan
    - What facility resources exist in the company?
    - What other projects will be using these same resources over the period of performance?
    - What time-phases facility resources will be available for this project?
- Logistics Plan
    - How will you acquire, distribute, store, package, and ship raw materials and finished goods?
    - How will replacements be handled?
- Management Plan
    - How will the project office and team be structured?
    - How will project management communicate with top management?
    - How will project management communicate with the customer?
    - What kind of in-house policies and procedures exist for management of projects?

This last item requires further comment. Regardless of technical competency and competitive costs, your proposal may be drastically downgraded (if not considered nonresponsive) unless you can demonstrate internal mechanisms for controlling projects. Many companies establish a *management cost and control system* (MCCS) guide to control and plan projects.

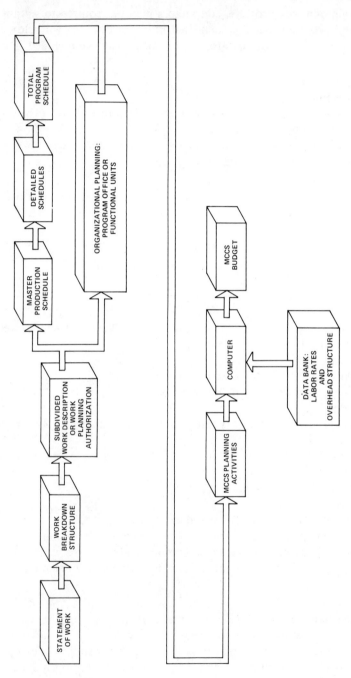

Figure 6–12. Labor planning flowchart.

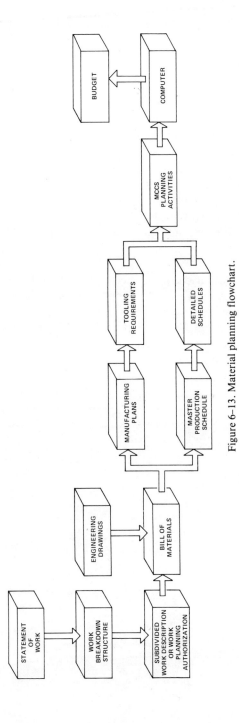

Figure 6–13. Material planning flowchart.

Table 6–5 identifies the type of information that would appear in this guide. The guide may be provided as a separate handout, an appendix to the management plan, or simply abstracted into the management plan.

- Manufacturing Plan
  - What are the time-phased manufacturing events?
  - How many units will be made?
  - What are the schedules manufacturing days?
  - How will the item be assembled, tested, and inspected?
  - What tolerance levels are acceptable and how will they be controlled?
- Procurement Plan
  - What are my sources for vendors?
  - Are they qualified vendors?
  - If the vendors are not qualified, what procedures can be used to qualify them?

If a make-or-buy decision is necessary, then the proposal should demonstrate that the contractor has employed sound technical and business judgment in arriving at such a decision. In addition, it is usually a good policy to show procurement logical flowcharts, such as Figure 6–14, to demonstrate to the customer that systematic procurement activities are employed as standard operating procedures.

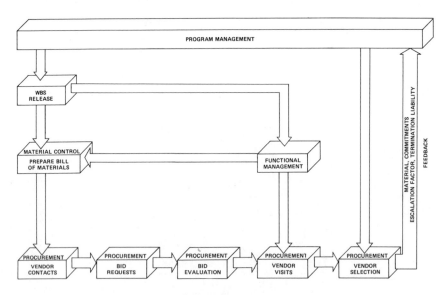

Figure 6–14. Procurement activity.

Table 6–5. Planning and Requirements Policies.

PROGRAM MANAGER	FUNCTIONAL MANAGER	RELATIONSHIP
Plans and Requirements Requests the preparation of the program master schedules and provides for integration with the Division Composite Schedules. Defines work to be accomplished through preparation of the Subdivided Work Description Package. Provides program guidance and direction for the preparation of program plans which establish program cost, schedule, and technical performance; and which define the major events and tasks to ensure the orderly progress of the program. Establishes priorities within the program. Obtains relative program priorities between programs managed by other programs from the director, program management, manager, marketing and product development, or the general manager as specified by the policy.	*Plans and Requirements* Develops the details of the program plans and requirements in conjunction with the program manager. Provides proposal action in support of program manager requirements and the program master schedule. With guidance furnished by the program manager, participates in the preparation of program plans, schedules, and work release documents which cover cost, schedule, and technical performance; and which define major events and tasks. Provides supporting detail plans and schedules. Negotiates priorities with program managers for events and tasks to be performed by his organization.	*Plans and Requirements* Program planning and scheduling is a functional specialty; the program manager utilizes the services of the specialist organizations. The specialists retain their own channels to the general manager but must keep the program manager informed. Program planning is also a consultative operation and is provided guidelines by the program manager. Functional organizations initiate supporting plans for program manager approval, or react to modify plans to maintain currency. Functional organizations also initiate planning studies involving trade-offs and alternative courses of action for presentation to the program manager. The program manager and program team members are oriented to his program, whereas the functional organizations and the functional managers are "function" and multi-program oriented. The orientation of each director, manager, and team member must be mutually recognized to preclude unreasonable demands and conflicting priorities. Priority conflicts that cannot be resolved must be referred to the general manager.

(continued)

Table 6-5. (cont.)

PROGRAM MANAGER	FUNCTIONAL MANAGER	RELATIONSHIP
Approves program contractual data requirements.	Conducts analysis of contractual data requirements. Develops data plans including contractor data requirements list and obtains program manager approval.	
Remains alert to new contract requirements, government regulations, and directives that might affect the work, cost, or management of the program.	Remains alert to new contract requirements, government regulations and directives which might affect the work, cost, or management of his organization on any program.	
Provides early technical requirements definitions, and substantiates make-or-buy recommendations. Participates in the formulation of the make-or-buy plan for the program.	Provides the necessary make-or-buy data; substantiates estimates and recommendations in the area of functional specialty.	Make-or-buy concurrence and approvals are obtained in accordance with current policies and procedures.
Approves the program bill of material for need and compliance with program need and requirements.	Prepares the program bill of material.	
Directs data management including maintenance of current and historical files on programmed contractual data requirements.		

Scheduling

Provides contractual data requirements and guidance for construction of program master schedules.

Concurs with detailed schedules constructed by functional organizations

Provides corrective action decisions and direction as required at any time a functional organization fails to meet program master schedule requirements or when by analysis, performance indicated by detail schedule monitoring, threatens to impact the program master schedule.

Scheduling

The operations directorate shall construct the program master schedule. Data should include but not be limited to engineering plans, manufacturing plans, procurement plans, test plans, quality plans, and protime spans for accomplishment of work elements defined in the work breakdown structure to the level of definition visible in the planned subdivided work description package.

Constructs detail program schedules and working schedules in consonance with program manager approved program master schedule. Secures program manager concurrence and forwards copies to the program manager.

Scheduling

The operations directorate constructs the program master schedule with data received from functional organizations and direction from the program manager. Operations shall coordinate program master schedule with functional organizations and secure program managers approval prior to release.

Program manager monitors the functional organizations detailed schedules for compliance with program master schedules and reports variance items which may impact division operations to the director, program management.

- Quality Assurance Plan
  - How will you guarantee that specifications will be met?
  - What is your general approach to quality assurance?
  - Do you have special facilities that are used for quality assurance testing and measurement?
  - Do you have a special quality assurance management team for the project?
- Research and Development Plan
  - Do you have a special organization for R&D?
  - What R&D activities are required?
  - Do you have standard formats for planning R&D activities?
  - How will R&D decisions be made?
  - What will be the role of the customer during the R&D decision-making process?
- Scheduling Plan
  - Are all critical dates accounted for?
  - Is there a standard method for updating schedules?
  - Will the project office maintain a single person responsible for updating all schedules? If so, how often will the schedules be updated?
- Tooling Plan
  - What are my time-phased tooling requirements?
  - Will they be made internally or purchased from the outside?
- Training Plan
  - How will training be administered?
  - Will training literature have to be developed?
  - Are there training schedules?
  - What is the cost of training?
- Transportation Plan
  - How will the goods and services be shipped?
  - Are there special carriers to be used?
  - Does the customer have preferred carriers?

There are several other types of plans that may be required such as reliability, maintainability, testing, systems engineering, and maintenance. Depending upon customer proposal requirements, it may be possible for each of these plans to be described in two or three paragraphs.

6.9 TIME/COST/PERFORMANCE TRADE-OFFS

The technical proposal must include a description of how trade-offs will be made. The following information must be included:

- Will the customer or contractor determine the priorities on time, cost, and performance?
- Will the customer or contractor make the final decision?

On the average, performance is usually the first to suffer. Customers seem to prefer changing performance specifications rather than missing major milestones or overrunning costs. Trade-off analysis cannot be accomplished in a realistic manner without

- A well-detailed and organized set of schedules that clearly delineate the project milestones, both major and minor
- A well-structured methodology for planned control of the major and minor trade-offs.

There are several possible combinations for trade-offs:

- *Cost is fixed and time is preferred to performance.* In this case, technical performance is reduced, which, in turn, should reduce time and possibly lower costs. If performance were preferred over time, then it seems only logical that the schedule must be pushed to the right. However, it is highly unlikely that costs can be maintained because management support time will increase.
- *Time is fixed and performance is preferred to cost.* Here, as one would expect, adding additional resources will almost always satisfy the time and performance constraints. This is in agreement with the adage: "Enough money can always guarantee performance." If cost is preferred to performance, then performance may have to be severely sacrificed in order to insure time constraints.
- *Performance is fixed and time is preferred over cost.* Here it is entirely possible that exponential cost increases will be incurred. If cost is preferred over time, then personnel must work at a higher position on the learning curve or else management support time increases the cost of the project.

Complete trade-off analysis often includes application of the rules of decision making under risk and uncertainty. It is best to define the trade-off analysis procedure as part of the technical proposal or project plan. The following rules should be considered:

- The exact process for trade-off analysis and implementation should be approved by the customer as early as possible in the program.

- The same control procedure that is utilized for major trade-offs should also be employed for minor trade-offs.
- During the design phase of a project, as many of the trade-off techniques as possible should be made.
- Use technical review meetings with the customer to control the major trade-offs.
- When trade-offs are necessary, show the customer that the trade-off will be implemented as fast as possible.

Quite often, technical proposals contain appendices that show the customer examples as well as diagrams of trade-off analyses that had been implemented on other projects. Figure 6–15 identifies the way that trade-off analysis is investigated. This section allows the customer to assign his own key personnel to interface with your personnel (perhaps on a one-to-one basis) during the planning stage so that valuable time is not lost downstream.

6.10 PROJECT CONTROL PROCEDURES

Both R&D and high-technology programs may undergo as many as 50 to 100 engineering change notices per month. It is not uncommon for large projects, such as weapons systems, to undergo 2,000 or more change orders monthly. The technical proposal must describe the method for controlling engineering changes. This process is often referred to as *configuration management.*

The major cause of schedule delays and cost overruns is often the result of ineffective change control. The government has tried to alleviate some of these potential problems with procedures as "design-to-cost," in which continuous cost/performance trade-offs are investigated.

Project control implies schedule control, cost control, performance control (i.e., configuration management), and the correlations among them. The technical volume usually describes only the configuration control items. This section must include three items:

- Item one calls for the establishment of a change control board. This includes the organizational structure for the board as well as a description of all members that have voting rights. Sample membership might be the assistant project manager for engineering (who may be acting as the chairman), engineering managers, manufacturing managers, procurement, cost accounting, and contract administration. This item should also describe the desired working relationship between the customer and contractor during the operation of the change control board.
- Item two describes the critical design review meetings that are estab-

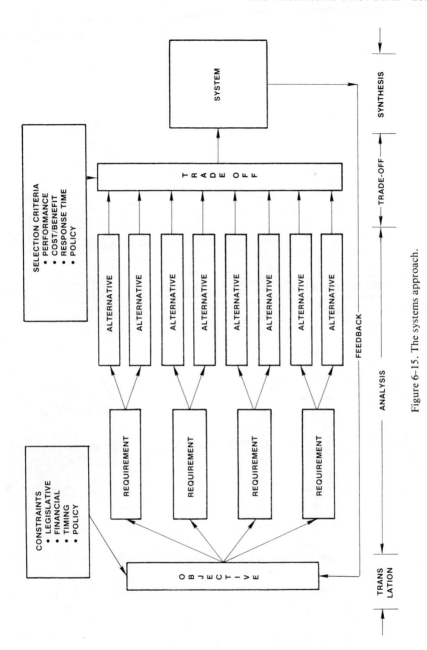

Figure 6–15. The systems approach.

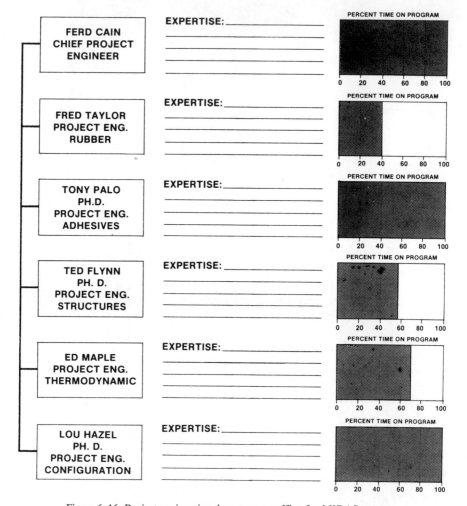

Figure 6–16. Project engineering department staffing for MIDAS program.

lished with the customer. The schedule should identify the point where the baseline design is "frozen."
- Item three is a description of the disciplined procedure for controlling and documenting the design changes.

6.11 RELATED EXPERIENCE

It is vitally important that both the management and technical proposals contain a section on related experience because the customer may evaluate the

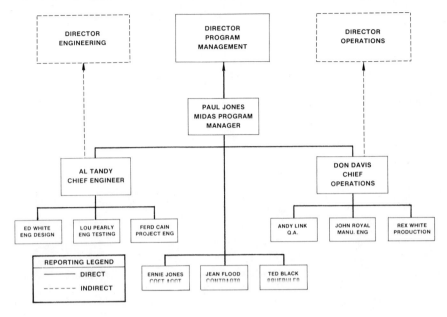

Figure 6-17. MIDAS program office.

management and technical proposals by different sides of the house. The related experience section should stress both past and current projects that are directly relatable to the one being bid, and provide credibility for the contractor's proposal.

6.12 KEY PROJECT PERSONNEL

Ideally, the best way of showing related experience is by assigning employees with the necessary experience to the key project positions. Resumés of key technical project personnel should be included in the technical proposal. Each resumé should be restricted to one page and, as a minimum, should include:

- Current position or assignments
- Related experience
- Responsibilities on new project
- Educational background and professional affiliations.

Sometimes, several key people can be summarized on one page, as shown in Figure 6-16. The percent time on project section is important to the customer because it shows that the company intends to utilize this person on the project and the employee's resumé is not being included simply to try to "eyewash" the customer. Of course, the employee may be reassigned to another at the last minute because of a major problem or a shift in priorities.

Organizational charts, such as Figure 6–17, should also be included to help clarify the exact positions of the key project personnel. The organizational charts in the technical proposal may be more of a summary nature whereas those in the management proposal may be more detailed.

Chapter 7

The Management Proposal

7.0 INTRODUCTION

The purpose of the management proposal is to explain to the customer precisely how you will manage the project and why you are qualified to do so. The management proposal should elaborate on such items as company history and experience, management capability, management philosophy, and available resources. The proposal must demonstrate that your company understands the environment surrounding the project and that your company will maintain a project organizational structure that can adapt readily to a changing environment.

The management proposal must convince the customer that your organization has a complete grasp of the problem and that you have the necessary resources and management expertise to satisfy or exceed your customer's requirements. The proposal should stress reality, not confusion or misunderstanding. Weaknesses in your proposal should be defined clearly as weaknesses, rather than concealed through mass confusion.

The management proposal should discuss the history and growth of the company. For high-technology packages, this section must describe the company's contributions to the state-of-the-art. This section should also provide emphasis on all past or present contracts that have characteristics similar to the one proposed.

The type of management that the company will use must be clearly shown in the proposal. This includes such items as organizational charts, reporting levels, resumés of key project personnel, and communication techniques with the customer. The type of structure selected should be based upon project size, complexity, importance, and interfacing adaptability to the customer's organization. The management structure selected must demonstrate flexibility in adapting to the customer's needs as well as changes in the environment.

Key to the management proposal is the description of the project office. Relationships must be identified among the project manager, the project team, and the functional units. The relationships must define authority, accountability, responsibility, direct and indirect reporting procedures, and levels of reporting. Furthermore, the proposal must show where the contractor's top management interfaces the project, especially with regard to time/cost/performance trade-offs.

The management proposal must show how the work will be performed and the resources to be used. Special attention should be given to the quality of the human resources. The proposal should identify those individuals with related experience and the percentage of time that they will be utilized on the project.

Management cost and control procedures must be identified with enough depth and detail that the customer is convinced thoroughly that accurate and timely information will be provided concerning the true status of the project. This information may be redundant with the information in the cost volume of the proposal. However, redundancy may be necessary because different customer personnel review each volume of your proposal.

There is usually better agreement among proposal writers as to the divisions of the management proposal as opposed to the cost and technical volumes. Below are the major divisions:

- Administrative management capability
- Program management
- Facilities
- Approvals and acceptances
- Cost and schedule controls
- History and experience.

These major divisions should not be taken lightly. While the cost and technical proposals may carry more weight than the management volume, an incomplete management volume may force the customer to consider your entire proposal as "nonresponsive," and you will be eliminated from further consideration.

If your proposal is in response to a customer request that includes bidding instructions, then you may wish to include an introduction to the management proposal. The introduction should contain a table that identifies the sections of the management proposal that satisfy the requirements of the bidding inquiries. This is shown in Table 7-1.

Some management proposals require only a few pages while others require separately bound volumes. If separate volumes are required, it is best to

Table 7-1. Response to bidding inquiries.

INFORMATION TO BIDDERS PARAGRAPH	PROJECT EXECUTION PROPOSAL SECTION
D-1	Company information
D-2	Company information
D-3	Technical qualifications and Project experience
D-4	Project work plan
D-5	Project organization
D-6	Manpower
D-7	Project schedule
D-8	Cost control
	Schedule control
	Material control
D-9	Subcontracting
D-10	Expediting
D-11	Project changes
D-12	Model
D-13	Confidentiality
E-1	Project experience
E-2	Project work plan
E-3	Labor management
E-4	Davis-Bacon Act
E-5	Project organization
E-6	Manpower
E-7	Cost control
	Schedule control
	Material control

develop a standard proposal front matter section that can be used for all three volumes.

7.1 ADMINISTRATIVE MANAGEMENT CAPABILITY

The purpose of the administrative management section is to identify the administrative information that has a direct bearing on your project, and to show the customer your compliance with general policies and procedures. This is of particular importance when bidding for government work. Typical information to be identified in the administrative information section would include:

- Organizational structure of the company
- Financial stability
- Accounting system
- Employee compensation policies

- EEO and Affirmative Action plans
- Employee safety and health programs
- Small business and labor surplus
- Quality assurance/control plan
- Confidentiality and security.

The purpose of providing a section on the organizational structure of your company is to identify the "solid" lines for management reporting. Most proposals identify this structure using block diagrams. The structure can be shown down through the lowest level of management.

It is also a good idea to identify the cost center accounts for each line organization together with the line function title. Thus, the customer can use the block diagrams to understand not only your management reporting structure, but also your method for accumulating costs.

This section should also contain brief resumés of your key personnel. Winning proposals contain resumés on

- Key upper-level managers
- The project sponsor (who may be an executive)
- The project manager
- All project office personnel
- Key middle and functional managers
- Other management personnel who will be concerned with monitoring and reporting progress.

Resumés may also be required of key functional personnel who have special qualifications even though they might be utilized only on a part-time basis. Unless requested by the customer, the resumés should not indicate the percent of time that the employee will spend on the project. Customers prefer not to see a person's resumé with many qualifications if that person is in fact going to spend only 5 percent of his or her time on the project. If there are alternate people for each key position, then you may wish to identify these individuals in the proposal, together with their resumés.

The financial stability of your organization should identify your method for satisfying financial obligations as well as your lines of credit. It is usually a good policy to include the latest stockholder report with profit and loss information. Small companies may be required to present profit/loss data for the past three years.

Most companies, especially if bidding on government work, have management cost and control systems (MCCS) that describe the accounting policies and procedures. The accounting methods must be related to the cost accounting codes in the organizational structure. If your accounting system has been audited by a government agency, indicate the date of the audit, by whom, and the results. Copies of government approval letters usually add merit to your proposal.

The section on employee compensation policies should be brief and should describe how these policies and benefits compare to other companies within your industry. If your employees receive below average wages, perhaps because of the fact that they reside in a low cost-of-living area, then your proposal should state this. This is imperative because the customer might feel that you do not have a quality professional community because of your below standard salary levels.

On government contracts, it is necessary to show that your organization is in compliance with EEO and Affirmative Action plans. Brief tables normally suffice. One effective way is to tabulate the information by showing the percentages of women and minorities in the management, professional, and blue collar ranks. If you can identify those individuals who will be assigned to your project, you add further credibility to your proposal.

Some companies are located in geographical areas where it may be difficult to satisfy EEO and Affirmative Action requirements. If this is the case, your proposal should show just cause for the violations.

The intent of the employee safety and health program section is to show compliance with OSHA and EPA regulatory requirements. This section should include a description of your company's

- Safety program
- Train program (for safety)
- Management and management support (for safety).

Providing historical "track record" data enhances your proposal. Your proposal should identify the areas in which your OSHA/EPA employees will be working. For a construction project, you may wish to include such items as:

- Air pollution control
- Solid waste disposal
- Water pollution control
- Surface drainage and erosion control
- Surface rehabilitation and revegetation
- Protection of fish and wildlife
- Aesthetic value considerations
- Fire protection and control
- Plans for oil clean-up and hazardous material handling
- Prevention of hazards to public health and safety for employees and neighboring populated areas.

The small business and labor surplus section is used to describe your certification (if applicable) and how you plan to use local labor. If you are a certified small business, the proposal should state by whom and how your certification was granted. If you intend to use local labor, state this in the proposal. If your program results in training local labor in higher skilled areas, you may have a competitive edge during proposal evaluation.

The quality assurance/control section is a description of your effectiveness in controlling the quality of the services or products for which you are bidding. The quality control portion should include:

- A brief description of your quality control activities, including the organizational structure
- A brief description of your quality control history, including both successes and methods for dealing with the problems.

The management volume must show clearly your ability to assure the quality of the project. Your proposal may be downgraded severely if you do not have good organizational structuring for the quality control group.

The control portion should describe briefly the items that will be controlled closely during the project and the methods of control. This section should not include an in-depth discussion of any management cost and control system (MCCS) that your company may utilize. The details of MCCS should be presented as part of the cost proposal. In the management proposal, the control portion might describe briefly control procedures for:

- Systems engineering
- Configuration management
- Engineering
- Manufacturing
- Subcontracting/procurement
- Quality control
- Reporting
- Performance testing
- Logistics
- Training
- Start-up
- Operations.

The last major section is confidentiality and security, and as a minimum should include the following:

- Reference to your security manual (if applicable) or reference to an appendix to the management proposal that contains your manual

- A description of your company's policies and procedures on security if a manual is not available
- A description of your security facilities
- The organization chart of your security teams, including resumés, if necessary
- All pertinent data regarding your security clearances, including granting agencies, dates, types of clearances, and so on.

Much of the information contained in the administrative management section is contained, in depth, in the technical and cost proposals. However, because different customer personnel may be reviewing the management proposal, each major topic should be discussed briefly with reference to the other volumes of the proposal.

7.2 PROGRAM MANAGEMENT

The program management section of the management proposal describes exactly the details of how you intend to manage the project. The major items included in this section are:

- Introduction or overview
- Plans or schedules
- Manpower staffing
- Subcontracting arrangements
- Procurement approach
- Management control techniques
- Project management.

The introduction and overview is a brief, narrative description of the tasks that will be performed to achieve the objective. This section can also list the basic approach, alternative approaches, and accompanying assumptions.

Generally, the management proposal is reviewed by nontechnical personnel and therefore should be written in nontechnical terms. Emphasis should be placed upon the fact that you understand the customer's requirements, goals, and objectives and that you have developed a detailed plan to achieve them.

The plan and schedule portion is a summary project master schedule that shows clearly that all customer major milestones will be met. Highly technical detailed schedules appear in the technical proposal and can be referenced here to support the master schedules.

Some customers prefer detailed project master schedules to be included in this section. If this is the case, make sure that the schedules follow the work breakdown structure. These schedules may simply be a duplicate of those in the cost and technical volumes. Brief reference should be made as to how the schedules were prepared and the confidence that your organization has in the ability of these schedules to satisfy all customer milestones.

Because customers are interested in how you intend to stay on schedule, you must include some brief description of your control techniques, such as PERT/CPM, or line of balance (LOB), and your internal policies and procedures for keeping management informed as to the status of the project. Another good technique is to provide historical data on your past experience in controlling projects and staying on schedule.

The manpower portion of the section should contain:

* Your present manpower capability
* Your monthly manpower availability (compared to project requirements)
* Turnover data (preferably by years)
* List of specialists in various areas
* Personnel resumés (if not included elsewhere in the proposal).

Your present manpower capability can easily be shown similar to Table 7-2. This staff experience profile is quite effective because, in addition to

Table 7-2. Staff experience profile

	NUMBER OF YEARS EMPLOYMENT WITH CONTRACTOR				
	0-1	1-2	2-3	3-5 YEARS	5 OR MORE YEARS
Process Engineers	2	4	15	11	18
Proj. Managers/Engineers	1	2	5	11	8
Cost Estimating	0	4	1	5	7
Cost Control	5	9	4	7	12
Scheduling and Scheduling Control	2	2	1	3	6
Procurement/Purchasing	4	12	13	2	8
Inspection	1	2	6	14	8
Expediting	6	9	4	2	3
Piping	9	6	46	31	22
Electrical	17	6	18	12	17
Instrumentation	8	8	12	13	12
Mechanical	2	5	13	27	19
Civil/Structural	4	8	19	23	16
Environmental Control	0	1	1	3	7
Engineering Specialists	3	3	3	16	21
Total	64	81	161	180	184

manpower capability, it shows length of employment and size of the functional units.

Another method for showing capabilities is to include a *skills matrix* as shown in Table 7–3. Although skills matrices can be developed for all company personnel, their most effective use is with potential project office personnel, key specialists, and possible alternates.

Manpower availability can be represented as in Table 7–4. This table can be effective also in identifying any independent consultants or "job shoppers" that will be used on your project.

Table 7–5 indentifies a relatively simple method to show the customer the turnover rate in your key areas. Low turnover rates enhance your company's position greatly. Obviously, you can take the best time period so as to identify the minimum turnover rates.

Some proposals include a great deal of depth in manpower planning by including:

- The number of departmental man-hours required each month for each element of the WBS
- Total manpower committed on other projects for the duration of this project.

Figure 7–1 can be used to satisfy the above mentioned items.

Resumés of your key specialists in the various areas should accompany the management proposal. The same resumés can also appear in the technical proposal. The specialists that you identify *must* be, for the majority, the same individuals that are assigned to the project. If the customer finds that 50 to 60 percent of the key people whose resumés were included in the proposal were not available at project initiation, then you may lose a great deal of credibility for future work.

Some companies include three or four resumés for each key position and allow the customer to choose. It is important that the position shown on the resumé correspond to or be of a higher stature than the position for which the person is nominated. Consideration should be given to the following:

- Does the person have specific knowledge of and experience in the type of project being bid?
- Is the person known to client? If so, how would he be received by the client in this position?
- Has the person worked on any other recent project in the geographical area?
- Does the person have overall qualifications for the work?

Table 7-3. Operations skills matrix

Functional Areas of Expertise	Able, J.	Baker, P.	Cook, D.	Dirk, L.	Easley, P.	Franklin, W.	Green, C.	Henry, L.	Imhoff, R.	Jules, C.	Klein, W.	Ledger, D.	Mayer, Q.	Newton, A.	Oliver, G.	Pratt, L.
Administrative Management		a				a		a			a	a			a	
Control and Communications	b		b	b	b		b	b		b	b	b		b	b	b
Environmental Impact Assessment	c	c	c						c		c		c			
Facilities Management		d					d				d		d			
Financial Management	e					e			e	e	e				e	e
Human Resources Management	f							f				f				
Industrial Engineering	g				g					g						
Intelligence and Security								h				h		h		
Inventory Control	i						i								i	i
Logistics			j		j			j				j				
OSHA	k									k			k			
Project Management	l			l		l					l				l	
Quality Control		m	m			m	m	m	m							
R&D		n	n	n							n		n			n
Wage and Salary Administration		o			o				o	o	o	o		o	o	

Table 7-4. Contractor's manpower availability

	TOTAL CURRENT STAFF		AVAILABLE FOR THIS PROJECT AND OTHER NEW WORK 1/83	ANTICIPATED GROWTH BY 1/83
	PERMANENT EMPLOYEES	AGENCY PERSONNEL	PERMANENT + AGENCY	PERMANENT + AGENCY
Process Engineers	93	-	70	4
Project Managers/Engineers	79	-	51	4
Cost Estimating	42	-	21	2
Cost Control	73	-	20	2
Scheduling/Scheduling Control	14	-	8	1
Procurement/Purchasing	42	-	20	1
Inspection	40	-	20	2
Expediting	33	-	18	1
Home Office Construction Management	9	-	6	0
Piping	90	13	67	6
Electrical	31	-	14	2
Instrumentation	19	-	3	1
Vessels/Exchangers	24	-	19	1
Civil/Structural	30	-	23	2
Other	13	-	8	0

NUMBER OF PERSONNEL

Table 7-5. Staff turnover data

	FOR TWELVE-MONTH PERIOD 1/1/82 TO 1/1/83	
	NUMBER TERMINATED	NUMBER HIRED
Process Engineers	5	2
Project Managers/Engineers	1	1
Cost Estimating	1	2
Cost Control	12	16
Scheduling/Scheduling Control	2	5
Procurement/Purchasing	13	7
Inspection	18	6
Expediting	4	5
Home Office Construction Management	0	0
Design and Drafting—Total	37	29
Engineering Specialists—Total	26	45
Total	119	118

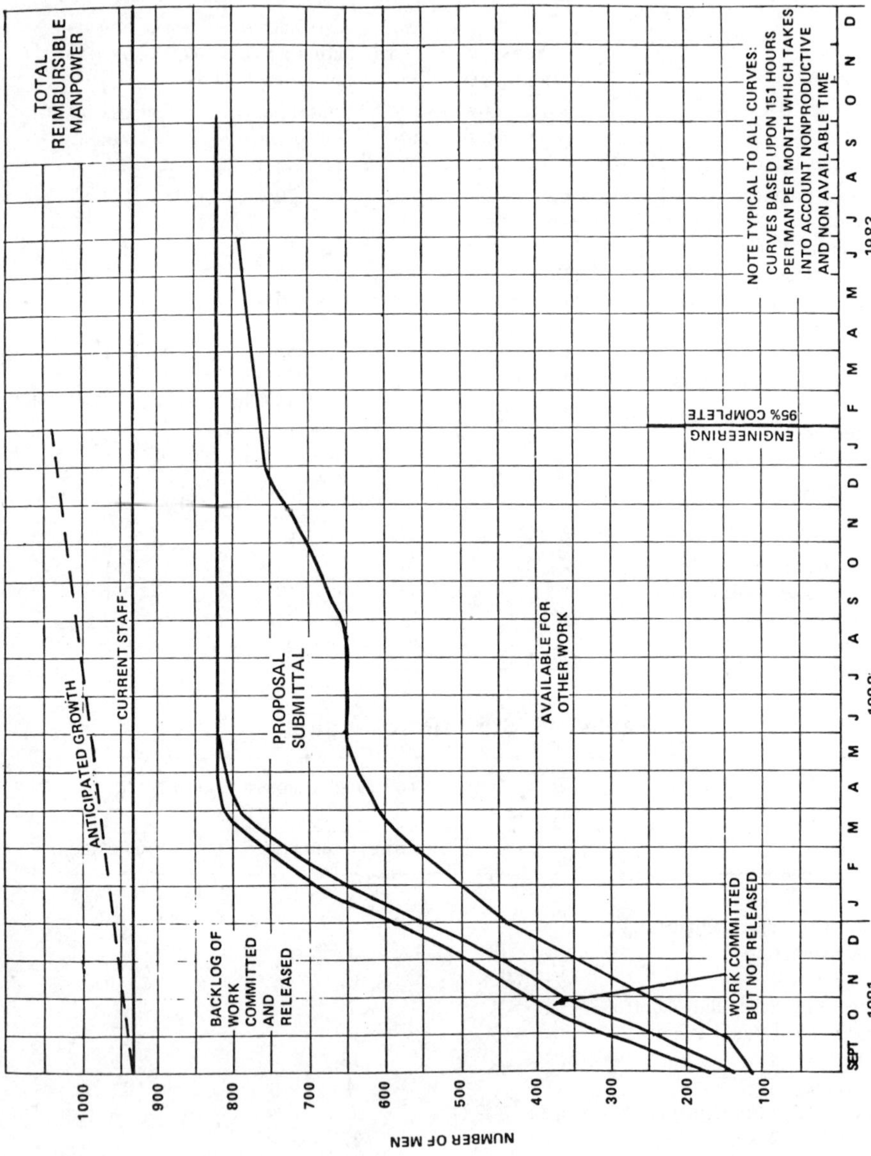

Figure 7-1. Total reimbursable manpower.

Optional information might include:

- Percentage of time devoted to the project
- Experience or education that is directly related to the proposed project.
- Educational history

Figure 7-2 shows the type of resumé that can be included. Some customers prefer short, abbreviated resumes. In this case, you may wish to combine your people in a format such as in Figure 7-3.

The subcontracting and procurement portion should emphasize your expertise, ability, and experience in selecting and qualifying vendors and subcontractors as well as in the methods for communications, monitoring, and follow-up. Communication is vital. You must show the customer that you will be monitoring the schedule, budget, and performance of all subcontractors closely. You may wish to identify periodic/scheduled meetings and data item requirements. Historical data can be used to support your information by including tabulated information regarding actual versus projected costs, actual versus projected delivery dates, and qualification test results.

The purpose of the management control techniques discussion is to convince the customer thoroughly that you have the necessary project management organization to control the project. Summary information is acceptable here. You might simply identify (and briefly describe) the following items with reference to the other volumes where specific details will be given:

- Management cost and control system (MCCS)
- Budgeting techniques (if computerized, state this)
- Mechanisms for time/cost/performance trade-offs
- PERT/time, PERT/cost, LOB
- Auditing procedures
- Variance analysis methods
- Status Reporting: Internal and External.

7.3 STRUCTURING THE PROJECT

There are a wide variety of organizational forms for structuring a project. The exact method depends upon the people in the organization, the company's product lines, and management's philosophy. A poorly structured project can sever communications channels that may have taken months or years to cultivate; cause a restructuring in the informal organization that leads to new power, status, and political position; eliminate motivation and job satisfaction; and totally alienate the customer such that there will be no follow-on

JOHN H. BENSON
Senior Project Engineer
30 Years Experience

GENERAL BACKGROUND

Mr. Benson has had 30 years of increasing responsibility in managing the design, procurement, construction, and start-up of large chemical, petrochemical, and refinery projects both in the U.S. and abroad. He has extensive project management, engineering, and design experience resulting from major assignments on a wide variety of projects. Because of the many duties he has performed, Mr. Benson has a thorough working knowledge of all functions necessary for successful project completion.

CURRENT EXPERIENCE

Mr. Benson is currently assigned as project director on a major chemical plant expansion for Shell in Europe. Previously, he served as project manager on two oil shale processing plant designs and was project manager for modification of a oil shale pilot facility. He has been project manager for the design of a large, commercial coal gasification plant.

Some of the other projects on which Mr. Benson has worked are:

- Amoco Chemical Corporation, Alvin, Texas: High-density polyethylene plant—project manager
- American Oil, Whiting, Indiana: Crude unit expansion—project manager.
- Olin Corporation, Charleston, Tennessee: Chemical expansion—senior project engineer
- Gulf Oil Corporation, Houston, Texas: Alkylation Unit—Project Engineer
- Goodyear Tire and Rubber Company, Akron, Ohio: Antiozonant Plant—Project Engineer

PREVIOUS EXPERIENCE

- Bates Engineering Company: Project manager responsibile for economic evaluation, design, construction, and start-up of chemical plants, including seven major prototype plants.
- Scientific Design Company, Inc.: Senior project manager, project engineer, and manager of engineering for major chemical, petrochemical, and energy projects. Project engineer for coal gasification unit in South Africa.
- Superior Engineering Company: Assistant manager of mechanical contracting division. Responsible for organizing the engineering, estimating, and procurement operations to support the field operations.
- Great Northern Chemical Company: Design supervisor and project engineer involved in the design, construction, and start-up of chemical plants.

PROFESSIONAL DATA

B.S., Chemical Engineering, University of Illinois
M.S., Chemical Engineering, University of Delaware
Registered Professional Engineer: Pennsylvania, Ohio, New York, Florida, and Texas.
Member: AIChE, AISE and PMI

Figure 7–2. Sample resume

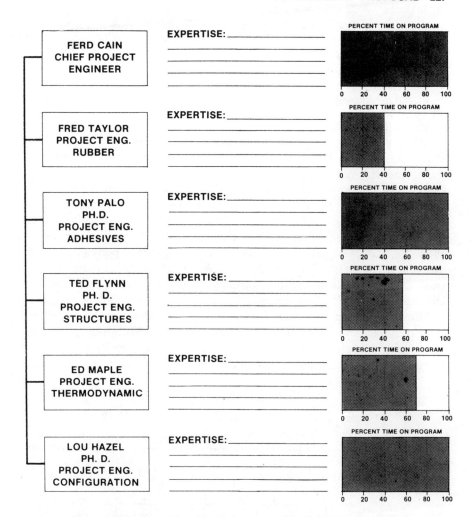

Figure 7-3. Project engineering department staffing for MIDAS program.

business. All customers consider the project organizational structure to be an extension of their own company.

There are two major criteria that must be considered in selecting the appropriate organization for the proposal:

- Because the customer considers the project team to be an extension of his own company, the project team (especially the project office) must be structured to be compatible with the customer's organization.
- The organizational form selected should not disrupt the ongoing, daily operations of the parent organization.

There are several methods for structuring projects. These include:

- Traditional structuring .
- Departmental control
- Divisional control
- Matrix control (discussed in Section 7.4).

Each method brings with it advantages as well as disadvantages. In the next several paragraphs, these methods are discussed not only to show the various structures, but to identify the way project organizations have matured over the past several years.

For more than two centuries, the traditional management structure has survived. However, recent business developments, such as the rapid rate of change in technology and position in the marketplace, as well as increased customer demands, have created strains on the existing organizational forms. Fifty years ago, companies could survive with only one or perhaps two product lines. The classical management organization, as shown in Figure 7-4, was found to be satisfactory for control and conflicts were at a minimum, but customer communications were poor.

However, as time progressed, companies found that survival depended upon multiple product lines (i.e., diversification) and vigorous integration of technology into the existing organization. As organizations grew and matured, managers found that company activities were not being integrated

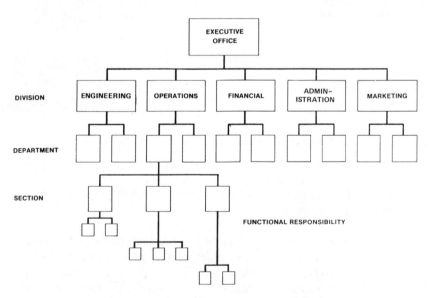

Figure 7-4. The traditional management structure.

effectively, and that new conflicts were arising in the well-established formal and informal channels. Managers began searching for more innovative organizational forms that would alleviate the integration and conflict problems.

Before a valid comparison can be made with the newer forms, the advantages and disadvantages of the traditional structure must be known. Table 7–6 lists the advantages of the traditional organization. As seen in Figure 7–4, the general manager has all of the functional entities necessary either to perform R&D or develop and manufacture a product. All activities are performed within the functional groups and are headed by a department (or, in some cases, a division) head. Each department maintains a strong concentration of technical expertise. Because all of the project must flow through the functional departments, each project can benefit from the most advanced technology, thus making this organizational form well suited for mass production. Functional managers can hire a wide variety of specialists and provide them with easily definable paths for career progression.

The functional managers maintain absolute control over the budget. They establish their own budgets, upon approval from above, and specify requirements for additional personnel. Because the functional manager has manpower flexibility and a broad base from which to work, most projects are normally completed within cost.

Both the formal and informal organizations are well established, and levels of authority and responsibility are clearly defined. Because each person reports to only one individual, communication channels are well structured.

Table 7–6. Advantages of the classical/traditional organization

- Easier budgeting and cost control
- Better technical control

- Specialists can be grouped to share knowledge and responsibility
- Personnel can be used on many different projects
- All projects will benefit from the most advanced technology (better utilization of scarce personnel)

- Provides flexibility in the use of manpower
- Provides broad manpower base to work with
- Provides continuity in the functional disciplines, policies, procedures, and lines of responsibility, which are more easily defined and understandable
- Readily admits mass production activities within established specifications
- Provides good control over personnel because each employee has one and only one person to report to
- Communication channels are vertical and well established
- Quick reaction capability exists, but may be dependent upon the priorities of the functional managers

If a structure has this many advantages, then why are we looking for other structures?

For each advantage there is almost always a corresponding disadvantage. Table 7–7 lists the disadvantages of the traditional structure. The majority of these are related to the fact that there is no strong central authority or individual responsible for the total project. Customers find it difficult to get quick answers to questions. As a result, integration of activities that cross functional lines becomes a difficult chore. Top-level executives become involved with this daily routine. Conflicts occur as each functional group struggles for power. The strongest functional group dominates the decision-making process. Functional managers tend to favor what is best for their functional group rather than what is best for the project. Many times, ideas remain functionally oriented with very little regard for ongoing projects. In addition, the decision-making process is slow and tedious.

Because there exists no customer focal point, all communications must be channeled through upper-level management. Upper-level managers then act in a customer relations capacity (i.e., project sponsor) and refer all complex problems down through the vertical chain of command to the functional managers. The response to the customer's needs therefore becomes a slow and aggravating process because the information must be filtered through several layers of management. If problem solving and coordination are required to cross functional lines, then additional lead time is required for the approval of decisions. All trade-off analyses must be accomplished through committees chaired by upper-level management.

Projects have a tendency to fall behind schedule in the classical organizational structure. Completing all projects and tasks on time, with a high degree of quality and efficient use of available resources, is all but impossible without continuous involvement of top-level management. Incredibly large lead times are required. Functional managers attend to those tasks that provide better

Table 7–7. Disadvantages of the classical/traditional organization

- No one individual is directly responsible for the total project (i.e., no formal authority; committee solutions)
- Does not provide the project-oriented emphasis necessary to accomplish the project tasks
- Coordination becomes complex and additional lead time is required for approval of decisions
- Decisions normally favor the strongest functional groups
- No customer focal point
- Response to customer needs is slow
- Difficulty in pinpointing responsibility; the result of little or no direct project reporting, very little project-oriented planning, and no project authority
- Motivation and innovation are decreased
- Ideas tend to be functionally oriented with little regard for ongoing projects

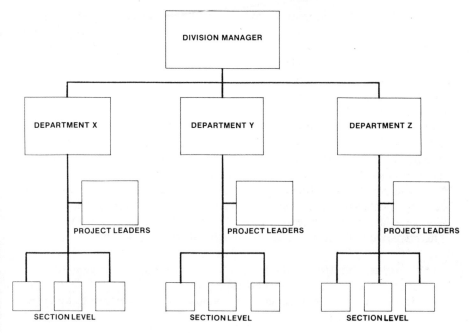

Figure 7-5. Departmental project management.

benefits to themselves and their subordinates first. Priorities may be dictated by requirements of the informal as well as formal departmental structure.

The first attempt to resolve the problems with the traditional structure was to develop project leaders or coordinators within each functional department, as shown in Figure 7-5. Section-level personnel were assigned temporarily as project leaders and would return to their former positions at project termination. This is why the term "project leader" is used rather than project manager, because the word "manager" implies a permanent relationship. This proved effective for coordinating and integrating work within one department, provided that the correct project leader was selected. Some employees considered this position as an increase in power and status, and conflicts occurred about whether assignments should be based upon experience, seniority, or capability. Several employees wanted the title merely so they could use it on their resumés. Furthermore, the project leaders had almost no authority and section-level managers refused to take directions from the project leaders. Many section managers were afraid that if they did take direction, they were admitting that the project leaders were next in line for the department manager's position.

When activities required efforts that crossed more than one functional boundary, say two or more sections or departments, conflicts arose. The project leader in one department did not have the authority to coordinate activities in any other department. Furthermore, the creation of this new position caused internal conflicts within each department.

Even though we have criticized this organizational form, it does not mean that it cannot work. Any organizational form (yes, *any* form) can work if the employees want it to work. As an example, a computer manufacturer has a midwestern division with three departments within it, as in Figure 7–5, and approximately 14 people per department. When a project comes in, the division manager determines which department will handle most of the work. Let us say that the workload is 60 percent department X, 30 percent department Y, and 10 percent department Z. Because most of the effort is in department X, the project leader is selected from that department. The project leader can almost always get the necessary resources from the other two departments. There are two reasons why this organizational form works here:

- The other department managers know that they may have to supply the project leader on the next activity.
- There are only three functional boundaries or departments involved (i.e., a small organization).

The next step in the evolution of project management was the *task force* concept. The rationale behind the task force concept was that integration could be achieved if each functional unit placed a representative on the task force. The group could then solve problems jointly as they occurred, provided that budget limitations were still observed. Theoretically, decisions could be made at the lowest possible levels, thus expediting information and reducing, or even eliminating, delay time.

The task force was composed of both part-time and full-time personnel from each department involved. Daily meetings were held to review activities and discuss potential problems. Functional managers soon found that their task force employees were spending more time in unproductive meetings than performing functional activities. In addition, the nature of the task force position caused many individuals to shift membership within the informal organization. Many functional managers then placed nonqualified and inexperienced individuals on task forces. The result was that the group soon became ineffective because they either did not have the information necessary to make the decisions, or lacked the authority (delegated by the functional managers) to allocate resources and assign work.

Development of the task force concept was a giant step toward conflict resolution: work was being accomplished on time, schedules were being maintained, and costs were usually within budget. But integration and coordination were still problems because there were no specified authority relationships or individuals to oversee the entire project through completion. Many attempts were made to overcome this by placing various people in charge of the task force; functional managers, division heads, and even upper-level management had opportunities to direct task forces. However, without formal project authority relationships, task force members maintained loyalty to their functional organizations, and, when conflicts came about between the project and functional organization, the project always suffered.

Although the task force concept was a step in the right direction, the disadvantages heavily outweighed the advantages. A strength of the approach was that it could be established very rapidly and with very little paperwork. Integration, however, was complicated; work flow was difficult to control, and functional support was difficult to obtain, because it was almost always controlled strictly by the functional manager. In addition, task forces were found to be greatly ineffective on long-range projects.

It soon became obvious that control of a project must be given to personnel whose first loyalty is directed toward the completion of the project. To do this, the project management position must be separated from any controlling influence of the functional managers. Figure 7–6 shows a typical line-staff organization.

Two possible situations can exist with this form of line-staff project control. In the first situation, the project manager serves only as the focal point for activity control, that is, a center for information. The prime responsibility

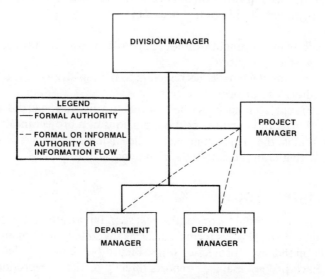

Figure 7–6. Line-staff organization.

of the project manager is to keep the division manager informed of the status of the project and to "harass" or attempt to "influence" managers into completing activities on time.

Only the project manager, not the functional manager, maintained monitoring authority, despite the fact that both reported to the same individual. Both work assignments and merit reviews were made by the functional managers. Department managers refused to take direction from the project managers because it seemed like an admission that the project manager was next in line to be the division manager.

The amount of authority given to the project manager posed serious problems. Almost all upper-level and division managers were from the classical management schools and therefore maintained serious reservations about how much authority to relinquish. Many of these managers considered it a demotion if they had to give up any of their long-established powers.

The second situation involves the amount of authority given to the project manager. The project manager (using the authority delegated by the division manager) can assign work to individuals in the functional organizations. The functional manager, however, still maintains the authority to perform merit reviews, but cannot enforce both professional and organizational standards in the completion of an activity. The individual performing the work is now caught in a web of authority relationships, and additional conflicts develop because functional managers are forced to share their authority with the project manager.

Although this second situation did occur during the early stages of matrix project management, it did not last because:

- Upper-level management was not ready to cope with the problems arising from shared authority.
- Upper-level management was reluctant to relinquish any of their power and authority to project managers.
- Line-staff project managers who reported to a division head did not have any authority or control over those portions of a project in other divisions; that is, the project manager in the engineering division could not direct activities in the manufacturing division.

7.4 THE MATRIX PROJECT

The matrix organizational form was the next step. It is an attempt to combine the advantages of all previous forms, and is ideally suited for companies such as construction that are "project-driven." Figure 7–7 shows a typical matrix structure. Each project manager reports directly to the vice president and general manager. Because each project represents a potential profit center, the power and authority used by the project manager come directly from the

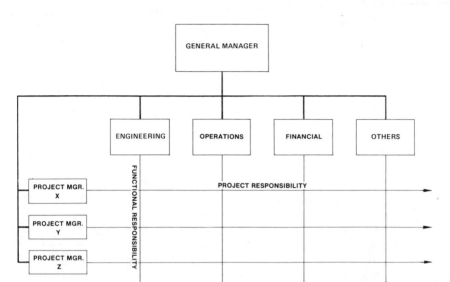

Figure 7-7. Pure matrix structure.

general manager. The project manager has total responsibility and account-ability for project success. The functional departments, on the other hand, have functional responsibility to maintain technical excellence on the project. Each functional unit is headed by a department manager whose prime respon-sibility is to insure that a unified technical base is maintained and that all available information can be exchanged for each project. Department managers must also keep their people aware of the latest technical ac-complishments in the industry.

Certain ground rules exist for matrix development:

- Participants must be assigned full time to the project; this insures a degree of loyalty.
- Horizontal as well as vertical channels must exist for making commit-ments.
- There must be a quick and effective method for conflict resolution.
- There must be communication channels and free access between managers.
- All managers must have an input into the planning process.
- Both horizontally and vertically oriented managers must be willing to negotiate for resources.
- The horizontal line must be permitted to operate as a separate entity ex-cept for administrative purposes.

These ground rules simply state some of the ideal conditions that matrix structures should possess. Each ground rule brings with it advantages and disadvantages.

Before describing the advantages and disadvantages of this structure, the organization concepts must be introduced. The basis for the matrix approach is an attempt to create synergism through shared responsibility between project and functional management. Yet this is easier said than done. The following questions must be answered before successful operation of a matrix structure can be achieved.

- If each functional unit is responsible for one aspect of a project, and other parts are conducted elsewhere (possibly subcontracted to other companies), how can a synergistic environment be created?
- Who decides which element of a project is more important?
- How can a functional unit (operating in a vertical structure) answer questions and achieve project goals and objectives that are compatible with other projects?

The answers to these questions depend upon the mutual understanding between the project and functional managers. Because both individuals maintain some degree of authority, responsibility, and accountability for each project, they must negotiate continuously. Unfortunately, the program manager might consider only what is best for his project (disregarding all others), whereas the functional manager might consider his organization as being more important than each project.

In the matrix:

- There should be no disruption because of dual accountability.
- A difference in judgment should not delay work in progress.

In order to get the job done, project managers sometimes need adequate organizational status and authority. A corporate executive contends that the organizational chart shown in Figure 7-7 can be modified to show that the project managers have adequate organizational authority by placing the department manager boxes at the tip of the functional arrowheads. The executive further contends that, with this approach, the project managers appear to be higher in the organization than their departmental counterparts but are actually equal in status. Executives who prefer this method must exercise due caution because the line and project managers may not feel that there still exists an equality in the balance of power.

Problem solving in this type of environment is a fragmented and diffused process. The project manager acts as a unifying agent for project control of resources and technology. Open channels for communication between the project manager and functional units as well as among functional units themselves must be maintained so as to prevent suboptimization of individual projects. The problems of routine administration can and do become a cost-effective requirement.

In many situations, functional managers have the power and means to make a project manager look good, provided that they can be motivated enough to think in terms of what is best for the project. Unfortunately, this is not always accomplished. This concept of "tunnel vision" can exist at all levels of management.

The project and functional environments cannot be separated; they must interact. The location of the project and functional unit interface is the focal point for all activities.

The functional manager controls departmental resources (i.e., people). This poses a problem in that although the project manager maintains the maximum control (through the line managers) over all resources, including cost and personnel, the functional manager must provide staff for the project's requirements. It is therefore inevitable that conflicts occur between functional and project managers.

The individual placed at the interface position has two bosses: the project manager and the functional manager. Merit reviews and hiring and firing responsibilities still rest with the department manager. Normally, merit reveiws are made by the functional manager after discussion with the program manager. The functional manager may not have the time necessary to measure the progress of this individual continuously. He must rely upon the word of the program manager for merit review and promotion. The interface members generally offer their loyalty to the person signing their merit review. This situation creates confusion, especially if conflicting orders are issued by the functional and project managers. The simplest solution is for the individual at the interface to ask the functional and project managers to communicate with each other to resolve the problem. This type of situation poses two problems for project managers:

- How does a project manager motivate an individual working on a project (either part-time or full-time) so that his loyalties are with the project?
- How does a project manager convince an individual to perform work according to project directions and specifications when these requests may be in conflict with department policy, especially if the individual feels that the functional manager may not look upon this too favorably?

There are many advantages to matrix structures, as shown in Table 7–8. Functional units exist primarily as support for a project. Because of this, key people can be shared and costs can be minimized. People can be assigned to a

Table 7-8. Advantages of a pure matrix organizational form

- The project manager maintains maximum project control over all resources, including cost and personnel.
- Policies and procedures can be set up independently for each project provided that they do not contradict company policies and procedures.
- The project manager has the authority to commit company resources provided that scheduling does not cause conflicts with other projects.
- Rapid responses are possible to change conflict resolution and project needs.
- The functional organizations exist primarily as support for the project.
- Each person has a "home" after project completion. People are more susceptible to motivation and end item identification. Each person can be shown a career path.
- Because key people can be shared, program cost is minimized. People can work a variety of problems (i.e., better people control).
- A strong technical base can be developed and much more time can be devoted to complex problem solving. Knowledge is available to all projects on an equal basis.
- Conflicts are minimal, and those requiring hierarchical referral are more easily resolved.
- Better balance between time, cost, and performance.

variety of challenging problems. Each person, therefore, has a "home" after project completion. Each person can be shown a career path in the company. People are more susceptible to motivation and end item identification. Functional managers find it easier to develop and maintain a strong technical base and can therefore spend more time on complex problem solving. Knowledge can be shared for all projects.

The matrix structure can provide rapid response to changes, conflicts, and other project needs. Conflicts are normally minimal, but those requiring resolution are easily resolved using hierarchical referral.

This rapid response is a result of the project manager's authority to commit company resources, provided that scheduling conflicts with other projects can be eliminated. Furthermore, the project manager has the authority to establish his own project policies and procedures independently, provided that they do not conflict with company policies. This eliminates much red tape and permits a better balance between time, cost, and performance.

The matrix structure provides us with the best of two worlds: the traditional structure and the matrix structure. The advantages of the matrix structure eliminate almost all of the disadvantages of the traditional structure. The word "matrix" often brings fear into the hearts of executives because it implies radical change, or at least they think that it does. If we take a close look at Figure 7-7, we can see that the traditional structure is still there. The matrix is simply horizontal lines superimposed over the traditional structure. The horizontal lines come and go as projects start up and terminate, but the traditional structure remains forever.

Matrix structures are not without their disadvantages, as shown in Table

7-9. The main disadvantages of the matrix organization is that more administrative personnel are needed to develop policies and procedures, and therefore both direct and indirect administrative costs increase. Each project organization operates independently. This poses a problem in that duplication of effort can easily occur; for example, two projects might be developing the same cost accounting procedure or functional personnel may be doing similar R&D efforts on different projects. Both vertical and horizontal communication is a must in a project matrix organization.

Functional managers are only human and therefore may be biased according to their own set of priorities. Project managers, on the other hand, must realize that their project is not the only one, and that a proper balance is needed; this includes a balance of power between functional and project units as well as a proper balance between time, cost, and performance.

One of the advantages of the matrix is a rapid response time for problem resolution. This rapid response generally applies to slow-moving projects in which problems occur within each functional unit. On fast-moving projects, the reaction time can become quite slow, especially if the problem spans more than one functional unit.

The matrix structure therefore becomes a compromise. In pure product management, technology suffer because there did not exist any single group for planning and integration. In the pure functional organization, time and schedule are sacrificed. Matrix project management is an attempt to obtain maximum technology and performance in a cost-effective manner and within time and schedule constraints.

We should note that with proper executive-level planning and control, all of the disadvantages can be eliminated. This is the only organizational form where this is possible. However, care must be taken with regard to the first disadvantage listed in Table 7-9. There is a natural tendency when going to a matrix to create more executive management positions than are actually necessary in order to get better control, which drives up the overhead rates. This

Table 7-9. Disadvantages of a pure matrix organizational form

- Companywide, the organizational structure is not cost effective because more people than necessary are required, primarily administrative.
- Each project organization operates independently. Care must be taken that duplication of effort does not occur.
- More effort and time is needed initially to define policies and procedures.
- Functional managers may be biased according to their own set of priorities.
- Although rapid response time is possible for individual problem resolution, matrix response time is slow, especially on fast-moving projects.
- Balance of power between functional and project organizations must be watched.
- Balance of time, cost, and performance must be monitored.

may be true in some companies, but there is a point where the matrix matures and less people are required at the top levels of management. When executives wish to reduce cost, they normally begin *at the top* by combining positions when slots become vacant. This is a natural fallout of having mature project and line managers with less top-level interference.

We identified the necessity for the project manager to be able to establish his own policies, procedures, rules, and guidelines. Obviously, with personnel reporting in two directions and to multiple managers, conflicts over administration can easily occur. According to Shannon.[1]

> When operating under a matrix management approach, it is obviously extremely important that the authority and responsibility of each manager be clearly defined, understood and accepted by both functional and program people. These relationships need to be spelled out in writing. It is essential that in the various operating policies, the specific authority of the program manager be clearly defined in terms of program direction, and that the authority of the functional executive be defined in terms of operational direction.

Most practitioners consider the matrix to be a two-dimensional system in which each project represents a potential profit center and each functional department represents a cost center. (This interpretation can also create conflict because functional departments may feel that they no longer have an input into corporate profits.)

Obviously, the matrix structure is the most complex of all organizational forms. Careful consideration must be given as to where and how the matrix organization fits into the total organization. Grinnell and Apple define four situations in which it is most practical to consider a matrix:[2]

- When complex, short-run products are the organization's primary output
- When a complicated design calls for both innovation and timely completion
- When several kinds of sophisticated skills are needed in designing, building, and testing the products, skills then need constant updating and development

---

[1] Shannon, Robert, "Matrix Management Structures," *Industrial Engineering,* March 1972, pp. 27–28. Published and copyright 1972 by the American Institute of Industrial Engineers, Inc., Norcross, Ga. 30092.

[2] Grinnell, S.K., and Apple, H.P., "When Two Bosses are Better Than One," *Machine Design,* January 1975, pp. 84–87.

- When a rapidly changing marketplace calls for significant changes in products, perhaps between the time they are conceived and delivered.

The matrix can take many forms, but are basically three common varieties. Each type represents a different degree of authority attributed to the program manager and indirectly identifies the relative size of the company. As an example, in the matrix of Figure 7–7, all program managers report directly to the general manager. This type of arrangement works best for small companies that have a minimum number of projects and assumes that the general manager has sufficient time to coordinate activities between his project managers. In this type of arrangement, all conflicts between projects are hierarchically referred to the general manager for resolution.

As companies grew in size and the number of projects, the general manager found it increasingly difficult to act as the focal point for all projects. A new position was created, that of director of programs or manager of programs or projects. This is shown in Figure 7–8. The director of programs was responsi-

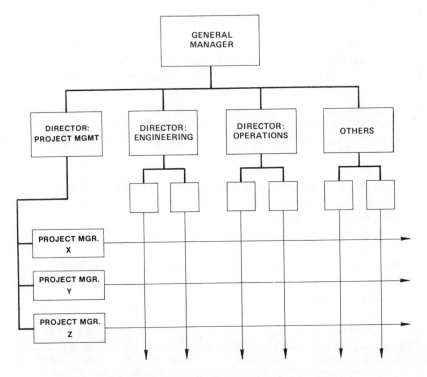

Figure 7–8. Development of a director of project management.

ble for all program management. The general manager was then free from the daily routine of monitoring all programs alone.

Beck has elaborated on the basic role of this new position, the *manager of project managers* (M.P.M.):[3]

> The M.P.M. is a project manager, a people manager, a change manager and a systems manager. In general, one role cannot be considered more important than the other. The M.P.M. has responsibilities for managing the projects, directing and leading people and the project management effort, and for planning for change in the organization. The Manager of Project Managers is a liaison between the Project Management Department and upper management as well as functional department management and acts as a systems manager when serving as a liaison.

Executives contend that an effective span of control is five to seven people. Does this apply to the director of project management as well? Consider a company that has 15 ongoing projects at once. There are three over $5 million, seven between $1 and $3 million, and five under $700,000. Each project has a full-time project manager. Can all 15 project managers report to the same person? The company solved this problem by creating a deputy director of project management. All projects over $1 million reported to the director and all projects under $1 million went to the deputy director. The director's rationale soon fell by the wayside when he found that the more severe problems were occurring on the smaller dollar-volume projects. If the project manager is actually a general manager, then the director of project management should be able to supervise more effectively than seven project managers. The desired span of control, of course, varies from company to company and must take into account:

- The demands imposed on the organization by task complexity
- Available technology
- The external environment
- The needs of the organizational membership.

Those variables influence the internal functioning of the company. Executives must realize that there is no one best way to organize under all conditions, including span of control.

As companies expand, it is inevitable that new and more complex conflicts arise. The control of the engineering functions poses such a problem: Should

---

[3] Beck, Dale R., "The Role of the Manager of Project Managers," *Proceedings of the Ninth Annual International Seminar/Symposium on Project Management,* October 24–26, 1977, Chicago, p. 141.

the project manager have ultimate responsibility for the engineering functions of a project, or should there be a deputy project manager who reports to the director of engineering and controls all technical activity?

Although there are pros and cons for both arrangements, the problem resolved itself in the company mentioned above when projects grew so large that the project manager became unable to handle both the project management and project engineering functions. Therefore, as shown in Figure 7-9, a chief project engineer was assigned to each project as deputy project manager, but remained functionally assigned to the director of engineering. The project manager was now responsible for time and cost considerations, whereas the project engineer was concerned with technical performance. The project engineer can be either "solid" vertically and "dotted" horizontal, or vice versa. There are also situations where the project engineer may be "solid" in both directions. This decision usually rests with the director of engineering. Of course, in a project where the project engineer would be needed on a part-time basis only, the picture would then be solid vertically and dotted horizontally.

This subdivision of functions is necessary in order to control large projects adequately. However, for small R&D projects, say $100,000 or less, it is quite common for an engineer to serve as the project manager as well as the project

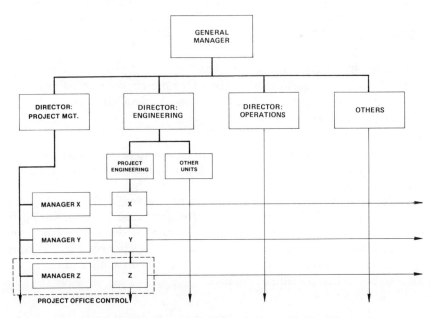

Figure 7-9. Placing project engineering in the project office.

engineer. Here, the project manager must have technical expertise, not merely understanding. Furthermore, this individual can still be attached to a functional engineering support unit other than project engineering. As an example, the mechanical engineering department receives a government contract for $75,000 to perform tests on a new material. The proposal is written by an engineer attached to this department. When the contract is awarded, this individual, although not in the project engineering department, can fulfill the role of project manager and project engineer while still reporting to the manager of the mechanical engineering department. This arrangement works best (and is cost-effective) for short-term projects that cross a minimum number of functional units.

Project management has matured as an outgrowth of the need to develop and produce complex and/or large projects in the shortest possible time, within anticipated cost, with required reliability and performance, and (when applicable) to realize a profit. Based upon the realization that modern organizations have become so complex that traditional organizational structures and relationships no longer allow for effective management, how can executives determine which organizational form is best, especially because some projects last for only a few weeks or months while others may take years?

To answer such a question, we must first determine whether or not the necessary characteristics exist for warranting a project management organizational form. Generally speaking, the project management approach can be effectively applied to a one-time undertaking that is:[4]

- Definable in terms of a specific goal
- Infrequent, unique, or unfamiliar to the present organization
- Complex with respect to interdependence of detailed tasks
- Critical to the company.

Once a group of tasks are selected and considered to be a project, the next step is to define the kinds of projects. These include individual, staff, and matrix or aggregate projects.

Unfortunately, many companies do not have a clear definition of what a project is. As a result, large project teams are often constructed for small projects when they could be handled more quickly and effectively by some other structural form. All structural forms have their advantages and disadvantages, but the project management approach, even with its disadvantages, appears to be the best possible alternative.

---

[4] John M. Stewart, "Making Project Management Work," *Business Horizons,* Fall 1965, p. 54.

Four fundamental parameters must be analyzed when considering implementation of a project organizational form:

- Integrating devices
- Authority structure
- Influence distribution
- Information systems.

Project management is a means of integrating all company efforts, especially research and development, by selecting an appropriate organizational form. Two questions arise when we think of designing the organization to facilitate the work of the integrators:

- Is it better to establish a formal integration department, or simply to set up integrating positions independent of one another?
- If individual integrating positions are set up, how should they be related to the large structure?

Informal integration works best if, and only if, effective collaboration can be achieved between conflicting units. Without any clearly defined authority, the role of the integrator is simply to act as an exchange medium across the interface of two functional units. As the size of the organization increases, formal integration positions must exist, especially in situations where intense conflict can occur (e.g., research and development).

Not all organizations need a pure matrix structure to achieve this integration. Many problems can be solved simply through the scalar chain of command, depending upon the size of the organization and the nature of the project. The actual size of organizations needed to achieve project control can vary from one person to several thousand. The organizational structure needed for effective project control is governed by the desires of top management and project circumstances.

Top management must decide upon the authority structure that controls the integration mechanism. The authority structure can range from pure functional authority (traditional management), to product authority (product management), and finally to dual authority (matrix management). From a management point of view, organizational forms are often selected based upon how much authority top management wishes to delegate or surrender.

Integration of activities across functional boundaries can also be accomplished by influence. Influence includes such factors as participation in budget planning and approval, design changes, location and size of offices, salaries, and so on. Influence can also cut administrative red tape and develop a much more unified informal organization.

Information systems also play an important role. Previously, we stated that one of the advantages of several project management structures is the ability to make both rapid and timely decisions with almost immediate response to environmental changes. Information systems are designed to get the right information to the right person at the right time in a cost-effective manner. Organizational functions must facilitate the flow of information through the management network.

Galbraith has described additional factors that can influence organizational selection. The factors are:[5]

- Diversity of product lines
- Rate of change of the product line
- Interdependencies among subunits
- Level of technology
- Presence of economies of scale
- Organizational size.

A diversity of product lines requires both top-level and functional managers to maintain knowledge in all areas. Diversity makes it more difficult for managers to make realistic estimates concerning resource allocations and the control of time, cost, schedules, and technology. The systems approach to management requires that sufficient information and alternatives be available so that effective trade-offs can be established. For diversity in a high-technology environment, the organizational choice might, in fact, be a trade-off between the flow of work and the flow of information. Diversity tends toward strong product authority and control.

Many functional organizations consider themselves as companies within a company and pride themselves on their independence. This poses a severe problem in trying to develop a synergistic atmosphere. Successful project management requires that functional units recognize the interdependence that must exist in order for technology to be shared and schedule dates to be met. Interdependency is also required in order to develop strong communications channels as well as coordination.

The use of new technologies poses a serious problem in that technical expertise must be established in all specialties, including engineering, production, material control, and safety. Maintaining technical expertise works best in strong functional disciplines, provided the information is not purchased outside the organization. The main problem, however, is how to communicate this expertise across functional lines. Independent R&D units can be

---

[5]Galbraith, Jay R., "Matrix Organization Designs," *Business Horizons,* February 1971, pp. 29–40.

established as opposed to integrating R&D into each functional department's routine efforts. Organizational control requirements are much more difficult in high-technology industries with ongoing research and development than with pure production groups.

The economies of scale and size can also affect organizational selection. The economies of scale are most often controlled by the amount of physical resources that a company has available. For example, a company with limited facilities and resources might find it impossible to compete with other companies on production or competitive bidding for larger dollar-volume products. Such a company must rely heavily on maintaining multiple projects (or products), each of low cost or volume, whereas a larger organization may need only three or four projects large enough to sustain the organization. The larger the economies of scale, the more the organization tends to favor pure functional management.

The size of the organization is important in that it can limit the amount of technical expertise in the economies of scale. While size may have little effect on the organizational structure, it does have a severe impact on the economies of scale. Small companies, for example, cannot maintain large specialist staffs and therefore incur a larger cost for specialization and lost economies of scale.

The four factors described previously for organizational form selections together with the six alternatives of Galbraith can be regarded as universal in nature. Beyond these universal factors, we must look at the company in terms of its product, business base, and personnel. Goodman has defined a set of subfactors related to R&D groups:[6]

- Clear location of responsibility
- Ease and accuracy of communications
- Effective cost control
- Ability to provide good technical supervision
- Flexibility of staffing
- Importance to the company
- Quick reaction capability to sudden changes in the project
- Complexity of the project
- Size of the project with relation to other work in-house
- Form desired by customer
- Ability to provide a clear path for individual promotion.

Goodman asked various managers to select from the above list and rank the factors from most important to least important in terms of how they

---

[6] Goodman, Richard A., "Organizational Preference in Research and Development," *Human Relations* Vol. 3, No. 4, 1970, pp. 279–298.

would be considered in designing an organization. Both general management and project management personnel were queried. With one exception, the flexibility of staffing, the responses from both groups correlated to a coefficient of 0.811. Clear location of responsibility was seen as the most important factor, and a path for promotion the least important.

Middleton conducted a mail survey to aerospace firms in an attempt to determine how well the companies using project management met their objectives.[7] Forty-seven responses were received. Tables 7–10 and 7–11 identify the results. Middleton stated:

> In evaluating the results of the survey, it appears that a company taking the project organization approach can be reasonably certain that it will improve controls and customer (out-of-company) relations, but internal operations will be more complex.

The way in which companies operate their project organization is bound to affect the organization, both during the operation of the project and after the project has been completed and personnel have been disbanded. The overall effects on the company must be looked at from a personnel and cost control standpoint. This is accomplished, in depth, in later chapters, Although project management is growing, the creation of a project organization does not necessarily insure that an assigned objective will be accomplished success-

Table 7–10. Major company advantages of project management

ADVANTAGES	PERCENT OF RESPONDENTS
• Better control of projects	92%
• Better customer relations	80%
• Shorter product development time	40%
• Lower program costs	30%
• Improved quality and reliability	26%
• Higher profit margins	24%
• Better control over program security	13%
Other Benefits	
• Better project visibility and focus on results	
• Improved coordination among company divisions doing work on the project	
• Accelerated development of managers because of breadth of project responsibilities	

(SOURCE: C. J. Middleton, "How to Set Up a Project Organization," *Harvard Business Review,* March–April 1967, pp. 73–82).

---

[7]C. J. Middleton, "How to Set Up a Project Organization," *Harvard Business Review,* March–April 1967, Copyright © 1967 by the President and Fellows of Harvard College, all rights reserved, pp. 73–82.

Table 7-11. Major company disadvantages of project management

DISADVANTAGES	PERCENT OF RESPONDENTS
• More complex internal operations	51%
• Inconsistency in application of company policy	32%
• Lower utilization of personnel	13%
• Higher program costs	13%
• More difficult to manage	13%
• Lower profit margins	2%
Other Disadvantages	
• Tendency for functional groups to neglect their job and let the project organization do everything	
• Too much shifting of personnel from project to project	
• Duplication of functional skills in project organization	

(SOURCE: C. J. Middleton, "How to Set Up a Project Organization," *Harvard Business Review,* March–April 1967, pp. 73–82).

fully. Furthermore, weaknesses can develop in the areas of maintaining capability and structural changes.

Middleton has listed four undesirable results that can develop from the use of project organizations, and affect company capabilities:[8]

- Project priorities and competition for talent may interrupt the stability of the organization and interfere with its long-range interests by upsetting the traditional business of functional organizations.
- Long-range plans may suffer as the company gets more involved in meeting schedules and fulfilling the requirements of temporary projects.
- Shifting people from project to project may disrupt the training of employees and specialists, thereby hindering the growth and development within their fields of specialization.
- Lessons learned on one project may not be communicated to other projects.

An almost predictable result of using the project management approach is the increase in management positions. Killian describes the results of two surveys:[9]

One company compared its organization and management structure as it existed before it began forming project units with the structure that existed afterward. The number of departments had increased from 65 to 106, while

---

[8] Ibid.
[9] William P. Killian, "Project Management—Future Organizational Concepts," *Marquette Business Review,* No., 2, 1971, pp. 90–107.

total employment remained practically the same. The number of employees for every supervisor had dropped from 13.4 to 12.8. The company concluded that a major cause of this change was the project groups [see footnote 8 for reference article.].

Another company uncovered proof of its conclusion when it counted the number of second-level and higher management positions. It found that it had 11 more vice-presidents and directors, 35 more managers, and 56 more second-level supervisors. Although the company attributed part of this growth to an upgrading of titles, the effect of the project organization was the creation of 60 more management positions.

Although the project organization is a specialized, task-oriented entity, it seldom, if ever, exists apart from the traditional structure of the organization.[10] All project management structures overlap the traditional structure. Furthermore, companies can have more than one project organizational form in existence at one time. A major steel producer, for example, has a matrix structure for R&D and a product structure elsewhere.

Accepting a project management structure is a giant step from which there may be no return. The company may have to create more management positions without changing the total employment levels. In addition, incorporation of a project organization is almost always accompanied by the upgrading of jobs. In any event, management must realize that whichever project management structure is selected, a dynamic state of equilibrium will be necessary. Regardless of which organizational structure is selected for the project, the project management section of the management proposal should contain:

- The organizational structure selected
- The relationship of the project organization to the overall company organization
- An outline of the project manager's responsibilities and authority. (This is discussed in Chapter 3.)

Figure 7–10 illustrates a method for identifying the relationship of the project to the overall company. If you are the proposal manager for Dalton Corporation, then Figure 7–10 is the organization chart that would be submitted for the MIDAS program. Two key points appear on this chart:

---

[10] Allen R. Janger, "Anatomy of the Project Organization," *Business Management Record,* November 1963, pp. 12–18.

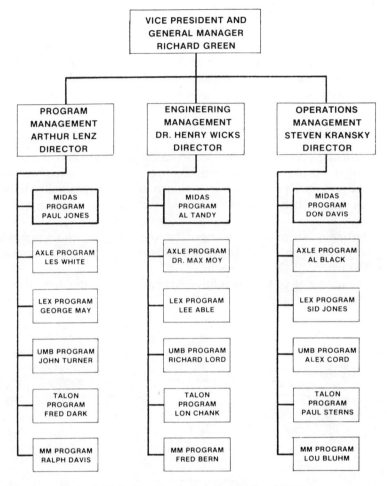

Figure 7-10. Dalton Corporation organizational structure.

- The MIDAS program appears at the top of the other projects, *regardless* of the priority. (Would you really expect the customer to be pleased if the project were to appear at the bottom of the list?)
- All information on these figures relating to the MIDAS program should be in **boldface** print in order to emphasize their location.

If you work for a small company in which one project manager may handle multiple projects, then you may wish to identify only the names of the key people on the proposed project. The customer may not be pleased to find his key people shared on several other projects.

The project office, as shown in Figure 7-11 should accompany Figure 7-10. Here, you may have to identify the percentage of time that each employee will spend in the project office. You may wish to refer to the resumés as in Figure 7-3.

7.5 COMPANY HISTORY

The intent of the company history section is not to develop a novel, but simply to summarize the birth of your company to the present time in order to convince the customer's evaluation team that your company is well qualified to perform the activities. At a minimum, this section should include:

- Pertinent data on the founding of the company (i.e., who, when, where, why, and so on), including information on original or current charter
- The nature of your past business
- The nature of your current business (size, complexity, diversity)
- Client references.

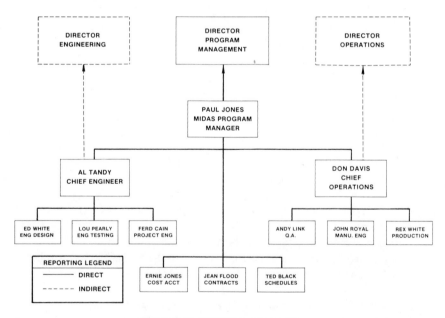

Figure 7-11. MIDAS program office.

The first item is important in that it provides the customer with sufficient data to be convinced that you are not a "fly-by-night" organization that came about simply to bid on this project. For small projects, a group of people may simply form a corporation in order to bid on some type of project. This is common for "training/seminar" projects where groups of consultants and university faculty members form special task forces. Today, for small projects that may be open only to corporations with sales less than $2 million, the government requires income statements for the past three years in order to show the solvency of the company. The government wants to limit their risk should your company fold before the project is scheduled for completion.

One of the best ways of demonstrating the nature of your current business is to provide a copy of your stockholder's report. In addition, make sure that you stress the successes that your company has had over the last 10 to 20 years. This should help establish credibility for your proposal.

The customer might wish to contact several of your clients to discuss working relationships and problems. Therefore, when you list your past and present clients, you may wish to include a high ranking customer representative who could be contacted to provide reference information. Project managers, project sponsors, and vice-presidents normally serve this purpose.

7.6 COMPANY CAPABILITIES AND OVERALL EXPERIENCES

The intent of this section is not only to identify to the customer your past successes, but to show that your organization possesses the necessary experience to achieve the contractual objectives. The customer must be convinced that your past successes were not "hit or miss" situations, but were achieved through methodical, well-organized logic based upon related past experiences.

In order to achieve this, you must show your achievement, expertise, and capability in certain areas. The question, of course, is which areas to describe. Some contractors describe all major items that could easily be developed into separate program plans. These include:

- Budgeting system
- Accounting system
- Management system
- Facilities utilization system
- Configuration management system
- Logistic support system
- Manufacturing system
- Procurement system

- Subcontracting system
- Quality assurance system
- Scheduling system
- Research and development system
- Tooling system
- Training system
- Transportation system
- Maintenance system
- Customer Liaison system.

At a minimum, the following information should be provided:

- *The size and type of contracts your company has successfully managed.*
- *The accuracy of your bidding history.* How close were you to your previous bids? What were your projected versus actual costs?
- *The accuracy of your delivery schedule.* How accurate were you in providing deliverables and meeting delivery dates? What were your planned versus actual delivery dates?
- *The accuracy of your procurement/subcontracting system.* How well have you worked with vendors and subcontractors in the past? Have they lived up to time, cost, and performance expectations?

Not all contractors have related past experience in each of these areas. In such cases, the contractor must stress general experience in order to show how it qualifies the organization to perform the project.

7.7 FACILITIES

The facilities section of the management proposal should describe the actual facilities your company has to satisfy the project requirements. It is necessary to describe only those facilities pertinent to the project. The facility section should also show the utilization rate of the facilities. As an example, several years ago a large production company bid on a government project. The facilities section showed that the major equipment and facilities were approaching maximum utilization and the government was quite concerned over the risk that they would be taking over the lifetime of the project. As part of the proposal effort, the customer agreed to spend a large amount of corporate dollars on a capital equipment plant expansion program should the contract be won.

A commonly forgotten portion of the facilities section is your graphic arts capability and your model shop. An important part of construction projects, for example, may be to provide the customer with a miniaturized model of the facilities. These types of facilities/capabilities may give you the competitive edge.

7.8 COST AND SCHEDULE CONTROLS

The intent of the cost and schedule controls section is to demonstrate not only your capabilities for controlling the project within time, cost, and performance, but your past successes in this area. Typical items included in this section would be:

- Budgeting procedures
- Scheduling procedures
- Control mechanisms.

The budgeting procedures should describe briefly your method for arriving at reasonable cost estimates for your proposals. You may wish to show some of your planning/budgeting documentation. Tabulated results can be used to show historical data of how your past budgeted costs have compared to actual costs at project termination.

The scheduling procedures should describe your experience with such tools and techniques as PERT/CPM, LOB, and others. You may wish to discuss your methods for updating schedules and graphs as well as any specialized symbolic notation your people use. If you maintain computer graphics capabilities, you may wish to add an appendix to the management proposal illustrating the types of computer graphics scheduling.

The control mechanisms should show your ability to compare actual to projected performance and cost continuously as a function of time. If your control system is computerized, you should state this. This section might also contain a description of your capability to determine project status as well as variance analysis accurately. Be sure to identify the capabilities of the system, such as level five of the work breakdown structure (see Section 6.6). Customers also like to see the types of control system status reports that will be provided to in-house management for decision making as well as to the customer for progress reporting.

7.9 SUBCONTRACTING AND JOINT VENTURES

If your proposed project includes subcontracting or a joint venture relationship, then your proposal should include a description of your proposed plan for controlling time, cost, and performance and your methods for subcontractor evaluation.

This section can be broken down into two parts. The first part will describe your history in working with subcontractors and how your joint venture operations work out. You should stress how decisions were made as well as all of your successes. Part two, which obviously will be based upon your successes from part one, will describe how you propose to work with this project's subcontractors and joint venture teams. Professional proposal evaluation teams will look for evidence in the following questions:

- How do you choose your criteria for selecting subcontractors?
- How closely will you be working with subcontractors and joint venture teams, especially during the initial planning stages?
- How will you be defining the requirements for your subcontractors or how will you be subdividing the responsibilites with the joint venture teams?
- How closely will you be monitoring the performance of your subcontractors or joint venture teams?
- How will you be obtaining status of the subcontractors. Will the information be obtained by written reports, regularly scheduled technical interchange meetings, or in-house representatives?
- How will you be providing the status information to the customer?

7.10 ONGOING WORK AND FUTURE OBJECTIVES

The stability and growth of your company can best be achieved by including a section on your company's ongoing work and future objectives. In this section, you should identify all ongoing work, not merely that which is directly related. However, you may wish to stress the related work.

If you have future plans to break into new areas, your proposal should state this. You may be pleasantly surprised to find out that your customer has plans to do the same, and this could easily give you the competitive edge because the customer may prefer to work with simply one contractor.

Chapter 8

The Cost Proposal

8.0 INTRODUCTION

The cost proposal must be regarded as equally as important as the technical and management proposals. When the customer intends to award a firm, fixed-price contract, the bottom line cost is the deciding factor in contract award. However, for a cost-reimbursable contract, the contract must be able to support all costs. In this case, the proposal must include supporting data for departmental direct labor man-hours, labor rates, escalation factors on salaries and raw materials, subcontracts, purchased parts, overhead rates, and profit percentages.

The purpose of the cost proposal is to provide the customer with sufficient cost and supporting data such that the customer will be convinced that the contractor's estimates are reasonable. The RFP will generally describe:

- The work breakdown structure against which costs must be provided
- The amount of cost data that must be furnished
- The amount of supporting data that must be furnished.

A customer-provided statement of work enables the customer to compare "apples with apples" when comparing the costs for the same WBS element in each bid. For example, if five of six bidders estimate approximately 6,000 man-hours for a given WBS element, and your bid comes in at 4,000 man-hours for the same task, the customer may question the validity of your bid and estimating techniques.

The cost proposal may very well be the most time-consuming proposal. There are several reasons for this:

- Estimates may have no relation to the expected cost or performance.
- Proposals may be priced out assuming unlimited resources whereas the functional managers know that such resources will not be available for the contract.
- The activity may be so unique to the company that accurate estimates cannot be made.
- Properly trained estimators may not be available.
- Functional managers may inflate their estimates to such a degree that the company will not be competitive.

It is not uncommon for the customer to give the contractor an additional two to four weeks for the preparation of the cost proposal. This time should be spent verifying the accuracy of the cost proposal, the risks to be incurred, and the compatibility of the cost and technical proposals.

Many contractors do not realize the full importance of the cost proposal. The proposal must be related to past performance and may be used by the customer as a basis for the future projects.

The actual content of the cost proposal depends upon the type of contract and the nature of the services to be proposed, whether they be a product, services, R&D, and so on. The following items may be included as part of the cost proposal:

- Abstract and/or title page
- Table of contents
- Introduction
- Summary
- Statement of work (or items to be furnished)
- Cost summary
- Supporting schedules
- Fee/profit statement
- Contractual terms and conditions
- Certifications and representations
- Government or customer-furnished equipment
- Elements of cost/cost breakdown
- Cost format
- Cost estimating techniques
- Supporting data
- Supplemental data (that may include MCCS)

8.1 BASIC CONSIDERATIONS: THE PRICING/PROFIT STRATEGY

Bidding can be defined as a competition for the right to perform services or to acquire property. For defense-related companies, contracts often provide the only source of revenue. The simplest case is when a government agency invites competitive bidding proposals. Each interested company must submit a bid, and the company with the lowest bid usually receives the contract. For large government contracts, the actual number of competitors is usually small and known. For small contracts, the exact number may be unknown and the contractor may have to alter both his estimating techniques, and his pricing/profit strategy.

The contractor's success is almost always based upon the ability to produce a low bid with adequate profit margin. When the contractor compiles a bidding estimate, target and overhead costs, as well as additional influential factors of the firm and that of the possible competitors, must be analyzed accurately. The contractor must be able to measure, with reasonable accuracy, the essential facts such as labor, material, overhead, and so on.

He must also be knowledgeable about the intangible and often unknown factors, especially those of his competitors. These unknown and intangible factors can, and often do, determine whether or not one should bid on a contract. As an example, a competitor who is faced with the possibility of having to lay off several employees may be awarded a government contract regardless of whether or not a lower bid is submitted. Essentially, the unknown and intangible factors are the contractor's judgment process of how the bid will be received and reviewed under these circumstances.

Any strategy that the company adopts as ground rules for competitive bidding must satisfy the objectives of the company. In other words, company objectives determine the strategy to be used in the bidding model. The strategy then dictates the parameters and constraints to be imposed. Table 8-1 lists some of the possible strategies resulting from company objectives. These, as well as others, serve as the objective function in competitive bidding.

The formulation and adoption of any type of competitive bidding approach, whether it is based upon game theory, decision theory, or Bayesian statistics, is usually designed to maximize the objective function. This for-

Table 8-1. Comparison of strategy-based objective functions.

TRADITIONAL MICROECONOMICS	COMPETITIVE BIDDING THEORY
1. Maximize profits	1. Maximize expected profits
2. Maximize sales subject to a profit constraint	2. Obtain a certain return on initial research and development
	3. Minimize expected losses
	4. Minimize expected profits of the competitors
	5. Obtain the contract, even at a loss, in order to maintain productivity and employment levels

mulation procedure can become a tedious task because it requires transforming the art of competitive bidding into a science. Any difficulties associated with the transformation are often counterbalanced by proper and realistic assumptions concerning the problem at hand.

The purpose of any competitive bidding model is an attempt to arrive at an optimum bid by quantifying as much information as possible concerning the goals of the firm. However, before competitive bidding can be quantified, the underlying assumptions must be explained in depth, otherwise the realistic dimensions of the model may be open to question. As is the case in any type of scientific endeavor, factual representation by assumption must be first described in a qualitative sense, because the validity of any model rests upon proper assumptions. The following are commonly used assumptions for determining pricing/profit strategy and estimating ground rules.

Assumption I: The Number and Identity of All Competitors are Known

In both microeconomic pricing theory and competitive bidding theory, the number and identity of all competitors are known. This takes an added significance for a closed consumer market because the contractor usually performs an analysis of the competitors to determine which have the capability of handling the contract.[1] Under some government contracts, the government announced, prior to the final bid, which companies will be bidding on each contract.

For the construction industry, a contractor may be inclined to feel that every possible contractor within a certain radius will bid on every contract, and only a given percentage of those, namely the firms that have the special equipment and manpower designated by the contract, will bid. In the aerospace industry, the field may be as narrow as 10 to 12 companies with only three or four competing. In an open consumer market, one company is interested only in the final product of the other company, not so much in potential abilities. However, for competitive bidding, both must be investigated in depth. Thus, it is reasonable to assume, in some cases, that the identity of all competitors in the field are known, as well as those expected to compete for the contract.

---

[1] In the defense industry, as the dollar value of the proposal increases, the number of competitors decreases. For small contracts (under $100,000), the total number of competitors are generally unknown, and several large companies will not compete, because their overhead rates exceed those of the smaller companies. Overhead rates become important for large contracts. If the capabilities are not present, the competitor must acquire them by using retained earnings. In this situation, overhead costs run high and must be included as capability costs in the bid.

Assumption II: The Prior Bidding History of All Competitors is Known

For any competitive bidding system to be valid, an accurate knowledge of competitor bidding history must be known. For competitive bidding on state and federal government contracts, bids may be a matter of public record. For other types of contracts, the necessary information may prove difficult to find.

Once the competitors' bids are known, work begins on the analysis. First, we must be able to separate the factual bids from the fantasy bids. This requires close scrutiny of the bidding spectrum of each bidder. Using the defense industry as an example, we can expect each competitor to submit a similar bid for a similar type of contract. If, however, we find bids at either the low or high extremes of the spectrum we analyze, if possible, the competitor's monetary situation at the time of the bid.

At the low-cost end of the scale, we must look at the relative importance of landing the bid. Certain questions must be answered. Will the competitor be operating at a loss? Is a future or follow-on contract anticipated? Is a negative profit acceptable for the sake of employing key personnel and holding together an organization? Or is it possible that the contractor wishes to become knowledgeable in a new field and is willing to operate at a loss to catch up with the competition and establish a reputation in the field?

At the high-cost end of the scale, there is generally only one conclusion, assuming that all other similar bids reflect a cluster of sorts. If the competitor is contract-rich at the moment, or does not want the contract because of insufficient resources in either equipment or personnel, "courtesy" bid is usually submitted, just to keep the firm's reputation alive. Often, government contracting agencies expect certain companies to bid on specified contracts, even though they have no real interest in the project.

Thus, it becomes important when analyzing the competitor's bidding history to investigate the time factor during which the bid was made. Current and future bidding strategies must consider how anxious or disinterested each competitor may have been during each bid. The necessity of determining the relevance and similarity of each competitor's bid may be the single most important factor in any competitive bidding model.

Wasson[2] has shown that implied in Assumptions I and II are the following points:

- Each bidder tends to follow a consistent pattern in his cost estimating procedure.

---

[2] Wasson, C. R., *Understanding Qualitative Analysis,* Appleton-Century-Croft, New York, 1969.

- Cost estimates made by competing bidders will be similar and reasonably parallel over time.
- If only winning bids are known directly, the competition was probably even enough that the losers' bids were close to those of the winner.
- As a result, the profit objective of each bidder can be approximated from any of his past bids if we have either knowledge of or a close estimate of his bid or an estimate of the project cost. While such an estimate will contain some degree of error, the error in a series of such estimates will be small.
- Each bidder makes his own bid without knowledge of the action of others and competitors' bids are therefore independent of each other. Thus the chances that each will enter a given bid is of the odds that others will enter that bid.

Wasson also states:

These assumptions would be familiar to anyone who has been making bids. All that competitive bidding strategy contributes, therefore, is a quantification of the inferences drawn about competitor behavior, in terms of a distribution of profit position values for all possible bids.

Assumption III: Target Costs Can Be Estimated With Reasonable Accuracy

The target cost is usually the principal independent variable in a competitive bidding strategy. Methods of estimating target costs are often a closely guarded secret. They are painstakingly prepared, checked, and rechecked. Target costs include man-hour costs, processing costs, equipment, and raw materials, as well as the mark-up functions of overhead costs. The mark-up costs may also include profits.

The accuracy with which one determines the target costs in usually dependent on the nature of the proposed contract. For the construction industry, it is not uncommon to bid on several similar contracts. Target cost estimates thus become more precise when competing on similar contracts. For the defense or aerospace industry, similar or repetitive contracts are few and far between. It therefore becomes a very risky procedure estimating target costs for new types of contracts.

Whenever the cost estimates are found to be higher than the competition, one of two general situations exists. First, the competition may be stiff enough such that almost all profit is slowly eliminated. This is common in the defense industry, where contract profits have declined sharply during the last 10 years. Second, we may find that our costs are always higher than the competition and that it behooves us to switch our interests to other types of projects.

Assumption IV: There Is No Collusion Among Competitors

No collusion by the competitors implies that we are playing an honest game. Each competitor can do all the work necessary to complete the contract. The Department of Justice has passed a variety of laws preventing collusion among competitors. In past years, there have been cases where several competitors would often band together and determine, either by territorial agreements or a rotation system, who would submit the low bid.

Although uncommon, competitive bidding sometimes produces identical bids on certain contracts. Although the government frowns on such bids and views them with mistrust, they can be, and often are, honest bids. Cook[3] has elaborated on five conditions that favor identical bids.

- Many industries are characterized by relatively few sellers. Identical bids are a manifestation of oligolpoly. When the competition is small, each competitor's habits are usually definable and deviations on the low-bid side may result in a price war.
- There is often reasonable opportunity for retaliatory action in American business.
- In many business situations, the product is well-specified.
- Often a product involves so small a transportation cost that the cost is typically absorbed by the seller, or else the product is transported by a common carrier or other transportation agency at costs determined from trade sources.
- Frequently, the quantities involved in individual bids are relatively small with respect to total output of the competitors, and/or the bid business is relatively small compared to the total output sold in other ways.

Also considered in Assumption IV is the disregarding of the commonly used "most-favored-customer" clause where the present purchaser must be given an opportunity retroactively to recompete at the low-bid price.

Assumption V: Bid Preparation Costs Are Not Included in the Estimation of Target Costs

In many government bidding situations, the government may occasionally reimburse each of the bidders a given percentage of the bidding costs. The percentage may be as high as 90 to 95 percent.

Occasionally, the bidder may wish to include the bid preparation costs in the target cost, or subsidize the costs out of previous profits. Bidding costs are

[3] Cook, Paul W., Jr., "Fact and Fantasy on Identical Bids," *Harvard Business Review,* 41 (January–February, 1963) pp. 67–72.

normally 0.5 to 2.0 percent of total costs.[4] Because this section concerns itself primarily with the comparison of models, bid preparation costs are not included in the target costs. There are additional assumptions to be made, other than those described here.

One of the most important factors in estimating costs and profits as well as determining bidding strategy is the type of contract expected. Usually, the ethics and confidence by which a bid is prepared depend on how much of a risk the contractor occurs both personally and through the contract.

Certain types of contracts provide relief for the contractor, especially if onerous risks exist.[5] The target cost must therefore consider how well the contract type covers certain high and low risk areas.

Prospective clients are always concerned when, during a competitive bidding process, one bid is much lower than the others. The customer may question the validity of the bid and whether or not the contract can be achieved for the low bid. In these cases, the customer usually includes safeguards such as incentive and penalty clauses in the contract.

Because of this risk factor, competitors often try to negotiate not only for the target cost figures, but also the type of contract involved, because risk protection is the predominant influential factor.

Once the competition is analyzed, the contractor must determine the amount of profit to bid for. The exact amount of profit may depend upon the type of contract. For example, on a firm, fixed-price contract, the contractor usually succeeds in obtaining a higher profit percentage than in a cost-reimbursable package because the contractor incurs a higher risk.

The three most common pricing techniques for profit are:

- A profit percentage of the totally burdened labor and raw material costs
- A total dollar value
- A dollar profit percentage per direct labor hour.

Some contractors prefer simply to negotiate the bottom line and a corresponding profit percentage. The value of this technique is that it is quick and simple. In the second technique, the proposal (if accepted) is expected to return a certain amount of dollars for the stockholder, rather than a profit

---

[4] It should be noted that research and development is almost always included in bidding costs. Because these costs become quite high on weapons systems development, government financing and reimbursement is essential.

Open consumer markets do not have bidding costs, but do have larger profits because R&D costs must be funded out of retained earnings. Usually large companies spend up to 2 to 3 percent of total sales on R&D.

[5] *Onerous risks* are unfair risks that the contractor may have to bear. Quite often, the contract negotiations may not agree on what is or is not an onerous risk.

percentage. This technique has a severe impact on the type of contract negotiated. For example, consider the following:

- Base cost = $20,000,000
- Cost-reimbursable contract with a 90/10 sharing ratio

You would like to make a profit of $1.6 million (which equals 8 percent of base cost) for the stockholders. Because of the sharing ratio, the contractor can agree to a negotiated base cost of $15 million with a 14 percent profit and still have the same profit of $1.6 million for the stockholders. However, a $5 million overrun will not be looked upon favorably by the customer for consideration during follow-on activities.

In the third technique, the contractor may simply request a profit between $2 to $6 for each direct labor hour worked. This technique, of course, depends upon the method of pricing out the work and rolling up the costs. In some companies, profits and overhead rates are applied to raw materials and purchased parts. The third technique is quite common in construction companies.

Pricing and profit strategy are therefore "married" to the type of contract, type of pricing, competitive situation, and negotiation techniques. Because of these factors, proposal managers must work closely with executives during the preliminary proposal stages so as to understand the basic pricing and profit strategies and their impact on the total pricing effort. The following five elements summarize these points:

- *Demand*. What will the customer pay?
- *Competition*. What is the competition selling it for?
- *Costs*. What additional costs are likely to be incurred?
- *Profit*. By how much money will this effort increase the company's economic outlook?
- *Benefits*. What long- or short-term benefits may be obtained from this effort?

8.2 ESTIMATING TECHNIQUES USED

Many proposals, even those which are not government-related, require descriptions of the estimating techniques used. The most efficient method is data tabulation. For example, for raw materials the proposal may state the

- Material
- Possible sources
- Recommended source
- Cost basis (i.e., vendor quote or past/present experience).

In addition, supplemental estimating techniques may be submitted for such items as overhead and general and administrative (G&A) costs. The estimating techniques may become the basis for contract negotiations. Government contracts are covered by the Truth in Negotiations Act.

The following information has to be estimated:

- Direct labor hours
- Divisional overhead rates
- Company G&A overhead rates
- Corporate overhead rates
- Material costs.

There are several factors to be considered in developing the estimating methods. The first item is the *historical data on previous activities.* This data should be based upon actuals and should include such things as scrap factors, breaks, spoilage, new equipment, facilities, or materials, special tooling, and learning curve improvements, whether a result of internal training or new employee hiring.

The second item is *future project rates.* This includes escalation factors for salaries and raw materials and any future trends that could have a bearing on costs such as labor union negotiations in your company as well as in the vendor's company. In this regard, many experienced managers read trade publications for guidance in price escalations.

Overhead rates may very well be the most difficult item to estimate. Table 8–2 shows the activities that may comprise an overhead rate.[6] Overhead rates are sensitive not only to salary/fringe benefit escalations, but moreso to the future business base. If the business base declines, the overhead rate may increase sharply. Many contracts allow for periodic renegotiation of the overhead rates should the contractor's business base change sharply. This topic, therefore, has a direct bearing upon the company's competitive situation.

The third item is the company's *physical assets.* This includes the design, layout, and proximity of the required materials, tools, facilities, equipment, and machinery. The estimates must consider the maintenance costs, comparative advantages of one facility over the next, and labor advantages.

The fourth item is the *overall learning curve efficiency* of the project team. The following questions must be answered:

- Do we have people with the necessary expertise?
- If not, do we have sufficient time to train employees?

---

[6]In some companies, entire divisions such as engineering are included in overhead rather than direct labor.

Table 8-2. Elements of Overhead Rates

Fringe benefits	Payroll taxes
Telephone/telegraph facilities	Reproduction facilities
Supervision	Clerical
Executive salaries	Vacation
Corporate salaries	Holiday
Group insurance	Sick leave
Office supplies	Utilities
Supplies/hand tools	Transportation
Building rent	Cafeteria
Building maintenance	Professional meetings
Depreciation of equipment	Retirement plans
Moving/storage expenses	Clubs/associations
Consulting services	Postage
Personnel recruitment	General ledger expenses
New business directors	Corporate auditing expenses

- Can we hire qualified personnel from the outside?
- If we have performed this effort before for the same customer, are the same employees available?
- If so, has there been a loss of learning in the time period between the two programs?
- If this is a follow-on effort, will the customer expect us to be performing at a higher position on the learning curve?

During contract negotiations in which an itemized breakdown of activities is needed, learning curve percentages are negotiated, especially for manufacturing operations and quality control. On large manufacturing projects, a change of as little as 5 percent in the learning curve could have an estimated impact of several million dollars in the final bid.

Once the ground rules are known, the next step is to determine the estimating procedure. There are generally three types:

- Detailed estimates
- Comparison estimates
- Group estimates.

Detailed estimates involve itemized analysis of each element of work, broken down to the smallest reasonable level. Detailed estimates are usually the best, but require large amounts of time for pricing, development of standards, and historical record keeping. Typical detailed standards might be:

- Materials property testing requires twenty (20) tests, each requiring six (6) hours. Testing includes clean-up, preparation time, and raw material

requisitioning. This estimate is based on the work performed under charge number D1375 on Project BL–23–55.
- This report requires 40 hours of preparation time. Reference time is based on charge numbers D3332 and D3341 on Project BN–33–21.

Comparison estimates are similar to detailed estimates but may differ by the degree of difficulty factor. For example:

- This report requires 50 hours of preparation time and is estimated to be 25 percent more difficult than the effort required on charge numbers D3332 and D3341 on Project BN–33–21. The reason for the increased degree of difficulty is the modification to the data item as requested by the customer in the statement of work.

Comparison estimates are both easy and hard to utilize effectively. They are easy in that they can be used on both similar and nonsimilar activities simply by including the degree of difficulty factor, and do not have to be used at the item-by-item level. For example, comparison estimates may be used at the project level, thereby eliminating detailed task estimating. The difficulty is in obtaining back-up justification for the degree of difficulty factor.

Group estimates are the easiest to develop but may be the highest risk. A group of individuals decides upon the "bottom line" cost. The group estimate may or may not contain detailed and comparison estimates. Group estimates are usually used for proposals that do not require back-up data or that need only a bottom line cost.

No matter how good the estimating system is, problems can occur. Below are common causes of downsteam cost problems that result from poor estimating:

- Poor estimating techniques and/or standards that result in unrealistic budgets
- Out-of-sequence starting and completion of activities and events
- Inadequate work breakdown structure
- No management policy on reporting and control practices
- Poor work definition at the lower levels of the organization
- Management reduces budgets or bids to be competitive or to eliminate "fat"
- Inadequate formal planning that results in unnoticed or often uncontrolled increase in scope of effort
- Poor comparison of actual versus planned costs
- Comparison of actual and planned costs at the wrong level of management

- Unforeseen technical problems
- Schedule delays that require overtime or idle time costing
- Material escalation factors that are unrealistic.

These factors can cause cost overruns in any phase of project development. Below are the most common causes for cost overruns:

- Proposal Phase
  - Failure to understand customer requirements
  - Unrealistic appraisal of in-house capabilities
  - Underestimate time requirement
- Negotiation Phase
  - Forcing a speedy compromise
  - Procurement ceiling costs
  - Negotiation team must "win this one"
- Contractual Phase
  - Contractual discrepancies
  - SOW different from RFP requirements
  - Proposal team different from project team
- Design Phase
  - Accept customer requests without management approval
  - Customer communications channels and data items
  - Design review meetings
- Production Phase
  - Excessive material costs
  - Specifications are not acceptable
  - Manufacturing and engineering disagreement

8.3 PRICING OUT THE WORK

The first integration of the functional unit into the project and proposal environments occurs during the pricing process. The total program costs obtained by pricing out the activities over the scheduled period of performance provides management with a fundamental tool for bidding and managing the project. During the pricing activities, the functional units have the option to consult the proposal manager for possible changes to work requirements as well as for further clarification.

Activities are priced out through the lowest pricing units of the company. It is the responsibility of these pricing units, whether they be sections, departments, or divisions, to provide accurate and meaningful cost data. Under ideal conditions, the work required (i.e., man-hours) to complete a given task is based upon historical standards. Unfortunately for many industries, projects and programs are so diversified that realistic comparison between previous activities may not be possible. The costing information obtained from each pricing unit, whether or not it is based upon historical standards, should be regarded only as an estimate. How can a company predict the salary structure three years from now? What will be the cost of raw materials two years from now? Will the business base (and therefore the overhead rates) change over the period of performance? The final response to these questions shows that costing out performance is related explicitly to an environment that cannot be predicted with any high degree of certainty.

Project management is an attempt to obtain the best utilization of resources within time, cost, and performance. Logical project estimating techniques are available. The following 13 steps provide a logical sequence in order to obtain better resource estimates. These steps may vary from company to company.

Step 1: Provide a complete definition of the work requirements.

Effective planning and implementation of projects cannot be accomplished without a complete definition of the requirements. For projects internal to the organization, the project manager works with the project sponsor and user (whether they be executives, functional managers, or simply employees) in order for the work to be defined completely. For these types of in-house projects, the project manager can wear multiple hats as project manager, proposal manager, and even project engineer on the same project.

For projects funded externally to the organization, the proposal manager (assisted by the project manager and possibly the contract administrator) must work with the customer to make sure that all of the work is defined completely and that there is no misinterpretation over the requirements. In many cases, the customer simply has an idea and needs assistance in establishing the requirements. The customer may hire an outside agency for assistance. If the activity is sole-source or perhaps part of an unsolicited effort, then the contractor may be asked to work with the customer in defining the requirements even before soliciting is attempted.

A complete definition of project requirements must include:

- Scope (or statement) of work
- Specifications
- Schedules (gross or summary).

The scope of work or statement of work (SOW) is a narrative description of all the work required to perform the project. The statement of work identifies the goals and objectives that are to be achieved. If a funding constraint exists, such as "this is a not-to-exceed effort of $250,000," this information might also appear in the SOW.

If the customer supplies a well-written statement of work, then the project and proposal managers will supply this SOW to the functional managers for dollar and man-hour estimates. Unless the customer maintains a staff of employees to provide a continuous stream of RFPs/RFQs, the customers must ask potential bidders to assist them in the preparation of the SOW. As an example, Alpha Company wishes to build a multimillion dollar chemical plant. Because Alpha does not erect such facilities on a regular basis, Alpha would send out inquiries instead of a formal RFP. These inquiries are used not only to identify potential bidders, but also to identify to potential bidders that they will have to develop an accurate SOW as part of the proposal process. This process may appear as a feasibility study. This is quite common especially on large dollar-value projects where contractors are willing to risk the additional time, cost, and effort as part of the bidding process. If the proposal is a sole-source effort, then the contractor may pass this cost on to the customer as part of the contract.

The statement of work is vital to proposal pricing and should not be taken lightly. All involved functional managers should be given the opportunity to review the SOW during the pricing process. Functional managers are the true technical experts in the company and best qualified to identify high-risk areas and prevent anything from "falling through the cracks." Misinterpretations of the statement of work can lead to severe cost overruns and schedule slippages.

The statement of work might be lumped together with the contractual data as part of the terms and conditions. The proposal manager may then have to separate out the SOW data from the RFP. This is vital for the pricing effort.

The second major item in the definition of the requirements is the identification of the specifications, if applicable. Specifications form the basis from which man-hours, equipment, and materials are priced out. The specifications must be identified so that the customer understands the basis for the man-hour, equipment, and materials estimates. Small changes in a specification can cause large cost overruns.

Another reason for identifying the specifications is to make sure that there will be no surprises for the customer downstream. The specifications should be the current revision. It is not uncommon for a customer to hire outside agencies to evaluate the technical proposal and to make sure that the proper specifications are being used.

Specifications are in fact standards for pricing out a proposal. If specifications either do not yet exist or are not necessary, then work standards should be included in the proposal. The work standards can also appear in the cost column of the proposal. Labor justification back-up sheets may or may not be included in the proposal, depending upon RFP/RFQ requirements.

For R&D proposals, standards may not exist and the pricing team may have to use educated guesses based upon the estimated degree of difficulty.

The technical standards and specifications may be called out by the customer. If it is a follow-on project, then the customer will expect you to perform the work within the estimate on the previous activity. If the standards or specifications will be different, then an explanation must be made or else the customer (and line managers) may feel that they have been "taken for a ride." Customers have the tendency of expecting standards to be lowered on follow-on efforts because the employees are expected to perform at an improved position on the learning curve.

The key parameter in explaining the difference in standards is the time period between the original cost estimate and the follow-on or similar cost estimate. The two most common reasons for having standards changes are:

- New technology which requires added effort
- Key employees with the necessary skills or expertise who have either left the organization or are not available.

In either event, justifications of the changes or modifications must be made so that the new ground rules are understood by all pricing and reviewing personnel.

The third item in the identification of the requirements is the gross schedule. In summary, the gross schedule identifies the major milestones of the project and include such items as

- Start date
- End date
- Other major milestone activities
- Data items and reports.

If possible, all gross schedules that are used for pricing guidelines should contain calendar start and end dates. Unfortunately, some projects do not have definable start and end dates and are simply identified by a time spread. Another common situation is where the end date is fixed and the pricing effort must identify the start date. This is a common occurrence because the customer may not have the expertise to determine accurately how long it takes to accomplish the effort.

Identifying major milestones can also be a tedious task for a customer. Major milestones include such activities as long-lead procurement, prototype testing, design review meetings, and any other critical decision points. The proposal manager must work closely with the customer or in-house sponsor either to verify the major milestones in the RFP or to identify additional milestones.

Major milestones are often grossly unrealistic. In-house executives from the customer and the contractor occasionally identify unrealistic end dates either because resources will be idle without the completion at this point in time, not enough money is available for a longer project, or management wants the effort completed earlier because it affects management's Christmas bonus.

All data items should be identified on the gross schedule. Data items include written, contractual reports and can be extended to include handout material for customer design review meetings and technical interchange meetings. Data items are not free and should be priced out accordingly. There is nothing wrong with including in the pricing effort a separate contingency fund for "unscheduled or additional" interchange meetings.

Step 2: Establish a logic network with checkpoints.

Once the work requirements are outlined, the project manager must define the logical steps necessary to accomplish the effort. The *logic network* (or *arrow diagram,* as it is more commonly called) serves as the basis for the PERT/CPM diagrams and the work breakdown structure. The arrow diagram simply shows the logical sequence of events, generally at the level which the project manager wants to control the program. Each logic diagram activity should not be restricted to specific calendar dates at this point because line managers should price out the work initially assuming unlimited resources and no calendar constraints.

If this is not done during the initial stages of pricing, line managers may commit to unrealistic time, cost, and performance estimates. After implementation, the project manager may find it impossible to force the line manager to meet his original estimates.

Step 3: Develop the work breakdown structure.

The simplest method for developing the work breakdown structure is to combine activities on the arrow diagram. If each activity on the arrow diagram is considered to be a task, then several tasks can be combined to form projects and the projects, when combined, become the total program. The WBS may contain definable start and end dates in accordance with the gross schedule at this point in time, although they may have to be altered before the final WBS is established solidly. Most project managers prefer to work at the task level of the WBS (level 3). The work is priced out at this level and costs are controlled at this level. Functional managers may have the option of structuring the work to additional levels for better estimating and control.

Often the arrow diagram and WBS are considered as part of the definition of the requirements, because the WBS is the requirement that costs be controlled at a specific level and detail.

Step 4: Price out the work breakdown structure.

The project manager's responsibility during pricing (as even during execution, for that matter) is to establish the project requirements that identify the "what," "when," and "why" of the project. The functional managers now price out the activities by determining the "how," "who," and "where" of the project. The functional managers have the right to ask the project manager to change the WBS. After all, the line managers are truly the technical experts and may wish to control their efforts differently.

Once the work breakdown structure and activity schedules are established, the program manager calls a meeting for all organizations that are required to submit pricing information. It is imperative that all pricing or labor costing representatives be present for the first meeting. During this kick-off meeting, the work breakdown structure describes in depth the responsibilities of each pricing unit manager during the program. The kick-off meeting also resolves the struggle-for-power positions of several functional managers whose responsibilities may be similar or overlap on certain activities. An example of this would be quality control activities. During the research and development phase of a program, research personnel may be permitted to perform their own quality control efforts, whereas during production activities, the quality control department or division would have overall responsibility.

Unfortunately, one meeting is not sufficient to clarify all problems. Follow-up or status meetings are held, normally with only those parties concerned with the problems that have arisen. Some companies prefer to have all members attend the status meetings so that all personnel will be familiar with the total effort and the associated problems. The advantage of not having all program-related personnel attend is that time is of the essence when pricing out activities. Many functional divisions carry this policy one step further by having a divisional representative together with possibly key department managers or section supervisors as the only attendees to this initial kick-off meeting. The divisional representative then assumes all responsibility for assuming that all costing data be submitted on time. This may be beneficial in that the program office need only contact one individual in the division to learn of the activity status, but may become a bottleneck if the representative fails to maintain proper communication between the functional units and the program office or if the individual simply is unfamiliar with the pricing requirements of the work breakdown structure.

During proposal activities, time is extremely important. There are many situations where an RFP requires that all responders submit their bids no later than a specific date, say 30 days. Under a proposal environment, the activities of the program office, as well as those of the functional unit, are under a schedule set forth by the proposal manager. The proposal manager's schedule has very little, if any, flexibility and is normally under tight time constraints in order that the proposal may be typed, edited, and published prior to date of submittal. In this case, the RFP defines indirectly how much time the pricing units have to identify and justify labor costs.

The justification of the labor costs may take longer than the original cost estimates, especially if historical standards are not available. Many proposals often require that comprehensive labor justifications be submitted. Other proposals, especially those that request an almost immediate response, may permit vendors to submit labor justification at a later date.

In the final analysis, it is the responsibility of the lowest pricing unit supervisor to maintain adequate standards, if possible, so that almost immediate response can be given to a pricing request from a program office.

The functional units supply their input to the program office in the form of man-hours. The input may be accompanied by labor justifications, if required. The man-hours are submitted for each task, assuming that the task is the lowest pricing element, and are time-phased per month. The man-hours per month per task are converted to dollars after multiplication by the appropriate labor rates. The labor rates are generally known with certainty over a 12-month period, but from there on are only estimates. How can a company predict salary structures five years hence? If the company underestimates the salary structure, increased costs and decreased profits will occur. If the salary structure is overestimated, the company may not be competitive. If the project is government-funded, then the salary structure becomes an item under contract negotiations.

The development of the labor rates to be used in the projection are based upon historical costs in business base hours and dollars for either the most recent month or quarter. Average hourly rates are determined for each labor unit by direct effort within the operations at the department level. The rates are only averages, and include both the highest-paid employees and lowest-paid employees together with the department manager and clerical support.[7] These base rates are then escalated as a percentage factor based upon past experience, budget as approved by management, and the local outlook in similar industries. If the company has a predominant aerospace or defense business base, then these salaries are negotiated with local government agencies prior to proposal submittal.

The labor hours submitted by the functional units are quite often overestimated for fear that management will "massage" and reduce the labor hours while attempting to maintain the same scope of effort. Many times management is forced to reduce man-hours either because of insufficient funding or just to remain competitive in the environment. The reduction of man-hours often provides heated discussion between the functional and program managers. Program managers tend to think in the best interests of the program while functional managers lean toward maintaining their present staff.

The most common solution to this conflict rests with the program manager. If the program manager selects members for the program team who are knowledgeable in man-hour standards for each of the departments, then an atmosphere of trust can develop between the program office and the functional department such that man-hours can be reduced in a manner which represents the best interests of the company. This is one of the reasons why program team members are often promoted from within the functional ranks.

The ability to estimate program costs involves more than just labor dollars and labor hours. Overhead dollars can be one of the biggest headaches in controlling program costs and must be estimated along with labor hours and dollars. Most programs have an assistant program manager for cost, whose responsibilities include monthly overhead rate analysis. The program manager can increase the success of the program drastically by insisting that each program team member understand overhead rates. For example, if overhead rates apply only to the first 40 hours of work, then, depending on the overhead rate, program dollars can be saved by performing work on overtime where the increased salary is at a lower burden.

The salary structure, overhead structure, and labor hours fulfill three of four major input requirements. The fourth major input is the cost for materials and support. Six subtopics are included under materials/support: materials, purchased parts, subcontract, freight, travel, and other. Freight and travel can be handled in one of two ways, both normally dependent on the size of the program. For small dollar-volume programs, estimates are made

---

[7] Problems can occur if the salaries of the people assigned to the program exceed the department averages. In many companies, department managers are included in the overhead rate structure, not direct labor, and therefore their salaries are not included as part of the department average.

for travel and freight. For large dollar-volume programs, travel is normally expressed as between 3 and 5 percent of all costs for material, purchased parts, and subcontracts. The category labeled other supports costs may include such topics as computer hours or special consultants.

The material costs are very time-consuming, moreso than the labor hours. Material costs are submitted via a bill of materials that includes all vendors from which purchases are made, project costs throughout the program, scrap factors, and shelf life for those products that may be perishable.

Information on labor is usually supplied to the project office in the form of man-hours/department/task/month. This provides a great degree of flexibility in analyzing total program costs and risks, and is well worth the added effort. Costs can be itemized per month, task, or even department. Computers, with forward pricing information, convert the man-hours to dollars. Raw materials are always priced out as dollars per month with the computer providing the forward pricing information for escalation factors.

Step 5: Review WBS costs with each functional manager.

Once the input is received from each functional manager, the project team integrates all of the costs to insure that all of the work is properly controlled without redundancy. An important aspect of this review is the time-phased manpower estimates. It is here that the project manager brings up the subject of limited rather than unlimited resources and asks the line managers to assess the various risks in their estimates.

As part of the review period, the project manager must ask the following questions:

- Was sufficient time allowed for estimating?
- Were the estimates based upon history or standards, or are they "best guesses?"
- Will the estimates require a continuous shifting of personnel in and out of the project?
- Will there be personnel available who have the necessary skills?

Obviously, the answers to these questions can lead into a repricing activity.

Step 6: Decide upon the basic course of action.

After the review with the functional managers, the project manager must decide upon the basic course of action or the base case. This is the ideal path that the project manager wishes to follow. Obviously, the decision is based on the risks on the project and the projected trade-offs that may have to be made downstream on time, cost, and performance.

The base case may include a high degree of risk if it is deemed necessary to satisfy contractual requirements. This base case approach and accompanying costs should be reviewed with the customer and upper-level management. There is no point in developing finalized, detailed PERT/CPM schedules and a program plan unless there is agreement on the base case.

Step 7: Establish reasonable costs for each WBS element.

Because the project will be controlled through the WBS, the project manager must define, with reasonable accuracy and confidence, the target costs for each WBS element, usually at level 3. Once the project is initiated, these costs become the basis for the project targets. The problem here is that the costs were based upon unlimited resources. Limited resources may require overtime or perhaps the work will have to be performed during higher cost escalation periods. These factors must be accounted for.

Step 8: Review the base case costs with upper-level management.

Once the base case is formulated, the pricing team member, together with the other program office team members, perform *perturbation analyses* in order to answer any questions that may come up during the final management review. The perturbation analysis is designed as a systems approach to problem solving, where alternatives are developed in order to respond to any questions that management may wish to consider during the final review.

The base case, together with the perturbation analysis costs, are then reviewed with upper-level management in order to formulate a company position for the program as well as to take a hard look at the allocation of resources required for the program. The company position may be to cut costs, authorize work, or submit a bid. If the program is competitive, corporate approval may be required if the company's chief executive officer has a ceiling on the dollar bids he can authorize to go out of house.

If labor costs must be cut, the program manager must negotiate with the functional managers as to the size and method for the cost reductions. Otherwise, this step may entail simply the authorization for the functional managers to begin the activities or to develop detailed plans.

Step 9: Negotiate with functional managers for qualified personnel.

Once the base case costs are established, the project manager must begin the tedious effort of converting all estimates to actual calendar dates and time frames based upon limited resources. Detailed schedules cannot be established without some degree of knowledge as to exactly which employees will be assigned to key activities. Highly qualified individuals may be able to accomplish the work in less time and may be able to assume added responsibilities.

Good project managers do not always negotiate for the best available resources because either the costs will be too great with those higher paid individuals or the project priority does not justify the need for such individuals.

Accurate, detailed schedules cannot be developed without some degree of knowledge as to who will be available for the key project positions. Even on competitive bidding efforts, customers require that the resumés of the key individuals be included as part of the proposal.

Step 10: Develop the linear responsibility chart.

Once the key employees are assigned to the activities, the project manager works with the functional managers in assigning project responsibilities. The project responsibilities may be assigned in accordance with assumed authority, age, experience on related efforts, maturity, and interpersonal skills.

The linear responsibility chart, if properly developed and used, is an invaluable tool not only in administering the project, but also in estimating the costs. The linear responsibility chart permits the project manager the luxury of assigning additional work to qualified personnel, of course upon approval of the functional managers. This additional work may be assigned to lower salaried individuals so that the final costs can come close to the departmental averages, assuming that the work was priced out in this fashion.

The linear responsibility chart development has a direct bearing upon how the costs are priced out and controlled. There are three methods for pricing out and controlling costs:

- Work is priced out at the department average and all work performed is charged to the project at the department average salary, regardless of who performed the work.
- Work is priced out at the department average but all work performed is billed back to the project at the actual salary of those employees who are to do the work.
- Work is priced out at the salary of those employees who will perform the work and the costs are billed back the same way.

Each of these methods has its advantages and disadvantages as well as a serious impact on the assignment of responsibilities.

Step 11: Develop the final detailed and PERT/CPM schedules.

Work standards are generally based upon the average employee. The assignment of above or below average employees can then cause the schedules to be shifted left or right. These detailed schedules are now based upon limited resources and provide the basis for accurate cost estimating. If at all possible, "fat" and slack time should be left in the schedules so as to provide some degree of protection for the line managers. "Fat" and slack time should be removed only as a last resort to lower costs, such as in the case of wanting to remain competitive or on buy-ins.

It should be obvious at this point that project pricing is an iterative process based upon optimization of time, cost, and performance together. After the detailed schedules are developed, the entire pricing process may have to be reaccomplished. Fortunately, the majority of the original estimates are usually salvagable and require only cosmetic modifications unless the customer provides major changes to specifications or quantity revisions because initial cost estimates were grossly unacceptable.

Step 12: Establish pricing cost summary reports.

Although the pricing of a project is an iterative process, the project manager must still burden himself at each iteration point by developing cost summary reports so that key project decisions can be made during the planning. There are at least two times when detailed pricing summaries are needed: in preparation for the pricing review meeting with management and at pricing termination. At all other times, it is possible that "simple cosmetic surgery" can be performed on previous cost summaries, such as perturbations in escalation factors and procurement cost of raw materials. The following list identifies the typical pricing reports.

- *A detailed cost breakdown for each WBS element.* If the work is priced out at the task level, then there should be a cost summary sheet for each task, as well as roll-up sheets for each project and the total program.
- *A total program manpower curve for each department.* These manpower curves show how each department has contracted with the project office to supply functional resources. If the departmental manpower curves contain several peaks and valleys, then the project manager may have to alter some of the schedules so as to obtain some degree of manpower smoothing. Functional managers always prefer manpower-smoothed resource allocations.
- *A monthly equivalent manpower cost summary.* This table normally shows the fully burdened cost for the average departmental employee carried out over the entire period of project performance. If project costs have to be reduced, the project manager performs a parametric study between this table and the manpower curve tables.
- *A yearly cost distribution table.* This table is broken down by WBS element and shows the yearly (or quarterly) costs that are required. This table, in essence, is a project cash flow summary per activity.
- *A functional cost and hour summary.* This table provides top management with an overall description of how many hours and dollars will be spent by each major functional unit, by division. Top management would use this as part of the forward planning process to make sure that there are sufficient resources available for all projects. This also includes indirect hours and dollars.
- *A monthly labor hour and dollar expenditure forecast.* This table can be combined with the yearly cost distribution, except that it is broken down by month, not by activity or department. In addition, this table normally includes manpower termination liability information for premature cancellation of the project by outside customers.
- *A raw material and expenditure forecast.* This shows the cash flow for raw materials based upon vendor lead times, payment schedules, commitments, and termination liability.

- *Total program termination liability per month.* This table shows the customer the monthly costs for the entire program. This is the customer's cash flow, not the contractor's. The difference is that each monthly cost contains the termination liability for man-hours and dollars, on labor and raw materials. This table includes the monthly costs attributed to premature project termination.

These tables are used both by project managers and upper-level executives. The project managers utilize these tables as the basis for project cost control. Top-level management utilizes these tables in selecting, approving, and prioritizing projects, as shown in Figure 8–1.

> *Step 13:* Document the results into a program plan.

The final step in cost estimating is to document all of the results into a project plan. The cost information is also the basis for the cost volume of the proposal. The logical sequence of events leading up to the program plan can be summarized as in Figure 8–2. Pricing is an iterative process, at best. The exact pricing procedure, of course, differs for projects external to the organization (as opposed to internal).

Regardless of whether or not you are managing a large or small project, cost estimating must be accomplished in a realistic, logical manner in order to avoid continuous panics. The best approach, by far, is to try to avoid the pressures of last-minute estimating, and to maintain reasonably updated standards for future estimating. Remember, project costs and budgets are only estimates based upon the standards and expertise of the functional managers.

8.4 COST BREAKDOWN/CODE OF ACCOUNTS

One of the unfortunate disadvantages of project management is that the contractor may have to maintain two sets of cost accounting books on each project; one for in-house use and another for the way that the customer wants costs reported back. Each company usually controls some degree of their costs in a consistent fashion such as by department, section, division, separate billing for raw materials, and so on. The problem occurs in the manner in which costs accounts are "rolled up" to provide a picture of the project status. Costs should be maintained in accordance with the work breakdown structure. Program costs are tracked according to the activity schedules which, in turn, follow the work breakdown structure. The WBS provides the basis for cost data collation and reporting.

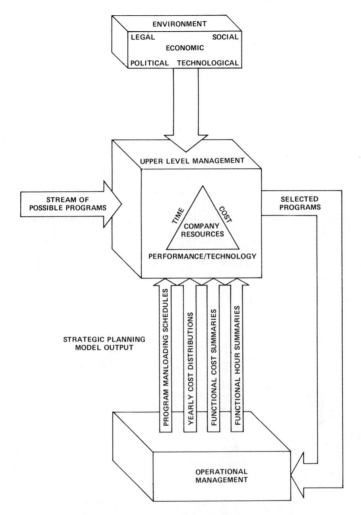

Figure 8-1. Systems approach to resource control.

The *actual cost* and the *budgeted cost of work Performed* (BCWP) for each contract or in-house project should be accumulated in detailed cost accounts by cost center and cost element, and reported in accordance with the flow-chart shown in Figure 8-3.[8] These detailed elements, for both actual costs incurred and the budgeted cost of work accomplished, are printed out monthly for all levels of the work breakdown structure. In addition, weekly sup-

---

[8] A complete description of these abbreviations is presented in Section 8.5.

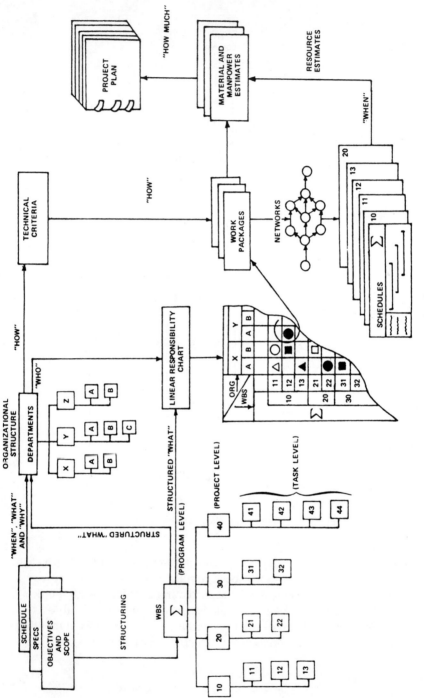

Figure 8-2. Project planning.

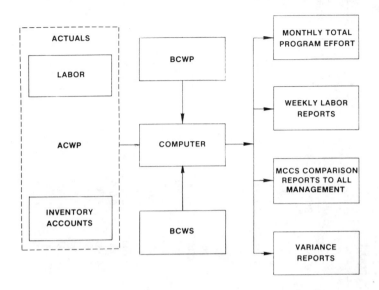

Figure 8–3. Cost data collection and reporting flowchart.

plemental direct labor reports can be printed to show the actual labor charges incurred and compared to the predicted efforts.

Table 8–3 shows a typical weekly labor report. The first column identifies the WBS number.[9] If more than one work order were assigned to this WBS element, then the work order number would appear under the WBS number. This procedure would be repeated for all work orders under the same WBS number. The second column contains the cost centers charging to this WBS element (and possibly work order numbers). Cost center 41XX represents department 41 and is a roll up of cost centers 4110, 4115, and 4118. Cost center 4XXX represents the entire division and is a roll up of all 4000-level departments. Cost center XXXX represents the total for all divisions charging to this WBS element. The weekly labor reports must list all cost centers authorized to charge to this WBS element, regardless of whether or not they incurred any costs over the last reporting period.

Most weekly labor reports provide current month subtotals and previous month totals. Although these also appear on the detailed monthly report, they may be included in the weekly report for a "quick-and-dirty" comparison. Year-to-date totals are usually not on the weekly report unless the users request it for an immediate comparison to the *estimate at completion* (EAC) and the work order release.

---

[9]Only three levels of cost reporting are assumed here. If work packages were used, then the WBS number would identify all five levels of control.

Table 8-3. Weekly labor report

WBS NO.	COST CENTER	H/$	WEEKLY ACTUAL	CURRENT MONTH SUBTOTAL	PREVIOUS MONTH		YEAR TO DATE			TOTAL EAC	WORK ORDER RELEASE
					ACWP	BCWP	ACWP	BCWP	BCWS		
01-03-06	4110	H	200	300	300	300	1,000	1,000	1,000	1,000	
		$	1,000	1,500	1,500	1,500	5,000	5,000	5,000	5,000	1,000
	4115	H	200	300	300	300	1,000	1,000	1,000	2,000	
		$	1,000	1,500	1,500	1,500	5,000	5,000	5,000	10,000	2,000
	4118	H	200	300	300	300	1,000	1,000	1,000	2,000	
		$	1,000	1,500	1,500	1,500	5,000	5,000	5,000	10,000	1,800
	41XX	H	600	900	900	900	900	900	900	5,000	
		$	3,000	4,500	4,500	4,500	4,500	4,500	4,500	25,000	4,800
	4443	H	100	200	400	360	800	700	1,400	2,000	
		$	600	1,200	2,400	2,260	4,800	4,200	8,400	12,000	1,800
	4446	H	200	400	1,000	1,200	2,000	2,000	2,300	3,000	
		$	800	1,600	4,000	4,800	8,000	8,000	9,200	12,000	2,500
	4448	H	300	600	1,000	1,200	2,000	2,000	2,300	3,000	
		$	1,500	3,000	5,000	6,000	10,000	10,000	15,000	15,000	3,000
	44XX	H	600	1,200	2,400	2,760	4,800	4,700	6,000	8,000	
		$	2,900	5,800	11,400	13,060	22,800	22,200	29,100	39,000	7,300
	4XXX	H	1,200	2,100	3,300	3,660	5,700	5,600	6,900	13,000	
		$	5,900	10,300	15,900	17,560	27,300	26,700	33,600	64,000	12,100
	XXXX	H	8,000	18,000	20,000	19,000	50,000	48,000	47,000	61,000	
		$	56,000	126,000	140,000	133,000	350,000	336,000	329,000	427,000	58,000

Weekly labor output is a vital tool for members of the program office in that these reports can indicate trends in cost and performance in sufficient time so that contingency plans can be established and implemented. If these reports were not available, then cost and labor overruns would not be apparent until the following month when the detailed monthly labor, cost, and materials output is obtained.

In Table 8–3 cost center 4410 has spent its entire budget. The work appears to be completed on schedule. The responsible program office team member may wish to eliminate this cost center's authority to continue charging to this WBS element by issuing a new *subdivided work description* (SWD) or work order cancelling this department's efforts. Cost Center 4115 appears to be only halfway through. If time is short, then Cost Center 4115 must add resources in order to meet requirements. Cost Center 4118 is similar to the costs required and incurred in cost center 4115 except that the work order released only 1,800 hours instead of the 2,000 hours planned for in the schedule. This identifies the management reserve. In this case, the responsible program team member feels that the work can be accomplished in less hours.

Work order releases are used to authorize certain cost centers to begin charging their time to a specific cost reporting element. Work orders specify hours, not dollars. The hours indicate the "targets" that the program office would like to have the departments shoot for. If the program office wished to be more specific and compel the departments to live within these hours, then the budgeted cost for work scheduled (BCWS) should be changed to reflect the reduced hours.

Whether or not any or all of the information presented here is shown to the customer depends upon the contractual terms and conditions. If the in-house reports are shown to the customer, then the cost proposal may have to contain a section on how to interpret and analyze the output information.

8.5 COST ACCOUNTING PROCEDURES

In Section 8.4, we defined one of the cost accounting procedures, namely that for analyzing direct labor, and how the costs were rolled up for each WBS element and level. In addition to direct labor, costs are normally accumulated for

- Materials
- Indirect labor
- Other direct labor categories
- Overhead.

The exact method for accumulating these may not be a requirement for the cost proposal, but the interpretation will be. Cost accounting procedures include not only the tracking of costs, but also the explanation of the cost deviations or variances. Variance analysis is an integral part of cost accounting and should be included in the proposal. Remember, the customer is probably interested more in the output of the cost accounting procedures (i.e., variance analysis) rather than in the detailed cost accounting methods of obtaining input.

A *variance* is defined as any schedule, technical performance, or cost deviation from a specific plan. Variances are used by all levels of customer and contractor management to verify the budgeting and scheduling systems. Both the budgeting and scheduling system variance must be compared together because:

- The cost variance compares deviations only from the budget and does not provide a measure of comparison between work scheduled and work accomplished.
- The scheduling variance provides a comparison between planned and actual performance but does not include costs.

In order to calculate variances, we must define the three basic variances for budgeted and actual costs for work scheduled and performed. Archibald defines these variables as follows:[10]

- *Budgeted cost for work scheduled* (BCWS) is the budgeted amount of cost for work scheduled to be accomplished plus the amount of level of effort or apportioned effort scheduled to be accomplished in a given time period.
- *Budgeted cost for work performed* (BCWP) is the budgeted amount of cost for completed work, plus budgeted for level of effort or apportioned effort activity completed within a given time period. This is sometimes referred to as an *earned value*.
- *Actual costs for work performed* (ACWP) is the amount reported as actually expended in completing the work accomplished within a given time period.

These costs can then be applied to any level of the work breakdown structure (i.e., program, project, task, subtask, work package) for work that is completed, in-program or anticipated. Using these definitions, the following variance definitions are obtained:

$$\text{Cost variance} = \text{BCWP} - \text{ACWP}$$
$$\text{Schedule/Performance variance} = \text{BCWP} - \text{BCWS}$$

---

[10]Russell D. Archibald, *Managing High Technology Programs and Projects,* New York: John Wiley and Sons, 1976, p. 176.

The schedule variance may be represented by hours, days, weeks, or even dollars.

Variances are almost always identified as critical items and are reported via *control system variance reports* to all organizational levels. Critical variances are established for each level of the organization in accordance with management policies. Variance controls may be different from program to program. Table 8–4 identifies a sample variance criteria for Program X. The customer should be made aware of this table so that the customer will know the criteria for preparing variance reports.

For many programs and projects variances are permitted to change over the duration of the program. For strict manufacturing programs (product management), variances may be fixed over the program time span using criteria as in Table 8–4. For programs that include research and development, larger deviations may be permitted during the earlier phases than during the later phases. Figure 8–4 shows time-phased cost variances for a program requiring research and development, qualification, and production phases. Because the risk should decrease as time goes on, the variance boundaries are reduced.

By using both cost and schedule variances we can develop an integrated cost/schedule reporting system that provides the basis for variance analysis by measuring cost performance in relation to work accomplished. This system assures that both cost budgeting and performance scheduling are constructed upon the same data base.

Figure 8–5 shows an integrated cost/schedule system. The figure identifies a performance slippage to date. This might not be a bad situation if the costs

Table 8–4. Variance Control for Program X

ORGANIZATIONAL LEVEL	VARIANCE THRESHOLDS*
Section	Variances greater than $750 and exceed 25% of costs
Section	Variances greater than $2,500 and exceed 10% of costs
Section	Variances greater than $20,000
Department	Variances greater than $2,000 that exceed 25% of costs
Department	Variances greater than $7,500 that exceed 10% of costs
Department	Variances greater than $40,000
Division	Variances greater than $10,000 that exceed 10% of costs

*Thresholds are usually tighter within the company reporting system than required external to government. Thresholds for external reporting are usually adjusted during various phases of program (% lower at end).

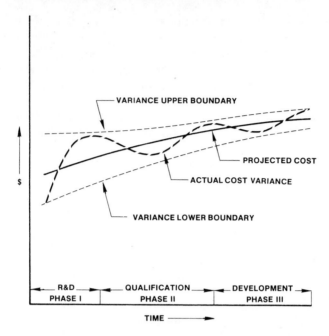

Figure 8-4. Project variance projections.

are proportionately underrun. However, from the upper portion of Figure 8-5, we find that costs are overrun (in comparison to budgeted costs), thus adding to the severity of the situation.

Also shown in Figure 8-5 is the management reserve. This is identified as the difference between the contracted cost for projected performance to date and the budgeted cost. Management reserves are contingency funds established by the program manager to counteract unavoidable delays that can affect the project's critical path. It is a natural tendency for functional managers (and some project managers) to inflate estimates substantially so as to protect the organization and provide a certain amount of cushion. Furthermore, if the inflated budget is approved, managers will undoubtedly use up all of the allocated funds, including reserves.

8.6 MANAGEMENT COST AND CONTROL SYSTEM (MCCS)

Many contracts, especially on cost-reimbursable packages, require that the customer maintain an "approved" (perhaps by the customer or sponsoring government agency) management cost and control system (MCCS) that describes not only the systematic method for pricing out the work, but also the method by which costs will be monitored and controlled after program go-

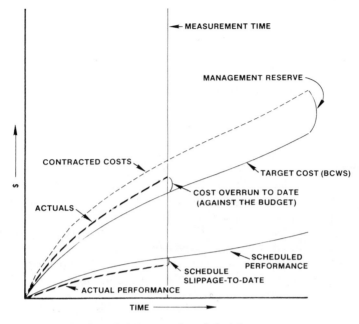

Figure 8–5. Integrated cost/schedule system.

ahead. Some companies refer to it as a planning and control system. The cost proposal provides the basis for the MCCS. It is usually a good policy for the cost proposal to include sections on how costs will be controlled after go-ahead, how cost control decisions will be made, and the types of cost control and status reports that will be provided to the customer. Some contractors maintain a separate MCCS volume that is added as an appendix to the cost proposal. The customer must be convinced, through your cost proposal, that accurate and timely information concerning the true status of the project will be submitted.

Effective management of a program during the proposal stage requires that a well-organized cost and control system be designed, developed, and implemented so that immediate feedback can be obtained for both the customer and contractor. In this way, the up-to-date usage of resources can be compared to those which were established as target objectives in the cost proposal. The requirements for an effective control system (for both cost and schedule/performance) should include:[11]

---

[11] Russell Archibald, *Managing High Technology Programs and Projects,* New York: John Wiley and Sons, 1976, p. 191.

- Thorough planning of the work to be performed to complete the project
- Good estimating of time, labor, and costs
- Clear communication of scope of required tasks
- Disciplined budget and authorization of expenditures
- Timely accounting of physical progress and cost expenditures
- Periodic reestimation of time and cost to complete remaining work
- Frequent, periodic comparison of actual progress and expenditures to schedules and budgets, both at the time of comparison and at project completion.

Management must compare the actual time, cost, and performance of the program to the budgeted time, cost, and performance not independently, but in an integrated manner. Being within budget at the proper time serves no useful purpose if performance is only 75 percent. Likewise, having a production line turn out 200 items exactly loses its significance if a 50 percent cost overrun was incurred. All three resource parameters (time, cost, and performance) must be analyzed as a group or else we might "win the battle but lose the war." Because of this, the use of the expression "management cost and control system" is vague in that the implication is made that only costs are controlled. This is not true. An effective control system monitors schedule and performance as well as costs by setting budgets, measuring expenditures against budgets and identifying variances, assuring that the expenditures are proper, and taking corrective action when required.

In Section 6.6 we defined the work breakdown structure as being the element that acts as the source from which all costs and controls must emanate. The work breakdown structure therefore serves as the tool from which performance can be subdivided into objectives and subobjectives. As work progresses, the WBS provides the framework from which costs, time, and schedule/performance can be compared against the budget for each level of the WBS.

The cost proposal must, therefore, include the WBS and the corresponding schedules which were developed around the WBS. In addition, the MCCS section of the cost proposal should identify pictorally all of the types of tables, figures, and charts that are used to determine project status and any corrective action to be taken. This insures the customer that the contractor understands the meaning of "control."

The first purpose of control therefore becomes a verification process accomplished by the comparison of actual performance to date with the predetermined plans and standards set forth in the planning phase and defined and documented in the cost proposal. The comparison serves to verify that:

- The objectives have been successfully translated into performance standards

- The performance standards are, in fact, a reliable representation of program activities and events
- Meaningful budgets are established such that actual versus planned comparisons can be made

In other words, the comparison verifies that the correct standards were selected and that they are properly used. This may very easily place the contractor in a favorable position for unsolicited follow-on work because the customer has confidence in the contractor's estimating techniques.

The second purpose of control is that of decision making. Three reports are required by management to make effective and timely decisions. These are:

- The project plan, schedule, and budget prepared during the planning phase (whether during proposal plannirg or project execution)
- A detailed comparison between resources expended to date and those predetermined. This includes an estimate of the work remaining and the impact on activity completion.
- A projection of resources to be expended out through program completion.

These reports are then supplied to both the managers and doers, and sometimes to the customer. Three useful results arise through the use of these three reports generated by a thorough decision-making stage of control:

- Feedback to management, the planners, and the doers and the customer
- Identification of any major deviations from the current program plan, schedule, or budget.
- The opportunity to initiate contingency planning early enough so that cost, performance, and time requirements can undergo corrective action without loss of resources to either the customer or contractor

The exact management cost and control system selected must be able to satisfy both the customer's and contractor's management needs and requirements in order that they can project accurately the status toward objective completion. The system must, therefore, provide information that:

- Gives a picture of true work progress
- Relates cost to scheduled performance
- Identifies potential problems as to their sources
- Provides information to the project manager and customer with a practical level of summarization

The management cost and control system, in addition to being a tool by which objectives can be defined (i.e, hierarchy of objectives and organization accountability), exists as a tool to develop planning, measure progress, and control change. As a tool for planning, the system must be able to be used to:

- Plan and schedule work
- Identify those indicators that are used for measurement
- Establish direct labor budgets
- Establish overhead budgets
- Identify management reserve.

As a tool for measuring progress and controlling change, the system must be able to

- Measure resources consumed
- Measure status and accomplishments
- Compare measurements to projections and standards
- Provide the basis for diagnosis and replanning.

Almost all management cost and control systems have identifiable design requirements. These include:

- Common framework from which to integrate time, cost, and technical performance
- Ability to track progress of significant parameters
- Quick response
- Capability for end-value prediction
- Accurate and appropriate data for decision making by each level of management
- Full exception reporting with problem analysis capability
- Immediate quantitative evaluation of alternative solutions

Even within a fully developed management cost and control system, there are numerous techniques that can be utilized. The appropriate technique must consider a cost/benefit analysis, and include such items as:

- Project Benefits
  - Management Cost and Control Techniques Facilitate:
    - Derivation of output specifications (project objectives)
    - Delineation of required activities (work)
    - Coordination and communication between organizational units
    - Determination of type, amount, and timing of necessary resources
    - Recognition of high-risk elements and assessment of uncertainties
    - Suggestions of alternative courses of action

- Realization of effect of resource level changes on schedule and output performance
- Measurement and reporting of genuine progress
- Identification of potential problems
- Basis for problem solving, decision making, and corrective action
- Assurance of coupling between planning and control
- Project Cost
  - Management Cost and Control Techniques Require:
    - New forms (new systems) of information from additional sources and incremental processing (managerial time, computer expense, etc.)
    - Additional personnel or smaller span of control to free managerial time for planning and control tasks (increased overhead)
    - Training in use of techniques (time and materials)

8.7 DEVELOPING THE SUPPORTING/BACK-UP COSTS

Not all cost proposals require back-up support. For those that do, the back-up support should be developed along with the pricing. Extreme caution must be exercised to make sure that the itemized prices are compatible with the supporting data. Government pricing requirements are a special case and are discussed in Chapter 11.

Most supporting data comes from external (subcontract or outside vendor) quotes. Internal data must be based upon historical data. This historical data must be updated continuously as each new project is completed. The supporting data should be traceable by itemized charge numbers.

Customers may wish to audit the cost proposal. In this case, the starting point might be with the supporting data. It is not uncommon on sole-source proposals to have the supporting data audited before the final cost proposal is submitted to the customer.

Not all cost proposals require supporting data. The determining factor is usually the type of contract. On a fixed price effort, the customer may not have the right to audit your books. However, for a cost-reimbursable package, your costs are an open book and the customer usually compares your exact costs to those of the back-up support.

Most companies usually have a choice of more than one estimate to be used for back-up support. In deciding which estimate to use, consideration must be given to the possibility of follow-on work.

- If your actual costs grossly exceed your back-up support estimates, you may lose credibility for follow-on work.
- If your actual costs are less than the back-up costs, then the customer will

expect you to perform the work at the same cost, if not lower, on follow-on efforts.

The moral here is that back-up support costs provide future credibility. If you have well-documented, "livable" cost estimates, then you may wish to include them in the cost proposal even if they are not required.

8.8 THE ESTIMATING MANUAL

Many companies try to standardize their estimating procedures by developing an estimating manual. The estimating is then used to price out the effort, perhaps as much as 90%. Estimating manuals are usually better estimates than industrial engineering standards because they include groups of tasks and take into consideration such items as down time, clean-up time, lunch, and breaks. Table 8–5 shows the table of contents for a construction estimating manual.

Table 8–5. Estimating Manual Table of Contents

Introduction
  Purpose and types of estimates
Major Estimating Tools
  Cataloged equipment costs
  Automated investment data system
  Automated estimate system
  Computerized methods and procedures
Classes of Estimates
  Definitive estimate
  Capital cost estimate
  Appropriation estimate
  Feasibility estimate
  Order of magnitude
  Charts—estimate specifications quantity
          and pricing guidelines
Data Required
  Chart—comparing data required for preparation
          of classes of estimates
Presentation Specifications
  Estimate procedure—General
  Estimate procedure for
      definitive estimate
  Estimate procedure for
      capital cost estimate
  Estimate procedure for
      appropriation estimate
  Estimate procedure for
      feasibility estimate

Estimating manuals, just as the name implies, provide estimates. The real question, of course, is "How good is the estimate?" Most estimating manuals provide accuracy limitations by defining the types of estimates. This is shown in Table 8-6. Using Table 8-6, we can now create Tables 8-7 and 8-8 that illustrate the use of the estimating manual.

Table 8-6. Classes of Estimates

CLASS	TYPES	ACCURACY
I	Definitive	± 5%
II	Capital Cost	± 10–15%
III	Appropriation (with some capital cost)	± 15–20%
IV	Appropriation	± 20–25%
V	Feasibility	± 25–35%
VI	Order of Magnitude	> ± 35%

Table 8-7. Checklist for Work Normally Required for the Various Classes of Estimate

ITEM	CLASS I	II	III	IV	V	VI
1. Inquiry	X	X	X	X	X	X
2. Legibility	X	X	X			
3. Copies	X	X				
4. Schedule	X	X	X	X		
5. Vendor inquiries	X	X	X			
6. Subcontract packages	X	X				
7. Listing	X	X	X	X	X	
8. Site visit	X	X	X	X		
9. Estimate bulks	X	X	X	X	X	
10. Labor rates	X	X	X	X	X	
11. Equipment and subcontract selection	X	X	X	X	X	
12. Taxes, insurance, and royalties	X	X	X	X	X	
13. Home office costs	X	X	X	X	X	
14. Construction indirects	X	X	X	X	X	
15. Basis of estimate	X	X	X	X	X	X
16. Equipment list	X					
17. Summary sheet	X	X	X	X	X	
18. Management review	X	X	X	X	X	X
19. Final cost	X	X	X	X	X	X
20. Management Approval	X	X	X	X	X	X
21. Computer estimate	X	X	X	X		

Table 8-8. Data Required for Preparation of Estimates

	CLASSES OF ESTIMATES					
	I	II	III	IV	V	VI
General						
Product	X	X	X	X	X	X
Process description	X	X	X	X	X	X
Capacity	X	X	X	X	X	X
Location—general					X	X
Location—specific	X	X	X	X		
Basic design criteria	X	X	X	X		
General design specifications	X	X	X	X		
Process						
Process block flow diagram						X
Process flow diagram (with equipment size and material)				X	X	
Mechanical P&I's	X	X	X			
Equipment list	X	X	X	X	X	
Catalyst/chemical specifications	X	X	X	X	X	
Site						
Soil conditions	X	X	X	X		
Site clearance	X	X	X			
Geological and meteorlogical data	X	X	X			
Roads, paving, and landscaping	X	X	X			
Property protection	X	X	X			
Accessibility to site	X	X	X			
Shipping and delivery conditions	X	X	X			
Major cost is factored					X	X
Major Equipment						
Preliminary sizes and materials			X	X	X	
Finalized sizes, materials, and appurtenances	X	X				
Bulk Material Quantities						
Finalized design quantity take-off		X				
Preliminary design quantity take-off	X	X	X	X		
Engineering						
Plot plan and elevations	X	X	X	X		
Routing diagrams	X	X	X			
Piping line index	X	X				
Electrical single line	X	X	X	X		
Fire protection	X	X	X			
Sewer systems	X	X	X			
Pro-services—detailed estimate	X	X				
Pro-services—ratioed estimate			X	X	X	
Catalyst/chemicals quantities	X	X	X	X	X	
Construction						
Labor wage, F/B, travel rates	X	X	X	X	X	
Labor productivity and area practices	X	X				
Detailed construction execution plan	X	X				
Field indirects—detailed estimate	X	X				
Field indirects—ratioed estimate			X	X	X	

Table 8-8. (cont.)

	CLASSES OF ESTIMATES					
	I	II	III	IV	V	VI
Schedule						
Overall timing of execution				X	X	
Detailed schedule of execution	X	X	X			
Estimating preparation schedule	X	X	X			
Miscellaneous						
Transportation rates	X	X				
Start up	X	X	X			
Insurance and taxes	X	X	X	X	X	
Royalties	X	X	X	X	X	X
Import/export duty rates	X	X	X	X	X	
Financing data	X	X	X	X	X	
Escalation						
Escalation analysis	X	X	X	X	X	
Contingency						
Identifiable risk analysis	X	X				

Not all companies can use estimating manuals. Estimating manuals work best for repetitive tasks or similar tasks that can use a previous estimate adjusted by a degree of difficulty factor. Activities such as R&D do not lend themselves to the use of estimating manuals other than for benchmark, repetitive laboratory tests. Proposal managers must make careful consideration as to whether or not the estimating manual is a viable approach. The literature abounds with companies that have spent millions trying to develop estimating manuals for situations that just do not lend themselves to the approach.

8.9 DATA ITEMS

All data items, such as quarterlies, monthlies, and technical reports should be priced out separately in the cost proposal. The following information should be included in estimating each report:

- Direct labor writing hours
- Number of pages per report
- Typing
- Editing and proofreading
- Graphic arts
- Reproduction services.

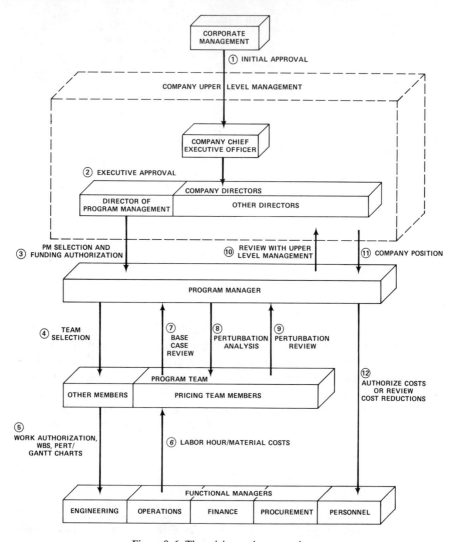

Figure 8–6. The pricing review procedure.

There is no such item as a "no-cost" report. Customers will "ask for the moon" if given the opportunity. By pricing out each report separately, you will identify for the customer:

- The expected number of pages per report
- The expected cost per report
- The expected cost for additional reports.

The biggest advantage of this technique is that the customer may severely reduce his demand for certain reports, especially on follow-on contracts.

8.10 THE PRICING REVIEW MEETING

The pricing review meeting is an integral part of cost proposal preparation. Regardless of how good the costs are, management's blessing is always necessary before the costs are submitted to the customer. If management feels that the costs are too low, then management may increase the costs in certain areas so as to eliminate certain risk or simply to avoid leaving any money "on the table."

More often than not, management arbitrarily slashes the costs so as to either remain competitive or to "buy in." This situation can prove to be a severe headache for the proposal manager because he must now return to the functional managers and tell them that they must reduce their man-hour estimates so as to remain competitive. If this simply requires that "fat" be removed from the estimates, then perhaps no major conflicts will occur. However, some estimates may already be lean and a severe conflict will be unavoidable.

Good proposal managers know where the "fat" is in the proposal before they enter into the pricing review meeting. Both the project and proposal managers must have alternatives and supporting data available to justify their position. However, the executives may already know how much money the customer has to do the job, and the cost proposal may have to be written for the money available. Quite often, executives have a lot more information available at their level than the proposal manager has. In this case, the executives allow the proposal team to estimate the job although management already knows what the final bid will be.

Figure 8–6 summarizes all of the steps from commitment to bid on the proposal to the pricing review meeting.

Chapter 9

Contracts

9.0 INTRODUCTION

Because the proposal is a formal offer to supply some service or production to a client, it is necessary to provide a section in the proposal that contains a draft contract or contract comments. In general, companies provide services or products based upon the requirements of invitations for competitive bids issued by the client or the results of direct contract negotiations with the client.

One of the most important factors in preparing a proposal and estimating the cost and profit of a project is the type of contract expected. The confidence by which a bid is prepared is usually dependent on how much of a risk the contractor will incur through the contract. Certain types of contracts provide relief for the contractor, especially as onerous* risks exist. The cost must therefore consider how well the contract type covers certain high- and low-risk areas.

Prospective clients are always concerned when during a competitive bidding process, one bid is much lower than the others. The client may question the validity of the bid and whether or not the contract can be achieved for the low bid. In cases such as this, the client usually imposes incentive and penalty clauses in the contract for self-protection.

Because of the risk factor, competitors must negotiate not only for the target cost figures, but also for the type of contract involved, since risk protection is the predominant influential factor. The size and experience of the client's own staff, urgency of completion, availability of qualified contrac-

---

Onerous risks are unfair risks that the contractor may have to bear. Quite often, the contract negotiations may not reach agreement on what is or is not an onerous risk.

tors, and other factors must be carefully evaluated. The advantages and disadvantages of all basic contractual arrangements must be recognized to select the optimum arrangement for a particular project.

Wherever possible, the proposal as amended at the time of contract award should be included among the contract documents referenced in the agreement.

Before you can analyze the various types of contracts, you should familiarize yourselves with the terminology found in contracts.

- The *target cost* or *estimated cost* is the level of cost that the contractor will most likely obtain under normal performance conditions. The target cost serves as a basis for measuring the true cost at the end of production or development.
  The target cost may vary for different types of contracts even though the contract objectives are the same. The target cost is the most important variable affecting research and development.
- *Target* or *expected profit* is the profit value that is negotiated for, and set forth in, the contract. The expected profit is usually the largest portion of the total profit.
- *Profit ceiling* and *profit floor* are the maximum and minimum values, respectively, of the total profit. These quantities are often included in contract negotiations.
- *Price ceiling* or *ceiling price* is the amount of money for which the government is responsible. It is usually measured as a given percentage of the target cost, and is generally greater than the target cost.
- *Maximum* and *minimum fees* are percentages of the target cost and establish the outside limits of the contractor's profit.
- The *sharing arrangement* or *formula* gives the cost responsibility of the government to the cost responsibility of the contractor for each dollar spent. Whether that dollar is an overrun or an underrun dollar, the sharing arrangement has the same impact upon the contractor. This sharing arrangement may vary depending on whether or not the contractor is operating above or below target costs. The *production point* is usually that level of production above which the sharing arrangement commences.

9.1 TYPES OF CONTRACTS

Because no single form of contract agreement fits every situation or project, companies normally perform work in the United States under a wide variety of contractual arrangements, such as:

- Cost-plus percentage fee
- Cost-plus fixed fee
- Cost-plus guaranteed maximum
- Cost-plus guaranteed maximum and shared savings
- Cost-plus incentive
- Fixed price or lump sum
- Fixed price incentive
- Fixed price for services, material, and labor at cost
- Time and material
- Bonus-penalty
- Combinations
- Joint venture.

At one end of the range is the *cost-plus,* a fixed fee type of contract where the company's profit, rather than price, is fixed and the company's responsibility, except for its own negligence, is minimal. At the other end of the range is the *lump sum* or *turnkey* type of contract under which the company has assumed full responsibility, in the form of profit or losses, for timely performance and for all costs under or over the fixed contract price. In between are various types of contracts, such as the guaranteed maximum, incentive types of contracts and the bonus-penalty type of contract. These contracts provide for varying degrees of cost responsibility and profit depending upon the level of performance. Contracts that cover the furnishing of consulting services are generally on a per diem basis at one end of the range and on a fixed price basis at the other end of the range.

There are generally five types of contracts to consider: fixed price (FP) cost-plus-fixed-fee (CPFF), or cost-plus-percentage-fee (CPPF), guaranteed maximum-shared savings (GMSS), fixed price-incentive-fee contracts (FPIF), and cost-plus-incentive-fee (CPIF). Each type is discussed separately.

- Under a *fixed price or lump sum contract,* the contractor must carefully estimate the target cost. The contractor is required to perform the work at the negotiated contract value. If the estimated target cost was low, the total profit is reduced and may even vanish. The contractor may not be able to underbid the competitors if the expected cost is overestimated. Thus, the contractor assumes a large risk.

  This contract provides maximum protection to the owner for the ultimate cost of the project, but has the disadvantage of requiring a long period for preparation and adjudications of bids. Also, there is the possibility that because of a lack of knowledge of local conditions, all contractors may necessarily include an excessive amount of contingency.

This form of contract should never be considered by the owner unless, at the time bid invitations are issued, the building requirements are known exactly. Changes requested by the owner after award of a contract on a lump sum basis lead to troublesome and sometimes costly extras.

- Traditionally, the *cost-plus-fixed-fee* contract has been employed when it was believed that accurate pricing could not be achieved any other way. In the CPFF contract, the cost may vary but the fee remains firm. Because, in a cost-plus contract, the contractor agrees only to use his best efforts to perform the work, good performance and poor performance are, in effect, rewarded equally. The total dollar profit tends to produce low rates of return, reflecting the small amount of risk that the contractor assumes. The fixed fee is usually a small percentage of the total or true cost. The cost-plus contract requires that the company books be audited.

With this form of contract the engineering-construction contractor bids a fixed dollar fee or profit for the services to be supplied by the contractor, with engineering, materials, and field labor costs to be reimbursed at actual cost. This form of bid can be prepared quickly at a minimal expense to contractor and is a simple bid for the owner to evaluate. Additionally, it has the advantage of establishing incentive to the contractor for quick completion of the job.

If it is a *cost-plus-percentage-fee,* the contract provides maximum flexibility to the owner and permits owner and contractor to work together cooperatively on all technical, commercial, and financial problems. However, it does not provide financial assurance of ultimate cost. Higher building cost may result, although not necessarily so, because of lack of financial incentive to the contractor compared with other forms. The only meaningful incentive that is evident today is the increased competition and prospects for follow-on contracts.

- Under the *guaranteed maximum-share savings* contract, the contractor is paid a fixed fee for his profit and reimbursed for the actual cost of engineering, materials, construction labor, and all other job costs, but only up to the ceiling figure established as the "guaranteed maximum." Savings below the guaranteed maximum are shared between owner and contractor, whereas contractor assumes the responsibility for any overrun beyond the guaranteed maximum price.

This contract form essentially combines the advantages as well as a few of the disadvantages of both lump sum and cost-plus contracts. This is the best form for a negotiated contract because it establishes a maximum price at the earliest possible date and protects the owner against being overcharged, even though the contract is awarded without competitive tenders. The guaranteed maximum-share savings contract is unique in that the owner and contractor share the financial risk and both have a real incentive to complete the project at lowest possible cost.

- *Fixed price incentive* contracts are the same as fixed price contracts except that they have a provision for adjustment of the total profit by a formula that depends on the final total cost at completion of the project and that has been agreed to in advance by both the owner and the contractor. To use this type of contract, the project or contract requirements must be firmly established. This contract provides an incentive to the contractor to reduce costs and therefore increase profit. Both the owner and contractor share in the risk and savings.
- *Cost-plus incentive* contracts are the same as cost plus contracts except that they have a provision for adjustment of the fee as determined by a formula that compares the total project costs to the target cost. This formula is agreed to in advance by both the owner and contractor. This contract is usually used for long duration or R&D type projects. The company places more risk on the contractor and forces him to plan ahead carefully and strive to keep costs down. Incentive contracts are covered in greater detail in Section 9.4.

Table 9–1 identifies the advantages and disadvantages of various contracting methods that are commonly used.

The type of contract that is acceptable to the client and your company is determined by the circumstances of each individual project and the prevailing economic and competitive conditions. Generally, when work is hard to find, clients insist on fixed price bids. This type of proposal is usually a burden to the contractor because of the proposal costs involved (about 1% of the total installed cost of the project), and the higher risk involved in the execution of the project on such a basis.

When there is an upsurge in business, clients are unable to insist on fixed price bids and more work is awarded on a cost-plus basis. In fact, where a special capability position exists, or where time is a factor, the client occasionally negotiates a cost-plus contract with only one contractor. Another technique used during time of high workload is to award a project on a cost-plus basis with the understanding that the contract will be converted at a later date, when the scope has been better defined and unknowns identified, to another form, such as a lump sum for services. This approach is appealing to both the client and the contractor.

As we mentioned earlier, the client frequently has a standard form of contract that is used as the basis of negotiation or the basis of requests for proposals. Your company should review the client's document carefully to assure yourself that you understand how the client's document differs from what is

Table 9-1. Contract Comparison

CONTRACT TYPE	ADVANTAGES	DISADVANTAGES
Cost-Plus Fee	• Provides maximum flexibility to owner • Minimizes contractor profits • Minimizes negotiations and preliminary specification costs • Permits quicker start, earlier completion • Permits choice of best qualified, not lowest bidding, contractor • Permits use of same contractor from consultation to completion, usually increasing quality and efficiency	• No assurance of actual final cost • No financial incentive to minimize time and cost • Permits specification of high-cost features by owner's staff • Permits excessive design changes by owner's staff increasing time and costs
Guaranteed Maximum-Share Savings	• Provides firm assurance of ultimate cost at earliest possible date • Insure prompt advice to owner of delays and extra costs resulting from changes • Provides incentive for quickest completion • Owner and contractor share financial risk and have mutual incentive for possible savings • Ideal contract to establish owner-contractor cooperation throughout execution of project	• Requires complete auditing by owner's staff • Requires completion of definitive engineering before negotiation of contract
Fixed Price-Lump Sum	• Provides firm assurance of ultimate cost • Insures prompt advice to owner of delays and extra costs resulting from changes	• Requires exact knowledge of what is wanted before contract award • Requires substantial time and cost to develop inquiry specs, solicit, and evaluate bids. Delays completion 3-4 months

(*continued*)

Table 9-1 (cont.)

CONTRACT TYPE	ADVANTAGES	DISADVANTAGES
	• Requires minimum owner follow up on work	• High bidding costs and risks may reduce qualified bidders
	• Provides maximum incentive for quickest completion at lowest cost	• Cost may be increased by excessive contingencies in bids to cover high-risk work
	• Involves minimal auditing by owner's staff	
Fixed Price for Services, Material, and Labor	• Essentially same as cost-plus-fee contract	• May encourage reduction of economic studies and detailing of drawings: produce higher costs for operation, construction, maintenance
	• Fixes slightly higher percentage of total cost	
	• Eliminates checking and verifying contractor's detailed invoices for services	• Other same disadvantages as cost-plus-fee contract
Fixed Price for Imported Goods and Services, Local Costs Reimbursable	• Maximum price assured for high percentage of plant costs	• Same extended time required for inquiry specs, quotations, and evaluation as fixed lump-sum for complete project
	• Avoids excessive contingencies in bids for unpredictable and highly variable local costs	• Requires careful definition of items supplied locally to insure comparable bids
	• Permits selection of local suppliers and subcontractors by owner	• No financial incentive to minimize field and local costs

your company's preferred position. Any additional duties or responsibilities assigned to your company merit careful scrutiny if the additional legal consequences and increased financial risks are to be evaluated properly.

It is important that you use an adequate and realistic description of the work to be undertaken and a careful evaluation and pricing of the scope of the work to be performed and the responsibilities and obligations assumed. The preparation of a proposal requires a clear understanding between the client and your company as to the rights, duties, and responsibilities of your company. The proposal defines what it intends to do and can do, what it neither intends doing nor is qualified to undertake, and the manner and basis of its compensation. Thorough analysis of these matters before, not after, submission of the proposal, is essential.

9.2 USING A CHECKLIST

To assist your company in evaluating inquiries and preparing proposals and contracts, a checklist of contract considerations and provisions can be helpful in the evaluation of each proposal and form of contract to insure that appropriate safeguards are incorporated. This checklist is also used for sales letters and brochures that may promise or represent a commercial commitment. The primary purpose of the checklist is to raise in the minds of those who use it the legal and commercial factors that should at least be considered in preparing proposals and contracts. Table 9–2 shows the typical major headings that would be considered in a checklist. A key word concept also provides an excellent checklist of the key issues to be considered for any contract. It will be useful as a reminder in preparation for contractor-client agreement discussions.

Contract provisions that would be critical in minimizing the major areas of inherent risk on projects, and that should be prepared for inclusion in proposals and contracts, are the following:

- Scope of services and description of project
- Contract administration
- Terms of payment
- Client obligation and supplied items

Table 9–2. Typical Main Heading for a Contract Provisions Checklist

I.	Definitions of Contract Terms
II.	Definition of Project Scope
III.	Scope of Services and Work to be Performed
IV.	Facilities to be Furnished by Client (for Service Company Use)
V.	Changes and Extras
VI.	Warranties and Guarantees
VII.	Compensation to Service Company
VIII.	Terms of Payment
IX.	Definition of Fee Base (Cost of the Project)
X.	State Sales and/or Use Taxes
XI.	Taxes (other than Sales/Use Taxes)
XII.	Insurance Coverages
XIII.	Other Contractual Provisions (including Certain General Provisions)
XIV.	Miscellaneous General Provisions

- Warranties and guarantees
- Liability limitation and consequential damages.
- Indemnity
- Taxes
- Patent indemnification
- Confidential information
- Termination provisions
- Changes and extras
- Assignments
- Delays, including *force majeure*
- Insurance requirements
- Arbitration
- Escalation (lump sum)
- Time of completion.

Because of the necessarily wide variations in detail among each proposal and contract, it is not feasible to prepare material specifically suited for each situation. It must also be realized that not only does each company have special situations and provisions that are applicable to its individual situation and clients, but in the changing world of today, new situations that require special handling arise constantly. Therefore, it is not practical to establish a standard form of contract and, only to a limited degree, standard provisions to be included in a contract.

However, under present-day conditions, an increasing number of clients have certain set ideas as to the content of the proposal and contract. In addition, many clients and prospective clients have their own contract forms that must be followed in order to be considered for project awards. Because the goal is a contract or proposal leading to maximum profit and minimum risk, it has not always been possible to differentiate between company policy, or commercial, technical, legal, financial, accounting, or other considerations. Therefore, it would be extremely helpful in your general approach to preparing proposals and contracts to develop a standard list and file of draft contract clauses that could be used with some modification for each bid. As these clauses are used and refined, the amount of changes required for each occasion will diminish. In addition, because clients occasionally ask for a "typical" contract, the draft clauses can be combined into a "typical" or "draft" contract that can be given to a client. Even though this "typical" contract agreement may not be sufficient for every situation, it can be a favorable starting place for your company. It would also be valuable to maintain a summary of commercially oriented company policies for reference in reviewing a client's contract provisions.

Negotiating for the type of contract is a two-way street. The contractor desires a certain type of contract to reduce risk. The client desires a certain type of contract to reduce costs. Often is the case where the client and contractor disagree. It is not uncommon in industry for prospective projects to be cancelled because of lack of funds, disagreements in contract negotiations, or changing of priorities.

9.3 PROPOSAL-CONTRACTUAL INTERACTION

It is critical during the proposal preparation stage that contract terms and conditions be reviewed and approved before submission of a proposal to the client. The contracts (legal) representative is responsible for the preparation of the contract portion of the proposal. Generally, contracts with the legal department are handled through or in coordination with the proposal group. The contract representative determines or assists with the following:

- Type of contract
- Required terms and conditions
- Any special requirements
- Cash flow requirements
- Patent and proprietary data
- Insurance and tax considerations
- Finance and accounting.

The sales department, through the proposal group, has the final responsibility for the content and outcome of all proposals and contracts that it handles. However, there are certain aspects that should be reviewed with others who can offer guidance, advice, and assistance to facilitate the effort. In general, contract agreements should be reviewed by the following departments:

- Proposal
- Legal
- Insurance
- Tax
- Project management
- Engineering
- Estimating
- Construction (if required)
- Purchasing (if required).

Responsibility for collecting and editing contract comments rests with the proposal manager. In preparing contract comments, consideration should be given to comments previously submitted to the client for the same form of agreement, and also previous agreements signed with the client.

Contract comments should be reviewed for their substance and ultimate risk to the company. It must be recognized that in most instances, the client is not willing to make a large number of revisions to his proposed form of agreement. The burden of proof that a contract change is required rests with you, and therefore each comment submitted must have a good case behind it.

Occasionally, you are confronted with a serious contract comment for which it is very difficult to express your position in words. In such instances, it is better to flag the item that you would like to discuss further with the client, and take it up at the conference table. A good example of this is taxes on cost plus foreign projects. Normally, when submitting a proposal for such work, you do not have sufficient definitive information to establish your position relative to how you would like to handle taxes, that is:

- What is client's position on taxes?
- Will one or two agreements be used for the work? Who will the contracting parties be?
- Time will not permit nor is the cost justifiable for a complete tax assessment.
- The client's position on tax matters is not known.
- Contract procedures have not been established. Would we buy in the name of the company or as agents without liability for the client?

Proposal personnel should become familiar with the legal considerations that should be taken into account in all proposals, contracts, and negotiations. Legal considerations are important because they can have financial impact.

Accordingly, effective communication between proposals and the legal department is essential so that legal consideration can be identified early and then minimized. To be effective, the legal department should be advised of information pertinent to their functions as promptly as possible as negotiations develop. Proposal personnel should also be familiar with the standard contract forms the company uses, its contract terms, and available conditions, including those developed jointly between sales and the legal department, as well as the functions, duties, and responsibilities of the legal department. In addition, key areas that are normally negotiated should be discussed so that proposal personnel have a better understanding of the commercial risks involved and why the company has certain positions.

By the time the client has reviewed the proposal, your legal position is fixed commercially if not legally. Therefore, sales and proposal personnel should understand and be prepared to put forward the company's position on commercially significant legal considerations, both in general and on specific issues that arise in connection with a particular project. In this way, sales will be in a position to assert, and sell the company's position at the appropriate time.

Proposals should send all bid documents, including the client's form of contract, or equivalent information, along with the proposal outline or instructions to the legal department as soon as possible, usually upon receipt of documents from the client. The instructions or outline should indicate the assignment of responsibility and include background information on matters that are pertinent to sales strategy or specific problems such as guarantees, previous experience with client, and so on.

Proposals should discuss briefly with the legal department what is planned by way of the project, the sales effort, and commercial considerations. If there is a "kick-off" meeting, a representative of the legal department should attend if it is appropriate or advisable. The legal department should make a preliminary review of the documents before any such discussion or meeting.

The legal department reviews the documents and prepares a memorandum of comment and any required contract documents, obtaining input where necessary or advisable. If the client has included a contract agreement with the inquiry, the legal department reviews it to see if it has any flaws or is against some set policy of the company. Unless a lesser level of effort is agreed upon, this memorandum will cover all legal issues that the legal department determines. This does not necessarily mean that all such issues must be raised with the client.

The purpose of the memorandum is to alert the proposal department to such issues. The memorandum suggests solutions to the legal issues raised, usually in the form of contract comments. The memo may make related appropriate commercial suggestions. If required, the legal department will submit a proposed form of contract, joint venture agreement, and so on. Generally, the legal department follows standards that have been worked out with sales and uses standard forms and contract language that were found to be salable in the past and to offer sufficient protection.

At the same time, proposals reviews the documents and advises the legal department of any pertinent issues known by or determined by proposals. This is essential not only because proposals has the final responsibility but also because proposals is responsible for providing information to and getting comments from others, such as purchasing, engineering, and estimating.

Proposals reviews and arranges for any other necessary review of the legal department's comments and documents. Proposals suggests the final form of comments, contract documents, and other relevant documents including the offer letter. Proposals reviews proposed final forms with the legal department as promptly as possible and prior to any commercial commitment.

Normal practice is to validate proposals for a period of 30 to 60 days following date of submission. Validation of proposals for periods in excess of this period may be required by special circumstances and should be done only with management's concurrence. Occasionally, it is desirable to validate a bid for less than 30 days. The validity period is especially important on lump sum bids. On such bids, the validity period must be consistent with validity times of quotations received for major equipment items. If these are not consistent, additional escalation on equipment and materials may have to be included in your lump sum price and your competitive position could thereby be jeopardized.

Occasionally, you may be requested to submit with your proposals a schedule covering hourly rate ranges for reimbursable personnel. For this purpose, you should develop a standard schedule covering hourly rate ranges and average rates for all personnel whom you consider to be in the reimbursable category. The hourly rate ranges are based upon the lowest paid person and the highest paid person in any specific job classification. In this connection, if there are any oddball situations, the effect of such is not included. Average rates are based upon the average of all personnel in any given job classification.

One area that is critical to the development of a good contract is the definition of the scope of work covered by the contract. This is of particular importance to the proposal manager, who is responsible for having the proper people prepared for the scope of work description. What is prepared during proposal production most likely governs the contract preparation and eventually becomes part of that contract. The degree to which the project scope of work must be described in a contract depends upon the pricing mechanism and contract form used.

A contract priced on a straight per diem basis or on the basis of reimbursement of all costs plus a fee does not normally require a precise description of either the services to be performed or the work to be accomplished.

Usually, a general description is adequate. This, however, is not the case if the contract is priced by other methods, especially fixed price, cost sharing, or guaranteed maximum. For these forms of contracts, it is essential that considerable care be taken to set forth in the contract documents the precise nature of the work to be accomplished as well as the services to be performed.

In the absence of a detailed description of the work prepared by the client, you must be prepared to develop such a description for inclusion in your proposal. When preparing the description of the work for inclusion in the contract documents, the basic premise to be followed must be that the language in the contract will be strictly interpreted during various stages of performance. The proper preparation of the description of the work as well as the evaluation of the requirements thereof requires coordination among sales, administration, cost, and technical personnel both inside and outside the organization. Technical personnel within the organization or technical consultants from outside must inform management whether or not there is an in-house capability to undertake the work and successfully solve the proper and timely completion of the work. Determination also must be made of whether or not suitable subcontracts or purchase orders can be awarded. In the major areas, firm commitments should be obtained. Technical projections must be effected relative to a host of problems, including delivery or scheduling requirements, the possibility of changes in the proposed scope of work, client control over the work, quality control, and procedures.

An inadequate or unrealistic description of the work to be undertaken or evaluation of the project requirements marks the beginning of an unhappy contract experience.

9.4 INCENTIVE CONTRACTS

To alleviate some of the previously mentioned problem areas, clients, especially the government, have been placing incentive objectives into their contracts. The fixed-price-incentive-fee (FPIF) contract is an example of this. The essence of the incentive contract is that it offers a contractor more profit if costs are reduced or performance is improved, and less profit if costs are raised or if performance goals are not met. Cost incentives take the form of a sharing formula generally expressed as a ratio. For example, if a 90/10 formula were negotiated, the government would pay for 90 cents and the contractor 10 cents for every dollar above the target cost. Thus, it benefits both the contractor and the government to reduce costs, because the contractor must consider that 10 percent of every dollar must be spent by the company. Expected profits can thus be increased by making maximum use of the contractor's managerial skills.

In the FPIF contract, the contractor agrees to perform a service at a given fixed cost. If the total cost is less than the target cost, then the contractor has made a profit according to the incentive fee formula. If the total cost exceeds the target cost, then the contractor loses money.

Consider the following example of an FPIF contract. All of the following dollars are in millions.

$$
\begin{aligned}
C &= \text{Target cost} = \$110 \\
P_{ex} &= \text{Expected profit} = 6\% \times C = \$6 \\
W &= \text{Price ceiling} = \$120 \\
CSP &= \text{Cost sharing point} = \$115 \\
R &= \text{Sharing formula} = 80/20
\end{aligned}
$$

Figure 9–1 represents the FPIF contract for the above data. The price ceiling is the maximum amount that the government will pay, $120. If the cost exceeds $120, the contractor has zero profit and must pay that difference. Between $120 and $115 (cost sharing point), the government may or may not bear the burden of any of the cost. In this case, the government bears the burden of 99 percent of the cost such that the contractor will make $1 profit for every $1 spent between the ceiling price and the cost sharing profit.

For costs below the cost sharing point, the sharing line of 80/20 is in effect. The contractor increases his profits by 20 cents on the dollar for every dollar spent below the CSP. Thus, it benefits the contractor to keep the costs to a minimum. To earn a profit of $10, the contractor would have to reduce costs by $20 (from the target cost). The important factor to be realized from Figure 9–1 is that the sharing formula provides the amount of fees payable to the contractor on the basis of expected (target) costs and true costs. There can be a different sharing formula for costs above and below the cost sharing point.

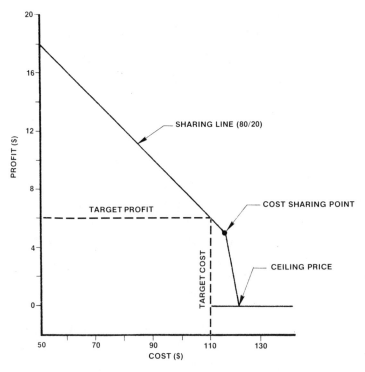

Figure 9–1. Fixed-price-incentive fee contract.

Another contract similar to FPIF, is the fixed-price-incentive-successive-targets (FPIS). In the FPIF contract, all negotiations revolved about the expected or target cost, which was agreed upon beforehand. This is often a tedious procedure because of the unknown factors that influence the cost estimation of the final product. In the FPIS contract, a "firm" target cost is decided upon after production begins and the product point is reached. This type of contract has built-in minimum and maximum profits.

As an example, consider

$$\begin{aligned}
C &= \$100 \\
P_{ex} &= \$8 \\
P_{max} &= \$9 \\
P_{min} &= \$7 \\
W &= \$130 \\
\text{Sharing formula} &= 95/5 \\
C_T &= \text{true cost}
\end{aligned}$$

After production begins and the product point is reached, a firm target cost is negotiated upon based on the up-to-date cost information. Quite often, this target cost equals the true cost. Assume $C_T = C = \$80$. The contractor has thus saved $20 and is entitled to 5 percent, or $1. Thus, adding this to the initial target profit yields a true profit of $9. It is also possible that the minimum profit, P_{min}, be guaranteed under the provision of the contract, regardless of the total cost or true cost.

The last type of contract is the cost-plus-incentive-fee (CPIF). Under this type of contract, the contractor is guaranteed a maximum or minimum fee that is a percentage of the true cost. The minimum fee may be based upon any type of profit level including zero or even a negative profit level. Consider the following cases.

$$\begin{aligned}
C &= 100 \\
TF &= \text{Target fee} = 6\% = \$6 \\
TF_{max} &= \$12 \\
TF_{min} &= 0 \\
\text{Sharing formula} &= 80/20
\end{aligned}$$

These data are represented in Figure 9-2. The target fees and target costs are negotiated beforehand. All other data are based upon percentages of the target costs and fees. If the true costs exceed $130, the contractor loses money. For true costs below $70, profits are constant. Thus, the range of incentive is between $70 and $130 where the profit is $2 out of every $10.

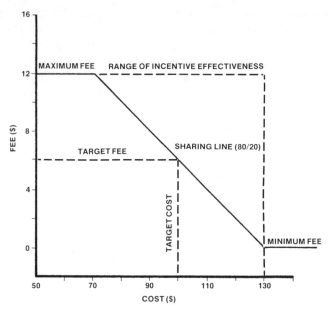

Figure 9-2. Cost-plus-incentive fee contract.

9.5 SUMMARY

While it is essential that companies obtain good contracts with a minimum of risk provisions, it is equally important that administration of those contracts be effective in order to achieve optimum results. Under current competitive and demanding conditions, it is imperative that all modern techniques of good contract administration are initiated.

The following guidelines can aid your company in preparing its proposals and contracts and administering operations thereunder:

- Use of the checklist in the preparation of all proposals and contracts
- Evaluation of risks by reference to the suggested contract provisions wherever appropriate
- Review by the legal department prior to submission to the client of all major proposals and contracts and of other contracts with questionable provisions
- Appropriate pricing or insuring of risks under the contract
- Improving contract administration at appropriate levels
- Periodic review and updating of the entire contract procedure including basic risk areas, administration, and so on.

Chapter 10

Proposal Design and Publication Techniques

10.0 INTRODUCTION

While the content and size of each proposal is different, the basic organization and format should be essentially the same. Just as it is important that the proposal be well written and carry a clear message to the client, it is just as important that the proposal be well organized and pleasant looking. The final product always reflects on how much time and money was spent on preparing it. But there are some steps you can take to upgrade the appearance of the proposal at very little additional cost. Your proposal should have a professional and finished look to it.

Because of the wide range of readers that reviews the proposal and possibly influences its outcome, a clear and logically presented proposal can only benefit from the extra effort. Instructions regarding format and organization of the proposal should be given to each participant at the start of the effort. These instructions must be followed strictly by all participants supplying input to the proposal to avoid a great deal of wasted time and effort. Some companies use a style guide that provides a consistent response and image from one proposal to another.

10.1 USING A FORMAT

To provide some degree of conformity and uniform look to the proposal, there are basic format requirements that should be followed. These basic requirements are the following:

- With the exception of the letter, all pages of all documents should be identified with the proposal number and dated in the upper right hand corner. All documents should bear the same date. Normally, proposals are dated *the day they are to be submitted.*
- The proposal should be written either in the "we-you" or the "contractor-owner" mode. Consistency throughout the proposal should be maintained.
- Identification of the specific project and its location should be standard throughout the entire proposal.
- The following margins should be maintained wherever practical on all proposal documents:

   Top = ¾ inch
   Bottom = 1-¾ inches
   Right Side = ¾ inch
   Left Side = 1-¼ inches

- Consistency of a proposal document is of the utmost importance. For this reason, an item should be covered in the proposal once and repeated elsewhere only when absolutely necessary.
- The proposal title page should be a duplicate of the cover except that it is black type on white paper (like the rest of the proposal).
- A table of contents should be used.

To provide a quality product in the short time allowed, the proposal manager should have a working knowledge of the typing, printing, and binding processes and equipment that are available. These services can be provided both internally and externally. Typists who are familiar with the proposal format may be assigned permanently to the proposal function. This would assure a consistency in the style of type used and the arrangement of text on the page. This arrangement would include margins, spacing, headings, paragraph indentations, and the page numbering method. Finally, the proposal should be attractively bound.

Some companies employ technical writers and graphics specialists to prepare documents for the proposal. Technical writers can be used to rewrite proposal sections prepared by contributing departments, but unless they are technical specialists themselves, all they can do is rewrite the sections so that they are better grammatically and are presented in a more meaningful and concise manner.

The proposal manager should provide the art specialist or draftsperson assigned to the effort with a complete list of the artwork requirements of the proposal as early as possible. This will allow the artists to prepare their own work schedule during that time frame. All proposal diagrams, illustrations, and other artwork should be functional, clear, uncluttered and pertinent to the proposal. Avoid using artwork that is not really necessary just because you think it looks impressive.

10.2 STANDARDIZING THE PROPOSAL

The following items can be considered as part of the standardization of the proposal format:

- Covers
  - Color of cover
  - Color of lettering
  - Material of cover
  - Layout, size, and style of lettering
  - Preprinted covers
- Tabs
  - Color of tabs
  - Color of lettering
  - Use of words, letters, or numbers
  - Layout, cut, and lettering style
  - Material
- Binding
  - Three-ring or multiring binder
  - Post binder
  - 19-Hole (spiral) binder
  - One standard size
  - Stock certain sizes
- Printing
  - In-house capability
  - Outside capability
  - Use of special techniques
  - Use of special equipment
  - Word processing equipment
- Paper
  - Quality (bond or xerox)
  - Size (reduce everything to 8-½ × 11)
  - Standard border with company logo
  - Color

It may be necessary, because of cost considerations and time constraints, to use different types of covers for different types of proposals. Examples of these different proposal types would be:

- Letter with some attachments
- Small quick effort
- Normal, fully tabbed, single volume
- Large effort with multiple volumes.

Regarding tabs, it seems preferable to use tabs with subject headings over numbers or letters. Subject headings give a better and more finished look, and make finding information in the proposal volume easier. But using subject headings prevents you from preordering and stocking, and probably will end up costing more. Because it takes time to order and receive the tabs, it requires good upfront organization and planning. The use of a standard size cut, say four or five on an 11-inch sheet, should be selected.

Typical requirements for binding would be:

- Lay flat when open
- Somewhat long lasting
- Attractive and not cheap looking
- Reasonably priced
- Stored standing up.

Three-ring or multiring binders are generally not acceptable because they can pop open and pages can tear out easily. Because these binders are one piece, they cannot be sent for printing until the final proposal size is determined, which adds more tightness to an already tight schedule. Also, because various sizes are required, storage becomes a problem. Spiral binders, on the other hand, are preferred because they can be printed in advance, have more flexibility, and are easier to stock. Because they take little space for storage, standard sizes can be stacked (i.e., ½ inch, ¾ inch, 1 inch, 1-1/8 inches) and so on.

To save time and help provide the professional image required in a proposal, boilerplate material can be put into proposal format and kept on file for future use. This information should be updated periodically to keep it current. Typical boilerplate would be:

- Qualifications and services
- Experience sheets and lists
- Corporate organization
- Resumés
- Corporate policies and procedures.

10.3 WORD PROCESSING EQUIPMENT

The selection of new equipment or systems for producing proposals or other documents must be viewed from two standpoints:

- To improve effectiveness and efficiency
- To improve quality in method of presentation and appearance.

The principal areas of improvement that are obtained by new equipment or systems are:

- *Word Processing.* How can we most effectively and efficiently get the typing job done, considering the need for editing and the repetitive nature of the work?
- *Graphics.* How can we obtain more flexibility and versatility in the graphical presentation of data and information? This encompasses charts, graphs, schedules, tables, and other visual aides.
- *Appearance.* How do we enhance the appearance of our proposals to get that most favorable first impression? This would encompass binding, typing style and format, covers, and so on.

In evaluating these three areas, consideration must be given to achieving a level of standardization and a uniform look in the proposal documents generated. The adage, "You don't get somethin' for nuthin'," must also be remembered.

One of the best and most effective tools available to improve efficiency in generating proposal documents is the *IBM Mag Card II Typewriter.* Use of the Mag Card II:

- Allows you to store standard and repetitive write-ups and other information such that it can be easily updated or modified to meet a specific presentation need
- Facilitates editing of documents while minimizing retyping and re-proofing
- Facilitates "last minute" changes or corrections with a minimum of delay
- Provides the base on which you can add downstream equipment to improve appearance and to attain greater flexibility in the area of graphics.

Two Mag Card II units facilitates the production of final masters for 100–150 pages on an eight-hour day. This should be adequate to handle one major bid or simultaneously two smaller bids.

In considering suppliers of word processing equipment and systems, IBM stands foremost because of:

- The wide range of equipment offered, especially that capable of recording on external media
- The reliability of their equipment and excellent servicing system

- The services they provide in training users personnel in how to use their equipment
- The wide use of IBM equipment.

Much can be said and done in the areas of graphics and appearance. Because they are interrelated, they should be considered jointly. They are integral to achieving a uniform look.

The IBM tape-driven composer is useful because it allows you to vary type style, size and density, and to justify right-hand margins. It also allows you to improve presentation of tables, charts, graphs, and so on.

10.4 REPRODUCTION

Regarding reproduction of materials used in proposals, the following considerations should be observed.

- All originals should be of the highest quality, commensurate with practicality and schedule. The quality of the finished product cannot be maintained if care is not taken in preparation of the original material.
- The responsibility for quality of material to be reproduced belongs to whomever prepares the originals for reproduction; however, it must rest ultimately with the proposal manager.
- The responsibility for quality of reproduced material rests with the reproduction machine operator. If, in the operator's judgment, the quality of the original does not permit a satisfactory copy, the requisitioning party should be notified immediately.
- The proposal manager decides if the schedule permits the original to be corrected, or if the faulty original must be used. Reproduction should be instructed not to reproduce material from inferior copy unless specifically told to do so by the proposal manager.
- Recognition is also given to the fact that quality suffers when too short a time is allotted for reproduction. Every effort should be made to allow adequate time to satisfactorily reproduce the material. If you know when an unusually heavy work order will be given to reproduction, you should advise them in advance. This is especially true when work is required outside of normal hours.
- In making paste-ups of copy, the completed pages should be reviewed carefully and all smudges, marks, dirt, and so on, should be removed prior to forwarding the material for reproduction. Copies in which type smudged, overly black, smeared, and so on, should be retyped.

While following the above procedures may cause a delay in the time it takes to complete the reproduction phase of the proposal material, it is well worth the effort. Considering the amount of money invested in preparation of proposals, they cannot be jeopardized by submission of a low quality piece of work to a prospective client. The proposal manager must plan for this in the proposal preparation schedule.

10.5 GRAPHICS

Graphic displays are usually the primary means for tracking cost, schedule, and performance. Good graphics makes the information easy to identify. Because communications with the customer is a vital part of any project, the graphic arts section may convince the customer that timely graphical data on project status is supplied, without having to wade through computer printouts or "wordy" reports.

Unfortunately, not all information can be displayed, and quite often any additional information requests require additional cost and effort. Proper graphical displays can result in:

- Cutting project costs and reducing the time scale
- Coordinating and expediting planning
- Eliminating idle time
- Obtaining better scheduling and control of subcontractor activities
- Developing better troubleshooting procedures
- Cutting time for routine decisions, but allowing more time for decision making.

It is therefore important that you show the customer that you possess the resources necessary to provide effective communications. The most common method is to illustrate the various graphical displays that you have used on previous contracts. You may wish to let the customer select the graphical methods that best satisfy the requirements. The graphic arts section can therefore serve as a "shopping list."

There exists between 30 and 40 different visual methods for representation of activities. The exact method chosen should depend upon the intended audience. For example, upper-level management may be interested in costs and integration of activities, with very little detail. Summary-type charts normally suffice for this purpose. Daily practitioners, on the other hand, may require that as much detail as possible be included in activity schedules. If the schedule is to be presented to the customer, then the representation should include cost and performance data.

The presentation of cost and performance data is both a science and an art. As a science, the figures and graphs should be describable in terms of symbols and expressions that are easily understandable. As an art, the diagram should rapidly bring across the intended message or objective quickly and elegantly.

In many organizations, each department or division may have its own method of scheduling activities. Research and development organizations prefer to show the logic of activities rather than the integration of activities that would normally be representative of a manufacturing plant.

The ability to communicate is a definite prerequisite for successful management of a program. Program review meetings, technical interchange meetings, customer summary meetings, and in-house management control meetings all require different representative forms of current program performance status. The final form of the schedule may be bar charts, graphs, tables, bubble charts, or logic diagrams. In the paragraphs that follow, a variety of charting techniques, together with their associated limitations, is described for various types of a program. The reader should be able to realize the advantages and disadvantages of each chart in relation to the proposal and program activities.

The most common type of display is the *bar* or *Gantt chart,* named for Henry Gantt who first utilized this procedure in the early 1900s. The bar chart is a means of displaying simple activities or events plotted against time or dollars. An activity represents the amount of work required to proceed from one point in time to another. An event is described as either the starting or ending point for either one or several activities.

Bar charts are most commonly used for exhibiting program progress or defining specific work required to accomplish an objective. Bar charts often include such items as listings of activities, activity durations, schedule dates, and progress-to-date. Figure 10–1 shows nine activities required to start up a production line for a new product. Each bar in the figure represents a single activity. Figure 10–1 is a typical bar chart that would be developed by the program office at program inception.

Bar charts are advantageous in that they are simple to understand and easy to change. They are the simplest and least complex means of portraying progress (or the lack of it) and can easily be expanded to identify those specific elements that may be either behind or ahead of schedule.

Gantt or bar charts provide only a vague description of how the entire program or project reacts as a system. There are three major discrepancies in the use of a bar chart. First, bar charts do not show the interdependencies of the activities, and therefore do not represent a "network" of activities. This relationship among activities is crucial for controlling program costs. Without this relationship, bar charts have little predictive value. For example, does the long-lead procurement activity in Figure 10–1 require that the contract be signed before procurement can begin? Can the manufacturing plans be written without the material specifications activity being completed? The second major discrepancy is that the bar chart cannot show the results of an early or late start in activities. How will a slippage of the manufacturing schedules

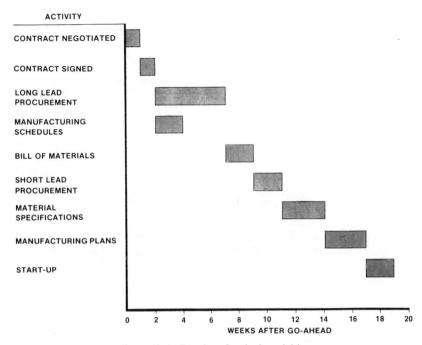

Figure 10–1. Bar chart for single activities.

activity in Figure 10–1 affect the completion date of the program? Can the manufacturing schedules activity begin two weeks later than shown and still serve as an input to the bill of materials activity?

What will be the result of a crash program to complete activities in 16 weeks after go-ahead instead of the originally planned 19 weeks? Bar charts do not reflect true project status because elements behind schedule do not mean that the program or project is behind schedule. The third limitation is that the bar chart does not show the uncertainty involved in performing the activity and, therefore, does not readily lend itself to sensitivity analysis. For instance, what is the shortest time that an activity might take? What is the longest time? What is the average or expected time to activity completion?

Even with these limitations, bar charts do, in fact, serve as a useful tool for program analysis. Even the earliest form of bar chart, as developed by Henry Gantt, has merit under certain circumstances. Figure 10–2 shows the conventional usage for work scheduled in a production facility for 12 days in January. On Thursday of the first week, the production facility was idle because of a lack of materials. By the end of the work day on Friday of the first week, only 280 out of the planned 300 units were produced. The production line was not available on either Saturday or Sunday, and operations resumed

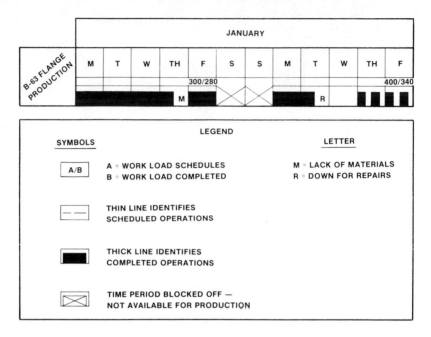

Figure 10-2. Manufacturing schedule for model B-63 flanges.

Monday. On Tuesday, the production line was down for repairs and did not resume operations until Thursday. Operations were sporadic on Thursday and Friday, and by the end of the day, only 340 out of a scheduled 400 units were completed.

Some of the limitations of bar charts can be overcome by combining single activities as shown in Figure 10-3. The weakness in this method is that the numbers representing each of the activities do not indicate the beginning or the end of the activity. Therefore, the numbers should represent events rather than activities, together with proper identification. As before, no distinction is made as to whether event 2 must be completed prior to the start of event 3 or 4. The chart also fails to clearly define the relationship between the multiple activities on a single bar. For example, must event 3 be completed prior to event 5? Often, combined activity bar charts can be converted to milestone bar charts by placing small triangles at strategic locations in the bars to indicate completion of certain milestones within each activity or grouping activities as shown in Figure 10-4. The exact definition of a milestone differs from company to company, but usually implies some point where either major activity begins or ends, or cost data becomes critical.

Bar charts can be converted to partial interrelationship charts by indicating (with arrows) the order in which activities must be performed. Figure 10-5

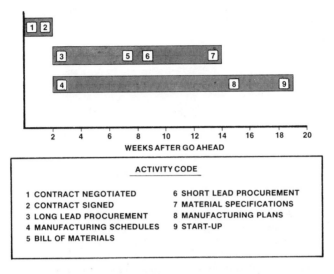

Figure 10–3. Bar chart for combined activities.

represents the partial interrelationship of the activities shown in Figures 10–1 and 10–3.

The most common method of presenting data to both in-house management and the customer is through the use of bar charts. Care must be taken to make the figures simple and understandable so that only one interpretation can exist. A great deal of information and color can be included in bar charts. Figure 10–6 shows a grouped bar chart for comparison of three projects performed during different years. When using different shading techniques, each area should be easily definable and no major contrast between shaded areas should exist except for possibly the current project. When grouped bars

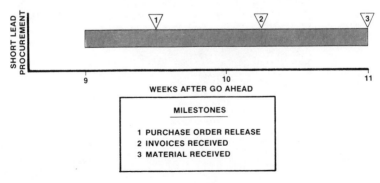

Figure 10–4. Bar/milestone chart.

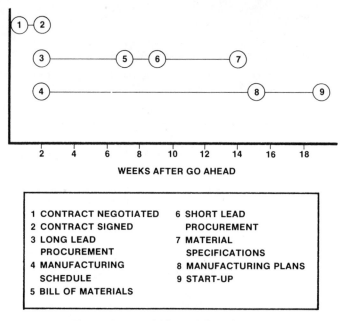

Figure 10–5. Partial interrelationship chart.

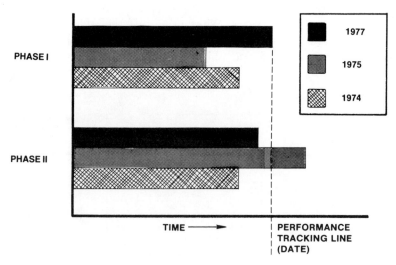

Figure 10–6. Grouped bar chart for performance comparison.

appear on one chart, nonshaded bars should be avoided. Each bar should have some sort of shading, whether it be cross-hatched or color-coded.

Contrasting shaded to nonshaded areas is normally used for comparing projected progress to actual progress as shown in Figure 10–7. The tracking date line indicates the time when the cost data/performance data were analyzed. Project 1 is behind schedule, project 2 is ahead of schedule and project 3 is on target. Unfortunately, the upper portion of Figure 10–7 does not indicate the costs attributed to the status of the three projects. By plotting the total program costs against the same time axis (as shown in Figure 10–7), a comparison between cost and performance can be made. From the upper section of Figure 10–7, it is impossible to tell the current program cost position. From the lower section, however, it becomes evident that the program is heading for a cost overrun, possibly because of project 1. It is generally ac-

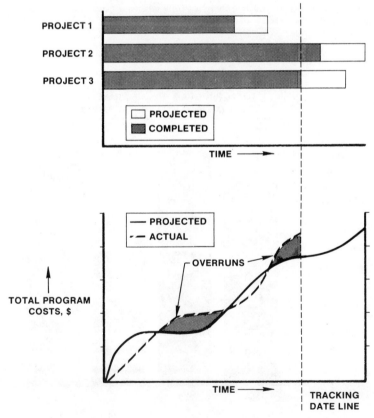

Figure 10–7. Cost and performance tracking schedule.

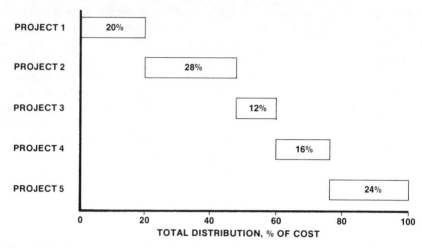

Figure 10-8. Step arrangement bar chart for total cost as a percentage of the five program projects.

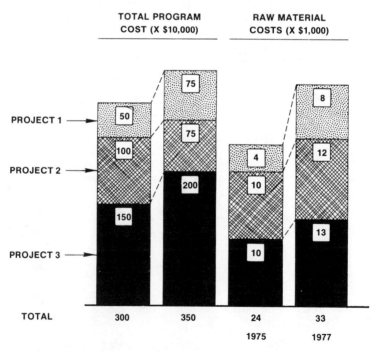

Figure 10-9. 1975 vs 1977 cost comparison.

ceptable to have the same shading technique represent different situations provided that clear separation between the shaded regions appears as in Figure 10–7.

Another common means for comparing activities or projects is through the use of step arrangement bar charts. Figure 10–8 shows a step arrangement bar chart for a cost percentage breakdown of the five projects included within a program. Figure 10–8 can also be used for tracking by shading certain portions of the step identifying each project. This is not normally done, however, because this type of step arrangement tends to indicate that each step must be completed before the next step can begin.

Bar charts need not be represented horizontally. Figure 10–9 indicates the comparison between the 1975 and 1977 costs for the total program and raw materials. Again, care must be taken to make proper use of shading techniques. Three-dimensional vertical bar charts are often the most beautiful to

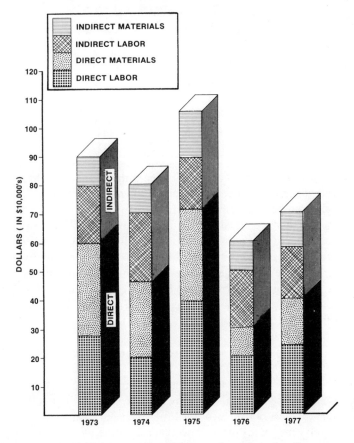

Figure 10–10. Direct and indirect material and labor costs breakdown for all programs per year.

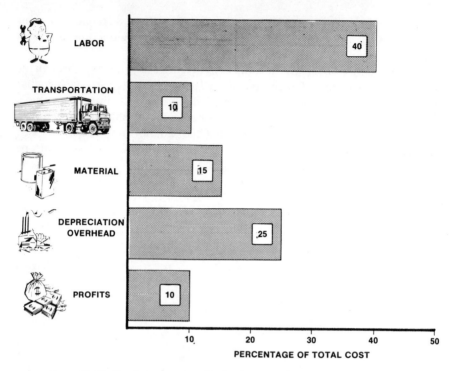

Figure 10–11. Total program cost distribution (quantitative-pictorial bar chart).

behold. Figure 10–10 shows a typical three-dimensional bar chart for direct and indirect labor and material cost breakdowns.

Bar charts can be made quite colorful and appealing to the eye by combining them with other graphical techniques. Figure 10–11 shows a quantitative-pictorial bar chart for the distribution of total program costs. Figure 10–12 shows the same cost distribution in Figure 10–11, but represented with the commonly used pie technique. Figure 10–13 illustrates how two quantitative bar charts can be used side by side to create a quick comparison. The right-hand side shows the labor hour percentages. Figure 10–13 works best if the scale of each axis is the same. Otherwise, the comparisons may appear distorted when, in fact, they are not.

The figures shown in this section are some of those previously used by the authors for customer interchange meetings and do not, by any means, represent the only method of presenting data in bar chart format. Several other methods exist, some of which are shown in the sections that follow.

Bar charts serve as a useful tool for presenting data at technical meetings. Unfortunately, programs must be won competitively or organized in-house before technical meeting presentations can be made. Competitive proposals

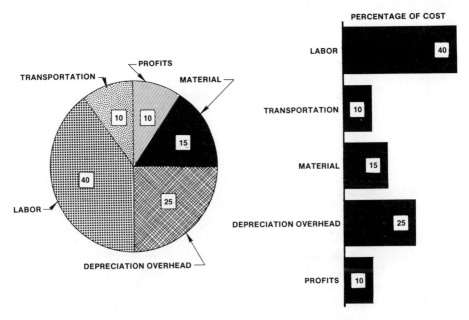

Figure 10–12. Distribution of the program dollar.

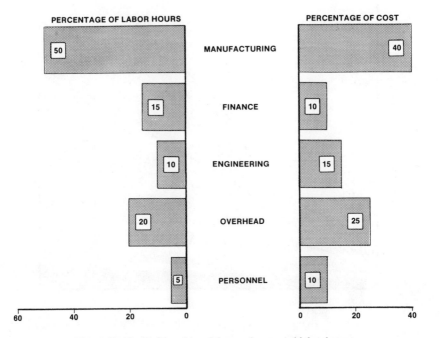

Figure 10–13. Divisional breakdown of costs and labor hours.

or in-house project requests should contain descriptive figures and charts, not necessarily representing activities, but showing either planning, organizing, tracking, or technical procedures designed for the current program or used previously on other programs. Proposals generally contain figures that require either some interpolation or extrapolation.

Figure 10–14 shows the breakdown of total program costs. Although this figure would also normally require interpretation, a monthly cost table accompanies it. If the table is not too extensive, then the table can be included with the figure. This is shown in Figure 10–15. During proposal activities, the actual and cumulative delivery columns, as well as the dotted line in Figure 10–15, would be omitted, but would be included after updating for use in technical interchange meetings. It is normally a good practice to use previous figures and tables whenever possible because management becomes accustomed to the manner in which data is presented.

Another type of schematic representation is the *work flowchart,* synonymous with the applications of flowcharting for computer programming. Flowcharts are designed to describe, either symbolically or pictorially, the sequence of events required to complete activity. Figure 10–16 shows the logic flow for production of molding VZ–3. The symbols shown in Figure 10–16 are universally accepted for several industries.

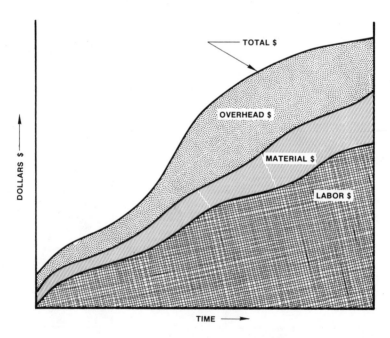

Figure 10–14. Total program cost breakdown.

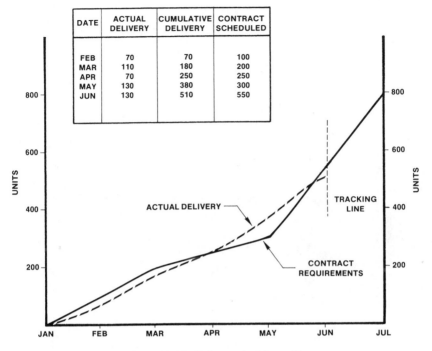

DATE	ACTUAL DELIVERY	CUMULATIVE DELIVERY	CONTRACT SCHEDULED
FEB	70	70	100
MAR	110	180	200
APR	70	250	250
MAY	130	380	300
JUN	130	510	550

Figure 10–15. Delivery schedule tracking.

Pictorial representation, although often a costly procedure, can add color and quality to any proposal. Pictorial sketches provide the customer with a proposal that is easier to identify than a logic or bubble chart. Customers may request tours during activities to relate the actual sites to the pictorial figures. If at all possible, program management should avoid pictorial representation of activities that may be off-limits to the customer, possibly because of security or safety.

Block diagrams can also be used to describe the flow of activities. Block diagrams can be used to show how information is distributed throughout an organization or how a process or activity is assembled. Figure 10–17 shows the testing matrix for propellant samples. Figures similar to this are developed when tours are scheduled during the production or testing phase of a program. Figure 10–17 shows the customer, not only where the testing will take place, but what tests will be conducted.

Block diagrams, schematics, pictorials, and logic flows all fulfill a necessary need for describing the wide variety of activities within a company. The figures and charts are more than descriptive techniques. They can also provide management with the necessary tools for decision making.

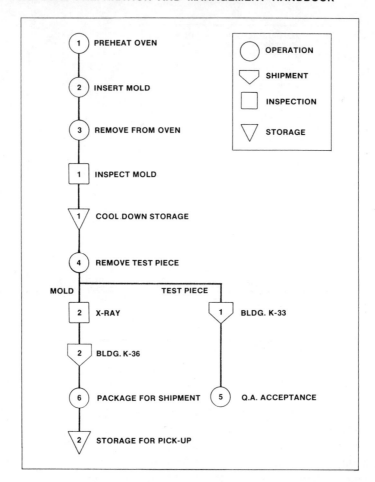

Figure 10–16. Logic flow for production of molding VZ–3.

Probably the most difficult figure to construct is the *logic diagram*. Logic diagrams are developed to illustrate the inductive and deductive reasoning necessary to achieve some objective within a given time frame. The major difficulty in developing logic diagrams is the inability to answer such key questions as: What happens if something goes wrong? Can I quantify any part of the diagram's major elements?

Logic diagrams are constructed similar to bar charts on the supposition that nothing goes wrong, and are usually accompanied by detailed questions, possibly in a checklist format, that require answers. The following questions

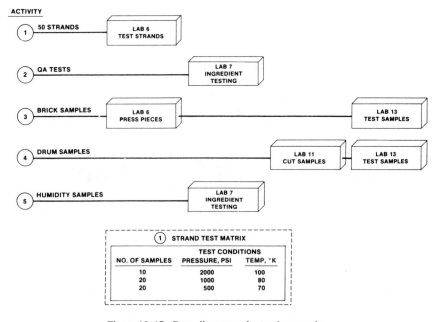

Figure 10–17. Propellant samples testing matrix.

would be representative of those that might accompany a logic diagram for a research and development project:

- What documentation is released to start the described activity and possibly the elements within each activity?
- What information is required before this documentation can be released (i.e., what prior activities must be completed, work designed, studies finalized, and so on)?
- What are the completion (or success) criteria for the activity?
- What are the alternatives for each phase of the program if success is not achieved?
- What other activities are directly dependent on the result of this activity?
- What are the key decision points, if any, during the activity?
- What other activities or inputs are required to perform this activity?
- What documentation signifies completion of the activity? (i.e., report, drawing, and so on)
- What management approval is required for final documentation?

These types of questions are applicable to many other forms of data presentation, not necessarily logic diagrams.

Chapter 11

Government Contracting

11.0 INTRODUCTION

The economic significance of federal procurement is truly massive. In fiscal year 1980, the U.S. Government spent approximately $80 billion through the procurement process, and during the same year distributed approximately $60 billion through federal grants.

Government procurement, while carried out in large part by the executive branch, must be conducted under laws enacted by the Congress. The federal government, like all governments, must act through agents; the U.S. government currently has more than 50 agencies to carry out its operations. These agencies are created by enabling acts of the Congress. Congress passes all laws authorizing the procurement of supplies and services and, in addition, it appropriates monies to pay for the contract services or products procured.

The government contracts area has three constituent elements: status, regulations, and contract clauses. Regulations cloth generally broad statutory language with specifics, dealing with the myriad esoteric details and contingencies on which Congress has neither the expertise nor the desire to legislate. Regulations provide a flexibility statutes cannot. The briefest experience in the government contracts field makes one aware of the constant changes in procurement regulations. Procurement status and regulations, however, generally have no impact on a government contractor unless implementing clauses are included in his contract.

The principal statutes and regulations governing federal procurement are:

- Armed services procurement regulations
- Federal procurement regulations
- NASA procurement regulations.

While there are regulations to be compiled with in the negotiated process as well as in the formal advertised process, in the former, rules are not as rigid and, in actuality, the process generally contemplates discussion. These discussions permit clarification of proposals to insure that offerors understand the government's requirements, as well as discussions or negotiations concerning the price or estimated cost at which the contractor agrees to perform the work.

The government contract imposes upon its contractors responsibilities with respect to subcontractors. These require suitable surveillance of subcontractors to insure proper performance. The government reviews the prime contractor's system of purchasing and/or subcontracting, and may require prior approval of any particular subcontract. The government may review the technical and financial proposals of a subcontractor to insure adequacy for the procurement, and may insist upon approving the subcontractor's billings prior to payment. The prime contractor is required to include certain clauses in the subcontract. Inspection, tests, and quality control procedures may thus by passed down. It has been said that the government exercise almost as much control over the subcontract as it does over the prime contract.

11.1 SIGNIFICANT DIFFERENCES

There are significant differences in contracting with the private sector as compared to contracting with the federal government and the resulting impact on the contracting process. Government procurement is very structured and complex in certain respects and problems can occur by failure to understand some basic principles of differences.

When contracts are entered into with the U.S. government, your company must take special care to acquaint itself with and to abide by voluminous governmental regulations. An experienced contract administrator is essential if the risk of losses and disallowances is to be controlled.

The language of government procurement is a combination of acronyms, words, and phrases from the fields of law, business, economics, accounting, and engineering, with a liberal sprinkling of the terminology used by the particular federal agency involved. Like any language, new words and terms are introduced through innovation of changes in the agency's mission. As with all professions, the language of procurement must be known in order to communicate effectively. More important, in procurement there are frequently monetary implications to the correct interpretation of words and terms.

The four basic differences which are significant to the evaluation and performance of government contracts are:

- Administrative
- Financial
- Legal
- Socioeconomic.

Selected aspects that are representative of the basic differences found in government contracts are shown below:

- Administrative Aspects
  - Procurement
  - The changes clause
  - Patent and technical data rights clauses
  - Government property
  - Acceptance and warranty
- Financial Aspects
  - Cost accounting standards
  - Defective pricing
  - Audit clause
  - Flowdown clauses
  - Penalties for violation
  - Changes
  - Escalation clauses
  - Progress payments
  - Renegotiation of profits
- Legal Aspects
  - Differences arising from sovereignty
  - Differences in the right to sue
  - Differences in administration of contracts
  - Subcontractors
  - Federal procurement statutes
  - Regulations governing procurement and property management
  - Boilerplate/required clauses
  - Bid protests and court actions
  - Contract disputes
- Socioeconomic Aspects
  - Special consideration for small business firms and labor surplus areas
  - Equal Employment Opportunity
  - Wage standards
  - Buy America act

- Environmental controls
- Occupational Safety and Health Act

11.2 GOVERNMENT PROCUREMENT PROCEDURES[1]

Introduction

The laws, regulations and policies governing the procurement of supplies and services for the United States government provide that the responsibility for the propriety of the action shall be fixed upon one individual, namely the contracting officer. However, while final responsibility is individually assigned, the solution of the wide variety of problems encountered in government contracting is beyond the ability of any one person. A government procurement action, therefore, is the result of the combined activities of specialists in particular fields who solve the financial, legal, and technical problems which arise.

In contracting with the government, it is important to recognize that, while the ultimate responsibility is upon the contracting officer, the contractor may never meet, personally, a contracting officer, but may deal, and does deal, continually with many persons representing him. With hundreds of government agencies performing a purchasing function, the procedures and the forms which they use may differ, but the basic system used will apply in general to all of them.

Responsibilites of the Procurement Office

After determining what is needed, securing the necessary approvals of higher authority, and insuring that the money is available for purchase, the initiator assigns the procurement to the procurement activity. The procuring contracting officer (PCO) is responsible for the initial negotiation of the contract. He is generally represented by a buyer or negotiator who is responsible for coordinating the actual procurement.

The technical initiator provides a procurement request which contains, to the extent that the information is available, the quantitative requirements, the specifications, delivery dates, place of delivery and other pertinent information. The contracts office will then usually convene a procurement review board composed of procurement, technical, small business, legal, and other specialists from the agency. It is the responsibility of this board to coordinate

---

[1] Section 11.2 has been summarized and adopted from Volume I, Chapter 1, *Contracting With the Federal Government,* by Paul R. McDonald. Reproduced by permission of Paul R. McDonald. For further information on this subject, the reader may contact Paul R. McDonald, Procurement Associated, Inc., 733 N. Dodsworth Avenue, Covina, California 91724.

the procurement to insure that departmental policies and procedures are followed, that all potential suppliers are given an opportunity to participate in the procurement, that all proposals are given adequate consideration, and that the award is made in the best interests of the government.

Selection of Bidders

In some cases, the question as to who will be asked to bid or propose on a procurement is left up to the contracting office. In other cases, the initiating technical section will specify either a single contractor to whom the proposal will be sent, and restrict the procurement to a particular contractor, or it may recommend to the contracting department a number of companies to be solicited.

If the procurement is not restricted to a sole source, the contracting agency selects a number of qualified companies from the bidder's list. The list of potential suppliers selected from the source files is screened to select only eligible contractors by screening them against the debarred and ineligible bidder's list. The regulations do not require that all qualified bidders receive a chance to bid on the invitation for bid or receive a copy of the request for proposal, but require only that a sufficient number be solicited to provide competition for the procurement. The procurement agencies are supposed to handle their bidder's list so that when the number of qualified bidders for a particular type of procurement is too large for them all to be notified, the invitation for bids or requests for proposals are rotated in some systematic fashion among them. The rotation principle does not always work in actual practice. Any contractor who learns about available procurement, whether advertised or negotiated, and who meets the appropriate requirements, can secure details of the procurement and the chance to bid on it, if he so requests.

Use of Formal Advertising

The contracting office then has to make a decision as to whether the procurement will be made by advertising or by negotiation. If the procurement meets the criteria for the use of formal advertising, (1) it is described by full and complete specifications to provide for full and free competition; (2) that there is an adequate number of suppliers who want the business to assure that effective competition will exist, and (3) that time is available for the detailed procedures of formal advertising, then that method will be used. The buyer prepares an invitation for bid (IFB), listing all pertinent data, and sends it out to a representative number of suppliers. When the bid opening date arrives, the bids are opened and the contract is awarded to the lowest, responsible, responsive bidder.

Prebid Conference

The prebid conference is a procedure which may be used, generally in complex procurements, as a means of briefing prospective bidders (e.g., where procurements which were formerly negotiated are to be formally advertised), and explaining complicated specifications and requirements to them as early as possible after the invitation has been issued and before the bids are opened. Since the invitation for bids itself must be sufficiently clear and complete to insure that bidders are bidding on the same basis, the need for this procedure is rare.

Two-Step Formal Advertising

If the available specifications or purchase descriptions are not sufficiently defining or complete to permit full and free competition without engineering evaluation and any necessary discussion of the technical aspects of the requirement, then "two step" formal advertising may be used. As its name implies, "two step" formal advertising is a method of procurement conducted in two phases. The first step consists of the request, submission, evaluation, and, if necessary, discussion of a technical proposal, without pricing, to determine the acceptability of the supplies or services offered. The second step consists of a formally advertised procurement, confined to those offerors who submitted an acceptable technical proposal in step one. An objective of the two-step procedure is to permit the development of a sufficiently descriptive statement of the government's requirements so that subsequent procurement may be made by standard formal advertising procedures.

Multiyear Procurement

Multiyear procurement is a method for competitive contracting for known requirements for military supplies in quantities not in excess of planned requirements for five years set forth in or in support of the Department of Defense Five Year Force Structure and Financial Program, even though the total funds ultimately to be obligated by the contract are not available to the contracting officer at the time of entering into the contract. Under this method, contract quantities are budgeted and accounted for in accordance with the program year in which each quantity is authorized.

Formal advertising, including two-step formal advertising, is the preferred method for use in multiyear procurement. However, negotiation can be used. In cases where the period of production is such that a contingency for labor and material cost in likely otherwise to be included in the multiyear contract price, the contracting officer may include a provision for price escalation.

Life Cycle Costing

This concept concerns itself with the influence that changes in suppliers may have on logistics costs and involves consideration of logistics costs in evaluating competitive bids. Traditionally, price has been the determining factor in competitive situations, and price competition has meant frequent changes in suppliers. Life cycle costing is a methodology for defining the other factors in a procurement in terms of logistics costs on the basis that is does not make sense to pay $10,000 for an equipment if the annual support costs amount to $50,000, when another equipment serving the same purpose can be acquired for $12,000 and an annual support cost of only $25,000.

Any time this technique is used for procurement, the solicitation will contain very precise information as to the factors to be used in bid evaluation. Some of the evaluation factors will be based on government studies as, for example, the cost of adding new items to the inventory. Others will be based on contractor-supplied data. This type of data will be verified by the government, usually by means of some form of demonstration.

Procurement by Negotiation

A large portion of government procurement does not meet the criteria for formal advertising and must be placed by negotiated procurement methods. The Procurement Act of 1947 provides that formal advertising is the preferred procurement method. If the determination is made to procure by negotiation, the procurement office must determine which of the 17 exceptions authorizing the use of negotiation listed in Section III, Part 2, of the ASPR covers the particular situation involved. The contracting officer must carefully document the procurement request with the facts pertaining to the justification for negotiation. This formal determination and findings, (D&F) with supporting data, is then reviewed by the legal division, or section, of the contracting office as to form and legality and then signed by the contracting officer. In some cases, the regulations provide that the secretary of the department concerned must approve the determination and findings.

Leader Company Procurement

Leader company procurement, as outlined in ASPR Section IV, Part 7, is an extraordinary procurement technique under which the developer or sole producer of an item or system (the leader company) furnishes manufacturing assistance and know-how or otherwise enables a follower company to become a source of supply for the item or system. A number of procedures are used.

One procedure is to award a prime contract to an established source (leader company) in which the source is obligated to subcontract a designated portion of the total number of end items required to a specific subcontractor (follower company), and to assist the follower company in that production.

A second procedure is to award a prime contract to the leader company for the requisite assistance to the follower company, and another prime contract to the follower company for production of the items.

A third procedure is to award a prime contract to the follower company for the items under which the follower company is obligated to subcontract with a designated leader company for the requisite assistance.

Preproposal Conferences

The preproposal conference is a procedure which may be used, generally in complex procurements, as a means of briefing prospective offerors after a solicitation has been issued but before offers or proposals are prepared. This procedure may be used when approved at a level higher than the contracting officer. Such a conference permits the government to explain or clarify complicated specifications and requirements to interested firms. It may also be used to provide an opportunity for interested firms to examine a model of the equipment being procured, where, for reasons such as security or limited quantities, the model can only be shown at a specific time and location. In some cases, a determination to hold a conference may be made as a result of questions and problems raised by prospective offerors. Adequate notice is given to all prospective offerors, and, if time permits, offerors may be asked to submit any questions that they may have in advance.

Request for Proposal

After the determination and findings is signed or approved by higher head-quarters, a request for proposal (RFP) is prepared by the contracting officer. This request for proposal should contain a complete and specific description of the items to be procured, together with all applicable specifications, quantities, time and place of delivery, method of shipment, specifications for preservation and packaging, technical instruction books and data required, and the material, if any, to be furnished by the government. It may request a quotation based on a particular type of contract, fixed price or cost type, but even if it does, this does not preclude the manufacturer from submitting a quotation on a different basis if he can convince the government buyer that his approach is in the best interest of the government. However, the contractor should respond to the request for proposal as requested and submit his alternate proposal separately. Prospective contractors are usually requested to submit a quotation supported by complete cost breakdown on a DD 633 Form or optional Form 60. Usually, 30 days are allowed the company to prepare and submit a proposal. However, shorter periods are not uncommon.

Cost or Pricing Data Requirements

ASPR provides that for contracts in excess of $100,000 prime contractors and subcontractors are required to submit actually or by specific identification in writing, cost, or pricing data, and sign a certificate that as of the date of agreement on price that the data is accurate, complete, and current, unless the contract is excepted on the basis that the price is based on competition, an established catalog or market price of a commercial item, the price is set by law or regulation, or the contract is exempted by the Secretary of the Department. If the contract is excepted, the contract must contain a price reduction clause which becomes operative with respect to any change or modification in excess of $100,000.

Cost or pricing data is defined as "all facts existing up to the time of agreement on price which prudent buyers and sellers would reasonably expect to have a significant effect on the price negotiations." If defective data is furnished, the government is entitled to an adjustment of the negotiated price, including profit or fee, to exclude any significant sums by which the price was increased because of the defective data. Properly supported and verified claims of "understated" cost or pricing data will be recognized, if such data was submitted in support of negotiation within the same pricing action, up to the amount of the government's claim for overstated cost or pricing data arising out of the same pricing action.

Unless the prime contract, subcontract, change, or modification is covered by one of the standard exceptions, certified cost and pricing data will have to be submitted. The contractor's estimating and pricing departments will have to be geared to develop proper cost and pricing data and be able to substantiate it.

The law and the regulation only require that accurate, complete, and current data be furnished. The contractor can still ask for any price for his services that he thinks he is entitled to and can get.

Prime contractors, who are required to submit and certify cost or pricing data, must also submit cost or pricing data from prospective subcontractors in support of each subcontract cost estimate included in the prime contractor's submission that is (1) $1,000,000 or more or (2) both more than $100,000 and more than 10 percent of the contractor's proposed prime contract. The prime contractor is responsible for submission of subcontractor cost or pricing data that is complete, accurate, and current as of the effective date of the prime contractor's certificate, and is responsible for updating a prospective subcontractor's data to the date on the certificate from the time of original submission by the subcontractor. Exemptions equivalent to those provided the prime contractor are recognized.

Only if the contracting officer determines that the data submitted was inaccurate, incomplete, or not current at the time of the signing of the certificate of current pricing can he invoke the defective cost or pricing data clause and require a reduction in price.

The fact that the contractor makes a greater dollar profit on a fixed price contract or a larger percentage of fee than was originally intended on a cost type contract based on the contractor's actual cost of performance means nothing, unless the increase can be shown to have occurred because the contractor's cost information was inaccurate, incomplete, or noncurrent at the time of the signing of the certificate of current cost or pricing data.

Preaward Surveys

When the contractor's bid or proposal is received, a preaward survey of the prospective supplier may be undertaken in accordance with the procedures outlined in Section I, Part 9, and Appendix K of ASPR. In other cases, the pre-award survey may not be made until after the initial analysis of proposals has shown that the contractor is in the zone of consideration, or in the case of an advertised procurement, that the contractor is the low bidder. In research and development procurement, the preaward survey may be made prior to sending out the request for proposal.

A preaward survey is an evaluation of a prospective contractor's capability to perform under the terms of a proposed contract. The evaluation may be accomplished by use of (1) data already on hand, (2) data from another government agency or commercial source, (3) an onsite inspection of plant and facilities to be used for performance of the contract, or (4) any combination of the three.

A preaward survey may involve the inspection of the plants and facilities with which the prospective contractor proposes to perform a contract and generally includes personal interviews with the contractor's personnel. The information provided by the contractor in his proposal regarding work load and financial capability is verified. The prime contractor is generally responsible for determining that he is dealing with responsible subcontractors. However, where subcontracting is important and represents a large percentage of the prime contract, government personnel may conduct what is, in essence, a preaward survey on the proposed subcontractor structure.

A preaward survey is made prior to letting any new contract. The extent of the survey is based on the complexity of the procurement and the amount of information already available in the agency. For large complex systems contracts, the preaward survey is usually made by the Source Selection Board.

In an advertised procurement, the preaward survey must determine that a contractor is a responsible contractor prior to the award of the contract. In a negotiated procurement, it must also be determined that the contractor is a responsible contractor. However, the preaward survey is only one of the factors that are taken into consideration.

Certificates of Competency

The purpose of the preaward survey is to determine that the contractor is responsible. If the bid or proposal of a small business concern is to be rejected because the contracting officer has determined the concern to be nonresponsible as to capacity or credit, the matter is referred to the Small Business Administration, if the proposed award exceeds $2,500. However, for awards exceeding $2,500.00, but not exceeding $10,000.00, referral is within the discretion of the contracting officer. Capacity means the overall ability of a prospective small business contractor to meet quality, quantity, and time requirements of a proposed contract and includes ability to perform, organization, experience, technical knowledge, skills, know-how, technical equipment, and facilities or the ability to obtain them.

The contracting officer is not required to refer the matter to the SBA if he determines that a small business concern is nonresponsible for a reason other than lack of capacity or credit, for example, lack of integrity, business ethics, or persistent failure to apply necessary tenacity or perseverance to do an acceptable job.

Analysis of Proposals

Each contracting officer is responsible for performing or having performed all administrative actions necessary for effective contracting. However, since he cannot expect to be an expert in all these fields, he must avail himself of the advice of specialists in the fields of contracting, finance, law, contract audit, packaging, engineering, traffic management, and price analysis. The contracting officer is responsible for the coordination of the specialists' efforts, but he cannot transfer his own responsibilities to them. Thus, the determination of the suitability of a contract price to the government always remains the responsibility of the contracting officer. However, the actual "deal" is usually made by the buyer/negotiator assigned to handle the procurement.

Upon receipt of the contractor's proposal, the buyer assigned to the procurement makes an initial analysis of the proposals received. A variety of techniques may be used by the contracting officer in the evaluation of offerors or contractors' proposals. Congress has established a statutory requirement for the submission of cost or pricing data by prospective contractors under certain conditions and for contracts above a certain size. These requirements are contained in ASPR Section III.

Price Analysis. Price analysis is the process of examining and evaluating a prospective price without evaluation of the separate cost elements and proposed profit of the individual prospective supplier whose price is being evaluated. It involves comparisons of the price quotation with current or past quotations for the same or similar items.

Cost Analysis. Cost analysis is the review and evaluation of a contractor's cost or pricing data and the judgmental factors applied in projecting from the data to the estimated costs in order to form an opinion on the degree to which the contractor's proposed costs represent what performance of the contract should cost, assuming reasonable economy and efficiency. It includes the appropriate verification of cost data, the evaluation of specific elements of costs and the projection of these data to determine the effect on prices of such factors as:

1. the necessity for certain costs
2. the reasonableness of the amounts estimated for certain costs
3. allowances for contingencies
4. the basis used for allocation of overhead costs
5. the appropriateness of allocations of particular overhead costs to the proposed contract
6. the contractor's compliance with his disclosed accounting practices and with the regulations and standards of the Cost Accounting Standards Board.

The Technical Officer

In addition to the administrative problems in connection with the contract, where technical problems may arise, a technical officer is usually assigned to coordinate with the contractor. It is important to remember that the technical officer may make decisions only within the scope of the contract and generally can make no decisions regarding administrative or cost matters in connection with the contract. It is the responsibility of the contractor to insure that he takes directions only from those government personnel authorized to give them.

The Defense Contract Audit Agency

The Defense Contract Audit Agency, under the staff supervision of the Assistant Secretary of Defense (Controller), is responsible for the performance of all necessary contract audit for the DOD and for providing accounting and financial advisory services regarding contracts and subcontracts to those DOD components responsible for procurement and contract administration activities. The auditor has the responsibility for securing information which requires access to the books of the contractor.

The Defense Contract Audit Agency is responsible for the following functions:

1. Audit, examine, and/or review the contractor's and subcontractor's accounts, records, documents and other evidence, systems of internal

control, accounting, costing, and general business practices and procedures; to the extent and in whatever manner is considered necessary to permit proper performance of the other functions described below.

2. Examine reimbursement vouchers received directly from contractors under cost type contracts, transmitting those vouchers approved for payment to the cognizant disbursing officer, and issuing DD Form 396 (Notice of Costs Suspended and/or disapproved) with a copy to the cognizant contracting officer with respect to costs claimed but not considered allowable. When the contractor disagrees with a suspension or disallowance action by DCAA and the difference cannot be resolved, the contractor may appeal in writing to the ACO, who will make a determination in writing. In addition, the contracting officer may direct the issuance of DCAA Form 1 (Notice of Costs Suspended and/or Disapproved) with respect to any cost which he has reason to believe should be suspended or disapproved.

3. Provide advice and recommendations to procurement and contract administration personnel on (a) acceptability of costs incurred under redeterminable, incentive, and similar type contracts; (b) acceptability of incurred costs and estimates of costs to be incurred, as represented by contractors incident to the award, negotiation, modification, change, administration, termination, or settlement of contracts; (c) adequacy of financial or accounting aspects of contract provisions; (d) adequacy of contractor's accounting and financial management systems; (e) adequacy of contractor's estimating procedures; and (f) adequacy of property controls.

4. Assist responsible procurement or contract administration activities in their surveys of the purchasing procurement systems of major contractors.

5. Direct audit reports to the government management level having authority and responsibility to take action on the audit findings and recommendations.

6. Cooperate with other appropriate Department of Defense components on reviews, audits, analysis, or inquiries involving contractor's financial position or financial and accounting policies, procedures, or practices.

7. Establish and maintain liaison auditors, as appropriate, at major procuring and contract administration offices.

8. Review General Accounting Office reports and proposed responses thereto which involve significant contract or contractor activities for the purpose of assuring the validity of appropriate, pertinent facts contained therein.

9. In an advisory capacity, attend and participate, as appropriate, in con-

tract negotiation and other meetings where contract cost matters, audit reports, or related financial matters are under consideration.

10. Provide assistance, as requested, in the development of procurement policies and regulations.

In addition, the Defense Contract Audit Agency makes postaward audits of contracts containing defective pricing provisions.

Inspection

The contract provides that all articles, materials, and workmanship are subject to inspection and test by government inspectors, to the extent practicable, at all times and places, including during manufacture and, in any event, prior to final acceptance. This inspection is generally conducted at the plant of the manufacturer. In some cases, where necessary, source inspection will be conducted at the plants of subcontractors who supply materials and major components. This inspection is carried out by the inspection personnel from the Defense Contract Administrative Services Region (DCASR), which has cognizance of the plant. The inspector's duty is to see that the government gets exactly what the contract calls for, down to the most minute specifications. His "bible" is his copy of the contract, including all documents incorporated in it by reference, such as "general specifications for inspection of material" and the drawings and detailed specifications for the equipment itself.

Changes

The Standard Changes Article in all government contracts provides that (1) the contracting officer may, at any time, by written order, make changes within the general scope of the contract, in the drawings designs or specifications, where the supplies to be furnished are especially manufactured for the government; (2) the method of shipping or packing; and (3) the place of delivery. In a large complex contract, these changes may run into the many hundreds. In some cases, they may cause an increase in the cost of the contract and, in other cases, a decrease. The pricing and negotiation of these changes may, in some cases, be more difficult than the negotiation of the original contract itself. The procedures for cost and price analysis, negotiation, board review, preparation, and executing of the modification of the contract required by a change, are the same as for the initial contract placement.

Contract Termination or Completion

During the period of contract performance, the contract may be either partially terminated or completely terminated for the convenience of the government. The clause in the contract entitled "Termination" outlines the rights and duties of both the contractor and the government with regard to termination and ASPR Section VIII, entitled "Termination of Contracts," gives the detailed procedures and forms required to implement the contract clause.

Conclusion

As may be seen from this brief summary of the contracts procedure used by the government, it is a very complicated process. A team composed of specialists in pertinent fields is utilized to prepare the groundwork for negotiation and conduct the actual negotiation with prospective contractors. It is important to note the number of personnel who are concerned with the procurement and who review the negotiations, many of whom have not participated in the actual negotiation itself. This same team concept is used to administer the contract after it is placed. The prospective contractor would be wise to protect his own interests by developing comparable team operation for the preparation of his proposals and the negotiation, administration, and renegotiation of his contracts.

11.3 SOCIOECONOMIC LEGISLATION

The government has enacted various laws that are intended to achieve beneficial social and economic goals through appropriate legislation. Many of these enactments affect the government contracts process. Various governmental objectives are realized by translating "socioeconomic" statutes into clauses for inclusion in contracts with the government. The contractor is thus confronted by numerous requirements related to the business of procurement.

The most significant areas in which contract clauses have been born of statutory enactments in the socioeconomic area are described in the following:

Small Business Firms

Congress has given a mandate to the executive branch that "a fair proportion of contracts shall be awarded to small business" (ASPR 1-702). In compliance with this mandate, contracting officers may designate particular procurements to be totally or partially set aside for small business (those not dominant in their field and owned independently).

By passage of the Small Business Act of 1953, 15 U.S.C. 631-647 (1970), Congress declared its policy of assisting and protecting small business. This policy is carried out in a variety of ways. Among them are direct loans, indirect loans (through small business investment companies), and management advice to small business concerns. In addition, the Act provides for assistance directly related to government procurement.

Labor Surplus Firms

Portions of procurement requirements may also be set aside for firms in areas of labor surplus. Only partial set-asides as available under this program. In order to assist certain geographical areas that have been hard-hit by unemployment, the Government has set aside certain contracts for labor surplus preference areas.

Typically, these areas face persistent underemployment. Such an area is classified by the Department of Labor as an "area of persistent unemployment," and a list of these areas is published in the department's publication *Area Trends in Employment and Unemployment.* Other areas faced with substantial unemployment can be designated labor surplus perference areas by the Department of Labor upon request of a prospective contractor.

Equal Employment Opportunity (EEO)

Federal procurement policy has for many years dictated insuring equal opportunity for all qualified persons, without regard to race, religion, color, sex, or national origin, employed by or seeking employment with government contractors. As early as June 1941, the government used its federal contracting powers to enforce this policy and eliminate discrimination. Although the source of that concern was an executive order, its perpetuation has been legislatively insured by Title VII of the Civil Rights Act of 1964.

Title VII applies generally to most business within the U.S. and the executive implementation of this policy declaration has particularly affected Government contractors.

Affirmative Action

The requirement for affirmative action on equal opportunity applies to all contractors subject to the Equal Employment Opportunity clause. However, not all contractors must develop (within 120 days after receiving contract award) and keep on file a written affirmative action compliance program. Only if a prime contractor has 50 or more employees and a contract of $50,000 or more must a written affirmative action program for each of its establishments be developed. In addition, the prime must notify each of his subcontractors having 50 or more employees and a subcontract of $50,000 or more of this requirement to develop such a written program. The prime contractor, however, is not required to inspect or evaluate such program of its subcontractors.

Chapter 12

Assuring Proposal Success

12.0 INTRODUCTION

One of the most difficult tasks is to assure that the proposal will be successful. Most goal-oriented managers look only at the time, cost, and performance paramenters. If an out-of-tolerance condition exists, then additional analysis is required to identify the cause of the problem. Looking only at time, cost, and performance might identify immediate contributions to profits, but will not identify whether or not the proposal itself was managed correctly. This takes on paramount importance if the survival of the organization is based upon a steady stream of successfully managed winning proposals. Once or twice a proposal manager may "luck out" with a successful proposal by being at the right place at the right time. After awhile, however, this effect becomes known for what it is. People will avoid working on proposals, and the company will lose in the long run.

To prepare the winning proposal, the company must develop a format, approach, and personnel that are professional. The team assigned must be knowledgeable in their area of responsibility and be motivated to strive for a winning proposal. Equally important, the parent company must recognize the importance of the proposal and give that activity all the support it needs. Generally, proposal success can be measured by the "actions" of three groups: the proposal manager and team, the parent organization, and the customer organization. The following sections discuss these key areas.

12.1 THE PROPOSAL TEAM

There are certain actions that the proposal manager and team can take in order to stimulate proposal success. These actions include the following:

- Insist upon the right to select key proposal team members.
- Select key team members with proven track records in their fields.
- Develop a commitment and sense of mission from the outset.
- Seek sufficient authority and a projected organizational form.
- Coordinate and maintain good relationship with client, parent, and team.
- Seek to enhance public's image of the project.
- Have key team members assist in decision making and problem solving.
- Develop realistic cost, schedule, and performance estimates and goals.
- Have back-up strategies in anticipation of potential problems.
- Team structure should be appropriate, yet flexible and flat.
- Go beyond formal authority to maximize influence over people and key decisions.
- Employ a workable set of proposal planning and control tools.
- Avoid overreliance on one type of control tool.
- Stress importance of meeting cost, schedule, and performance goals.
- Give priority to achieving the mission or function of the end items.
- Keep changes under control.
- Seek to find ways of assuring job growth for effective team members.

To insure that the proposal prepared will be a win, the proposal manager must exhibit the qualities of leadership, motivation, and the desire to do an outstanding effort. The proposal manager must be a manager, not a doer. The proposal manager should not write any parts of the draft material unless it is a small effort; work and responsibility must be delegated wisely. The proposal manager and the proposal team must adhere to the following considerations:

- Read the inquiry document and understand completely the specific requirements
- Plan and organize the proposal so that it gets off to a strong start
- Recruit for and organize the proposal
- Develop and use a proposal outline
- Define and develop a plan to obtain all needed data and information
- Enforce the schedule and budget
- Get management support behind the proposal
- Use a checklist as a guide

- Allow adequate time to prepare redrafts and reviews
- Review all sections of the proposal
- Determine if final proposal is completely responsive.

In addition, to aid in the preparation of a winning proposal, the proposal team should follow the points discussed in Table 12–1, the "Ten Commandments" for effective proposal writing.[1]

Table 12-1. Ten Commandments for Effective Proposal Writing

1. **GET YOUR STORY ACROSS EARLY.** A cardinal rule of effective communication is to come on strong, to spark the reader's interest early. This can be done by providing him with all your best information and most persuasive arguments right from the start. Sure, they have to be justified and elaborated, but this can be done later after you've shown him you have something to say. Establish your theme here too and let it permeate your whole proposal. Consistency of thought and enthusiasm will pay dividends.

2. **EMPHASIZE CUSTOMER BENEFITS.** Your message must emphasize the customer's gain in whatever you propose. The advantages that accrue to him from your approach must be obvious. You should always write in terms which satisfy his needs—technical, financial and managerial. If you are not selling something that he wants to buy, he is not going to be interested in reading about your engineering skill or factory capacity.

3. **BE SPECIFIC.** Sell one idea and sell it hard. Don't just describe a variety of possible approaches, and let the customer try to feel out what it is you really recommend. If you have thoroughly studied his problem and your range of capabilities to meet it, and have made a careful trade-off analysis, you know there is only one best approach that you can provide to meet his specific need.

4. **WRITE IN A POSITIVE STYLE.** Too many proposals are defensive, negative and apologetic. They are so filled with qualification, conditions and elaborate discussions of problem areas that their total effect is almost to unsell the reader. If you are going to bid on a job, you must be confident that you are a qualified bidder with a sound approach. If you can't write a positive proposal, you shouldn't be writing one at all.

5. **TALK THE CUSTOMER'S LANGUAGE.** Don't assume the evaluator is familiar with all details of your technique or with all your terminology. Provide background so he can understand your approach. Demonstrate clearly your familiarity with his program, and do so in a language familiar to him. Too often proposals are filled with highly specialized technical jargon. Your abbreviations, device model numbers, and newly coined words for technologies, are not necessarily clear to your customer. If you must use your pet names, and acronyms, be sure you define them as often as necessary throughout the document to make your meaning clear.

   Give the evaluator the words he needs to sell your ideas to his management. The easier you make his job, the more appreciative he's likely to be. Consider his position. He must have logical reasons for making his selection. They should be obtainable from, and substantiated by your proposal without a struggle.

---

[1] Paul R. McDonald, *Proposal Preparation Manual,* Pp. II–6–17 and II–6–18. Reproduced by permission of Paul R. McDonald, Procurement Associates, Inc., 733 N. Dodsworth Ave., Covina, California 91724.

6. **BE FRANK AND DIRECT.** Vague proposals confuse customers. Quality, dignity, simplicity, coherence and clarity are basic. If you don't intend to meet certain requirements, don't think you'll fool the evaluator by failing to discuss them. Clearly state any aspects of your approach which deviate from the stated requirement. But then explain: (1) the reasons why you aren't meeting all requirements, (2) why you feel that nonetheless your total approach is acceptable, and (3) actions you plan to take, prior to and after program go-ahead, to cover any possible deficiencies. If you've interpreted an ambiguous requirement, say so.

7. **KEEP THE PROPOSAL SHORT.** One handicap in writing a good proposal is the scarcity of time usually available. Rather than resulting in a short proposal, the reverse typically happens. This is because the authors, in their attempt to cover everything, write frantically and voluminously. They feel that they don't have the time to spare and as a result, they don't. Brevity must be measured relatively—a brief proposal could run 300 pages, depending on the complexity of the proposed program and hardware. But many proposals are plagued by unnecessary length. Too much supporting information is provided, usually because the writer thinks it is better to throw in a little extra to impress the customer, possibly hoping that the reviewer or the editor will trim it back to size. The reviewer or editor may hesitate to delete supporting data, particularly highly specialized and technical material because he assumes that the contributor felt it essential to the message.

In a multi-contributor effort this effect can snowball out of reasonable proportion. Supporting data not essential to the basic proposal argument should be submitted under separate cover—in a volume of appendixes, an attachment or in a technical memo.

8. **USE BRIEF, ACTIVE LANGUAGE.** Technical proposals are extremely sophisticated in their subject matter and terminology. However, they don't have to be written in stuffy, overly formal, impersonal and inflated language. Put on your conversational hat when you write proposals. Tell your story in a direct, straightforward way. After you have written a section, go back over it, test each word to see if it is a "working" one. If it isn't, throw it out. Cut overlong sentences in two. Don't let paragraphs cover entire pages. Watch your frequency of use of the passive tense. Too many passive statements create an air of diffidence and remoteness in your writing.

The reader of a proposal is certain to be influenced, if only subconsciously, by the quality of its writing. A neat, dignified, effective illustrated, and well-polished approach has never offended anyone, perhaps because it appears to represent best the nature of the originator.

9. **MAKE ORGANIZATION OBVIOUS.** If you have a well-constructed outline and write according to it, you can easily convert all of your topic headings, even to the very lowest level, into headlines which will guide the reader naturally and effectively through the desired thought process. Give him every sign-post you can. Don't assume that he is motivated to read your precious prose. Some ill-informed proposal writers say, "All the data is there—the reader will get the message if he just looks for it." Well, he just may not bother to look for it. . . .

10. **BE ORIGINAL.** It is too easy to retread old proposal texts for new applications. The odds of succeeding are against you if you want an effective document. Maybe the proposal you are stealing from was poorly done in the first place. Perhaps the application was just different enough that the whole slant of the document is wrong, even though it is describing generally the same subject matter. If you are writing a proposal is must be addressed to a specific customer for an application which is somewhat unique. Old proposal material might be a good starting point to give you information, but be extremely wary about using it verbatim. Particularly watch for (1) topics that are not directly and necessarily applicable to your message, (2) reference to programs, agencies and concepts which will not be familiar to the new

customer. Always try to go an old proposal one better by injecting new facts and ideas—or at least new words.

12.2 THE PARENT/CLIENT ORGANIZATION SUPPORT

We have stated that a proposal cannot be successful unless it is recognized as a project and has the support of top-level management. Top-level management must be willing to commit company resources and provide the necessary administrative support so that the proposal easily adapts to the company's day-to-day routine of doing business. Furthermore, the parent organization must develop an atmosphere conducive to good working relationships among the proposal manager, parent organization, and client organization.

With regards to the parent organization, there exists several variables that can be used to evaluate parent organization support. These variables include:

- A willingness to coordinate efforts
- A willingness to maintain structural flexibility
- A willingness to adapt to change
- Effective strategic planning
- Rapport maintenance
- Proper emphasis on past experience
- External buffering
- Prompt and accurate communications
- Enthusiastic support
- Identification to all concerned parties that the proposal does, in fact, contribute to parent capabilities.

The mere identification and existence of these variables do not guarantee proposal success in dealing with the parent organization. Instead, it implies that there exists a good foundation to work with such that if the proposal manager, the proposal team, and the parent organization take appropriate actions, then proposal success is likely. The following actions must be taken:

- Select at an early point a proposal manager with a proven track record of technical skills, human skills, and administrative skills (in that order) to lead the proposal team.
- Develop clear and workable guidelines for the proposal manager.
- Delegate sufficient authority to the proposal manager so that important decisions can be made in conjunction with key team members.
- Demonstrate enthusiasm for and commitment to the proposal and team.
- Develop and maintain short and informal lines of communication.
- Avoid excessive pressure on the proposal manager to win contracts.

- Avoid arbitrarily slashing or ballooning proposal team's cost estimate.
- Avoid "buy-ins."
- Develop close, not meddling, working relationships with the principal client contact and proposal manager.

Both the parent organization and the proposal team must employ proper managerial techniques to insure that judicious and adequate, but not excessive, use of the planning, controlling, and communications systems can be made. These proper management techniques must also include preconditioning, such as:

- Clearly established specifications and designs
- Realistic schedules
- Realistic cost estimates
- Avoidance of "buy-ins"
- Avoidance of over-optimism

A client organization can have a great deal of influence toward proposal success by minimizing meetings, making rapid responses to requests for information, and simply by letting the contractor "do his thing" without any interference. The variables that exist for the client organization include:

- A willingness to coordinate efforts
- Rapport maintenance
- Establishment of reasonable and specific goals and criteria
- Well-established procedures for changes
- Prompt and accurate communications
- Commitment of client resources
- Minimization of red tape
- Providing sufficient authority to the client contact (especially for decision making).

With these variables as the basic foundation, the following actions should result:

- Encourage openness and honesty from the start from all participants.
- Create an atmosphere that encourages healthy, but not cut-throat, competition, or "liars" contests.
- Plan for adequate funding to complete the proposal.
- Develop clear understandings of the relative importance of cost, schedule, and technical performance goals.

- Develop short and informal lines of communication and flat organizational structure.
- Delegate sufficient authority to the principal client contact and allow prompt approval or rejection of important decisions.
- Reject "buy-ins"
- Make prompt decisions regarding contract award or go-ahead.
- Develop close, not meddling, working relationships with proposal participants.
- Avoid arms-length relationships.
- Avoid excessive reporting schemes.
- Make prompt decisions regarding changes.

By combining the relevant actions of the proposal team, parent organization, and client organization, we can identify the fundamental lessons for management. These include:

- *When starting off in proposal management, plan to go all the way.*
  - Recognize authority conflicts: resolve
  - Recognize change impacts: be an agent for change
- *Match the right people for the right job.*
  - No system is better than the people that implement it
- *Allow adequate time and effort for laying out the proposal groundwork and defining work.*
  - Work breakdown structure
  - Network planning
- *Insure that work packages are the proper size.*
  - Manageable and organizational accountability
  - Realistic in terms of effort and time
- *Establish and use planning and control systems as the focal point of proposal implementation.*
  - Know where you're going
  - Know when you've gotten there
- *Be sure information flow is realistic.*
  - Information is the basis for problem solving and decision making
  - Communication "pitfalls" are the greatest contributors to proposal difficulties
- *Be willing to replan.*
  - The best laid plans can go astray
  - Change is inevitable
- *Tie together responsibility, performance, and rewards.*
  - Management by objectives
  - Key to motivation and productivity

- *Long before proposal ends, plan for its end.*
  - Disposition of personnel
  - Disposal of material and other resources
  - Transfer of knowledge
  - Closing out work orders
  - Customer/contractor financial payments and reporting

Having defined proposal success, we can now identify some of the major causes for the failure of proposal management. These causes include:

- *Selecting a concept that was not applicable.* Since each application is unique, selecting a project that does not have a sound basis, or forcing a change when the time is not appropriate, can lead to immediate failure.
- *The wrong person selected as proposal manager.* The individual selected must be a manager, not a doer. He must place emphasis on all aspects of the work, not merely technical.
- *Upper management not supportive.* Upper management must concur in the concept and must behave accordingly.
- *Inadequately defined tasks.* There must exist an adequate system for planning and control such that a proper balance between cost, schedule, and technical performance can be maintained.
- *Management techniques misused.* There exists the inevitable tendency in technical communities to attempt to do more than is initially required by contract. Technology must be watched and individuals must buy only what is needed.
- *Proposal completion not planned.* By definition, each proposal must stop. Completion must be planned so that the impact can be identified.

It is often said that more can be learned from failure than from success. The lessons that can be learned from project failure include:[2]

- When starting off in project (proposal) management, plan to go all the way.
- Do not skimp on the project (proposal) manager's qualifications.
- Do not spare time and effort in laying out the project (proposal) groundwork and defining work.
- Insure that the work packages in the project (proposal) are of proper size.
- Establish and use network planning techniques, having the network as the focal point of project (proposal) implementation.

---

[2] Ivars Avots, "Why Does Project Management Fail?" *California Management Review*, Vol. 12, 1969, pp. 77–82

- Be sure that the information flow related to the project (proposal) management system is realistic.
- Be prepared to continually replan jobs to accommodate frequent changes on dynamic programs.
- Whenever possible, tie together responsibility, performance, and rewards.
- Long before a project (proposal) ends, provide some means for accommodating the employees' personal goals.
- If mistakes in project (proposal) implementation have been made, make a fresh try.

12.3 USING A CHECKLIST

The hazards of a eleventh-hour proposal that is inadequately prepared immediately prior to the due date are very severe. A proposal must be prepared with the view that it may be accepted "as is." To prepare a proper proposal, there must be an opportunity for initial drafts, redrafts, and revisions of the proposal and some period for the requisite reviews and evaluations before the proposal is put into final form and delivered to the client. The need to review and evaluate the proposal before it can be sent to a client cannot be overemphasized. No company, no matter how many proposals it has done, is so successful that they can avoid this effort.

Many companies have developed a detailed checklist of key areas to help them go through the proposal preparation process without missing importance considerations because of a tight time schedule. A checklist also allows you to be consistent in the proposals you turn out as a company, and not a reflection of the individual who prepared them.

There can be many forms of checklists and the amount and type depends on your organization and the size and complexity of the proposals you prepare. Your organization could prepare checklists for the following areas:

- Technical proposal
- Management proposal
- Cost proposal
- Contract
- Proposal request (inquiry)
- Project approach
- Capabilities and staffing
- Overall responsiveness
- Control and Reporting
- Format and editing
- Publication and final assembly.

Even though there may be many individual kinds of checklists, they can be grouped together into four basic types of checklists that relate to the key phases of a proposal life. These four types of checklists are:

- The inquiry analysis checklist
- The proposal preparation checklist
- In-house evaluation of final proposal
- Customer evaluation of proposal.

We have included sample checklists for these four key areas in Appendices A through D. While these checklists have been prepared for use in bidding to the federal government, which would probably be the most complex or tedious situation, they can easily be applied by a contractor in bidding non-government work.

While it may be true that many parts of an inquiry, especially for repeat clients, are the same, each request for proposals should be carefully reviewed on an individual basis. It is very important that the contractor review the request thoroughly. Appendix A contains a checklist that may be used to review a proposal request to insure that the major contract areas are covered both in the initial review and subsequent negotiation and drafting of the contract. It is also used to insure that the proposal contains all the information that is required to prepare a completely responsive proposal. To be most effective, the request for proposals should become the most read document by the whole proposal team.

Another area in which a checklist can aid in increasing the chances of a successful proposal is in proposal preparation. This checklist gives the proposal team a step-by-step guide for review and verification of the proposal development, including the preparation of drafts and redrafts. Appendix B contains a proposal preparation checklist that covers all aspects of the preparation process.

In many cases, the various company elements concerned with proposal preparation operate independently or with limited coordination. Because of this, it is extremely important that sufficient time be allowed for a thorough internal analysis and review of the proposal to insure that a completely responsive proposal is prepared. All proposals should be carefully reviewed prior to being forwarded to the client. The proposal plan should always allow time for analysis and review. The review should not be made by the persons responsible for the development of the proposal because they tend to read into the proposal what they intended to say rather than what it actually says. The checklist contained in Appendix C can be used to evaluate a proposal prior to forwarding it to a customer. It can also be used to analyze the reasons behind the lack of success of a particular proposal effort.

Almost as important as the review of the proposal before it is sent to the customer is the review of the reasons for the company's success or failure after the contract has been awarded to either the company or to a competitor. In the first case, it is important to know what you did well in order that you can do it that way again. In the event of failure, it is important to know what you did wrong so that the same mistakes can be avoided in the future. In today's highly competitive market, it is important that the company submit proposals completely responsive to the customer's wishes. So even where the proposal is successful, the customer should be asked for an evaluation of why it was successful. Such an analysis can be used to determine the customer's attitude toward the firm in order that strengths can be exploited and weaknesses corrected. Appendix D contains a checklist or guide used by clients to review proposals. This checklist can also be used by contractors to prepare proposals that are responsive from the client's point of view.

In general, whether a large or small effort is required, each proposal should be prepared using some sort of checklist. A simplified checklist that can be kept in mind when preparing all proposals to insure better end results is the following:

- Prepare and implement a proposal plan
- With sales, arrive at a winning market strategy
- Prepare and follow a schedule and budget
- Develop direct contact with client
- Review technical approach with client
- Review management approach with client
- Recruit and organize proposal team
- Brief proposal team members
- Identify and work out problems critical to the proposal
- Determine alternate approaches
- Check facility and equipment requirements
- Check manpower requirements
- Record all decisions.

Appendices

Appendix A

Analysis of the Procurement Request[1]

CHECKLIST
I. Identify the requirement: if you have not made a similar item before, endeavor to see the item before you prepare your quotation. Know what you are going to sell. Review specifications to see that:
  1. They are clear, complete and explicit.
  2. No conflicting statements have been made.
  3. No uncertain requirements are included which might possibly result in future problems or exceptions.
  4. The specifications used are up to date.
  5. Determine if quantities or delivery data will adversely effect price.
II. Examine the effect of the contract on your operations. Project this effect over the life of the contract.
  1. Is plant capacity available?
  2. Alternative uses for capacity.
  3. Determine need for facilities, special tooling and financial assistance.
  4. Equipment available.
  5. Is any special machinery required?
  6. Employees experienced in the type of work required.
  7. Are tolerances within the capability of the available equipment and employees?
  8. Are the engineering and design within the capabilities of present technical personnel?

---

[1] Paul R. McDonald, *Proposal Preparation Manual,* Section II, Chapter 2, "Analysis of the Procurement Request." This section has been reproduced by permission of Paul R. McDonald, Procurement Associates, Inc., 733 N. Dodsworth Avenue, Covina, California 91724.

9. Will any special or critical material be needed? If so, does the IFB or Request For Proposal provide for priority assistance in securing it?
10. Examine the extent and nature of the subcontracting involved. Check the availability of capacity for specialized requirements.
11. Is the firm's quality control inspection system adequate to meet Government requirements or will costly changes be necessary?
12. If the price quotation is to be on a cost type or redeterminable basis, does the firm's cost accounting system meet Government requirements for this type of contracting?
13. Is the firm's purchasing system adequate?
14. Is cash available to finance the contract?
15. Effect of Renegotiation and Vinson-Trammell Acts on profits.

III. Review the Procurement Request.
1. F.O.B. Terms—Multiple destinations.
2. Delivery schedules—required or target.
3. Time discounts.
4. Packaging and marking requirements.
5. Inspection and acceptance points.
6. Priorities and allocations.
7. Time for submission of proposals.
8. The Government's right to reject bids (advertised).
9. The method of price quotation desired (Fixed Price or Cost Type).
10. Whether alternative methods of price quotation will be considered.
11. The extent of the cost information desired.
12. What performance provisions will be included?
13. Inspection requirements.
14. Insurance requirements.
15. Patents and copyrights; the possible effect of patents and copyright articles. What proprietary data must be supplied with proposal or after award of contract?
16. Royalty requirements.
17. Whether the Davis-Bacon Act or Service Contract Act is applicable; if so what the applicable wage rates are; whether Walsh-Healey Public Contracts Act is applicable.
18. Whether Government-owned property will be available. If so, where it may be inspected. Availability of facilities, special tooling, and Government-furnished material.
19. Will facilities be furnished under a separate facilities contract (over $50,000) or under the terms of the applicable Property Clause?
20. Determine necessity for special break outs of facility and special tooling costs.
21. Bond requirements.
22. Effect of taxes, local, State and Federal, on price.
23. Type of financing contemplated.
24. Availability of Government financing assistance.
25. Security requirements.
26. Effect of special clauses.

IV. Discuss the request for proposal with Government personnel, if possible:
1. Clarify any omissions or discrepancies.
2. Obtain background information.
3. Learn about similar previous or current procurements. In particular, check on past or current prices of same or similar items.
4. Check on availability of manufacturing process studies or possible assistance from other Government Contractors making the same or similar items.
5. Review the results of any research and development contracts.
6. Determine the basis of the evaluation of bids or proposals.

V. Prepare proposal.
   Circulate proposal to all departments concerned. Develop proposal team, engineering, manufacturing, inspection, accounting and legal personnel.

VI. Check Proposal.
1. All questions are answered.
2. Cost data is as requested.
3. Delivery dates meet the requirements.
4. Unit of measure does not differ from that specified in the request.
5. Proposal reflects all changes in the original request.
6. Additions, extensions, etc., are correct.
7. Acceptance time is specified.

VII. Forward Proposal.
   Make sure proposal is complete and forwarded in proper format.

VIII. Prepare for Negotiations.
1. Determine bargaining limits.
2. Determine relative bargaining position of both parties.
3. Determine firm's position on all important issues.
4. Develop alternative proposals for all questionable areas.
5. Determine price and delivery schedule.

IX. Negotiate Price and Terms.
1. Financing (if required).
   a. Discuss need and best method to obtain adequate financing; guaranteed loan, progress payments or advance payments.
2. Patents and Royalties.
   a. Determine acceptability of royalty charges.
   b. Arrange for reporting royalties, if required.
   c. Determine if any infringement is required.
   d. Decide if inclusion of Patent Indemnity clause is necessary.
   e. Discuss patent rights. Distinguish carefully between the Department of Defense and industry's definition of foreground patents.
   f. Carefully explore effect of any patent clause included in the contract and need for any special coverage.
3. Copyrights.
   a. Discuss interest in copyright material and decide if firm is to retain interest in any copyrights developed under the contract.
4. Labor.
   a. Determine need and allowability of overtime required to meet contract schedule.

      b. Discuss Non-Discrimination Clause.

      c. Determine any applicable wage determinations under the Walsh-Healey Act.

      d. Check wage rates under Davis-Bacon Act when applicable.

      e. Check wage rates under Service Contract Act, when applicable.

5. Restrictions.

      a. Determine the application of Renegotiation and Vinson-Trammel Acts. Determine if exemption is possible.

      b. Check requirements of Act in respect to record keeping.

6. Facilities.

      a. If Government facilities are involved, make provision for the fact that the Government generally accepts no obligation to restore or pay for the costs of restoring any premises affected by installation or removal of facilities.

      b. Discuss retention of facilities. Government generally has the right to remove any items of the facilities at any time.

      c. Determine possibility and possible effect on costs of abandonment.

      d. Stand-by provisions.

      e. Contractor receives no profit on purchased facilities, direct costs will be reimbursed only up to ceiling, when ceiling is established.

      f. Requirements of Davis-Bacon Act when it applies.

      g. Determine precisely the degree of maintenance required.

      h. Check property record requirements.

      i. Determine policy on use of facilities for other Department of Defense work or commercial work.

      j. Determine rental requirements.

      k. Inspect any government facilities or equipment to determine condition and conformance to requirement.

7. Special Tooling.

      a. Discuss type and cost of special tooling.

      b. Determine the method of providing for tooling under a fixed price contract and whether Government will take title.

      c. Inspect any Government tooling offered.

8. Government-furnished material.

      a. Make sure material in Government inventory has been inspected.

      b. Determine effect of insurance requirements.

      c. Determine effect of furnished Government property on price.

      d. Decide on method of provision.

9. Taxes.

      a. Ensure a clear understanding as to exclusion or inclusion in price.

      b. Excise taxes.

      c. State and Local Taxes.

10. Insurance.

      a. Determine whether there are any special problems in regard to allocation of risk, adequacy of coverage, reasonableness of cost, etc.

11. Pricing Terms.

Determine the proper pricing terms; if redetermination is involved, establish target and ceiling; if escalation, determine amount and coverage; if incentive provision, establish target, ceiling and profit formulas; if cost, provide contractually for any special cost problems.

X. Review contract before signature to insure that it clearly covers the agreements reached. Any questionable areas should be clarified in transmittal letter.
   1. If changes in the contract are agreed to, have contract rewritten or amended and treat in the same manner as when the contract was first written.

XI. When confirmed copy of the contract is received, notify all interested personnel.

XII. Maintain the following records for each procurement:
   1. A complete history of the case from receipt of the procurement request until the contract is finally closed out completely.
   2. Memoranda on each important telephone call and conference. Each memorandum should indicate date, persons involved, who they represent, matters discussed, agreements reached, information given, and other pertinent information.
   3. Copies of each letter or memo written in connection with the procurement.
   4. Set up proper filing system.

Appendix B

Proposal Preparation Checklist[1]

I. Know The Customer
   A. In attempting to fully understand and appreciate the desires of the customer, the proposing firm should determine the following:
      1. During the preparation of a qualitative operational requirement, what does the using command think it will need in the future (even though this desire may never see the light of a proposal)?

      This is important from two standpoints—it affords an opportunity to influence the customer to include information on equipments or techniques that can be supplied and it provides an opportunity to guide company internal research and development programs. In addition, since the using command probably will be represented on the Source Evaluation Group, this will provide information on the operational orientation of the user.

      2. At the level of operational requirements director, what important military systems are likely to be favored and what factors are considered most important?
      3. At the System/Program Office Level, what operational and technical features are likely to be favored?
      4. At the level of research and engineering director, what engineering and technical approaches and features are favored? Also, what is the company's image as a contractor and what, if necessary, can be done to improve that image?

---

[1] Paul R. McDonald, *Proposal Preparation Manual,* Section II, Chapter 8; reproduced by permission of Paul R. McDonald, Procurement Associates, Inc., 733 N. Dodsworth Avenue, Covina, California 91724.

5. At the Comptroller level, what money has been, or is likely to be, approved on a major program?
6. At what level has the Source Selection Authority been designated?
7. At the Joint Chiefs of Staff level, what elements in the various program areas are receiving most attention and support from an operational viewpoint?
8. At the Secretarial level (Service and DOD), what political factors may influence the Source Selection Authority?
9. At Congressional and Department of Commerce level, what political and economic factors may influence the placing of large defense contracts?
10. Will the President's Scientific Advisor of the President's Scientific Advisory Committee be brought into the decision-making process on a particular program?

II. Analysis Of The Request For Proposal (RFP)
  A. Upon receipt of the RFP, a complete analysis such as the following should be made:
    1. Define program and pertinent instructions.
    2. Specify the basic elements of the proposal.
    3. Detail the manner in which the program should be broken down.
  B. Clearly and unambiguously spell out all unusual directions necessary for proposal preparation:
    1. Are existing tools and facilities to be used?
    2. Are special tooling or facilities required?
    3. Will manufacturing use the company's engineering development capability?
    4. Will sketches be used?
    5. What Government Furnished Equipment (GFE) will be used?
    6. What are the documentation requirements?
    7. What are the reliability requirements?
    8. What are delivery requirements?
    9. Are there any special test or unusual acceptance requirements?
  C. The proposal management team members responsible for these areas should query themselves on the following factors:
    1. What does the contract require for reliability and maintainability? Can we meet these requirements? Can we exceed them, and if so, to what degree?
    2. Are there any unusual specifications for inspection requirements?
    3. Are the means for securing approvals clearly defined?
    4. Are the requirements of text and demonstration clearly stated?
    5. What kind of reliability, testing inspection, and acceptance requirements will be placed on vendors and subcontractors?
    6. Are the bases for acceptance of all contract items clearly stated? When final acceptance occurs subsequent to delivery or installation, does the company have a provisional acceptance that protects the company against damage due to acts of God, customer negligence, and so forth?

      7. Compatibility of subcontractor type of pricing with the company's expected contract type with the customer?

      8. Are warranties compatible with program requirements?

      9. Special conditions such as options?

    10. Compatibility of subcontract terms and conditions with expected customer's contract and its provisions?

III. Program Schedule

  A. All proposal management team members should study applicable procurement documents to determine any unknowns or special problems that may affect their inputs. The team should determine jointly where it is being fully responsive to the RFP, and if it meets the minimum specification requirements. If not, the team should jointly establish a sound basis for making exceptions and requesting waivers.

  B. The team should list all deliverable contract items and plot the schedule milestones for each item. The following deliverable items should be considered when compiling this schedule:

      1. Monthly or quarterly progress reports, other presentations, films, and so forth.

      2. Engineering study reports.

      3. Movies, models, required lecture aids.

      4. Required mockups.

      5. Applicable specifications for breadboards.

      6. Prototype or engineering models.

      7. Applicable specifications for finished equipment.

      8. Applicable specifications for drawings, including vendor documentation.

      9. Applicable specifications for instruction books, maintenance and operation manuals.

    10. Installation requirements.

    11. Services—Engineering, integrated logistic support, and so forth.

    12. Modified GFE to be delivered.

    13. Training programs.

    14. Test tools and test equipment—stated or implied.

    15. Spare parts and assemblies.

    16. Test reports and qualification test data.

    17. Type and amount of effort associated with each deliverable contract item.

    18. Itemization of all travel required.

    19. Specific packing and shipping requirements.

  C. It is highly desirable that a well-structured milestone type of schedule be established. It should consider the following:

      1. Does the contract require any approvals, formal or otherwise, prior to proceeding to the next step such as preliminary design approval, final design approval, or environmental test approval? Will these cause gaps in the schedule?

2. Do test specifications have to be submitted for formal approval before testing can be started? Is a special format required?
3. Do parts or equipment designations have to be obtained?
4. Is the basis for acceptance clear?
5. Will additional shifts or premium overtime be required for any part of the program? For example, will environmental testing have to be run around the clock? Do facilities limitations and schedule requirements demand multiple shifts? Is final assembly space available for this program and has it been scheduled and phased in properly?
6. What is the schedule for receipt of GFE?
7. Have vendor deliveries been scheduled to assure availability and, simultaneously, minimize inventory, storage, and maintenance costs? Have long-lead items been phased in promptly enough?
8. What size organization will be required to handle the proposed program?
9. What are the skills and man-loading required by each company element for such tasks?
10. If we do not have all the specialized skills or capabilities needed, how will we obtain them? (Personnel recruiting, subcontracting, consultants, or team of associate companies)?
11. Will the Government have to supply any personnel or services other than those normally involved in technical and legal contract administration?
12. Have we presented a clear explanation of organization functions and procedures in the proposal presentation?

IV. Facilities
   A. A list of all facilities required to accomplish the proposed program should be compiled by the proposal management team. These should be scheduled and phased-in with other contractual commitments. The following questions should be answered:
   1. Are these facilities now company-owned capital equipment or must they be procured?
   2. Will any part of the operation require the use of Government sites, aircraft, test ranges, or whatever?
   3. Are these facilities from 2. above Government-owned? Will their use be allowed on this program? Will additional Government facilities be required? Can these be made available? Rent-free use?
   4. Will any part of the operation require the use of specialized engineering or manufacturing test equipment including capitalized items?
   5. Are company laboratory calibration facilities adequate? If not, what capabilities must be met? Can adequate calibration be accomplished elsewhere; if so, at what cost in money and time?
   6. Do we have adequate engineering and factory space for this program? If not, how much additional space is required? Does it have to be specially air conditioned, dust-free, RF noise free, clean rooms, con-

trolled atmospheric conditions, gas purging system and facilities for explosives?

7. Do any materials require special handling or storage? Security requirements?

8. Do we have to subcontract to someone who has specialized facilities?

9. Does the program require computer time? Can this be phased in properly?

V. Management Section

  A. The following checklist should be used to assure full, complete and objective management proposals. These include the following major sections of the management proposal:

    1. Personnel Survey.

    2. Program/Project Management Organization.

    3. Management Procedures.

    4. Facilities.

    5. Schedule and Program Plan.

    6. Related Experience.

    7. General Business Situation.

  B. Personnel Survey

  Have you:

    1. Shown the applicable experience of the key individual assignees as related to this task?

    2. Shown that the past performance of your assignees indicates a capability to cope with unexpected problems?

    3. Balanced your team between practical experience and theoretical capability?

    4. Indicated the availability of required specialists/consultants?

    5. Left any holes in your aggregate team experience, with reference to the types of technical/manufacturing/subcontractor management which is key or peculiar to this program?

    6. Shown management resources of sufficient quality, stature, and availability? Do not promise to utilize personnel the customer knows very well will not be made available.

    7. Wrongly assumed customer prior knowledge of our capability?

    8. Shown a program manager who can devote full time to the project?

    9. Carefully avoided making biographies sound like boilerplate material?

    10. Shown how any new personnel required will be secured? Do not rely on rapid hiring programs—the customer has bogeys for how fast he believes you can hire. Shown realistic plans for intracompany transfers? The customer knows that there are practical limits.

    11. Included key subcontractor personnel in biographies/organization chart?

VI. Program/Project Management Organization

  A. Have you:

    1. Shown your willingness to commit resources?

2. Shown top management interest in and support for this program?
3. Improperly assumed customer prior knowledge of the company and thus failed to display all our resources?
4. Aligned our organization with that of the customer to specifically show the points of interface?
5. Shown enough objectivity/organizational independence of value engineering, quality control and reliability functions?
6. Shown the interrelationships of the contributing functions to the overall program control?
7. Shown a management organization that covers the full spectrum of the program requirements? Shown requirements to fill each organizational block and what percent of time each individual will be employed on the program?
8. Shown a Program Manager reporting at a high-enough level to have authority to get the job done and to have top management attention and help if needed to resolve problems? Show this clearly and honestly—don't try to hoodwink the customer. Remember to consider future growth of the program in setting the Program Manager's reporting level.
9. Shown other companies which are potential or recommended subcontractors? Shown how their program management interfaces with our program management? Shown the specific subcontractor controls within our organization (i.e., who controls funding to the subcontractor? Who controls technical specifications?) Have we played up our major subcontractor's strengths as well as our own?
10. Shown only the program organization assignment of people?
11. Specifically defined the Program Manager's duties, authorities (including limitations), lines of responsibility and review from top management?
12. Shown an organization vertical enough to satisfy the customer? Shown the required degree of one man control?
13. If the proposed team (including subcontractors) is one that has been in place working as a team for a considerable time, have we played up their experience in working together and their availability for immediate application?

VII. Management Procedures
  A. Have you:
    1. Stated where and when you will review decisions with the customer?
    2. Incorrectly assumed customer prior knowledge of our procedures and their value?
    3. Clearly identified which company/industry-wide procedures will specifically be used in each phase of the program and for what purposes?
    4. Taken the boilerplate flavor out of writeups of management techniques to be employed?
    5. Shown a management approach to value engineering which is suffi-

ciently detailed to assure proper and thorough consideration throughout all phases of the program?
6. Erroneously included management control procedures which will not
be used on this program?
7. Included important policies/instructions of primary interest?
8. Demonstrated past use of management procedures intended for use
on this program?
9. Clearly indicated internal reporting and communication methods to
be used?
10. Shown an objective attitude toward make or buy by providing a detailed account of the procedures and analysis made prior to decision?
11. Given direct reference to the use of specific management tools for the
solution of anticipated or known problem areas?
12. Shown special management attention for those program variables tied
to incentives? Defined and recommended incentive provisions which
are not so complex as to put the customer in the position of being
unable to settle a contract within a reasonable period of time?
13. Specifically shown our provisions for configuration control per the
applicable customer document?
14. Specifically discussed provisions for handling program changes?
15. Shown our understanding of applicable customer approval procedures?
16. Discussed relationships of our customer to our subcontractors?
17. Shown provision for in-plant liaisons?
18. Shown procedures for obtaining information from industry as
required? Shown methodology for objective review of this data? Set
up a credible and objective system for obtaining and handling data
from potential subcontractors who might normally be regarded as
competitors?
19. Shown procedures for obtaining materials and assuring their quality?

VIII. Facilities
   A. Have you:
      1. Shown that all computation, test, measuring, recording, reproduction,
and other equipment necessary for completion of engineering tasks is
adequate and available?
      2. Shown access to all necessary special equipment not normally
available?
      3. Shown the production capability and capacity to implement a full-scale
production program for the system/equipment involved in this
proposal?
      4. Improperly assumed customer prior knowledge of the adequacy/ad-
vantages of our facilities?
      5. Specifically indicated any requirements for additional GFE facilities,
tooling, or equipment to perform the job? Included plans to retain
GFE currently on site for other programs?

      6. Taken the boilerplate flavor out of the writeups by detailing the key program-related facilities and separately listed the routine floor area type of statistics.

      7. Shown a factory floor plan indicating the location of key manufacturing functions for the subject program? Shown the number of square feet required for production and storage? Shown the geographical location of facility proposed for this program?

      8. Shown the relation of other programs/contracts which affect the facilities required for this program? In particular, have we resolved any real or imagined facility conflicts which may concern our customer?

IX. Schedule And Program Plan

  A. Have you:

      1. Supported the schedule by analyses and comparisons with previous known major program schedules (both in-house and other programs)?

      2. Avoided changing the customer's schedule (if you are concerned about meeting it) but shown the risks and cost penalties involved in adhering to his schedule? Have you offered possible alternatives and tradeoffs? A cost/time tradeoff is a very effective way to analyze and present this consideration.

      3. Shown a development plan for the engineering effort to be conducted to insure that the system/equipment produced will meet customer functional and reliability requirements? Have you shown the methodology for getting the job done (simulations, computations, or tests)? Does your development plan include the data, field support equipment development, test methods, maintainability and reliability analyses as well as hardware?

      4. Shown an estimated number of man years for each major task that will clearly accomplish the job? Shown the distinction between management/professional/specialists categories?

      5. Shown check and control points to assure the adequate, accurate and timely data submittals as required by the program?

      6. Incorporated time for customer approval cycles?

      7. Incorporated schedule time and events for customer furnished information?

      8. Specifically accounted for all items and services to be supplied to the customer?

X. Related Experience

  A. Are there sections on:

      1. Past engineering and manufacturing accomplishments similar to those required by the proposed program? Does this section show that we are a leader in the field and completely abreast of the state of the art? If we are not a leader, have we discussed or concluded a team relationship or located a vendor in order to increase our capability? Have we highlighted the past accomplishments for this customer? Have we shown that the accomplishments were of equal or greater complexity? Have

we included past experience of our major subcontractors/ vendors? Have we included exploratory or advanced programs already accomplished and indicated their impact on the proposed program relative to risk and alternatives? Have we shown our experience in delivering data, training, test equipment, field service, as well as equipment? Have we shown our experience with technical direction agencies if applicable? Have we shown our experience with incentive contracts?

2. Past schedule performance and our proposed schedule control?
3. Our demonstrated capability to effectively control the efforts of major subcontractors by direction, coordination, and integration?
4. Past cost performance and our proposed cost control methods?

B. General Business Situation
Have you included your:
1. Surplus labor area designation?
2. Small business, and minority support record and proposed use of small businesses?
3. Capital situation (where applicable)?

XI. Kickoff Meeting
A. The Proposal Director should prepare for kickoff meetings by checking the following:
1. Representatives from the following areas:
   a. Proposal Support
   b. Contract Administration
   c. Finance/Cost Estimating
   d. Manufacturing
      Preplanning
      Assembly Planning
      Metal Parts Manufacturing Planning
      Production Control
      Integrated Electronics Manufacturing
      Quality Control Test Equipment Engineering
      Materials
      Quality Control Engineering
      Quality Assurance
   e. Engineering
      Engineering Development Shop
      Systems Engineering
      Environmental Engineering
      Reliability Engineering
      Spare Parts Engineering
      Instruction Books
      Logistics
      Technical Publications
      Product Service
      Specialty Design Engineering
      Engineering Design and Drafting Standards

2. Proposal Summary:
   a. Identify proposal by number
   b. Identify potential customer
   c. Proposal items—quantities and delivery dates
   d. Functional description of items involved
   e. Abridged version of technical requirements
   f. Highlights and peculiarities of the RFP
3. Historical Review:
   a. History of the project in the customer's organizations.
   b. History of the project, or of allied programs, in the company.
4. Competition:
   a. Major competitors
   b. Competitor's strengths—particularly as related to proposed program.
   c. Company versus competitors' capabilities.
   d. Anticipated features of competitors' proposals.
5. Sales Potential:
   a. Sales and growth potential underlying this particular program.
   b. Sales potential in allied or complementary fields.
   c. Additional benefits that may be accrued from winning this competition (i.e., incremental and business considerations).
6. Political Climate:
   a. Does the political climate put any competitor in a preferred position?
   b. Is there a specific political reason why our company would not be considered acceptable?
   c. How can we improve our political position in relation to this program?
   d. Should we propose alone, or is it politically expedient to submit a team or associate proposal?
7. Pricing:
   a. Contract price envisaged by the customer.
   b. Contract price envisaged by the Proposal Director.
   c. Historical pricing information.
   d. Pricing philosophy: shall major emphasis be placed on price? To what level of detail shall pricing be accomplished? Should pricing considerations be tied in with some kind of milestone planning?
8. Engineering:
   a. Consideration of alternative proposals.
   b. Evaluation of trade offs.
   c. Specific steps to be taken, such as hiring consultants or joining forces with an associate company to solve these problems.
9. Manufacturing:
   a. Specific steps to be taken, such as fabricating sample or prototype units and other measures phased-in to solve difficult problems.
   b. Make-or-buy decisions should be coordinated with purchasing.

      c. Based on the type of program involved and the sales potential, determine where the manufacturing will be accomplished—model shop, quick reaction shop, regular manufacturing facilities, or some combination of these facilities.

10. Procurement:
    a. Subcontract complete packages?
    b. Can GFE be used? Do these require modification? What are the overall GFE requirements?

11. Sales:
    a. Sales effort required for presentation.
    b. Sales contacts to be made during the proposal preparation period.
    c. Sales inputs required during proposal preparation.
    d. Sales effort required during interim between proposal submission and contract award.
    e. Management contacts and participation required during preproposal and postproposal periods.

12. Contract Requirements:
    a. Specific contract or technical requirements, including specifications that should be examined for exceptions and waivers.
    b. Type of contract anticipated—fixed-price of cost-reimbursement category.
    c. Contract incentive provisions (if any).

13. Proposal Strategy And Decisions:
    a. Review of the reasons underlying the proposal decision.
    b. Factors to be emphasized (i.e., price, delivery, performance, experience, facilities, or whatever).
    c. Teaming up with key subcontractors or associate companies.
    d. Specific assignments proposed and the reasons underlying them.

14. Customer:
    a. Stress the cooperative attitude toward working with and for the customer.
    b. Prime considerations for proposal evaluation.
    c. Cost effectiveness philosophy.
    d. Availability and magnitude of funds.
    e. Our rating in relation to competition.
    f. Probability of eventual procurement.

XII. Proposal Hints
  A. The following hints may assist in developing a complete, responsive technical proposal:
    1. Don't half bid.
    2. Don't be stereotyped. Think! It may not be desirable to do it as we always have in the past.
    3. Know the customer—his habits, prejudices, and interpolitics.
    4. Don't mix winning a proposal competition with negotiation.
    5. A last-minute estimate of cost, where cost is a decisive factor, does not make for a winning proposal.
    6. Be frank—technically and otherwise.

7. Don't deviate from the main strategy for minor or irrelevant reasons.
8. Avoid a false technical opinion of self-capability. Prove technical capability by illustrating accomplishments in related fields.
9. All functions of the company may not be required. Weed out the unnecessary ones early in the game.
10. Complicated organizational structures presented in a proposal are not readily understood nor desired by the average customer. Customize the program organization plan so that it's tailored to the job and to the customer.
11. Give objective thought to the use of subcontractors.
12. Consider the value of submitting as a subcontractor or associate.
13 An inventive or novel approach doesn't necessarily make a good or winning proposal. The customer may actually want the tried and proved.
14. Evaluate several proposal approaches rather than choosing the first one considered. Consider alternatives.
15. Make sure you know the role of any Government laboratories in subsequent proposal evaluation.
16. Customer contact, especially in the technical area, is most beneficial before the Government initiates proposal action. But customer contact, especially in the technical areas, is least beneficial after the Government initiates proposal action.
17. Sell your capabilities to the customer before starting the proposal. A written proposal is a poor place to introduce and sell unknown capabilities to a customer. In such a case, it is better to use an associate already known to the customer.
18. Don't operate in a vacuum with respect to the customer or to the competition.
19. Proficiency in research-type efforts does not necessarily prepare an organization for accomplishing a development-type program.
20. Familiarity with a subject through analytical techniques is a poor substitute for experimental efforts.
21. Show willingness to consider other contractors and recognize the fact that no one contractor has the best of everything.
22. Do not touch on possible tradeoffs and fail to pursue them to show why you did or did not consider them.
23. Recognize where flexibility is required to reduce design freeze risk to a minimum.
24. Be sure that scope of test plan is complete in recognizing the role and participation of the many agencies involved.
25. Avoid use of percentages that actually are educated guesses in presenting any cost information to the customer.
26. Follow RFP format and instructions to the letter. Give the customer the information he is looking for.
27. Keep to the facts and minimize the flag waving.
28. Find unique examples to portray the company's technical know-how and resource capability.

29. Recognition for past accomplishments from high level sources may be used, but only with caution to avoid the accusation of "name dropping."
30. Do not develop charts or graphs that are so large and complex that they will be difficult to read after reduction in the proposal document.
31. Review program plan for any extras not necessarily required to meet the RFP or the design and mission requirements prior to final pricing.
32. Avoid presentation of uncertain or unsubstantiated financial data that will generate more requests for financial data.
33. The content of the proposal is more important than the form of presentation.
34. Do not hinder technical understanding and/or technical clarity by using excessive technical elegance and/or meticulous technical detail.

B. Most of the check-items listed are incorporated automatically into a proposal by fulfilling the dictates implicit in the following questions:
1. Have we followed what we genuinely believe is the customer's wish, or have we tried to sell him on our "pet" approach?
2. Have we eliminated all the excess in the proposal—not just in dollars but in design, methods, and so forth? Remember, the more we propose to do, the more it will cost.
3. Have we sufficiently coordinated the proposed design with all company functions concerned to establish that our plan is the best that we can possibly submit within the permitted time?
4. Is it precisely clear what we are proposing to do? Have we stated it concretely and unequivocally?
5. Have we offered realistic alternatives (if still responsive) rather than trying to convince the customer that he doesn't know what he is talking about or what he wants and that he should listen to our ideas instead?
6. Have we taken fullest advantage of our good points in what we have said in the proposal, or have we taken for granted that the customer already appreciates the company's capabilities?
7. Have we told the customer clearly just what we intend to do for him—made it crystal clear precisely what he can expect to get for his money?
8. Have we recognized the problem areas and offered realistic alternative approaches to overcome them?

XIII. Proposal Content
A. Following is a checklist to further assist in the actual preparation of the proposal:
1. Cite exploratory and advanced programs already accomplished and their impact relative to risk, alternatives, and schedule performance.
2. Avoid changing customer schedule (assuming it can't be met) but show risks involved in adhering to his schedule. Offer possible alternatives and tradeoffs.
3. Show history of analogous type programs to support the position that proposed schedules and decision points are realistic.
4. Show technical risk versus schedule risk.

5. Be truthful about risks (especially those already known to the customer).

6. Solutions to problems should, wherever possible, relate to previous successful applications.

7. Show highest level of company management participation in the program to convince the customer that this program is receiving necessary attention. It is not enough to have just an expression of initial interest. Show how this interest will permeate the organization and be followed throughout the life of the program.

8. Tailor the management approach to the specific program and its problem areas.

9. Identify the management process by which total company resources will be used to maximize the benefits of all talents.

10. Show company organization in such a way as to provide sufficient understanding of the company.

11. Show responsibilities of key personnel in the program/project organization—that they have key tasks and functions in an organization with a solid foundation.

12. Biographies should show accomplishments of the individual, not just the jobs that he has held. Relate these accomplishments and experience to the proposed program.

13. Show the valuable contributions that the individuals you have selected can make to this program.

14. Indicate communication channels and interrelationship that will be exercised between co-contractors, subcontractors and vendors to assure complete integration and cooperation.

15. Show principal management controls that the Program/Project Manager will have to do his job effectively.

16. Demonstrate responsiveness to program changes, the ability of the Program/Project Manager to control funds, and the impact on the program of both.

17. Show a working organization with key people in place.

18. Show manpower projections, program loading and resources capabilities in words and charts.

19. Show specific technical subsystem uncertainties along with plans for solution.

20. Identify total systems management capability.

21. Show specific cost objectives for the efforts of cost improvement and value analyses.

22. Avoid boilerplating generalities and stress what is unique and different. Customer highlighted subjects such as Reliability, Value Engineering, and Integrated Logistic Support require particular attention.

23. Stress techniques to be used to assure that all objectives will be accomplished during the test program.

24. Give coverage in detail and scope for all support requirements. Understanding of the total system and its needs will be assessed by the customer.

25. Stress full capability of field programs. Installation and checkout plans may be of high importance to the customer. Thoroughness, scope, and level of detail will reveal depth of understanding, past experience and effort devoted to this critical phase.
26. Provide curves in support of manpower requirements to demonstrate realism in costs.
27. Show available facilities in detail (photographs, schematics, or whatever).
28. Stress willingness to use company-owned facilities with minimum of Government requirements.
29. Avoid guilt complex and negative attitude. Do not bring up problems, such as limited funds.

XIV. Costing Information Requirements
    A. The following checklist is a guide for the Proposal/Project Manager to ensure that necessary information is desseminated to those responsible for cost estimating.
    B. Customer Requirement Summary
       1. Type of system or equipment.
       2. Type of anticipated contract—fixed-price or cost-reimbursement category.
       3. Anticipated date of award.
       4. Previous requisitions.
       5. Proposed Item.
          a. Segregated by work scope.
          b. Description of item and specifications.
          c. Quantity.
          d. Unit having task responsibility.
       6. Applicable military and/or customer specifications.
       7. Responsibility for design specification.
       8. Proposed delivery schedule for all proposed items.
       9. CFE or GFE material.
      10. Technical exceptions.
      11. Special estimating instructions.
      12. Other instructions (i.e., subcontract items).
    C. Design Specification Summary
       1. Release schedule.
       2. Equipment content, weight and power.
       3. Packaging techniques.
       4. Electrical and mechanical description.
       5. Parts list.
       6. Items subcontracted.
       7. Special testing on components and subcontracted items.

XV. Material for Final Management Briefing
    A. In preparation for the final management briefing, the proposal management team should provide the following:
       1. Completed technical proposal.
       2. Summary of salient technical features.
       3. Completed cost estimates.

4. Recommended total selling price.
5. List of assumptions.
6. Itemization of risks.
7. Incremental pricing effect.
8. Summary of selected strategy
   Customer
   Competitor
   Internal
9. Tradeoffs or cost effectiveness calculations.
10. Alternative proposals considered.
11. Investment (i.e., dollars, people and facilities).
12. Recommended negotiation tradeoffs.
13. Eventuality plans.
14. Recommended continuing effort.

XVI. Technical Proposal Evaluation
    A. The following checklist might be used to evaluate the completeness, accuracy and clarity of presentation of the technical proposal:
        1. In the summary, have you:
           a. Demonstrated familiarity with the customer's problem?
           b. Presented the crux of the solution in simple direct language?
           c. Indicated unique competence to do the job?
           d. Highlighted your program or hardware and company experience to be applied?
           e. Given the development/producibility status of each major component?
           f. Given a physical description of the system or equipment including a photograph or sketch of all major components? Given a summary table of equipment size, weight, power, reliability, life, mean-time-to-repair, or whatever the need requires?
           g. Specified any major deviations you feel you must take to the specification?
           h. Enumerated any new or important features?
           i. Demonstrated conclusively why the customer should buy from us?
           j. Identified any alternatives to be offered, briefly told why, and indicated where they are covered?
        2. Have you analyzed and documented in the proposal the technical risk versus the schedule risk and financial risk for each alternative solution proposed?
        3. Have you shown the key technical decision tree for the program and substantiated this in detailed sections? Have you indicated preferred results?
        4. For each alternative considered (and in the summary or a separate section), have you clearly listed the key technical advantages of the approach compared to others considered?
        5. Have you highlighted your responsiveness to the RFP?
        6. Have you demonstrated objectivity in key decisions?
        7. In what way are tradeoffs utilized and made clear to top level evaluators?

8. Are you sure we have not misread or misinterpreted the customer's statement of desired work? Have we clearly stated all assumptions and interpretations?

9. Does the program we propose solve the problem the customer stated or does it emphasize another problem and another solution?

10. Have we proposed a "pet" idea rather than investigating all possible solutions and picking the best one?

11. Do we have open for investigation several approaches rather than picking one? Is this really necessary?

12. Do we merely state we "will comply" with customer requirements or do we also show how?

13. Will the variations, exceptions and deviations to the customer's desired statement of work benefit the Government or will they prejudice the adequate performance of the program?

14. Have we shown originality in concept in the proposal? Have we made recommendations for program improvement?

15. Have we shown specific theoretical models to be employed in technical tradeoffs? Have we given their current status and summarized how they will be applied?

16. Have we recognized and addressed the military/aerospace problem involved? Have we shown the integration with other systems?

17. Have we recognized, considered and identified the limitations of the state of the art?

18. Have we demonstrated our consideration of the economics involved?

19. Have we demonstrated our understanding of the logical integration of human factors? Have we stated the personnel profiles being considered?

20. Have we correctly identified all required laboratory apparatus, test equipment, and measuring or recording equipment required and available? Have we shown that they are sufficiently accurate?

21. Have we demonstrated our ability to conduct the requisite operational analyses?

22. Did we describe the process of solving the technical problems including the alternative approaches rejected and why they were rejected?

23. Have we shown adequate and convincing background for our recommended solution including analytical work and applicable test/operational experience?

24. Have we met all specifications as well as general written or implied?

25. Have we analyzed each military or customer specification for our ability to comply, for its appropriateness to the customer's problem, and for the cost of such compliance?

26. Have we expanded the definition of implied customer requirements?

27. Have we demonstrated how we designed (or will design) for maintainability and reliability and have we described these design features?

28. Have we leaned toward the customer's
    a. Engineering concepts?

   b. Specially developed components or devices?
   c. General purpose test and handling equipment?
29. Have we demonstrated:
   a. The pertinence of our system to the problem?
   b. The completeness of our system?
   c. The quality of our system?
   d. The integration of the subsystem elements of our system?
   e. The technical competence of our subsystem designs?
30. Have we used too much (or too many):
   a. Propaganda?
   b. Technical jargon?
   c. Inconsistent forms or styles?
   d. Duplication or ambiguity?

XVII. Review Of Material And Data
   A. In preparation for the final management review briefing, the program management team should provide the following:

	Pre-RFP	RFP Receipt	Final Proposal	Dept. Staff
1. Sales Plan	X	X	X	
2. Opportunity Information Log	X	X	X	
3. RFP Requirements including Hardware				
Preliminary	X			
Final		X	X	X
4. Competitive Evaluation	X	X	X	X
5. Customer Climate and Organization	X	X	X	X
6. Assumptions	X	X	X	X
7. Program Organization				
8. Proposal Plan and Schedule				
Preliminary	X			
Final		X	X	X
9. Technical Features		X	X	X
10. Costs				
Bogeys	X	X		
Estimates			X	X
11. Recommended Selling Price and Pricing				
Strategy			X	X
12. Incentive Proposal			X	X
13. Risks	X	X	X	X
14. Tradeoffs or Cost Effectiveness	X	X	X	X
15. Alternative Proposals	X	X	X	X
16. Investment:				
Dollars-Proposal Cost	X	X	X	
Dollars-Program Cost	X	X	X	X
People	X	X	X	X
Facilities	X	X	X	X
17. Negotiation Tradeoffs			X	X
18. Alternative Courses of Action		X	X	X
19. Continuing Action Plans			X	X

XVIII. Do's And Don'ts Of Oral Presentations
   A. Do not give a general or capability pitch (unless specifically requested). Do not give a laundry list. Do not present a solution looking for a problem.
   B. Make sure that a pitch is specific and that it is something that will solve the customer's problems.
   C. Start oral communication at the Program/Project Engineer level and work yourself up.
   D. At the outset of every presentation, tell the customer why you are there and what you want.
   E. Tailor each presentation to the audience and to the objectives.
   F. Dry-run all presentations.
   G. Make sure the customer knows (beforehand) what you intend to present and that he agrees with it.
   H. Be frank.
   I. Consider problems after delivery and maintain communications.
   J. Present earnestly and confidently. And above all, knowledgeably. Remember that the difference between the right word and the almost-right word is like the difference between lightning and the lightning bug.

Appendix C

In-House Evaluation of Proposals [1]

I. TECHNICAL APPROACH

This section should provide an analysis of the problem a discussion of the operational environment and an accurate and clear technical description of the proposed system and/or hardware, including drawings or sketches of the proposal configuration. The following should be considered:

1. Is there a clear concise statement of the technical requirements which the proposal fulfills, or in the case of an unsolicited proposal, the particular areas involved?

2. Is the technical problem as seen by the customer clearly delineated?—not simply "parroted" from RFP? Is the proposal responsive to the technical requirement?

3. Does the proposal convincingly show a depth of understanding of the problem?

4. Is there a brief discussion of alternate solutions which were explored and rejected and the reason for their rejections?

5. Is there a discussion of technical approaches to be explored and why the company's approach may be expected to yield the desired results?

6. Have unrealistic and unreasonable performance requirements been indentified and alternatives suggested?

[1] Paul R. McDonald, *Proposal Preparation Manual.* Adapted from "Customer's Evaluation of Proposals," Section VIII, Chapter 2, pp. VIII–2–1 through VIII–2–12. Reproduced by permission of Paul R. McDonald, Procurement Associates, Inc. 733 N. Dodsworth Avenue, Covina, California 91724.

7. In event of deviations or alternates, is the detailed logic for these recommendations given? Especially in terms of benefits, such as enhanced performance, lower costs, greater producibility, earlier delivery and simpler maintenance?

8. In the event that certain problem objectives are to some extent incompatible with other problem goals (e.g., simplicity vs. accuracy) does the proposal unequivocally show that the optimum solution, all factors considered, has been attained?

9. Have the more difficult areas been identified and detail provided showing how performance requirements never before achieved will be met?

10. Have excessive costs or time delays required to meet certain specific requirements been clearly pointed out?

11. If originality has been spelled out as a requirement, does the proposal represent a unique, imaginative approach?

12. Is there a description of novel ideas or technical approaches?

13. Is there a statement of major technical problems which must be solved with an indication as to the amount of effort budgeted to each?

14. Is the relation of proposed solution to the broader over-all system with which it will operate shown?

15. Is there a description of the hardware which the contractor expects to furnish?

16. Is there a conservative estimate of the item's performance?

17. Does the proposal state where the company intends to deviate from standard military specifications? How much? Why?

18. Does the proposal show that proper consideration has been given in the operational concept to serviceability and ease of maintenance?

19. Is an estimate furnished of maintenance procedures and schedule showing to what extent special test or support equipment will be required?

20. Does the approach consider the viewpoints of logistics, long-range maintenance, retrofitting, problems of the using command?

21. If new components must be developed, does the proposal explain why existing ones cannot be used?

22. Are unique or unusual component reliability requirements exceeding those obtainable from conventional components described and justified?

23. If hardware is to be supplied, does the proposal indicate whether it will be suitable for production or whether partial or complete re-engineering effort would be needed before the design could be placed in production?

24. In the event proprietary data or techniques will be designed in, does the proposal explain why?

25. Is an estimate provided as to the likelihood of the program resulting in usable hardware?

26. Is convincing technical substantiation of the design proposed?

27. Does the approach avoid over-engineering and over-sophistication?

28. Is a manhour estimate (not costs) included in the technical portion of the proposal?

II. TECHNICAL ABILITY

This Section should clearly demonstrate the overall technical competence of the company to successfully complete the specific project involved.

1. Does the proposal provide convincing assurance of specific technical competence for this project?
2. Does the proposal give specific examples of similar projects successfully completed?
3. Is information provided as to the relation of the proposed hardware to existing or previous programs which the company has done for other customers, indicating the customer, project, and funds already spent?
4. Do the biographies relate specific experience of personnel to the specific needs of this project? Has extraneous biographical information been eliminated?
5. Is the availability of specific people clearly detailed—in terms of manhours for both full-time and part-time people?
6. Since the customer knows that the same personnel are used for different proposals, does the proposal show a depth of qualified personnel?
7. Are areas of technical weakness identified and does the proposal show how this will be compensated for—for example by subcontracting or the use of consultants?
8. Does the proposal clearly indicate that there is adequate technical space and facilities, both general and special to perform work efficiently and on schedule?
9. Does the proposal outline the availability of the facilities, Government-owned, owned, or leased, necessary for the specific project, for research, development, production and testing?
10. Are special technical facilities (such as dust-free laboratories, temperature controlled rooms, data processing equipment, special laboratory equipment) required by the project clearly spelled out?
11. Is it clearly indicated that all required facilities will be available when required for this project?
12. Where Government-furnished equipment is required, are these needs clearly justified?
13. Is a facility plan provided showing layout, tests, dollar value and square footage?
14. Where tie-ins with subcontractors are proposed, is specific evidence given of the subs' commitment to make technical people and facilities available when required?

III. DELIVERY REQUIREMENTS AND SCHEDULING

Delivery is most important. The proposal must not only state that the delivery schedule will be met, it must show how it will be met.

1. Does the proposal provide convincing assurance that the customer's delivery dates will be met or bettered?
2. Is sufficient detail regarding master scheduling, programming, followup, and other like functions given to reinforce the foregoing assurance?

3. Where subcontractors and major suppliers are involved, are sufficient safeguards built into proposed scheduling system to insure sub-schedule compliance with master program?

IV. PROJECT DIRECTION AND MANAGEMENT

The proposal should show the company's Method of Management. It should elaborate on organization, personnel manpower controls. It must demonstrate that the company has an understanding of the external organization relations with the Government or Prime Contractor and with subcontractors necessary to the accomplishment of the project. It must outline the overall management concepts employed by the company and the specific type of management that will be provided for the proposal project.

1. Does the proposal clearly demonstrate an understanding of the customer's concern with the management of this project?
2. Are details provided on corporate experience, facilities and personnel?
3. Does the proposal demonstrate that top-level management will continue a high level of interest and assume responsibility for successful accomplishment of the program?
4. Does the proposal provide convincing evidence that the company is properly oriented and organizationally structured to meet the specific management needs of this project? Especially in terms of providing the requisite functions of communication (internal and external) and of integration of all project phases and pieces?
5. Is evidence given of management's understanding of how the specific project fits into the customer's over-all needs?
6. Does the proposal indicate that management first has taken a completely objective and detached look at the entire problem prior to thinking in terms of specific solutions?
7. Is it clear that management has honestly examined its own areas of competence and incompetence?
8. Are details provided on management objectives, policies, participation, and reliability concepts?
9. Does the proposal show the capabilities of the management to handle a project of the size contemplated?
10. Is evidence given that top-level management has full control of its organization?
11. Does the proposal show how the interest of the company in this specific project ties in with the company's long-range plans as well as with past experience?
12. Does the proposal outline the type of management to be provided for the project, viz; whether a special management group will be formed or whether there will be company-wide participation?
13. Does the proposal show the position of the program manager or group in the over-all company organization and the limits of authority and responsibility?

14. If no over-all group is to be formed, does the proposal show the method of operation within the over-all company structure?
15. Does the proposal delineate the requisite numbers (neither over- or under-managed) of the right types of management people?
16. Where organizational charts are presented, is it clearly shown how the project management will operate effectively on a day-to-day basis?
17. Is information furnished as to the type, frequency, and effectiveness of management controls and methods for corrective action?
18. Do the manpower buildup charts clearly explain the methods of manpower acquisition, particularly skilled manpower requirements?
19. Is a total manpower plan and individual plans for engineering, manufacturing and quality control furnished?
20. Is information furnished showing how the present project will phase in with current and future business?
21. Is a Make-Or-Buy Program provided?
22. Is evidence given that supports the selection of subcontractors—not only from the standpoint of their technical and manufacturing capabilities, but also their management philosophy and talent?
23. If the proposal involves systems management, does the proposal show how the subcontractor's management will be integrated into the program?
24. Are organization charts furnished of first and second tier subcontractors which show clearly their relationship to the prime and to other subcontractors?
25. Is evidence given of the complete support of the subs' management for an arrangement wherein the company would be the system manager?
26. If subcontractors will be used for major parts or subsystems, is a copy of their proposal furnished or evidence to show their proposal has been properly developed and evaluated?
27. Has provision been made for horizontal consultation between subcontractors?

V. QUALITY ASSURANCE, QUALITY CONTROL AND RELIABILITY
The term "Quality Assurance" covers all the actions necessary to adequately determine that product requirements are met. "Quality Control" is the system and management function by which the Contractor ascertains and controls the quality of supplies or services. "Reliability" is the ability of item to function without failure. The proposal should carefully delineate the company's programs in these areas.
   1. Does the proposal describe the company's quality control plan including organization, policies, facilities, operational system, technical capabilities, and records system?
   2. Is it clear that the customer's quality control requirements will be achieved by the company's quality control system, organization, concept and approach?
   3. Are deviations from customer requirements satisfactorily explained?

4. Does the proposal show that customer reliability requirements can be achieved by the company's concept and approach, including a specific program for meeting or surpassing these requirements?

5. Is it clearly shown how the reliability organization and project responsibility fit into the proposed program?

6. Are reliability monitoring points (breadboard, experimental, development, service test, prototype and production) clearly delineated so that customer surveillance may be effectively exercised?

7. Does the proposal show an understanding of reliability prediction techniques and spell out in detail how predicted goals will be met?

8. Is creative ingenuity reflected in the proposal by pointing out reliability approaches to particular development phases?

9. Does the proposal discuss the company's facilities and measuring equipment?

10. Does the proposal fully utilize the sales value of the company's reliability concepts including the use of in-plant and outside standard laboratories?

VI. PRICE

The price or cost estimate should not be arrived at by adding the raw estimates of the various company departments, but should be based on the lowest price which will make the business acceptable to the company in the light of available alternatives, adjusted to take into account the long-run benefits and drawbacks.

1. Is this the lowest possible price? Considering (*a*) long-range potential vs. immediate return; (*b*) probable competitive price range?

2. Have all "make-or-buy" aspects been considered?

3. Is there complete satisfaction that subcontractors and vendors have submitted their lowest realistic cost estimates?

4. Is it a certainty that manhour, space, facility and other cost factors have not been over-estimated?

5. Are overhead and burden rates and fees completely reasonable for this type of project?

6. Is the extent of pricing detail given consistent with the importance of these details?

7. Has consideration been given to the dollar value placed on the project by the customer and the funds available for it?

VII. FIELD SUPPORT

The field support which will be or can be provided to place the item in service and maintain it in operation must be fully described.

1. Does the proposal adequately cover all aspects of support required for the stated program? The following items should be considered; maintenance, engineering, technical training, technical data, installation support, depot support and implementation, sustaining engineering and product improvement, field representation, provisioning of unit spares and maintenance and operating parts, test, and other ground support equipment.

2. Does the proposal highlight the magnitude and scope of the company's field service and support capability?

3. Are recommended support aspects accurately described and delineated?

    4. Does the proposal provide specific examples of accomplishment in the field service and support area?

    5. Does the proposal describe the type of support which will be required from the customer?

VIII. MANUFACTURING

The proposal should show the company's competence to manufacture the item. Some information in this field is important even in proposals for research and development which may not involve any quantity production since the buyer must usually give consideration to and plan for future production quantities.

    1. Does the proposal describe the company's manufacturing organization responsibilities, tool policy and plan, fabrication and assembly plan, quality assurance, and configuration and manufacturing controls?

    2. Does the proposal explain the system and procedures used for schedule planning and operational controls?

    3. Does the proposal provide convincing assurance of specific manufacturing competence in terms of this project? Does the biographical data relate the specific experience of the manufacturing people to the specific work areas of this project?

    4. Does the proposal give specific examples of similar projects successfully completed by the company?

    5. Does the proposal clearly indicate the varying availabilities of these manufacturing people to the project? If subcontractors and/or consultants are involved, does the proposal provide assurance of their availability?

    6. Does the proposal clearly indicate that the company has adequate manufacturing space and facilities, both general and special, to perform the work efficiently and on schedule?

    7. Are specialized equipment and processes required for the project given sufficient prominence in the proposal through photographs and descriptive information?

    8. Does the proposal clearly delineate the work flow paths from the time the engineering is released to the time that items are shipped?

    9. Does the proposal show evidence of an effective manufacturing control system?

    10. Does the proposal indicate a clearly defined procedure under which the company can move quickly to meet any emergency with a minimum of program disruption?

    11. Does the proposal call attention to the high standards of the production test procedures used?

    12. Does the proposal specifically state that all required facilities are available for the project at this time?

    13. Does the proposal provide evidence that the company utilizes the most advanced methods in its manufacturing and manufacturing support areas?

IX. EDITING AND FORMAT

Usually no arithmetic rating is assigned to editorial calibre and format of the proposal; however, their importance cannot be over-emphasized. The information required by the proposal must be presented in a logical pleasing manner that will give the required emphasis. The proposal is the point of sale and should be prepared and presented to the customer with that in mind.

1. Has the proposal been checked for clarity, logic of presentation, consistency, completeness, accuracy and emphasis?
2. Does the proposal follow the organization of the subject matter in the Request For Proposal?
3. Has the editing removed all unessential, trivial and repetitive material?
4. Is the proposal easy to read? Does it have short, logical paragraphs, frequent headings, and dividers for major sections? Is the use of abbreviations confined to standard words and are alphabetical abbreviations not readily understood by non-technical and/or technical personnel removed?
5. Have consistent page and figure numberings been used?
6. Has a Table of Contents and Index been provided consistent with the size and complexity of the proposal?
7. Have non-technical synopsis of the various sections been provided for the guidance of non-technical evaluators?
8. Does the proposal quote references rather than cite them?
9. Do the illustrations contribute to the "story line" of the proposal? Do they add to its readability and are they functional?
10. Is the completed proposal an "attractive sales package"?

Appendix D

Customer's Evaluation of Proposals[1]

Table D-1. General Quality and Responsiveness of the Proposal

a. COMPLETENESS AND THOROUGHNESS

Considerations:

1. Have all essential data required by the Request for Proposal been included?
2. Is the proposal easily legible, well organized, clear and concise; or is it an uncoordinated collection of unrelated data, hastily assembled and haphazardly edited?
3. Is all data pertinent and significant, or is much of it irrelevant data collected from past proposals for the purpose of impressing by volume alone?
4. Is the proposal presented in a manner which will simplify evaluation, or does it diffuse and confuse the essentialities?

b. GRASP OF PROBLEM

Considerations:

1. Does the proposal recognize and differentiate between the simpler and the more difficult performance requirements?
2. Does it evidence recognition of inherent maintenance and supply problems?
3. Does it demonstrate an awareness of human and environmental factors affecting the scope of work?

[1] Paul R. McDonald, *Proposal Preparation Manual.* Adapted from "Customer's Evaluation of Proposals," Section VIII, Chapter 1, Pages VIII-1-17 through VIII-1-25. Reproduced by permission of Paul R. McDonald, Procurement Associates, Inc. 733 N. Dodsworth Avenue, Covina, California 91724.

4. Does it evidence a recognition of relationships with other contractors and agencies, and the coordination and liaison problems involved?
5. Is the estimate of professional, technical, and administrative manpower requirements in consonance with the project requirements? Is there a reasonable balance between professional personnel and technicians?
6. Is there evidence of appropriate utilization of scientific and professional personnel; or conversely are technicians offered where highly qualified professional specialists are required?

c. RESPONSIVENESS TO TERMS, CONDITIONS AND TIME OF PERFORMANCE

Considerations:

1. Is there adequate evidence of intent to meet all terms and conditions specified in the Request for Proposal with regard to reporting requirements, proprietary rights, documentation disclosures, and any other special technical conditions cited in the RFP?
2. Does the proposed delivery schedule conform with mandatory or target schedule requirements? Where time of performance is of the essence and is a competitive evaluation factor, is the proposed delivery schedule adequately supported by the technical proposal?
3. To what extent is the offeror willing to commit himself on the firm requirements, and on the "best efforts" portions of the Technical Scope Of Work?
4. If award is contingent upon the existence of a follow-on production capability, is the proposal responsive to the data requested in the RFP? Does data submitted substantiate production capability and cost estimates?

Table D-2. Organization, Personnel and Facilities

a. EVIDENCE OF GOOD ORGANIZATION AND MANAGEMENT PRACTICES

Considerations:

1. Does the proposal evidence the breadth and depth of management capability appropriate to the project? Is there evidence of stability of job tenure in upper management echelons?
2. How does the proposed task organization integrate into the overall organization in terms of effective lines of authority and communication, and in terms of effective integration of research, development, design, drafting, technical writing, reliability, and test functions.

b. QUALIFICATIONS OF PERSONNEL

Considerations:

1. Does the proposal include definite plans for the assignment of specific key personnel?
2. Do assigned key personnel possess the experience, educational background and record of past accomplishment appropriate to the scope of work?
3. Is the quality of personnel as set forth in the proposal generally supported by the salary scales?
4. Is the proposal dependent upon any substantial recruitment of key personnel? If so, would such recruitment result in high cost of performance, or might it adversely affect other vital contracts in the geographical areas of the offeror?
5. Is the success of the project excessively dependent upon subcontract or temporary consultants? If so, to what extent are subcontract plans firm and reasonably irrevocable?

c. ADEQUACY OF FACILITIES

Considerations:

1. Are the proposed laboratory, pilot manufacturing, and test facilities adequate for the requirements of the Technical Scope of Work?
2. Are the proposed facilities conveniently available to engineering personnel?
3. Is the proposal contingent upon Government-furnished capital equipment beyond that set out in the RFP?

d. EXPERIENCE IN SIMILAR OR RELATED FIELDS

Considerations:

1. Is the normal commercial or Government business of the offeror closely related to the proposed work?
2. Is the offeror experienced with practices and procedures of the contracting agency to an extent which would increase the effectiveness of his performance?
3. Does the company enjoy a respected reputation in the field to which the proposal relates?

e. RECORD OF PAST PERFORMANCE

Considerations:

1. Has the offeror held previous contracts with the agency or other Government establishment?
2. Were schedule commitments generally met?
3. Did the contractor solve his own technical problems, or did he rely heavily upon the technical staff of the agency?
4. Was there an unusually high number of contractual problems which might be attributed to inflexibility, naivete, or lack of cooperation on the part of the contractor?
5. If there were significant cost over-runs, were they due to an incompetently low initial cost estimate, or to valid problems which could not have been anticipated?

f. POTENTIAL AS A PRODUCTION FACILITY

Considerations:

1. Does the proposal present adequate evidence of the existence of physical plant, personnel, and financial resources to permit transition from development to production?
2. Do other mobilization planning commitments of the offeror preclude proposed production of the item under mobilization conditions?
3. Does the close proximity of a production facility reflect in valuable feedback to development engineers? If so, is the production-orientation of development engineers of significance to the successful completion of the proposed work?

g. GEOGRAPHIC LOCATION

Considerations:

1. Will the location of the facility result in excessive inconvenience, expense and lost time in the conduct of liaison and supervision?

2. Is the plant located in a critical defense area? If so, is it significant to future production plans?

h. PLANT SECURITY

Considerations:

1. Will extensive alterations be required to physical facilities to meet security requirements of the contract?

Table D-3. Technical Approach

a. PROJECT PLANNING

Considerations:

1. Does the proposal demonstrate detailed and realistic scheduling of the various technical phases of the project?
2. Does the proposal demonstrate effective review, evaluation and control at specific check-points?
3. Are proposed schedules in line with available personnel resources?
4. Are parallel investigations proposed on critical problems, and avoided on more routine problems?
5. Are breadboard tests planned early in the program in vital design areas?

b. RELIABILITY

Considerations:

1. Is proposal based on proven components and techniques?
2. Is redundancy provided in critical functional features?
3. Will design be based upon "worst-case" analysis?
4. How are theoretical reliability analyses and reliability testing integrated into the design program?

c. MAINTAINABILITY

Considerations:

1. Have self-checking features been considered in the proposal?
2. Are high mortality components intended to be easily accessible and fully interchangeable?
3. Are requirements for special tools, fixtures and test equipment expected to be minimal?
4. Has adequate consideration been given to "throwaway" of low-cost modules, and field repair of high-cost modules?
5. Has consideration been given to field modification for probable future changes?
6. Does the proposal avoid excessive dependence upon periodic field adjustment or calibration?

d. PRODUCIBILITY AND ECONOMY

Considerations:

1. Does proposal evidence maximum design simplicity?
2. Does proposal evidence the elimination of special precision components, selection of fits, matched pairs, etc.?
3. Is proposed design overly dependent upon special capital production equipment, critical process controls and critical materials?
4. Does the proposal adequately consider maximum use of standard components and indicate procedures for screening of selected components against existing standard items?
5. If production cost estimates were requested, are these reasonable, and are they adequately supported by the technical proposal?

e. TECHNICAL DATA AND DOCUMENTATION

Considerations:

1. Does the proposal contain assurances that drawing, specifications and other technical data to be supplied under terms of the Request For Proposal will be complete, thoroughly checked for accuracy, and generally suitable for competitive procurement purposes?
2. Does the proposal contain any reservations on full technical disclosure, or restrictions on use of such data?
3. Are proposed man-hours for drafting and technical writing consistent with requirements for adequate documentation?

f. SPECIFIC SUB-FACTORS

The evaluation sub-factors are generally applicable to many R&D proposals. Fully as important as these factors, however, are those directly related to the primary requirements of the Request for Proposal. Examples of such "peculiar" factors, selected at random, are: Overall Size and Weight; Shock Resistance; Power Consumption, Accuracy, Facility and Speed of Operation; Environment Limits, Radiation Shielding; Man-Portability; Fail-Safe Provisions; Lubrication Requirements; Graze Sensitivity; Compatibility with existing equipment. These factors should be determined based upon a review of the Technical Scope of Work, and included in the evaluation plan.
etc.

Only such subfactors will be included as are necessary and desirable for adequate evaluation. While the more subfactors that are included the more objective will be the evaluation, no factors should be included which are not necessary to evaluate the specific procurement in question. Neither should subfactors be included covering the mandatory aspects of the procurement, for example, the compliance of bidders with proprietary rights requirements or with mandatory delivery schedules, since proposals are normally either responsive or non-responsive to these requirements and there is usually no permissible graduation of compliance.

The inclusion of a large number of subfactors to which all bidders must comply if their proposal will be considered has the effect of leveling the final technical rating so that the point spread between the best and worst proposal will be deceptively small. To

EVALUATION FACTORS	WEIGHT
I. General Quality and Responsiveness of Proposal	
a. Completeness and Thoroughness	5
b. Grasp of Problem	10
c. Responsiveness to Terms, Conditions and Time of Performance	3
II. Organization, Personnel and Facilities	
a. Evidence of Good Organizational and Management Practices	5
b. Qualifications of Personnel	10
c. Adequacy of Facilities	8
d. Experience in Similar or Related Fields	5
e. Record of Past Experience	5
f. Geographic Location	5
III. Technical Approach	
a. Reliability	10
b. Maintainability	5
c. Producibility and Economy	5
d. Technical Data and Documentation	5
e. Overall Size and Weight	10
f. Power Consumption	10
g. Environmental Range	3
h. Sheilding Techniques	8
IV. Final Technical Evaluation	
D-1 General Quality and Responsiveness of Proposal	1
D-2 Organization, Personnel and Facilities	2
D-3 Technical Approach	3

be of greatest possible value, the evaluation plan should be designed to result in the greatest possible point spread between good and poor proposals.

Specifying Relative Weights

The assignment of weights for both the three Primary Evaluation Factors, or their supporting subfactors is the responsibility of the technical evaluation agency. The numerical weights assigned will depend upon the relative importance of each of the evaluation factors.

The first step in the assignment of numerical weights is to decide upon the relative importance of each of the three primary factors. A spread of "ten" (10) is usually adequate for expressing this relationship. A typical example of the establishment of weight for the three primary factors would be:

Table D-1 GENERAL QUALITY AND RESPONSIVENESS
OF PROPOSAL   4

In some cases, the possible technical approaches may be so stereotyped as to be less significant than Organization, Personnel and Facilities, in which case the Technical Approach would be assigned a lower numerical weight, such as:

The assignment of numerical weights to the supporting subfactors is accomplished in a similar manner. It should be noted, however, that it is necessary to consider only the relative importance of subfactors within each of the primary groupings. It is not necessary to consider the relative importance of any of the subfactors under "Organization, Personnel and Facilities" as compared with the subfactors under "Technical Approach", but only as compared with other subfactors under "Organization, Personnel and Facilities".

In the event that proposals for performance of a second phase of contract effort are to be considered in the evaluation for placement of a Phase I contract, the technical evaluation panel will at that time establish the relative weight of the final Phase I and Phase II evaluation.

Proposal Preparation Bibliography

1. American Management Associations, Inc., *Writing Reports That Work,* 1969.
2. Ammon-Wexler, Jill, "Writing a Winning Proposal," *Electronic Warfare,* May-June 1977.
3. Ammon-Wexler, Jill and a.p. Carmer, Catherine, *How to Create a Winning Proposal.* Mercury Communications, Inc., 1976.
4. Beverage, J.M., *Anatomy of a Win,* Playa Del Rey, California: J.M. Beverage and Associates, Inc.
5. Close, R.N., *Developing and Implementing a Winning Proposal Strategy,* 1976.
6. Cook, D.F. and Blanton, L.B., *Writing to Win,* General Electric Company, 1975.
7. DeGeorge, William F., "Ingredients for Successful Proposals," *Machine Design,* April 3, 1969.
8. Dycus, Robert D., "Improving the Evaluation Score of Your Proposals," *Technical Communication,* 1977.
9. Dycus, Robert D., "The Relative Effectiveness of Proposal Approaches—An Experimental Study," *Technical Communication,* first quarter, 1975.
10. Dycus, Robert D., "Relative Efficacy of a One-Sided vs. Two-Sided Communication in a Simulated Government Evaluation of Proposals," *Psychological Reports,* 1976.
11. Englebret, David, "Storyboarding a Better Way of Planning and Writing Proposals," *IEEE Transactions of Professional Communication,* December, 1972.
12. Goodson, G. and Hart, S., *How to Storyboard* (pamphlet, 19 pp.), TRW Systems Group, 1970.
13. Gunning, Robert, *How to Take the Fog out of Writing,* Chicago: Dartnell Corporation, 1964.
14. Loring, Roy J., "The Proposal Manager's Work," *Chemical Engineering,* August 24, 1970.
15. Loring, Roy J., "Cost of Preparing Proposals," *Chemical Engineering,* November 16, 1970.
16. Morris, Steele, "Engineering Proposals," *Machine Design,* May 13, 1965.
17. Procurement Associates, Inc., "Proposal Planning Document," *Proposal Manager's Handbook,* 1973.

18. Renner, Stan, *Introduction to The Stop Technique as Applied to Organizing and Writing Proposals,* SESW–S69, Sylvania Electronics Systems, Western Division, 1970.
19. Robinson, W.L., Jr., *R&D Proposal Preparation Guide,* Data Publications, 1962.
20. Rugh, D.E. and Manning, R.E., *Proposal Management Using the Modular Technique,* Manning and Rugh Associates, 1977.
21. Shnitzler, R.K., "Making Your Technical Proposal More Effective—Section I," *Journal of the Society of Technical Writers and Publishers,* April 1963.
22. Shnitzler, R.K., "Making Your Technical Proposal More Effective—Section II," *Journal of the Society of Technical Writers and Publishers,* July 1963.
23. Simmons, S.A., *Proposal Preparation Guide,* AVCO Corporation, 1965.
24. Strunk, William Jr. and White, E.B., *The Elements of Style,* New York: Macmillan, 2nd ed., 1972.

A Project Management/ Systems Management Bibliography

1. Abt Associates Inc., *Applications of Systems Analysis Models: A Survey.* Washington, D.C.: Technology Utilization Division, Office of Technology Utilization, National Aeronautics and Space Administration, 1968.
2. Ackoff, Russell Lincoln, and Emery, Fred E., *On Purposeful Systems.* Chicago: Aldine/ Atherton, 1972.
3. Ackoff, Russell Lincoln, *Redesigning the Future: A Systems Approach to Societal Problems.* New York: John Wiley, 1974.
4. Alderfer, Clayton P., *Change Processes in Organizations.* New Haven, Connecticut, Department of Administrative Sciences, Yale University, 1971.
5. Allen, Louis A., *The Professional Manager's Guide,* (USA: Louis A. Allen Associates, 1969).
6. Anthony, Robert N. Planning and Control Systems: *A Framework for Analysis* Boston: Division of Research, Graduate School of Business Administration, Harvard University, 1965.
7. Archibald, Russell D. *Managing High-Technology Programs and Projects.* New York: John Wiley, 1976 pp. 55, 82, 176, 191.
8. Argyris, Chris, "How Tomorrow's Executives Will Make Decisions." *Think,* 33, 18–23. (November-December, 1967).
9. Argyris, Chris "Resistance to Rational Management Systems," *Innovation,* issue 10: (1969), pp. 28–42.
10. Argyris, Chris, "Today's Problems with Tomorrow's Organizations," *Journal of Management Studies* 4: (February, 1967), pp. 31–55.
11. ARINC Research Corporation. *Guidebook for Systems Analysis/Cost Effectiveness.* Washington, D.C.: U.S. Department of Commerce, National Bureau of Standards: distributed by Clearinghouse for Federal Scientific and Technical Information, 1969.

12. Association for Systems Management. *An Annotated Bibliography for the Systems Professional.* 2nd ed. Cleveland: Association for Systems Management, 1970.
13. Avots, Ivars, "Why Does Project Management Fail?" *California Management Review* 12 (Fall, 1969), pp. 77–82.
14. Avots, Ivars, "Making Project Management Work: The Right Tools For the Wrong Project Manager," *S.A.M. Advanced Management Journal,* 40, 20–26, (Autumn, 1975).
15. Bachman, J., *et al.,* Bases of Supervisory Power: A Comparative Study in Five Organizational Settings," in *Control in Organizations,* A. Tannenbaum, ed. New York, McGraw-Hill, 1968, pp. 229–238.
16. Baker, Frank, ed. *Organizational Systems; General Systems Approaches to Complex Organizations* Homewood, Illinois, R.D. Irwin Series in Management and the Behavioral Sciences, 1973.
17. Barnes, Lewis B., "Project Management and the Use of Authority: A Study of Structure, Role, and Influence Relationships in Public and Private Organizations," Ph.D. Dissertation, University of Southern California, 1971.
18. Baumgartner, John Stanley, *Project Management,* Homewood, Illinois, R.D. Irwin series, 1963.
19. Beckett, John A., *Management Dynamics: The New Synthesis.* New York: McGraw-Hill, 1971.
20. Benne, K.D. and Birnbaum, M., "Principles of Changing" in *The Planning of Change,* New York, Holt, Rinehart, and Winston, 1969.
21. Benningson, Lawrence, "The Team Approach to Project Management," *Management Review* 61, (January 1972), pp. 48–52.
22. Benningson, Lawrence, *Project Management,* New York: McGraw-Hill, 1970.
23. Bennis Warren G., "The Coming Death of Bureaucracy." *Think* 32: 30–35. (November-December 1966).
24. Benton, John Breen, *Managing the Organizational Decision Process,* Lexington, Mass, Lexington Books, 1973.
25. Berlinski, David J., "On Systems Analysis: An Essay Concerning the Limitations of some Mathematical Methods in the Social, Political, and Biological Sciences," Cambridge, Mass., M.I.T. Press, 1976.
26. Berrien, F. Kenneth, *General and Social Systems,* New Brunswick, N.J., Rutgers University Press, 1968.
27. Bertalanffy, Ludwig von, *General Systems Theory; Foundations, Development, Applications,* New York, G. Braziller, 1972.
28. —*General Systems Theory,* New York, G. Braziller, 1968.
29. Bingham, John E., and Davies, G.W.P. *A Handbook of Systems Analysis.* London. Macmillan, © 1972, 1974. Distributed in North America by Halsted Press, a division of John Wiley, New York and Toronto.
30. Blake, R.R. and Mouton, J.S., *The Managerial Grid,* Gulf Publishing, 1964.
31. Blankstein, Charles Sidney, "The Base Level Development Assistance Project: A Managerial Perspective," 1972. Cambridge, Mass: M.I.T., Thesis, M.S.
32. Block, Ellery B. "Accomplishment/Cost: Better Project Control." *Harvard Business Review* 49: (May 1971), pp. 110–24.
33. Bobrowski, T.M., "A Basic Philosophy of Project Management." *Journal of Systems Management,* May-June 1974.
34. Boulding, Kenneth, "General Systems Theory—The Skeleton of Science," *Management Science,* (April 1956), pp. 197–208.
35. Bowman, R.R., "An Analysis of Project Management Concepts in the Missile/Space Industry," MBA Thesis, Utah State University, 1967.

36. Boyatzis, R.E., "Building Efficacy: An Effective Use of Managerial Power," *Industrial Management Review,* 11, 1: 65–75, 1969.

37. —, "Leadership: The Effective Use of Power", *Management of Personnel Quarterly.* Graduate School of Business Administration, University of Michigan (Fall, 1971), pp. 21–25. Reprinted in Richards, Max D., and William A. Nielander, *Readings in Management,* fourth edition, (Cincinnati, Southwestern Publishing Co., 1974), pp. 623–629.

38. Brandon, Dick H., and Gray, Max, *Project Control Standards,* Princeton, Brandon/Systems Press, 1970.

39. Burke, R.J., "Methods of Resolving Interpersonal Conflict," *Personnel Administration,* July-August, 1969, pp. 48–55.

40. —, "Methods of Managing Superior-Subordinate Conflict," *Canadian Journal of Behavioral Science,* 2,2: 124–135, 1970.

41. Burke, W.W. and Hornstein, H.A., *The Social Technology of Organization Development.* Fairfax, Virginia, NTL Learning Resources Corporation, 1972.

42. Burt, David N., "Getting the Right Price With the Right Contract." *Management Review* 24–34, (May, 1976).

43. Butler, Arthur G., Jr., "Project Management: A Study in Organizational Conflict," *Academy of Management Journal* 16, 84–101, (March, 1973).

44. —, "Behavioral Implications for Professional Employees of Structural Conflict Associated with Project Management in Functional Organizations." Ph.D. Dissertation, University of Florida, 1969.

45. Butler, D., and Miller, N., "Power to Reward and Punish in Social Interaction," *Journal of Experimental Social Psychology,* 1, 4: 311–322, 1965.

46. Cicero, John P., and Wilemon, David L., "Project Authority: A Multidimensional View," *IEEE Transactions on Engineering Management,* EM–17: 52–57, (May 1970).

47. Chapman, Richard L., *Project Management in NASA; the System and the Men,* Washington: Scientific and Technical Information Office, National Aeronautics and Space Administration; for sale by the Superintendent of Documents, U.S. Government Printing Office, 1973.

48. Chen, Gordon K., and Kaczka, Eugene E., *Operations and Systems Analysis: A Simulation Approach.* Boston, Allyn and Bacon, 1974.

49. Churchman, Charles West, *The Systems Approach,* New York, Dell Publishing Company, 1968.

50. Cleland, David I., "Organizational Dynamics of Project Management," *IEEE Transactions on Engineering Management,* EM–13: 201–5, (December, 1966).

51. —, "The Deliberate Conflict," *Business Horizon,* 11, 1: 78–80, (1968).

52. —, "Project Management in Industry: An Assessment," *Project Management Quarterly,* 5, 2, 3: 19–21, (1974).

53. —, "Defining A Project Management System," *Project Management Quarterly,* 8, 4: 37–40, (1977).

54. —, "Why Project Management?" *Business Horizons,* 7: 81–88, (Winter, 1964).

55. Cleland, David I., and King, William R., *Management: A Systems Approach.* New York, McGraw-Hill, 1972.

56. —, *Systems Analysis and Project Management,* New York, McGraw-Hill, 1968.

57. —, *Systems Analysis and Project Management,* New York, McGraw-Hill, 1975. pp. 271, 371–380.

58. —, *Systems Organizations, Analysis, Management: A Book of Readings,* New York, McGraw-Hill, 1969.

59. Couger, J. Daniel, and Knapp, Robert W., (eds.) *System Analysis Techniques.* New York, John Wiley, 1974.
60. Crowston, Wallace B., "Models for Project Management," *Sloan Management Review,* 12: pp. 25–42, (Spring, 1971).
61. Cullingford, G. and Prideaux, J.D.C.A., "A Variational Study of Optimal Resource Profiles," *Management Science* 19: 1067–81, (May, 1973).
62. Dahl, R., "The Concept of Power," *Behavioral Science,* 2: 201–215, (July, 1957).
63. Datz, Marvin A. and Wilby, L.R., "What Is Good Project Management?" *Project Management Quarterly, 8,* 1: (March 1977).
64. Davis, Keith, "The Role of Project Management In Scientific Manufacturing," *Arizona Business Bulletin 9:* (May 1962), pp. 1–8.
65. —, "The Role of Project Management in Scientific Manufacturing." *IRE Transactions on Engineering Management,* 9, 3, (1962).
66. Davis, S., "An Organic Problem-Solving Method of Organizational Change," *Journal of Applied Behavioral Science,* 3–21, (January, 1967).
67. Davis, Stanley, "Two Models of Organization: Unity of Command Versus Balance of Power," *Sloan Management Review,* (Fall, 1974), pp. 29–40.
68. Davis, S.M., and Lawrence, P.R., *Matrix,* Reading, Mass, Addison-Wesley, 1977.
69. De Greene, Kenyon Brenton, *Sociotechnical Systems: Factors in Analysis, Design, and Management.* Englewood Cliffs, N.J., Prentice-Hall, 1973.
70. —, (ed.) *Systems Psychology,* New York: McGraw-Hill, 1970.
71. Delbecq, André L., Schull, Fremont A., Filley, Alan C., and Grimes, Andrew J., *Matrix Organization: A Conceptual Guide to Organizational Variation,* Wisconsin Business Papers No. 2. Madison, University of Wisconsin, Bureau of Business Research and Service, 1969.
72. Delbecq, André L., and Filley, Alan C. *Program and Project Management in a Matrix Organization: A Case Study,* Madison, University of Wisconsin, Bureau of Business Research and Service, 1974.
73. Dibble, E.T. and Suojanen, Waino, "Project Management in a Crisis Economy," *Infosystems-Spectrum,* 23: 44–46, (January, 1976).
74. Doering, Robert D., "An Approach Toward Improving the Creative Output of Scientific Task Teams," *IEEE Transactions on Engineering Management,* EM-20: 29–31, (February, 1973).
75. Earle, V.H., "Once Upon a Matrix: A Hindsight on Participation," *Optimum* 4, 28–36, 1973.
76. Eirich, Peter Lee, "An Information System Design Analysis for a Research Organization." Cambridge, Mass., M.I.T. M.S. Thesis, 1974.
77. Emery, F.E., *Systems Thinking: Selected Readings.* New York, Penguin Education, 1974.
78. Emery, J.C., *Organizational Planning and Control Systems,* New York, Macmillan, 1969.
79. Emshoff, James R., *Analysis of Behavioral Systems,* New York, Macmillan, 1971.
80. *European Conference on the Management of Large Space Programs,* (Paris, 1970), New York, Gordon and Breach Science Publishers, 1971.
81. Evan, W.M., "Conflict and Performance in R&D Organization," *Industrial Management Review,* 7: 37–45, (1965).
82. Evan, W.M., "Superior-Subordinate Conflict in Research Organizations," *Administrative Science Quarterly,* 52–64, (July, 1965).
83. Exton, William, *The Age of Systems: The Human Dilemma.* New York, American Management Association, 1972.
84. Fiore, Michael V., "Out of the Frying Pan into the Matrix," *Personnel Administration* 33, 3: 4–7, (1970).

85. Fisher, Gene Harvey, *Cost Considerations in Systems Analysis*. New York, American Elsevier, 1971.
86. Fitzgerald, John M. and Ardra F., *Fundamentals of Systems Analysis,* New York, Wiley, 1973.
87. Flaks, Marvin, and Archibald, Russell D., "The EE's Guide to Project Management," *Electronic Engineer* 27: 28 + (April, 1968); 20 + (May); 27–32 (June); 33–34 + (July); 33 + (August).
88. Forrester, Jay W., "A New Corporate Design," *Industrial Management Review* 7: 5–17 (Fall, 1965).
89. Frankwicz, Michael J., "A Study of Project Management Techniques," *Journal of Systems Management* 24: 18–22, (October, 1973).
90. French, J.R., Jr., and Raven, B., "The Bases of Social Power," in *Studies in Social Power,* D. Cartwright, (ed.), Ann Arbor, Mich: Research Center for Group Dynamics, 1959, pp. 150–165.
91. Fried, Louis, "Don't Smother Your Project in People," *Management Advisor* 9: 46–49, (March, 1972).
92. Friend, Fred L., "Be A More Effective Program Manager," *Journal of Systems Management,* 27: 6–9, (February, 1976).
93. Fuller, R. Buckminster, *Synergetics: Explorations in the Geometry of Thinking.* New York, Macmillan, 1975.
94. Gaddis, P.O., "The Project Manager," *Harvard Business Review,* May-June, 89–97, (1959).
95. Galbraith, Jay R., "Matrix Organization Designs-How to Combine Functional and Project Forms," *Business Horizons,* February, 1971.
96. Geisler, M.A., "How to Plan for Management in New Systems," *Harvard Business Review,* September-October, 1962.
97. Gemmill, G., "Managerial Role Mapping," *The Management Personnel Quarterly,* 8, 3: 13–19, (Fall, 1969).
98. Gemmill, G., and H. Thamhain, "The Power Styles of Project Managers: Some Efficiency Correlates," *20th Annual JEMC, Managing for Improved Engineering Effectiveness* (Atlanta, Ga., Oct. 30–31, 1972), pp. 89–96.
99. Gemmill, G.R. and Thamhain, H.J., "Project Performance as a Function of the Leadership Styles of Project Managers: Results of a Field Study," *Convention Digest. 4th Annual Meeting of the Project Management Institute,* Philadelphia, October 18–21, 1972.
100. —, "Influence Styles of Project Managers: Some Project Performance Correlates," *Academy of Management Journal,* 17, 2: pp. 216–224, (June, 1974).
101. Gemmill, Gary, and Thamhain, Hans J., "The Effectiveness of Different Power Styles of Project Managers in Gaining Project Support," *IEEE Transactions on Engineering Management* EM-20, 38–44, (May, 1973).
102. —, "Interpersonal Power in Temporary Management Systems," *Journal of Management Studies,* (October, 1971).
103. —, and Wilemon, David L., "The Power Spectrum in Project Management," *Sloan Management Review* 12: pp. 15–25, (Fall, 1970).
104. Gemmill, Gary and David Wilemon, "The Product Manager as an Influence Agent," *Journal of Marketing,* 36: 26–31, (January, 1972).
105. Gibson, James L., (ed.) *Readings in Organizations: Structure, Processes, Behavior,* Dallas, Business Publication, 1973.
106. Gildersleeve, Thomas R., *Data Processing Project Management,* New York, Van Nostrand Reinhold, 1974.

107. Gill, P.G., *Systems Management Techniques for Builders and Contractors,* New York, McGraw-Hill, 1968.
108. Goggin, William C., "How the Multidimensional Structure Works at Dow Corning." *Harvard Business Review,* pp. 54–65, (January-February 1974).
109. Goodman, Richard A., "Ambiguous Authority Definitions in Project Management," *Academy of Management Journal* 10: 395–408, (December, 1967).
110. Goodman, Richard A., "Organizational Preference in Research and Development," *Human Relations* 23: 279–298, 1970.
111. Goodman, R., "Ambiguous Authority Definition in Project Management," *Academy of Management Journal,* 10: 395–407, (1967).
112. Grinnell, S.K., and Apple, H.P., "When Two Bosses are Better than One," *Machine Design,* 9: 84–87, (January, 1975).
113. Grimes, A., S. Klein, and F. Shull, "Matrix Model: A Selective Empirical Test," *Academy of Management Journal,* 15, 1: 9–31, (March, 1972).
114. Gross, Paul F., *Systems Analysis and Design for Management,* New York, Dun-Donnelley, 1976.
115. Gullet, C. Ray, "Personnel Management in the Project Organization," *Personnel Administration and Public Personnel Review* 1: 17–22, (November, 1972).
116. Hall, D.M., *Management of Human Systems,* Cleveland, Ohio: Association for Systems Management, 1971.
117. Hall, H. Lawrence, "Management: A Continuum of Styles," *S.A.M. Advanced Management Journal* 33: pp. 68–74, (January, 1968).
118. Hansen, J.J., "The Case of the Precarious Program," *Harvard Business Review,* (January-February, 1968).
119. Center For Health Research, "Health Research: The Systems Approach," New York, Springer, 1976.
120. Hellriegel, Don and John W. Slocum, Jr., "Organizational Design: A Contingency Approach," *Business Horizons,* 16, 2: pp. 59–68, (April 1, 1973). Reprinted in Richards, Max, D., and William A. Nielander, *Readings in Management,* fourth edition, (Cincinnati, Southwestern, 1974), pp. 516–527.
121. Hersey, Paul, and Blanchard, K.H., "The Management of Change," *Training and Development Journal,* 26, 1: (January, 1972); 26, 2: (February, 1972); and 26, 3: (March, 1972).
122. Hlavacik, James D., and Thompson, Victor A. "Bureaucracy and New Product Innovation," *Academy of Management Journal* 16: 361–72. (September, 1973).
123. Hodgetts, Richard M. "An Interindustry Analysis of Certain Aspects of Project Management," Ph.D. dissertation, University of Oklahoma, 1968.
124. —, "Leadership Techniques in the Project Organization," *Academy of Management Journal* 11: 211–19, (June, 1968).
125. Hoge, R.R. "Research and Development Project Management: Techniques for Guiding Technical Programmes Towards Corporate Objectives," *Radio and Electronic Engineer* 39: pp. 33–48, (January, 1970).
126. Holland, Ted, "What Makes a Project Manager?" *Engineering* 207–262, (February 14, 1969).
127. Hoos, Ida Russakoff, *Systems Analysis in Public Policy: A Critique,* Berkeley, University of California Press, 1972.
128. Hopeman, Richard J., *Systems Analysis and Operations Management,* Columbus, Ohio, Merrill, 1969.
129. Hopeman, R.J. and D.L. Wilemon, *Project Management/Systems Management-Concepts and Applications,* Syracuse, Syracuse University/NASA, 1973.

130. Horowitz, J., *Critical Path Scheduling—Management Control Through CPM and PERT.* New York, Roland Press, 1967.
131. Houre, Henry Ronald, *Project Management Using Network Analysis.* New York, McGraw-Hill, 1973.
132. Hynes, Cecil V., "Taking a Look at the Request For Proposal," *Defense Management Journal,* (October, 1977), pp. 26–31.
133. International Congress for Project Planning by Network Analysis, *Project Planning by Network Analysis,* Amsterdam, North-Holland Publishing Company, 1969.
134. Ivancevich, J., and J. Donnelly, "Leader Influence and Performance," *Personal Psychology,* 23: 539–549, (1970).
135. Jacobs, Richard A., "Project Management—A New Style For Success," *S.A.M. Advanced Management Journal,* 41: (Autumn 1976), pp. 4–14.
136. —, "Putting Management Into Project Management," Paper presented at A.S.M. Workshops in Detroit, Tulsa, Oakland and Las Vegas (1976).
137. Janger, Allen R., "Anatomy of the Project Organization," *Business Management Record,* 12–18, (November, 1963).
138. Jantsh, Erich, *Design for Evolution: Self-Organization and Planning in the Life of Human Systems.* New York, G. Braziller, 1975.
139. Jenett, E., "Guidelines for Successful Project Management," *Chemical Engineering,* 70–82, (July 9, 1973).
140. Johnson, James R., "Advanced Project Control," *Journal of Systems Management,* 24–27, (May, 1977).
141. Johnson, Marvin M., (ed.) *Simulation for Manufacturing Industries,* La Jolla, California: The Society for Simulation, Simulation Councils Inc., 1973.
142. Johnson, Richard Arvid, Newell, William T., and Vergin, Roger C., *Operations Management; A Systems Concept,* Boston, Houghton-Mifflin, 1972.
143. Johnson, R.A., Kast, E.E., and Rosenzweig, J.E., *The Theory and Management of Systems,* New York, McGraw-Hill, 1973.
144. Jonason, Per, "Project Management, Swedish Style," *Harvard Business Review,* 104–109, (Nov/December, 1971).
145. Kahn, R.L., Wolfe, D.M., Quinn, R.P., Snock, J.D., and Rosenthal, R.A., *Organizational Stress: Studies in Role Conflict and Ambiguity,* New York, John Wiley, 1964.
146. Kast, Fremont E., and Rosenzweig, James E., "Organization and Management of Space Programs," in *On Advances in Space Science and Technology,* edited by Frederick I. Ordway III, New York, Academic Press, 1965.
147. —, *Organization and Management; A Systems Approach.* 2nd ed. New York, McGraw-Hill, 1974.
148. Kast, F.E. and Rosenzweig, J.E., *Contingency Views of Organization and Management,* Science Research Associates, 1973.
149. Kast, D., "The Motivational Basis of Organizational Behavior," *Behavioral Science, 9,* 2: 131–143, (1964).
150. Kerzner, Harold, *Project Management: A Systems Approach to Planning, Scheduling and Controlling,* New York, Van Nostrand Reinhold, 1979.
151. Kerzner, Harold, *Project Management for Bankers,* New York, Van Nostrand Reinhold, 1980.
152. Kerzner, Harold, "Systems Management and the Engineer." *Journal of Systems Management,* 18–21, (October, 1977).
153. Killian, William P., "Project Management—Future Organizational Concepts." *Marquette Business Review* 2: 90–107, (1971).

154. Kindred, Alton R., *Data Systems and Management: An Introduction to Systems Analysis and Design,* Englewood Cliffs, N.J., Prentice-Hall, 1973.

155. Kingdon, Donald R., "The Management of Complexity in a Matrix Organization: A Socio-Technical Approach to Changing Organizational Behavior," Los Angeles, University of California, M.S. thesis, 1969.

156. —, *Matrix Organization: Managing Information Technologies,* London, Tavistock Publications, 1973.

157. Kirchner, Englebert, "The Project Manager." *Space Aeronautics,* 43: 56–64, (February, 1965).

158. Klir, George, J., *Trends in General Systems Theory,* New York: John Wiley, 1972.

159. Koplow, Richard A., "From Engineer to Manager—And Back Again," *IEEE Transactions on Engineering Management,* EM-14: 88–92, (June, 1967).

160. Larsen, Niels Ove, "An Evaluation of Managerial Strategies for Dealing with Work Pressure in a Project Oriented Environment," Ph.D. dissertation, M.I.T., Alfred P. Sloan School of Management, 1969.

161. Laszlo, Ervin, *A Strategy for the Future: The Systems Approach to World Order,* New York, G. Braziller, 1974.

162. Lawrence, Paul R. and Lorsch, Jay W., "New Management Job: The Integrator," *Harvard Business Review,* 142, (November/December, 1967).

163. Lawrence, P.R. and Lorsch, J.W., *Organization and Environment,* Boston, Division of Research, Harvard Business School, 1967.

164. Lazer R.G., and A.G. Kellner, "Personnel and Organizational Development in an R and D Matrix-Overlay Operation," *IEEE Transactions on Engineering Management,* EM-11: 78–82, (June, 1964).

165. Ler, Alec M., *Systems Analysis Frameworks,* New York, Wiley, 1970.

166. Lewin, K., "Frontiers in Group Dynamics," *Human Relations,* 1. 1, (1947).

167. Lewin, K., "Group Decision and Social Change," in Maccoby, E.E., *et al., Readings in Social Psychology,* New York: Holt, Rinehart, and Winston, 1958, pp. 197–211.

168. Livingstone, G.S. "Weapon System Contracting," *Harvard Business Review,* (July-August, 1959).

169. Lock, D., *Project Management,* London, Gower Press, 1969.

170. Logistics Management Institute, *Introduction to Military Program Management,* Washington, D.C.: Superintendent of Documents, U.S. Government Printing Office, 1971.

171. London, Keith R., *The People Side of Systems: The Human Aspects of Computer Systems,* New York, McGraw-Hill, 1976.

172. Ludwig, Ernest E., *Applied Project Management for the Process Industries.* Houston, Texas, Gulf Publishing Company, 1974.

173. Lutes, Gerald Scott, "Project Selection and Scheduling in the Massachusetts Department of Public Works," M.S. Thesis M.I.T. Alfred P. Sloan School of Management, 1974.

174. McGregor, D., *The Professional Manager,* New York, McGraw-Hill, 1967.

175. McMillan, Claude, and Gonzalez, Richard F., *Systems Analysis: A Computer Approach to Decision Models,* Irwin, Homewood, Ill., 1973.

176. Majeli, Vincent, "Management by Hindsight: Diary of a Project Manager," *Management Review,* 60: 4–14, (June, 1971).

177. —, "Sowing the Seeds of Project Cost Overruns," *Management Review,* 61: 7–14, (August, 1972).

178. Maier, N.R., and Hoffman, L.R., "Acceptance and Quality of Solutions as Related to Leader's Attitudes Toward Disagreement in Group Problem Solving," *Journal of Applied Behavioral Science.* 373–386, (1965).

179. Marquis, D.G., and Straight, Jr., D.M., "Organizational Factors in Project Performance," Working Paper pp. 133–65, Cambridge, M.I.T., School of Management, 1965.

180. Martin, Charles C., *Project Management: How to Make It Work,* New York, Amacom, 1976, pp. 41, 137.

181. Martin, James Thomas, *Systems Analysis for Data Transmission,* Englewood Cliffs, Prentice-Hall, 1972.

182. Martino, R.L., *Project Management,* Wayne, Pa., MDI Publications, Management Development Institute, 1968.

183. —, *Resources Management.* Wayne, Pa., MDI Publications, Management Development Institute, 1968.

184. Matthies, Leslie H., *The Management Systems: Systems are People,* New York, Wiley, 1976.

185. Mechanic, D., "Sources of Power of Lower Participants in Complex Organizations," *Administrative Science Quarterly,* 7: 349–364, (December, 1962).

186. Mee, John F., "Project Management," *Business Horizons* 6: 53–55, (Fall, 1963).

187. —, "Matrix Organization," *Business Horizons,* 70, (Summer, 1964).

188. Melchner, Arlyn J., (ed.), *General Systems and Organization Theory: Methodological Aspects,* Kent, Ohio, Kent University Press, 1975.

189. Melchner, Arlyn J., and Kayser, Thomas A., "Leadership without Formal Authority: The Project Department," *California Management Review.* 13, 2: 57–64, (1970).

190. Meinhart, W.A., and Delionback, Leon M., "Project Management; An Incentive Contracting Decision Model," *Academy of Management Journal,* 11: 427–34, (December, 1968).

191. Metz, William W., "Identification and Analysis of Research and Development Project Management Problems Based on Nonnuclear Munitions Development in the Air Force," Ph.D. dissertation, George Washington University, 1970.

192. Middleton, C.J., "How to Set Up a Project Organization," *Harvard Business Review* 45: 73–82, (March-April, 1967).

193. Miller, E.J., *Systems of Organization,* New York, Barnes and Noble Book Company, 1967.

194. Moder, Joseph J., and Phillips, Cecil R., *Project Management with CPM and PERT,* 2nd ed., New York, Van Nostrand Reinhold, 1970.

195. Mordlea, Irwin, "A Comparison of a Research and Development Laboratory's Organization Structures," *IEEE Transactions on Engineering Management,* EM-14, 170–76, (December, 1967).

196. Morgan, John, "Coping with Resistance to Change," *Ideas for Management,* Cleveland, Ohio, Association for Systems Management, 1971.

197. Morton, D.H., "The Project Manager, Catalyst to Constant Change: A Behavioral Analysis," *Project Management Quarterly,* 6, 1: 22–3, (1975).

198. Mungo, B.B., "Management Studies in the Field of Aeronautics: Management of Projects," *Journal of the Royal Aeronautical Society* 71, 334–36: 336–38, (May, 1967).

199. Myers, S.M., Conditions for Manager Motivation, *Harvard Business Review,* 58–71, (Jan-Feb. 1966).

200. NATO Institute on Decomposition as a Tool for Solving Large-Scale Problems, Cambridge, England, *Decomposition of Large-Scale Problems,* Amsterdam, North-Holland Publishing Company, 1973.

201. Neuschel, Richard F., *Management Systems for Profit and Growth,* New York, McGraw-Hill, 1976.

202. O'Brien, James B., "The Project Manager: Not Just a Firefighter," *S.A.M. Advanced Management Journal,* 39: 52–56, (January, 1974).
203. Optner, Stanford L., *Systems Analysis for Business and Industrial Problem Solving,* Englewood Cliffs, N.J., Prentice-Hall, 1965.
204. —, *Systems Analysis for Business Management,* Englewood Cliffs, N.J., Prentice-Hall, 1968.
205. —, *Systems Analysis for Business Management,* Englewood Cliffs, N.J., Prentice-Hall, 1975.
206. —, "Organizational Preference in Research and Development," *Human Relations,* 23: 279–98, (August, 1970).
207. Oyer, David William, "The Use of Automated Project Management Systems to Improve Information Systems Development, Cambridge, Mass.: M.S. Thesis, Alfred P. Sloan School of Management, M.I.T. 1975.
208. Pastore, Joseph M. "Organizational Metamorphosis: A Dynamic Model," *Marquette Business Review 15:* 17–31, (Spring, 1971).
209. Patchen, M., *Some Questionnaire Measures of Employee Motivation and Morale: A Report on their Reliability and Validity,* Ann Arbor, Michigan: Institute for Social Research, 1965.
210. Paul, W.J., K. Robertson, and F. Herzberg, "Job Enrichment Pays Off," *Harvard Business Review,* 47, 2: 61–78, (1969).
211. Peart, Alan Thomas, *Design of Project Management Systems and Records,* London, Gower Press, 1971.
212. —, *Design of Project Management Systems and Records.* Boston, Cahners Books, 1971.
213. Pegels, C. Carl, *Systems Analysis for Production Operations,* New York, Gordon and Science Publishers, 1976.
214. Pondy, L.R., "Organizational Conflict: Concepts and Models," *Administrative Science Quarterly,* 298–307, (September, 1967).
215. Potter, William J., "Management in the Ad-hocracy," *S.A.M. Advanced Management Journal,* 39: 19–23, (July, 1974).
216. Reeser, Clayton, "Some Potential Human Problems of the Project Form of Organization," *Academy of Management Journal,* 12: 459–68, (December, 1969).
217. Rogers, L.A., "Guidelines for Project Management Teams," *Industrial Engineering,* 12, (December, 1974).
218. Rudwick, Bernard II., *Systems Analysis for Effective Planning: Principles and Cases.* New York, Wiley, 1969.
219. Rubin, Irwin M., and Seilig, Wychlam, "Experience as a Factor in the Selection and Performance of Project Managers," *IEEE Transactions on Engineering Management* EM 131–35, (September, 1967).
220. Sadler, Philip, "Designing an Organization Structure," (publication source unknown).
221. Sapolsky, Harvey M., *The Polaris System Development: Bureaucratic and Programmatic Success in Government,* Cambridge, Mass., Harvard University Press, 1972.
222. Sayels, Leonard R., and Chandler, Margaret K., *Managing Large Systems: Organizations for the Future,* New York, Harper and Row, 1971.
223. Schaller, L.E., *The Change Agent,* New York, Abington Press, 1972.
224. Schoderbek, Peter P., Kefalas, A.G., and Schoderbek, Charles G., *Management Systems: Conceptual Considerations,* Dallas, Business Publications, 1975.
225. Schmidt, Joseph William, *Mathematical Foundations for Management Science and Systems Analysis,* New York, Academic Press, 1974.
226. Schroder, Harold J., "Making Project Management Work," *Management Review,* 54: 24–28, (December, 1970).

227. —, "Project Management: Controlling Uncertainty," *Journal of Systems Management,* 24: 28-29, (February, 1975).
228. Seiler, J.A., "Diagnosing Interdepartmental Conflict," *Harvard Business Review,* 121-132, (September-October 1963).
229. Shah, Ramesh P., "Project Management: Cross Your Bridges Before You Come to Them," *Management Review,* 60: 21-27, (December, 1971).
230. Sharad, D., "About Delays, Overruns and Corrective Actions," *Project Management Quarterly,* 21-25, (December,1976).
231. Shannon, Robert E., "Matrix Management Structures," *Industrial Engineering* 4, 26-29, (March, 1972).
232. Sheriff, M., "Superordinate Goals in the Reduction of Intergroup Conflict," *American Journal of Sociology,* 63: 349-358, (1958).
233. Shrode, William A., and Voich, Dan Jr., *Organization and Management: Basic Systems Concepts,* Homewood, Illinois, R.D. Irwin, 1974.
234. Shull, Fremont, and Judd, R.J., "Matrix Organizations and Control Systems," *Management International Review* 11, 6: 65-72, (1971).
235. Shull, Fremont A., *Matrix Structure and Project Authority for Optimizing Organizational Capacity,* Business Science Monograph No. 1. Carbondale, Business Research Bureau, Southern Illinois University, 1965.
236. Simmons, John R., *Management of Change: The Role of Information,* (based on a research project sponsored by the Institute of Office Management), London, Gee & Company, 1970.
237. Sivazlian, B.D., and Stanfeld, L.E., *Analysis of Systems in Operations Research,* Englewood Cliffs, N.J., Prentice-Hall, 1973.
238. Smith, G.A., "Program Management—Art or Science?" *Mechanical Engineering 96,* 18-22, (September, 1974).
239. Smith, Michael Gary, *PCS: A Project Control System,* Ph.D. thesis, M.I.T., Cambridge, Mass., 1973.
240. Smith, William N., "Problem-Solving and Bargaining as Modes of Constructive Conflict Resolution in Aerospace Matrix Organizations," Ph.D. thesis, University of California, Los Angeles, 1972.
241. Smyster, Craig H., "A Comparison of the Needs of Program and Functional Management" (unpublished masters thesis), School of Engineering, Wright-Patterson Air Force Base, Air Force Institute of Technology, 1965.
242. Starr, Martin Kenenth, *Production Management: Systems and Synthesis,* 2nd ed. Englewood, N.J. Prentice-Hall, 1972.
243. Stasch, Stanley F., *Systems Analysis for Marketing Planning and Control,* Glenview, Illinois, Scott, Foresman, 1972.
244. Steger, W.A., "How to Plan for Management in New Systems," *Harvard Business Review,* (September-October), 1962.
245. Steiner, George A., "Project Managers' Problems with the Development of High Performance Aerospace Systems," *Astronautics and Aeronautics,* 75-76, (June, 1966).
246. —, and Ryan, William G., *Industrial Project Management.* New York, Macmillan, 1968, p. 24.
247. Stewart, John M., "Making Project Management Work," *Business Horizons* 8: 54-68, (Fall, 1965).
248. Stopher, Peter R., and Meyburg, Arnim H., *Transportation Systems Evaluation,* Lexington, Massachusetts, Lexington Books, 1976.
249. Tannenbaum, Robert and Warren H. Schmidt, "How to Choose a Leadership Pattern," *HBR Classic,* 162-180, (May-June, 1973).

250. Taylor, W.J., and Watling, T.F., *Successful Project Management,* London, Business Books, 1970, p. 32–; 1972.
251. —, "Teamwork Through Conflict," *Business Week,* 44–45, (March 20, 1971).
252. Thamhain, Hans J., and Wilemon, David L., "Diagnosing Conflict Determinants in Project Management," *IEEE Transactions on Engineering Management,* EM–22, 35–44, (February, 1975).
253. —, and Gemmill, Gary R., "Influence Styles of Project Managers: Some Project Performance Correlates," *Academy of Management Journal,* 17, 216–24, (June, 1974).
254. Thamhain, H.J., and Wilemon, D.L., "Conflict Management in Project-Oriented Work Environments," *Proceedings of the Sixth International meeting of the Project Management Institute,* Washington, D.C., September 18–21, 1974.
255. —, "Conflict Management in Project Life Cycles," *Sloan Management Review,* 31–50, (Summer, 1975).
256. —, "The Effective Management of Conflict in Project-Oriented Work Environments," *Defense Management Journal* 11, 3: 975, (1978).
257. Thompson, J.D., *Organization in Action,* New York, McGraw-Hill, 1967.
258. Thompson, Victor A., "Bureaucracy and Innovation," *Administrative Science Quarterly* 10: 1–20, (June, 1965).
259. Toellner, John, "Project Estimating," *Journal of Systems Management,* 6–9, (May, 1977).
260. Trower, Michael H., "Fast Track to Project Delivery: Systems Approach to Project Management," *Management Review* 62: 19–23, (April, 1973).
261. Tsai, Martin Chia-Ping, "Contingent Conditions for the Creation of Temporary Management Organizations," M.S. thesis, Alfred P. Sloan School of Management, M.I.T., Cambridge, Mass., 1976.
262. Vaughn, Dennis Henry, "Key Variables of a Management Information System for a Department of Defense Project Manager," M.S. thesis, Alfred P. Sloan School of Management, M.I.T., Cambridge, Mass., 1976.
263. —, "Understanding Project Management," *Manage* 19, 9: 52–58, (1967).
264. Wadsworth, M., *EDP Project Management Controls,* Englewood Cliffs, N.J., Prentice-Hall, 1972.
265. Walton, R.E., and Dutton, J.M., "The Management of Interdepartmental Conflict: A Model and Review," *Administrative Science Quarterly,* 14, 1: 73–84, (March, 1969).
266. Walton, R.E., Dutton, J.M., and Cafferty, T.P., "Organizational Contest and Interdepartmental Conflict," *Administrative Science Quarterly,* 14, 4: 522–542, (December, 1969).
267. Webb, James E., "NASA as an Adaptive Organization," in *On Technological Change and Management,* ed. by David W. Ewing, Cambridge, Massachusetts, Harvard University Press, 1970.
268. Weinberg, Gerald M., *An Introduction to General Systems Thinking,* New York, Wiley, 1975.
269. Wetzel, John Jay, "Project Control at the Managerial Level in the Automotive Engineering Environment," M.S. thesis, Alfred P. Sloan School of Management, M.I.T. Cambridge, Mass., 1973.
270. Whitehouse, Gary E., "Project Management Techniques," *Industrial Engineering* 5: 24–29, (March, 1973).
271. —, *Systems Analysis and Design Using Network Techniques.* Englewood Cliffs, N.J., Prentice-Hall, 1973.
272. Whiting, Richard J., "In Defense of Functional Organization," *Management Review, 58,* 7: 49–52, (July, 1969).

273. Wilemon, David L., "Managing Conflict in Temporary Management Systems," *Journal of Management Studies 10:* 282–96, (October, 1973).
274. Wilemon, D.L., "Project Management Conflict. A View from Apollo," *Third Annual Symposium of the Project Management Institute,* Houston, Texas, (October, 1971).
275. —, "Managing Conflict on Project Teams," *Management Journal,* 28–34, (Summer, 1974).
276. Wilemon, D.L., "Project Management and its Conflicts: A View from Apollo," *Chemical Technology,* 2, 9: 527–534, (September, 1972).
277. —, and Gary R. Gemmill, "Interpersonal Power in Temporary Management Systems," *Journal of Management Studies,* 8: 315–28, (October, 1971).
278. —, and Cicero, John P., "The Project Manager: Anomalies and Ambiguities," *Academy of Management Journal* 13: 269–82, (September, 1970).
279. Willoughby, Theodore C., *Business Systems,* Cleveland, Association for Systems Management, 1975.
280. —, and Senn, J.A., *Business Systems,* The Association for Systems Management, 1975.
281. Wilson, Ira Gaulbert, *Management Innovation and System Design,* Princeton, Auerbach, 1971.
282. Woodgate, Harry Samuel, *Planning by Network: Project Planning and Control Using Network Techniques,* London, Business Publications, 1967.
283. Wooldridge, Susan, *Project Management in Data Processing,* 1st ed. New York, Petrocelli/Charter, 1976.
284. Wrong, D., "Some Problems in Defining Social Power," *American Journal of Sociology.* 73, 6: 673–681, (May, 1968).

Competitive Bidding Bibliography

1. Anderson, R.M., "Handling Risk in Defense Contracting," *Harvard Business Review* (1969), pp. 90–98.
2. Arps, J.J., "A Strategy for Sealed Bidding," *Journal Petroleum Technology,* 1033, (September, 1965).
3. Baumgarten, R.N., "Discussion for Opbid-Competitive Bidding Strategy Model" by Morin and Clough, *Journal of the Construction Division of ASCE 96,* 88, (1970).
4. Benjamin, N.B.H., "Competitive Bidding for Building Construction Contracts," Technical Report No. 106, Department of Civil Engineering, Stanford University, June 1969.
5. Bell, L.B., "A System for Competitive Bidding," *Journal of Systems Management 20,* 26–29, (1969).
6. Bristor, J.D., "Discussion for Bidding Strategies and Probabilities, by Gates" (March, 1967), *Proceedings of the American Society of Civil Engineers Journal,* Construction Division 94, 109, (1968).
7. Bristor, J.D., "Discussion for "Bidding-Work Loading Game' by Torgersen, *et al.''* (October, 1968), *Proceedings of the American Society of Civil Engineers Journal,* Construction Division 95, 139–140, (1969).
8. Broemser, G.M., "Competitive Bidding in the Construction Industry," Ph.D. dissertation, Stanford University, California, 1968.
9. Brown, K.C., "A Theoretical and Statistical Study of Decision-Making under Uncertainty-Competitive Bidding for Leases on Offshore Petroleum Lands," Ph.D. dissertation, Southern Methodist University, Dallas, Texas, 1966.
10. Casey, B.J. and L.R. Shaffer, "An Evaluation of Some Competitive Bid Strategy Models for Contractors," Report No. 4, Department of Civil Engineering, University of Illinois, Urbana, Illinois.
11. Christenson, C., *Strategic Aspects of Competitive Bidding for Corporate Securities,* Boston, Mass., Division of Research, Harvard, University School of Business.

12. Clough, R.H., *Construction Contracting,* Appendix L, 2nd Ed., New York, John Wiley, 1969.
13. Cook, Paul W., Jr., "Fact and Fancy on Identical Bids," *Harvard Business Review, 41,* 67–72 (January–February, 1963).
14. Crawford, P.B., "Pattern of Offshore Bidding," Society of Petroleum Engineers of AIME, Paper No. 2613, Dallas, Texas, 1969.
15. Crosby, A.R., "The Client/Contractor Syndrome," *Chemical Engineering Program 61,* 11, 44–48, (1965).
16. Edelman, F., "Art and Science of Competitive Bidding," *Harvard Business Review 43,* 53–66, (July–August, 1965).
17. Emerick, R.H., "How to Find the Unforeseen in Competitive Bidding," *Power Engineering 69,* 45–46, (August, 1965).
18. Flueck, J.A., "A Statistical Decision Theory Approach to a Seller's Bid Pricing Problem under Uncertainty," Ph.D. thesis, University of Chicago, School of Business, 1967.
19. Frey, J.B., "Competitive Bidding on General Construction Contracts," Ph.D. thesis, University of Delaware, 1962.
20. Friedman, L., "A Competitive Bidding Strategy," *Operations Research 4,* 104–112, (1956).
21. Gates, M., "Aspects on Competitive Bidding," Connecticut Society of Civil Engineers, 1959.
22. Gates, M., "Statistical and Economic Analysis of a Bidding Trend," *Journal of the Construction Division,* ASCE, Paper 2651, 13–35 (November, 1960).
23. Gates, M., "Bidding Strategies and Probabilities," *Journal of the Construction Division,* ASCE, Paper 5159, *93,* 75–107, (1967); and subsequent closure, p. *96,* 77–78 and 93, (1970).
24. Green, P., "Bayesian Decision Theory in Pricing Strategy," *Journal of Marketing 27,* 5–14, (1963).
25. Griesmer, J.H. and M. Shubik, "The Theory of Bidding," IBM Research Report, RC–629, IBM Research Center, Yorktown Heights, N.Y., (March 1, 1962).
26. Griesmer, J.H. and M. Shubik, "The Theory of Bidding II," IBM Research Report, RC–688, IBM Research Center, Yorktown Heights, N.Y., (May 25, 1962).
27. Griesmer, J.H. and M. Shubik, "The Theory of Bidding III," IBM Research Report, RC–874, IBM Research Center, Yorktown Heights, N.Y., (January 29, 1963).
28. Griesmer, J.H., R.E. Levitan, and M. Shubik, "Towards a Study of Bidding Processes, Part Four, Unknown Competitive Costs—," IBM Research Paper RC–1532, IBM Research Center, Yorktown Heights, N.Y., (January, 1966).
29. Hanssman, F. and Rivett, B.H.P., "Competitive Bidding," *Operations Research, Quarterly 10,* 49–55, (1959).
30. Harsanyi, J.C., "Games with Incomplete Information Played by Bayesian Players, Parts I–III," *Management Science 14,* 159–182, 320–334, 486–502, (1967–68).
31. Hugo, G.R., "How to Prepare Bids for Crown Lease Sales," *Oil Week 16,* 56–60, (1965).
32. Lavalle, I.H., "A Bayesian Approach to an Individual Player's Choice of Bid in Competitive Sealed Auctions," *Management Science 13,* A584–597, (1967).
33. Moriguti, S. and S. Suganami, "Notes on Auction Bidding," *J. Opns, Res. Soc. (Japan), 2,* 43–59, (1959).
34. Morin, T.L., and R.H. Clough, "Opbid—Competitive Bidding Strategy Model," *Journal of Construction Division,* ASCE, Paper 6690; (June, 1970) and subsequent discussion, pp. *96,* 88–97.
35. Ortega-Reichert, A., "Models for Competitive Bidding under Uncertainty," Technical Report No. 103, Department of Operations Research, Stanford University, Stanford, California, January, 1968.

36. Park, W.R., "How Low to Bid to Get Both Job and Profit," *Engineering News-Record 168*, 38–40, (April 19, 1962).

37. Park, W.R., "Less Bidding for Bigger Profits," *Engineering News-Record 170*, 41 (February 14, 1963).

38. Park, W.R., "Bidders and Job Size Determine Your Optimum Markup, *Engineering News-Record 170*, 122–123, (June 13, 1963).

39. Park, W.R., "Bidding: When to Raise and When to Fold," *The Modern Builder*, Kansas City, Mo., (July, 1963).

40. Park, W.R., "The Problem of Breaking Even," *The Modern Builder*, Kansas City, Mo. (September, 1963).

41. Park, W.R., "The Strategy of Bidding for Profit," *The Modern Builder*, Kansas City, Mo. (September, 1963).

42. Park, W.R., "Better Bidding Will Beget Bigger Profits," *The Modern Builder*, Kansas City, Mo. (October, 1963).

43. Park, W.R., "How Much to Make to Cover Costs," *Engineering News-Record 171*, 168–170, (December 19, 1963).

44. Park, W.R., "It Takes a Profit to Make a Profit," *Mid-West Contractor*, Kansas City, Mo. (March 11, 1964).

45. Park, W.R., "Profit Optimization Through Strategic Bidding," *AACE Bulletin, 6, 5* (December, 1964).

46. Park, W.R., *The Strategy of Contracting for Profit*, Englewood Cliffs, N.J., Prentice-Hall, 1966.

47. Rothkopf, M.H., "A Model of Rational Competitive Bidding," *Management Science 15*, 362–373, (1969).

48. Sakaguchi, M., "Mathematical Solutions to Some Problems of Competitive Bidding," *Proceedings of the Third International Conference on Operational Res.* (Oslo, 1963), 1964, pp. 179–191, Dunod (Paris) and English University Press (London).

49. Schlaifer, R., *Probability and Statistics for Business Decisions*. New York, McGraw-Hill, 1959.

50. Simmonds, K., "Adjusting Bias in Cost Estimates," *Opnal. Res. Quart., 19*, 325–327, (1968).

51. Simmonds, K., "Competitive Bidding—Deciding the Best Combination of Non-Price Features," *Operational Research Quarterly 19*, 5–15, (1968).

52. Stark, Robert M., "Competitive Bidding: A Comprehensive Bibliography," *Opns. Res. 19*, 484–490, (1971).

53. Symonds, G.H., "A Study of Management Behavior by Use of Competitive Business Games," *Management Science 11*, 135–153, (1964).

54. Vickrey, W., "Counterspeculation, Auctions, and Competitive Sealed Tenders," *Journal of Finance 16*, 8–37, (1961).

55. Wasson, C.R., *Understanding Qualitative Analysis*, New York, Appleton-Century-Crofts, 1969.

56. Wilson, R.B., "Competitive Bidding with Disparate Information," Working Paper No. 114, Graduate School of Business, Stanford University, October 1966.

57. Wilson, R.B., "Competitive Bidding with Asymmetrical Information," *Management Science 13*, A816–820, (1967).

58. Wilson, R.B., "Competitive Bidding with Disparate Options," *Management Science 15*, 46–48, (1969).

Subject Index